I0796148

TAYLOR SWIFT ALL THE SONGS

TAYLOR SWIFT ALL THE SONGS

THE STORY BEHIND EVERY TRACK

DAMIEN SOMVILLE & MARINE BENOIT

BLACK DOG
& LEVENTHAL
PUBLISHERS
NEW YORK

Contents

When she was young, Taylor Swift discovered country singer LeAnn Rimes, then went on to listen to Shania Twain, Faith Hill, and the Dixie Chicks (now known as the Chicks).

TAYLOR SWIFT: BIRTH OF A STAR AND AN EMPIRE

An Enchanted Childhood

Taylor Alison Swift was born on December 13, 1989, in West Reading, Pennsylvania. Her early years were something of a fairytale. She spent them on a Christmas tree farm overlooking a lake on the outskirts of Wyomissing, a town near Reading. Her father, Scott Kingsley Swift, was a financial advisor with Merrill Lynch, and her mother, Andrea Gardner Swift, née Finlay, was a mutual fund marketing executive. Taylor Swift lacked nothing materially and received love in abundance. Her younger brother, Austin, who she is still very close to, was born when she was two and a half.

As a child, she competed in horseback-riding competitions, but her main pastime was making up stories and singing Disney songs. She discovered a LeAnn Rimes record when she was six years old and began listening to it, over and over again. This first contact with country music was a revelation to her. She then turned to other female artists who would have a pivotal influence on her own music, which she began to create: Shania Twain, Faith Hill, and the Dixie Chicks (now known as the Chicks) were among her favorite singers for a long time. In her early teens she began performing in a theater troupe but realized that acting wasn't as fun as moments spent with her friends in front of a karaoke microphone. So, at the age of eleven, she determined to sing in front of an audience wherever she could. For a year and a half, she performed every week in a karaoke contest at the Pat Garrett Roadhouse, an amphitheater where country music events were held. Her perseverance paid off and she won the contest's top prize: a show opening for the Charlie Daniels Band, the Nashville singer best known for his song "The Devil Went Down to Georgia" (1979). After this exhilarating experience, Taylor Swift, more emboldened than ever, sought to perform the national anthem at any local sporting event. She even landed a contract with her favorite NBA team, the Philadelphia 76ers.

Mockery and Ostracism

With this kind of exposure, one would think that the angelic-faced preteen would be one of the most popular girls in her school. Not so: Taylor Swift struggled to fit in and was mocked by some of her classmates for her love of country music, which was not popular with her age group at the time (pop and R&B reigned supreme in the charts). This rejection had a deep impact on her. The gaze of others, the feeling of isolation, and the desire for recognition became recurring themes in her lyrics, even twenty years later. "Anything that makes you different in middle school makes you weird," she told *Rolling Stone* magazine (March 5, 2009). "My friends turned into the girls who would stand in the corner and make fun of me." Her lifeline—and object of emotional support—became a 12-string guitar, an instrument she was given by her parents. She was determined to master it even before she could play a 6-string. Holed up in her room, thinking about her classmates mocking her and telling her wouldn't go far, she pushed her practice sessions to the point of bleeding fingers. But for her, the effort was worth it: Now she was able to play the cathartic songs she wrote when she got home, creating a personal diary set to music.

Propelled Toward Nashville

When their daughter was fourteen, Scott and Andrea Swift decided to settle permanently in Hendersonville, a suburb of Nashville, Tennessee. Their intention was to give their daughter every chance of making it big in the country

No artist has been able to bring together a community as passionate as Taylor Swift's. Here for the release of *Red (Taylor's Version)* in 2021.

music world. Taylor was already on the radar of the music industry, having been on a development contract with RCA Records since 2004. The aim of a development contract is to enable artists just starting out to hone their skills with a variety of professional songwriters. Taylor Swift began polishing her lyrics with Liz Rose, the songwriter credited on many of her early hits. Taylor Swift's real breakthrough came when she met Scott Borchetta, a former DreamWorks Records executive who was about to launch his own label, Big Machine Records. Borchetta spotted the singer in Nashville, at the Bluebird Cafe, at a show organized, among other things, for professionals to spot young talent. Convinced that this very young girl was a real gem, he took the gamble of signing her in 2005. This decision was by far the most strategically important in Scott Borchetta's professional life.

Taylor Swift's first album, titled *Taylor Swift*, was produced by Nathan Chapman, who had already produced several of her demos. Released in October 2006, it received good reviews despite the artist's very young age, something that can sometimes lead to a degree of mistrust in the industry. Although assisted by Liz Rose, Taylor Swift wrote the lyrics for each of the eleven tracks. The themes of these songs would follow her throughout her career: love and its vicissitudes, friendship, and the judgments of others, to which she was about to be exposed even more by putting herself in the spotlight. She built up a solid online fan base, via the various emerging social networks. On MySpace in particular, she took the time to respond sincerely and directly to every message she received. This proximity to the public won her an increasing number of new listeners, so much so that five of her singles topped the pop and country charts, keeping her album in the Billboard 200 for 157 weeks, making it the longest-lasting Billboard album of the 2000s.

A Meteoric Rise

Her next two albums, *Fearless* and *Speak Now*, released in 2008 and 2010 respectively, set the stage for her meteoric rise in the music world. The former, with its catchy melodies and storytelling accessible to an audience far beyond country music, became not only her first No. 1 on the Billboard 200 but also the most award-winning country album of all time. It earned her very first Grammy for Album of the Year 2010. Somewhat reluctantly, Taylor Swift also found herself making headlines around the world around the same time, following her performance at the 2009 MTV Video Music Awards. Onstage to collect her award for Video of the Year, she was interrupted by rapper Kayne West, who felt that the award should have gone to Beyoncé. While this episode propelled her further into the limelight, reinforcing her image as a humble, mature young artist, it was also, regrettably, the beginning of a long series of

After *Fearless* (2008) and *Speak Now* (2010), Taylor Swift's career takes off in a series of resounding successes.

controversies that followed her for almost ten years, but from which she emerged, largely victorious and bigger and stronger for all that.

A commercial and critical success, *Speak Now*, which this time she wrote entirely on her own, consolidated her standing as a talented singer-songwriter, capable of producing deep, introspective lyrics despite her youth. Her writing generated a certain fascination among some observers, who were surprised that such a young girl, whom life at the time seemed not to have dented too much, was capable of conveying universal messages with such force. *Red*, her fourth studio album, was the final overwhelming evidence for anyone who still doubted her songwriting ability. When it was released in October 2012, it exceeded all expectations, selling over 1 million copies in its first week, an achievement all the more remarkable at a time when record sales in general were in steep decline. It was also the last of her discography to be described as country pop.

Birth of a Pop Legend

The following years of Taylor Swift's career were a string of successes, each more resounding than the last, both commercially and critically. With the release of her fifth album, *1989* in October 2014, she embarked upon a change in artistic direction that marked her definitive move into pop. Inspired by the sounds of the 1980s, the album sent shockwaves through the music industry, cementing the singer's status as a global superstar. Singles such as "Shake It Off," "Blank Space," and "Style" became instant worldwide hits. They were also songs in which she made fun of the criticism she regularly received, particularly concerning her hectic love life. And yet Taylor Swift was still perceived as a humble artist, always striving to renew herself. Her extraordinary creativity extended to organizing ever more elaborate treasure hunts for her fans, who were encouraged to decipher hidden messages and follow the clues she scattered throughout her videos, social media posts, and album inserts. Over the years, these interactions steadily strengthened the loyalty of her fans, proving her ability to transform each of her projects into a global event. In the history of music, no artist has been able to bring together a community as active and impassioned as that of Taylor Swift.

Resilience

However, 2016 marked the singer's first—and up till now, only—difficult phase, despite the fact that everything had always gone her way. Drawn once again into a new chapter of the media-publicized conflict with Kanye West and, this time also with Kim Kardashian, the rapper's wife at the time, she became the target of an extremely brutal viral smear campaign. The hashtag #TaylorSwiftIsOverParty made the rounds on social networks, jeopardizing her

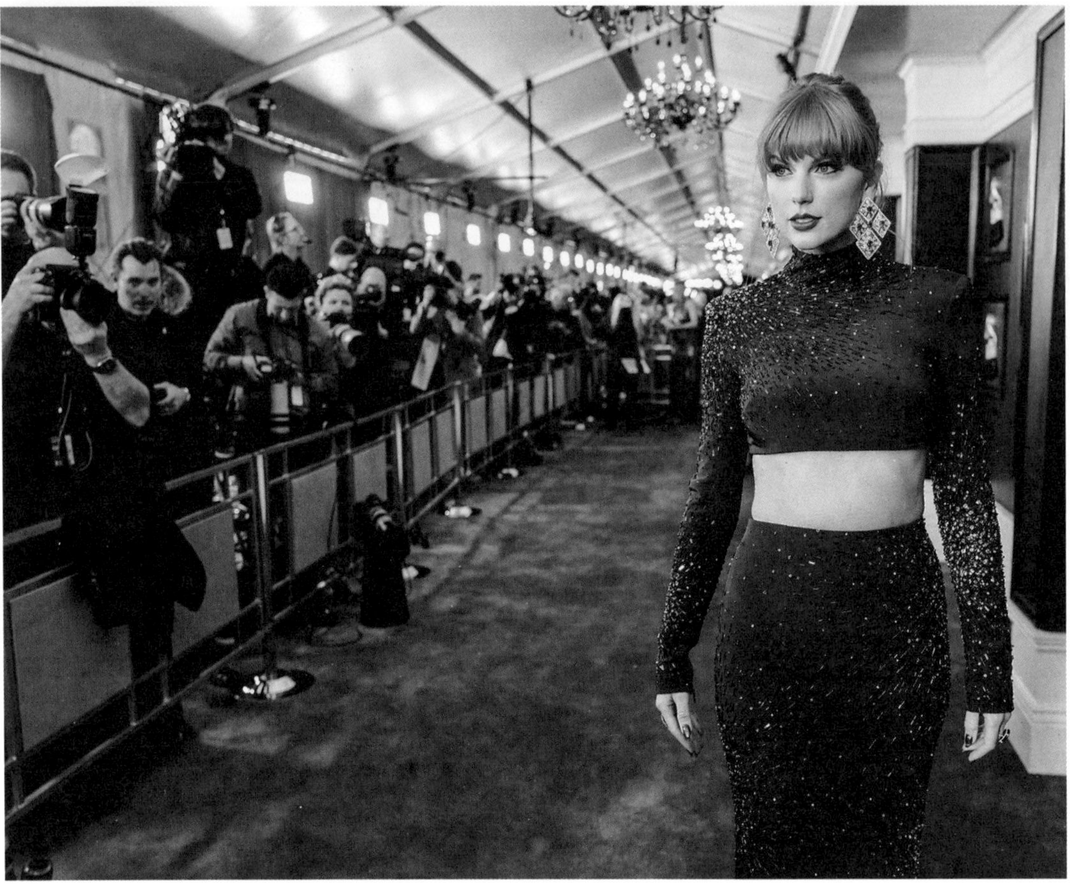

Taylor Swift in 2023. This year marks the start of "The Eras Tour," her world tour.

image and, by extension, her entire career. Once again she showed great strength of spirit during this dark period and managed to turn the storm into a creative inspiration: namely *Reputation* (2017), which remains one of her most daring and liberating albums. The resulting stadium tour broke ticket sales records and proved, if proof were still needed, that the "new Taylor" was also dominant in the global music scene.

An Artistic Renaissance

At the end of this electric phase, the artist embraced some gentler, calmer periods. First came the colorful *Lover* (2019), a joyful album celebrating love in all its forms. Then, in the midst of a global pandemic, she surprised the world with *Folklore*, and *Evermore* (2020), twin albums released just a few months apart, whose folk and indie sounds are relatively far removed from her previous pop productions. These intimate records, consisting of poetic stories and fictional characters, revealed a new facet of her creative genius: her ability to tell stories that are no longer just her own. With *Folklore*, she won the Grammy for Album of the Year 2021, making her the first woman to win the award three times. This was followed by *Midnights* (2022) and *The Tortured Poets Department* (2024), accomplished albums in which she extended her mastery of storytelling even further. In these recent productions, she seemed to have achieved what might now be called the "Taylor Swift sound." She had been developing it for almost ten years with her friend and loyal collaborator Jack Antonoff and, more recently, with Aaron Dessner, one of the masterminds behind the rock band The National. It is a warm voice that plays brilliantly with the meaning and sound of words, a host of organic instruments and compelling melodies, often imbued with emotional intensity.

The "Eras Tour" Phenomenon

During the "Eras Tour," a record-breaking world tour starting in 2023, the singer gave her fans the opportunity to celebrate every era of her career. During 149 extraordinary shows, veritable musical marathons lasting over three hours and featuring monumental decors

The pop star receives the Global Icon Award at the 2021 BRIT Awards, a recognition for an exceptional career.

and dazzling stage outfits, Taylor Swift once again demonstrated that she deserves her status as a global cultural phenomenon. In fact, the previous year, in January 2022, she was the subject of a course at New York University's Clive Davis Institute (taught by Brittany Spanos of *Rolling Stone* magazine, who covered the artist's evolution as an entrepreneur and master marketer). That same year, the university awarded Taylor Swift an honorary Doctorate in Fine Arts degree for her work and achievements.

A Transgenerational Figure

For any who might still have doubts, Taylor Swift is more than simply a prolific musician. She is an artist of rare generosity who transcends genres, generations, and borders, and whose legacy, at just thirty-six years of age, is already colossal. She has also become one of America's most powerful spokespersons, publicly calling for votes for progressive candidates and regularly denouncing social injustice, discrimination, and patriarchy. Finally, she is one of the most fervent advocates of artists' rights in a music industry now subject to streaming platforms and algorithms. She even re-recorded her first six albums to regain ownership of them. Taylor Swift has indeed built an empire, but a benevolent one, where power is in tune with the hope of one day living in a better society.

Notice

In view of Taylor Swift's imposing discography, we have chosen to concentrate on the analysis of the original songs recorded in the studio, and only the discographic objects will be dealt with (the music videos, documentaries, and live films could themselves be the subject of a book in their own right). Nor will we list the many official (and unofficial) thematic playlists available on streaming, as these titles are dealt with individually in these pages. Finally, we have listed tracks appearing on various compilations or film soundtracks in the "non-album singles" section at the end of the book.

Only the most significant rankings are listed. Where not indicated, the reference ranking for Taylor Swift albums is *Billboard 200*.

Next page spread: The *Reputation* era, 2018. A liberation of speech after a period of silence.

RELEASE DATES
United States: October 24, 2006
(ref.: Big Machine Records BMR120702)
***United States reissue: March 18, 2008**
(ref.: Big Machine Records BMR079102)
Best Ranking: 5

ALBUM

Taylor Swift

Tim McGraw · Picture to Burn · Teardrops on My Guitar · A Place in This World · Cold As You · The Outside · Tied Together with a Smile · Stay Beautiful · Should've Said No · Mary's Song (Oh My My My) · Our Song · I'm Only Me When I'm with You* · Invisible* · A Perfectly Good Heart* · Beautiful Eyes / I Heart? (EP)

At the age of sixteen, Taylor Swift caused a sensation at the 2006 CMT Music Awards in Nashville, heralding her rise to fame in country pop music.

FOR DISCERNING SWIFTIES

Originally, the singer wanted to call her first album *A Place in This World*. In the end, she decided to call it *Taylor Swift*.

A DEBUT ALBUM OF PRECOCIOUS MATURITY

"Hey, can we move to Nashville?" Taylor Swift asked her parents, Scott and Andrea Swift, this question when she was just ten years old. She had seen an episode of *Behind the Music*—the VH1 documentary series that traces the careers of musicians—about country singer Faith Hill, and since then had only one idea in mind: to move to Nashville and make her mark. Like so many others, Faith Hill managed to launch her career in the city, the cradle of country labels, artists, and festivals dedicated to the country genre. "I would watch these biographies on Faith Hill or the Dixie Chicks or Shania Twain or LeAnn Rimes, and the thing I kept hearing was that they had to go to Nashville," recalled Taylor in a 2008 interview with *Entertainment Weekly*.

Going to Nashville, a Childhood Dream

While Taylor's parents were very supportive of their daughter's passion for music, neither of them really knew how determined she was to turn her dream of becoming a singer into reality. The following year, her mother agreed to go with her to Nashville for a few days during a school vacation, to distribute her demo—which was essentially her singing karaoke—to various record companies. According to the 2008 article in *Entertainment Weekly*, Taylor recalled: "I took my demo [...], where I sound like a chipmunk—it's pretty awesome—and my mom waited in the car with my little brother while I knocked on doors up and down Music Row. I would say, 'Hi, I'm Taylor. I'm eleven; I want a record deal. Call me.'" No one called her. Taylor nevertheless remained undeterred. After realizing that simple karaoke songs would not make her stand out from the crowd, she decided to compose her own songs and play them on the guitar. At the age of twelve, she set herself the goal of learning the twelve-string guitar, even before learning how to play a six-string guitar. Her parents told her that her hands would be too small to play the twelve-string, and that was all the challenge she needed. Taylor began playing four hours a day on weekdays and six on weekends, to the point where her fingers bled and she had to protect them with tape to be able to keep practicing. Unsurprisingly, it wasn't until a few years later that she first strummed a six-string with ease.

First Contract with RCA Records

In 2002, the year she turned twelve, in her teenage bedroom, Taylor wrote her very first song, "The Outside," about how she always felt excluded from her peers. The

Taylor Swift wrote her first songs in her childhood home in Wyomissing, Pennsylvania, which was put up for sale in 2013.

Only a handful of artists can claim to have been noticed from their very first attempt at songwriting, and Taylor is one of them. In 2004, the Maybelline cosmetics brand asked her to contribute "The Outside" to a sponsored album showcasing young female talent. Around the same time, she composed "Christmas Must Be Something More" for a Christmas EP released exclusively for Target in 2007.

following year, she reached a milestone when the country label RCA, which collaborated with Joe Galante and Renee Bell, two legendary figures in the Nashville country music industry, offered her a one-year development contract (consisting of coaching and providing resources to define and strengthen her as a musician and recording artist. Once the deal was signed, the Swift family, who had been leading a peaceful existence between their spacious main residence in Wyomissing, Pennsylvania, and their vacation villa in Stone Harbor, New Jersey, realized that the young woman's future might well lie more than six hundred miles from home. After signing the contract with RCA, Scott and Andrea finally decided to grant their daughter's wish. They moved to the Nashville suburb of Hendersonville, to a plush house near a lake familiar to Johnny Cash.

An Innate Talent for Songwriting

Taylor enrolled at the local Hendersonville High School. Until then, she had not had many friends, but she was better integrated in her new environment. She also took part in songwriting sessions as part of the support provided by RCA. She wrote under the supervision of many experienced Nashville composers, including Troy Verges, Brett Beavers, and the Warren Brothers. She also met songwriter and producer Liz Rose, who played a crucial role in the early years of her career. Although Liz Rose readily admits that she had little input into the lyrics Taylor shared with her, she and the young artist were a benevolent duo that ended up being formidably effective. They met every Tuesday after Taylor's classes to co-write. By this time, Taylor was already attracting a great deal of interest from country music professionals. She was said to be remarkably mature for her age, and her ability to use language to express more than just teenage torments was impressive. Sensing that the tide was turning, Taylor decided to free herself from her agreement with RCA when her development contract came to an end in 2005. She worried she'd be stuck in the status of "artist in development" for several more years. Also, RCA wanted her to record songs composed by others, which she did not want to do. She was right to follow her instincts: In May of the same year, after she had just been released from her contract with RCA, Sony/ATV Publishing, the world's number one music publisher, contacted her with an offer to write lyrics for some of its artists. She accepted without hesitation, becoming, at the age of fifteen, the youngest songwriter ever hired by the company. Arthur Buenahora, the former Sony/ATV executive who signed that first contract, recalls in the *New Yorker* that the "songs were great, but it was her, really. She was a star. She lit up the room."

Borchetta Enters the Scene

At a showcase at Nashville's Bluebird Cafe, Taylor caught the eye of Universal Music executive Scott Borchetta, who already had a twenty-year career under his belt. In an interview with the CBS television network, Borchetta confided that he feared that night that another producer would "catch" the young artist before he did. For her part, Taylor was delighted at the prospect of working with the most

During the pretelecast of the Grammy Awards in January 2010, Taylor Swift shared the stage with Liz Rose for having cowritten "White Horse."

powerful label on the planet. A few weeks later, Borchetta called with both good and bad news. The good news was that he wanted to sign with her, and the bad news was that it would not be with Universal Music. The producer had already decided to leave the company and set up his own label, Big Machine Records. Taylor, who accepted the proposal, was no doubt urged on by her parents, who appreciated Borchetta's ideas and audacity. She was also convinced that a small structure like Big Machine would be able to offer her special attention, even though, at the same time, she had to adapt to the constraints posed by the launch of any company. "[Big Machine] only had ten employees when it started out, so when they released my first single ["Tim McGraw"], my mother and I came along to help put the CDs in envelopes to send to the radio stations," she told *Entertainment Weekly* in 2008. "We did all this sitting on the floor because there was no furniture in the record company offices yet."

A Hard-Hitting Nugget

For the writing of this eponymous first album (*Taylor Swift*), which Big Machine Records undertook to produce, Taylor Swift surrounded herself with the presence of Liz Rose. Their joint work produced the hits "Teardrops on My Guitar," "White Horse," "You Belong with Me," and, above all, "Tim McGraw," the track that propelled Taylor permanently into the limelight, thanks in part to Scott Borchetta's strategy of getting it on the playlists of all the country radio stations. But the success of this first single was not only due to the fact that it was a "hit as hard as gems," to use the words of critic Rob Sheffield in *Blender* magazine. Taylor went to great lengths to ensure her track's online visibility, particularly on the MySpace social network, frequented by many teenagers and young adults in search of musical discoveries. Taylor spent hours replying to all the fan messages she received and personally thanking the radio hosts who played her tracks. In the summer of 2006, "Tim McGraw" reached number six on the Hot Country Songs chart and number forty on the Hot 100. Her debut album, a collection of bittersweet ballads in which she examines the difficulties of relationships, whether in love or friendship, was a huge commercial and critical success. It remained on the Billboard 200 chart for 157 consecutive weeks.

Hidden Messages

Up until the album *Reputation* in 2017, Taylor slipped riddles into the booklets of her albums. Figuring them out could reveal the identity of a person, or the moral of the story. For example, from *Fearless* (2008) to *Red* (2012), the messages can be deciphered by taking the capital letters introduced in the lyrics in order. For *1989* (2014), lowercase letters were used, and the thirteen messages resulting from this decryption form a coherent whole. Taylor had found a playful way of encouraging her fans to read her songs with the utmost attention. It was also a way for her to engage her with fans in a conversation that has gone a long way toward creating and cementing the Swifties community.

Taylor Swift onstage at the Stagecoach Festival in Indio, California, May 2008.

Bridgestone Arena in Nashville, September 2011: Taylor Swift onstage with Tim McGraw, the man who inspired her first single.

SINGLE

TIM MCGRAW

Taylor Swift, Liz Rose / 3:52

Musicians
Taylor Swift: vocals, backing vocals
Nathan Chapman: acoustic guitar, banjo, bass, drums, electric guitar, backing vocals, mandolin
Bruce Bouton: dobro
Mike Brignardello, Tim Marks: bass
Nick Buda, Shannon Forrest: drums
Gary Brunette: electric guitar
Eric Darken: percussion
Dan Dugmore: pedal steel
Rob Hajacos, Wanda Vick: fiddle
Tony Harrell: keyboards
Jeffrey Hyde: banjo
Andy Leftwich: fiddle, mandolin
Liana Manis: backing vocals
Lex Price: mandolin
Joshua Whitmore: dobro, pedal steel
Ilya Toshinsky: acoustic guitar, banjo
John Willis: banjo, mandolin, high-strung acoustic guitar
Recorded
Quad Studios and Sound Cottage (Nashville), 2006
Technical Team
Producer: Nathan Chapman
Executive Producer: Scott Borchetta
Mixing: Chuck Ainlay, Jeff Balding
Sound Engineers: Nathan Chapman, Chad Carlson, Allen Ditto, Clarke Schleicher, Sandi Spika
Mastering: Hank Williams
Single Releases
CD single, US, June 19, 2006—BMRTS0101
CD single and vinyl, limited edition of 4,000 hand-numbered copies, US (2019)—BMRTS0101V
Best Rankings: Hot Country: 6; Hot 100: 40

Genesis

This single was produced by Nathan Chapman, the providential one-man band and musical director of an album designed to conquer the airwaves. The song "Tim McGraw" was sketched out in around twenty minutes on the piano by the sixteen-year-old Taylor Swift, then co-written with songwriter Liz Rose. This staple of the star's repertoire pays tribute to country songwriting couple Tim McGraw and Faith Hill, who have greatly influenced Taylor Swift's songwriting. Written as soon as she arrived at Hendersonville High School (Tennessee) in 2004, the lyrics are dedicated to her boyfriend at the time, who was about to leave for college, and their imminent separation. Taylor hopes he will think of her when he hears her favorite song on the radio: Tim McGraw's "Can't Tell Me Nothin'" (from the album *Live Like You Were Dying*, released in 2004). When she played this song on ukulele alone in front of Scott Borchetta, CEO of Big Machine, her original label, he declared: "We've got your first single."

On the radio edit version, Taylor Swift had no hesitation in changing the phrase of the last chorus, "Someday, you'll turn your radio on," replacing "your radio" with the name of the local radio station.

Production

Between modern and traditional country, this midtempo ballad begins with an acoustic guitar riff right in the center of the stereo field, enhanced on the right-hand side by a slide-played dobro part. The rich, brilliant sound of both instruments immediately immerses the listener in the Nashville sound of the 2000s, while the *I-VI-IV-V* chord progression (in this case *C*, *A* minor, *F*, *G*), reminiscent of late-1950s doo-wop (a subgenre of R'n'B), adds a nostalgic touch to the composition. At 0:13, Taylor's voice softly makes its entrance, and the acoustic guitar follows with delicate strumming, quickly joined by a few mandolin licks that open up the stereo field on the left. At 0:38, the bass completes the spectrum, playing the tonic of the chords until the drums and the chorus, sung by Nathan

Chapman himself, first enter the scene. At the start of the second verse, the snare drum finally marks beats 2 and 4 to affirm the binary pulse. From 1:48 onward, the fiddle arrangement envelops the pre-chorus, setting the stage for the long-awaited takeoff of the second chorus, to which electric guitar arpeggios add some top end. After the bridge and climax of the third chorus (see "On Your Headphones"), a final, intimate verse cycle enables Taylor and her velvety voice to elegantly bring her storytelling full circle: "He said the way my blue eyes shined / Put those Georgia stars to shame that night / I said, 'That's a lie.'"

ON YOUR HEADPHONES

At 2:35, the bridge arrangement rekindles the listener's attention with the entrance of an instrument uncommon in country music: the *tubular bells*. Just a few of their notes are enough to pull the harmonic spectrum upward. They take the tension up a notch before the start of the third chorus, which starts out very subdued, then builds to a climax between 3:02 and 3:27.

Hidden Message

Can't tell me nothin'.

Partly thanks to Nathan Chapman, Taylor Swift has consolidated her status as a revolutionary country pop artist

At the 43rd CMA Awards in 2009, Taylor Swift receives several major awards for *Fearless*, produced in part by Nathan Chapman.

NATHAN CHAPMAN, THE CRAFTSMAN IN THE SHADOWS

Born in Nashville in 1976 to musician and producer parents, Nathan Chapman grew up in country music recording studios. In 2004, he began working with Taylor, a fourteen-year-old artist under a development contract with the RCA label. Although his talent as a studio guitarist was already recognized, he was still far from being the renowned and in-demand producer he would become after his collaboration with the singer. At the time, Chapman had yet to produce an album in his own name and had only been asked to produce the teenager's demo. Taylor said, in a 2015 interview during a listening session for the *1989* album at the Grammy Museum, that working with him "was actually a shock"—so much so that she convinced Scott Borchetta to leave him in charge of her first album. Taylor proved once again that she knew how to make winning choices, as their duo would partly shape not only the sound that was to become her trademark, but also that of modern country-pop music as a whole—the metallic, slamming guitars, backing violins, and percussive rhythms are now characteristic of the sound.

Taylor's Main Producer Until 2014

Nathan Chapman was lead producer on the singer's first three studio albums—*Taylor Swift* (2006), *Fearless* (2008), and *Speak Now* (2010)—and contributed some songs as producer and musician on *Red* (2012) and *1989* (2014). His crowning achievement came in 2010, when, as co-producer with the star, he won the Grammy Award for Album of the Year for *Fearless*. Even after their professional separation, which coincided with Taylor's desire to evolve musically by exploring new sound horizons and working with other producers, Taylor would never tire of praising him. "This Love," featured on *1989*, was the last track he produced for Taylor. Nathan Chapman did not collaborate on Taylor's Versions. Although she has never said why, one of the reasons seems obvious: Nathan Chapman still worked for Big Machine, which she had been in a dispute with since the resale of her masters.

A Career Well Launched

Chapman's work with Taylor Swift had given a major boost to his career. He went on to produce entire albums or songs for artists such as Keith Urban, Kylie Minogue, Shania Twain, Madeline Merlo, and the young country singer Callista Clark, whom the current Big Machine Label Group aimed to make the new rising star of country music.

Left: Cleveland, Ohio, April 2007: Taylor Swift sings the national anthem.

Opposite: Signed photos displayed at The Bluebird Cafe, an intimate club in Nashville that has been a springboard for many artists.

SINGLE

PICTURE TO BURN

Taylor Swift, Liz Rose / 2:53

Musicians
Taylor Swift: vocals, backing vocals
Nathan Chapman: acoustic guitar, electric guitar, backing vocals
Nick Buda: drums
Eric Darken: percussion
Scotty Sanders: pedal steel
Rob Hajacos: fiddle
Jeffrey Hyde: banjo
Tim Marks: bass
John Willis: mandolin, high-strung acoustic guitar

Recorded
Castle Studios A (Nashville), 2006

Technical Team
Producer: Nathan Chapman
Executive Producer: Scott Borchetta
Mixing: Chuck Ainlay
Sound Engineers: Nathan Chapman, Chad Carlson
Mastering: Hank Williams

Single Releases
CD single, US, February 4, 2008—(ref. ?)
CD single and vinyl, a limited edition of 4,000 hand-numbered copies, US and Europe, December 20, 2019—BMRTS0104V
Best Rankings: Hot Country: 3; Hot 100: 28

Genesis

For this single (which was certified double platinum), Taylor and her team decided to choose a song with a rock sound perfectly suited to the subject matter: a story of love's revenge, which singularly distances the listener from the sweet bitterness expressed in the song "Tim McGraw." With "Picture to Burn," the singer takes pleasure in ridiculing her ex-boyfriend, mocking his redneck side as well as his main attribute: the famous pickup truck he never let her drive. At the tender age of sixteen, Taylor was already attacking clichés of virility and a certain idea of America, foreshadowing her political coming-out and stance ten years later, during the 2018 midterms.

Production

In stark contrast with "Tim McGraw," the saturated guitars and high tempo of "Picture to Burn" evoke the dense atmosphere of 1970s Southern rock. From the very first chorus, at 0:31, the banjo and pedal steel make their appearance, adding the country spice without which this track would sound resolutely pop rock.

Hidden Message

Date nice boys.

Kimmie Rhodes
Sunbird Records
VINCE MELAMED
TAYLOR SWIFT
ROSIE FLORES
Sam Russell
LYNN WHITE
JUDE JOHNSTONE
MICHAEL LILLE
Gary Burr
DONNA SUMMER
PATRICIA CONROY
Morningstar
Jen Cohen

Taylor Swift performs in Sydney, Australia, March 2009. The Sound Relief concert was organized in support of the victims of the Victoria bushfires.

SINGLE

TEARDROPS ON MY GUITAR (RADIO SINGLE REMIX)

Taylor Swift, Liz Rose / 3:23

Musicians
Taylor Swift: vocals, backing vocals
Nathan Chapman: acoustic guitar, banjo, bass, electric guitar, backing vocals
Eric Darken: percussion
Nick Buda: drums
Dan Dugmore: pedal steel
Rob Hajacos: fiddle
John Willis: high-strung acoustic guitar

Recorded
Sound Cottage (Nashville), 2006

Technical Team
Producer: Nathan Chapman
Executive Producer: Scott Borchetta
Mixing: Chuck Ainlay, Jeff Balding
Sound Engineers: Nathan Chapman, Chad Carlson, Allen Ditto, Clarke Schleicher, Sandi Spika
Mastering: Hank Williams

Single Releases
CD single, promo, US, February 20, 2007—BMRTS0102
Best Ranking: Hot 100: 13

Genesis

"Teardrops on My Guitar" was Taylor Swift's first song to reach the Mainstream Top 40. Certified triple platinum, it is her first crossover single—it also won Song of the Year at the 2008 BMI Country Awards. In this song, the singer describes her secret feelings for classmate Drew Hardwick during her freshman year at Hendersonville High School. Taylor has no hesitation in calling him by his real first name here, always preferring her lyrics to be grounded in reality. The two teenagers make a habit of sitting next to each other in class, and quickly become friends. Drew spends all his time talking about a girl he is madly in love with; he thinks that he has found the perfect girl, he tells her. Taylor listens patiently and supports him in his choice, despite her feelings for him. They remain friends until they part ways. One day, after hearing "Teardrops on My Guitar" on the radio, Drew tried to contact her by phone; they met again two years later, when he was waiting for her outside her home. Their exchanges were brief but cordial. Was he trying to renew a friendly bond, or to show that he was finally available romantically? Although she has moved on, Taylor admits to having wondered about this for a long time.

Production

This ballad, which has had numerous versions and remixes, is an excellent example of country-pop crossover, revealing the young songwriter's multiple influences. The song's structure and harmonic and melodic development fit perfectly into the codes of mid-2000s pop music, while the arrangements and production are typical of modern country and the sound developed in the Nashville studios since the late 1990s. The particular grain of the electric guitar evokes that of the Nobles ODR-1 overdrive pedal, the best-kept secret of Nashville session guitarists, here well highlighted by Chapman's short solo at the end of the second chorus.

To keep the narrative in a hushed atmosphere, acoustic instruments dominate the verses: strummed high-strung and standard guitars positioned at either end of the stereo

field, mandolin counterpoints, banjo arpeggios, and drums played with brushes. The choruses take flight with the impetus of Dan Dugmore's pedal steel, Rob Hajacos's discreet fiddle, Nathan Chapman's slightly distorted electric guitar, Nick Buda's drums, which support beats 2 and 4 on the snare drum, and the rounded bass. Supported in this way, Taylor Swift is able to fully exploit the top end of her range, with a confident voice that is comforting for the listener, who may also have their heart broken.

Hidden Message

He will never know.

FOR DISCERNING SWIFTIES

A 2:59 pop remix version was included, at track 15, in the international rerelease of the album issued in 2008. Traditional country instruments were scrapped (exit the mandolin, dobro, pedal steel, and banjo), with the exception of a violin arrangement whose classical playing has a completely different character from the expressivity of the fiddle playing on the original version. The acoustic drums are replaced with a programmed drum machine, and layers of synthesizers further emphasize the pop feel. All that remain are the strummed acoustic guitar, electric guitar, bass, and Taylor Swift's voice loaded with effects (delay and reverb), characteristic of the mainstream pop of the time.

FOR DISCERNING SWIFTIES

Robert Ellis Orrall, who co-wrote the definitive version of "A Place in This World" with Angelo Petraglia, revealed on his Instagram account that the demo version of this song was recorded on January 15, 2004, with two other tracks: "I'm Only Me When I'm with You" (as a bonus track on the Deluxe reissue of the first album, released in 2007) and "What Do You Say" (as yet unreleased, except on one of Taylor Swift's demo CDs in 2004).

A PLACE IN THIS WORLD

Taylor Swift, Robert Ellis Orrall, Angelo Petraglia / 3:22

Musicians

Taylor Swift: vocals, backing vocals
Nathan Chapman: acoustic guitar, banjo, bass, drums, electric guitar, backing vocals, mandolin
Bruce Bouton: dobro
Mike Brignardello, Tim Marks: bass
Nick Buda, Shannon Forrest: drums
Gary Brunette: electric guitar
Eric Darken: percussion
Dan Dugmore: pedal steel
Rob Hajacos, Wanda Vick: fiddle
Tony Harrell: keyboards
Jeffrey Hyde: banjo
Andy Leftwich: fiddle, mandolin
Liana Manis, Robert Ellis Orrall: backing vocals
Lex Price: mandolin
Joshua Whitmore: dobro, pedal steel
Ilya Toshinsky: acoustic guitar, banjo
John Willis: banjo, mandolin, high-strung acoustic guitar

Recorded

Castle Studios A (Nashville, Tennessee), 2006

Technical Team

Producer: Nathan Chapman
Executive Producer: Scott Borchetta
Mixing: Chuck Ainlay, Jeff Balding
Sound Engineers: Nathan Chapman, Chad Carlson, Allen Ditto, Clarke Schleicher, Sandi Spika
Mastering: Hank Williams

Genesis

Taylor Swift wrote this song when she was thirteen, in November 2003. She dreamed of succeeding in Nashville as a professional singer and songwriter. In 2004, her dream started to come true when RCA Records offered her a development contract. The young singer and her family moved to Nashville shortly after that.

Production

After an opening guitar chord, we are straight into the heart of the matter, with Taylor's voice ("I don't know what I want") and no fewer than three guitars supporting her first verse: a strumming acoustic guitar in the center, backed by two rhythmic electric guitars placed to the right and left of the stereo field—plus an arpeggiated banjo also in the center. The same formula is used on the pre-chorus, to which bass is added, then, at 0:27, into the chorus: a straight drumbeat, pedal steel, and electric guitar gimmick echo Taylor's voice. We find the same ingredients as on "Picture to Burn." The intensity goes up a notch and does not come down again until the bridge, at 1:49, after the electric guitar solo at the end of the second chorus. A few notes of tubular bells and mandolin tremolos later, and the musicians redouble their energy on the third chorus, ending with a highly orchestrated ad lib. "Oh, I'm just a girl," Taylor Swift repeats, but it is clear she already knows what she wants.

Hidden Message

I found it.

"Cold As You" marks the beginning of a famous Swiftian tradition: From now on, every fifth track on every album will be the designated vulnerable, moving ballad.

Taylor Swift performs at Country Thunder USA, July 2008, in Twin Lakes, Wisconsin.

COLD AS YOU

Taylor Swift, Liz Rose / 4:01

Musicians

Taylor Swift: vocals, backing vocals
Nathan Chapman: acoustic guitar, banjo, bass, drums, backing vocals, mandolin
Bruce Bouton: dobro
Mike Brignardello, Tim Marks: bass
Nick Buda, Shannon Forrest: drums
Eric Darken: percussion
Dan Dugmore: pedal steel
Rob Hajacos, Wanda Vick: fiddle
Tony Harrell: keyboards
Jeffrey Hyde: banjo
Andy Leftwich: fiddle, mandolin
Lex Price: mandolin
Joshua Whitmore: dobro, pedal steel
Ilya Toshinsky: acoustic guitar, banjo
John Willis: banjo, mandolin, high-strung acoustic guitar

Recorded

Dark Horse Recording (Franklin, Tennessee), 2005–2006

Technical Team

Producer: Nathan Chapman
Executive Producer: Scott Borchetta
Mixing: Chuck Ainlay, Jeff Balding
Sound Engineers: Nathan Chapman, Chad Carlson, Allen Ditto, Clarke Schleicher, Sandi Spika
Mastering: Hank Williams

Genesis

"Cold As You" tackles the theme of disillusionment in love with a directness that has become a hallmark of Taylor Swift's songwriting. In a publicity interview, the singer said: "I conceived this song with Liz [Rose] and I think the lyrics are some of the best I've ever come up with." She recalls that moment when you realize someone is not at all the person you thought they were; she describes how you try to make excuses for them when they do not deserve it. Some people will never really love you is what she confides in her lyrics. As she is putting her words down on paper, Taylor begins to sing: "And now that I'm sitting here thinking it through / I've never been anywhere cold as you."

Production

"Cold As You" is the first track on the album to include a piano score. Played by Tony Harrell, it essentially carries the song on its shoulders, giving the harmonic spectrum a hitherto unheard-of density. The usual elements are also present: drums played with brushes, a round, minimalist bass and airy pedal steel, dobro strokes in counterpoint, and ample, supple acoustic guitar strumming. Two notable facts, however: the absence of electric guitar and the greater presence of the fiddle, whose embellishments help to sublimate this highly emotional arrangement.

Hidden Message

Time to let go.

Taylor Swift onstage at the Vault Concert Stages of the 2008 CMA Music Festival, an event that celebrates the diversity and richness of the country music scene.

THE OUTSIDE

Taylor Swift / 3:27

Musicians

Taylor Swift: vocals, backing vocals
Nathan Chapman: acoustic and electric guitars, banjo, bass, drums, backing vocals, mandolin
Bruce Bouton: dobro
Mike Brignardello, Tim Marks: bass
Nick Buda, Shannon Forrest: drums
Gary Brunette: electric guitar
Eric Darken: percussion
Dan Dugmore: pedal steel
Rob Hajacos, Wanda Vick: fiddle
Tony Harrell: keyboards
Jeffrey Hyde: banjo
Andy Leftwich: fiddle, mandolin
Liana Manis, Robert Ellis Orrall: backing vocals
Lex Price: mandolin
Joshua Whitmore: dobro, pedal steel
Ilya Toshinsky: acoustic guitar, banjo
John Willis: banjo, mandolin, high-strung acoustic guitar

Recorded

2005–2006

Technical Team

Producers: Nathan Chapman, Robert Ellis Orrall
Executive Producer: Scott Borchetta
Mixing: Chuck Ainlay, Jeff Balding
Sound Engineers: Nathan Chapman, Chad Carlson, Allen Ditto, Clarke Schleicher, Sandi Spika
Mastering: Hank Williams

Genesis

For Taylor Swift, the "outside" is the world she does not belong to, that of the "cool kids." Very tall for her age, a fan of country karaoke, and always on the road to sing at a festival, Taylor wonders every day if anyone will come and talk to her. While her early (unrecorded) lyrics often described idealized love relationships, stories she had not experienced, "The Outside" is the first song she wrote observing reality, in a painful introspection that is honest and surprisingly mature for a twelve-year-old. But Taylor Swift has always considered herself lucky, because, through music, she has never needed alcohol or drugs to escape.

Production

"The Outside" starts off at full speed, with all the guitars in play and the rhythm section to the fore. The track's upbeat feel and sense of speed are accentuated by the mandolin's sixteenth-note rhythm, which acts as a kind of harmonic high hat. This type of fast playing, usually reserved for bluegrass music, is an interesting production trick in the context of a country-pop arrangement like this. At 2:19, the lead part played on baritone guitar brings an original texture that is particularly pleasing to the ear. In addition to the heavy production work on the electric guitars, at 2:35 we notice the presence of a piano played in the upper register to finish the track with an extra touch of brilliance, in contrast to the very rich bass sounds of the baritone guitar. Producer Robert Ellis Orrall co-produced this track with Nathan Chapman, and the richness of the arrangement proves that they were able to work well as a team.

Hidden Message

You are not alone.

Taylor Swift has always been committed to maintaining a special relationship with her audience.

A CHILD OF THE INTERNET

Born in 1989, Taylor Swift belongs to the first generation that grew up around social media. She knew early in her musical career that she could use these tools to spread her music and her image. Taylor opened her MySpace account, which was a key site at the time for emerging artists, on August 31, 2005, the day before the official launch of the Big Machine label. Over the following months, she amassed more than forty-five million streams, a figure that Big Machine president and CEO Scott Borchetta was only too happy to quote to prove to skeptical radio stations that there was indeed an audience for his artist.

Abolishing Distance Between Artist and Audience

MySpace was soon to become a key element in Taylor's early marketing strategy, which was initially not really a strategy at all: Like many teenagers, she simply enjoyed regularly updating her page. She posted video montages and photos during her tours and other work sessions, and she made it a point of honor to reply personally to the fan messages she received, often indulging in confessions or sharing cat photos. This direct and sincere engagement was totally innovative at a time when a distance between artists and their public was still the norm. When she was eighteen, in the intro on her MySpace page (now defunct but accessible from the Internet Archive), she wrote: "In my spare time, I like to conduct random baking experiments in my kitchen and write letters to people. I really love people who like my music. They're number 1 on my favorite things list." This was Swift's tour de force: giving her fans the feeling that she is not only an artist they appreciate, but also a young woman as "normal" as they are, someone they can connect with.

Sharing Her Personal Life

MySpace was not the only social network she embraced. In 2008, just as the platform was beginning to be abandoned by users, she created her Twitter account, where she posted both her latest news and comments on her personal life. In 2011, she launched her Instagram account. Her page has now become one of the most followed accounts in the world, with 282 million followers. In 2014, she first appeared on the microblogging site Tumblr, which she uses to interact with the public in greater depth. She shared photos and more developed thoughts and wrote lengthy responses to fans.

The Birth of the Swifties

From the very first years of her success, her fan base has been appreciative of this closeness. Their commitment and

Swifties dream of winning a VIP ticket to a concert by their musical and cultural icon.

loyalty to the artist is unique in the music industry. Swifties, as her fans often call themselves, are, among other things, impervious to any form of influence exerted by the media, preferring to follow the artist's news directly on her social networks. It has to be said that Taylor gives her fans plenty to chew on: She announces album releases, music videos, and tour dates, of course, but she also regularly distills hidden messages that her fans like to decipher—a habit she has been developing since her first album.

A Strong and Independent Woman

The deep bond Taylor has been able to forge with her public has allowed her to create her own media ecosystem. It not only gives her a way to better control her narrative by delivering her version of events directly on her networks, but it also has allowed her, in the most difficult moments of her career, to almost completely free herself from the media. For example, around 2016, after a yearlong retreat from the spotlight, she orchestrated her comeback solely on her Instagram account. She deleted all the content on her account and, a few days later, posted a series of cryptic videos in which we can make out a snake's coiling tail (see the *Reputation* album). She radically changed the atmosphere and, focusing on a single social media channel, showed she was taking back control of her public image.

During the 2008 CMA Music Festival, Taylor Swift takes part in a question-and-answer session about her musical transition to a more mature style.

TIED TOGETHER WITH A SMILE

Taylor Swift, Liz Rose / 4:08

Musicians

Taylor Swift: vocals, backing vocals
Nathan Chapman: acoustic guitar, banjo, bass, drums, backing vocals, mandolin
Bruce Bouton: dobro
Mike Brignardello, Tim Marks: bass
Nick Buda, Shannon Forrest: drums
Eric Darken: percussion
Dan Dugmore: pedal steel
Rob Hajacos, Wanda Vick: fiddle
Tony Harrell: keyboards
Jeffrey Hyde: banjo
Andy Leftwich: fiddle, mandolin
Lex Price: mandolin
Joshua Whitmore: dobro, pedal steel
Ilya Toshinsky: acoustic guitar, banjo
John Willis: banjo, mandolin, high-strung acoustic guitar

Recorded

2005–2006

Technical Team

Producer: Nathan Chapman
Executive Producer: Scott Borchetta
Mixing: Chuck Ainlay, Jeff Balding
Sound Engineers: Nathan Chapman, Chad Carlson, Allen Ditto, Clarke Schleicher, Sandi Spika
Mastering: Hank Williams

Genesis

In "Tied Together with a Smile," Taylor Swift tells the story of her friend, a beauty queen with an eating disorder. All the girls want to look like her, all the boys want to be with her, but, alone in front of her mirror, the young woman dislikes what she sees. This empathetic song tells the story of self-esteem and the difficulty of facing up to the gaze of others.

Production

In this predominantly acoustic ballad, the slow tempo is driven by brushes on the drums, in symbiosis with the folk guitar rhythm. Right from the introduction, almost all the acoustic instruments are present, with fiddle, dobro, banjo, and arpeggiated acoustic guitar responding in turn; the only thing missing is the mandolin, which makes its entrance on the first chorus to flesh out the binary rhythm on the left-hand side in response to the acoustic guitar strumming positioned on the right. Electric guitar, bass, pedal steel, and a layer of Hammond organ gently reinforce the choruses, broadening the stereo field and adding depth to a nuanced arrangement that perfectly suits the subject: "[...] and no one knows / That you cry, [...] / And you're tied together with a smile."

Hidden Message

You are loved.

STAY BEAUTIFUL

Taylor Swift, Liz Rose / 3:56

Musicians
Taylor Swift: vocals, backing vocals
Nathan Chapman: acoustic guitar, banjo, bass, drums, backing vocals, mandolin
Bruce Bouton: dobro
Mike Brignardello, Tim Marks: bass
Nick Buda: drums
Eric Darken: percussion
Dan Dugmore: pedal steel
Shannon Forrest: drums
Rob Hajacos, Wanda Vick: fiddle
Tony Harrell: keyboards
Jeffrey Hyde: banjo
Andy Leftwich: fiddle, mandolin
Lex Price: mandolin
Joshua Whitmore: dobro, pedal steel
Ilya Toshinsky: acoustic guitar, banjo
John Willis: banjo, mandolin, high-strung acoustic guitar

Recorded
2005–2006

Technical Team
Production: Nathan Chapman
Executive Producer: Scott Borchetta
Mixing: Chuck Ainlay, Jeff Balding
Sound Engineers: Nathan Chapman, Chad Carlson, Allen Ditto, Clarke Schleicher, Sandi Spika
Mastering: Hank Williams

Genesis

"Stay Beautiful" is the story of Cory, an enigmatic young man whom Taylor Swift has never dated but has watched from afar. As described by the singer, Cory seems every inch the deep-eyed, athletic young male fantasy figure every teenage girl is secretly in love with: "These pretty girls on every corner / They watch him as he's walking home / Saying, 'Does he know?'" Taylor writes this song like a letter she will never send, perhaps hoping that one day, the handsome Cory will hear it and recognize himself in it.

Production

This is the first ternary track (subdivision of the quarter note into three beats: In this case, a mid-tempo country shuffle ternary) on the album, giving it a more pronounced country-folk feel. A few bluegrass accents are thrown in for good measure, notably with the banjo's clawhammer-like playing, the dobro, and the fiddle's constant double-stopping to highlight the ritornello of the choruses. It is only a matter of time before the arrangement confines itself to acoustic instruments; here, only the Hammond organ (generally very discreet, except on the bridge) and the bass are electrified. Between 2:18 and 2:36, the bridge arrangement clearly stands out from the other parts, incorporating a tremolo mandolin and, above all, a descending arpeggio that seems to be played on the top of a Fender Rhodes keyboard or by a celesta and doubled by pedal steel. The effect is quite magical and conducive to reverie, ideal for a song in praise of beauty.

Hidden Message

Shake 'n' bake [as in the breadcrumb mixture].

During the American Music Awards, November 2007, in Los Angeles.

SINGLE

SHOULD'VE SAID NO

Taylor Swift / 4:02

Musicians

Taylor Swift: vocals, backing vocals
Nathan Chapman: acoustic guitar, electric guitar, backing vocals
Tim Marks: bass
Nick Buda: drums
Eric Darken: percussion
Scotty Sanders: pedal steel
Rob Hajacos: fiddle
John Willis: banjo

Recorded

Dark Horse Recording (Franklin, Tennessee), August 2006

Technical Team

Producer: Nathan Chapman
Executive Producer: Scott Borchetta
Mixing: Chuck Ainlay, Jeff Balding, Jeremy Wheatley
Sound Engineers: Nathan Chapman, Chad Carlson
Programming: Alexis Smith, Richard Adlam
Mastering: Hank Williams, Jeremy Wheatley

Single Releases

CD single, US, May 18, 2008
7-inch vinyl, 45 rpm, single, 4,000-copy hand-numbered limited edition, white vinyl, January 24, 2020—BMRTS0106V
Best Rankings: Hot Country: 1; Hot 100: 33

Genesis

Released on May 18, 2008, "Should've Said No" is the fifth and final single from the album. Taylor Swift wrote the song—which went platinum—at the age of sixteen, after learning that her boyfriend at the time had cheated on her. The title came first, then the choruses, which she composed in five minutes. According to Taylor herself, most of the lyrics correspond exactly to the words she would have used at the time of the confrontation with her boyfriend. Faithful once again to one of her favorite writing methods: sticking as closely as possible to reality when the context allows. Similar in theme to her song "Picture to Burn," the tone here is more moralistic and less focused on expressing anger: "You shouldn't be begging for forgiveness at my feet / You should've said no."

Production

Deceptively, "Should've Said No" kicks off with a short, 100 percent acoustic intro, with the clear intention of exposing the listener to the melody of the chorus, a heady gimmick that imprints itself throughout the song. Initially played by the banjo alone, this theme is doubled by the fiddle as soon as the full band arrives, after a drum break reminiscent of 1990s rock. The electric guitars take center stage, the sound is full-bodied, and the volume of the amps and the overdrive pedals is pushed further than usual. Acoustic instruments once again take center stage on the first verse and the pre-chorus; the playing is restrained. This contrast enables the explosion of the first chorus and its instrumental coda. The same recipe is applied to the rest of the arrangement, with Nathan Chapman and his musicians taking care not to let the tension fade. Taylor Swift is thus able to unfold her narrative and gradually build up the intensity, demonstrating that her vocal tone holds up perfectly to this type of rock orchestration. At 2:57, after the epic electric guitar solo at the end of the second chorus, the bridge enables Nick Buda to develop a drum part, mainly centered on the toms, reminiscent of the heavy, powerful playing of grunge rock drummers from the first half of the 1990s (such as Matt Cameron of Soundgarden or Jimmy Chamberlin of the Smashing Pumpkins, to name but two).

Hidden Message

Sam Sam Sam Sam Sam Sam.

Taylor Swift onstage in Kansas City, May 2007, one of her first major performances on tour.

MARY'S SONG (OH MY MY MY)

Taylor Swift, Liz Rose, Brian Maher / 3:33

Musicians

Taylor Swift: vocals, backing vocals
Nathan Chapman: acoustic guitar, banjo, bass, drums, backing vocals, mandolin
Bruce Bouton: dobro
Mike Brignardello, Tim Marks: bass
Nick Buda, Shannon Forrest: drums
Eric Darken: percussion
Jeffrey Hyde: banjo, mandolin
Lex Price: mandolin
Joshua Whitmore: dobro
Ilya Toshinsky: acoustic guitar, banjo
John Willis: banjo, mandolin, high-strung acoustic guitar

Recorded

2005–2006

Technical Team

Producer: Nathan Chapman
Executive Producer: Scott Borchetta
Mixing: Chuck Ainlay, Jeff Balding
Sound Engineers: Nathan Chapman, Chad Carlson, Allen Ditto, Clarke Schleicher, Sandi Spika
Mastering: Hank Williams

Genesis

"Mary's Song (Oh My My My)" is a tribute to eternal love. Taylor Swift was inspired to write it by a couple who lived next door to her. At a family dinner, the couple told their story of how they met as children, aged seven and nine. Taylor found them so touching that she decided to put into song what this solid, pure love inspired in her.

Production

A new example of a guaranteed 100 percent acoustic intro, this country-pop ballad kicks off with the sound of mandolin and dobro, with delicate strumming of folk guitar and banjo played with a discreet picking style. At 0:11, Taylor's voice makes its entrance, immersing the listener in a subdued atmosphere conducive to telling the

story of Mary and her lifelong companion. After the intimate arrangement of the first verse, the chorus opens the floodgates: Electric guitars, bass, and drums weave an orchestration perfectly calibrated to conquer US country and mainstream radio. Despite these qualities, "Mary's Song (Oh My My My)" was never released as a single.

Hidden Message

Sometimes love is forever.

Taylor Swift performing "Our Song" at the 41st CMA Awards in 2007 at the Sommet Center in Nashville.

FOR DISCERNING SWIFTIES

Since "Our Song" ends with the phrase "Play it again," Taylor Swift decided it would be an ideal closing track. It is like a direct and, at the same time, subliminal suggestion to play the album again, as soon as it is finished.

SINGLE

OUR SONG

Taylor Swift / 3:22

Musicians
Taylor Swift: vocals, backing vocals
Nathan Chapman: acoustic guitar, electric guitar, banjo, backing vocals
Bruce Bouton: dobro
Tim Marks: bass
Nick Buda: drums
Eric Darken: percussion
Rob Hajacos: fiddle

Recorded
Quad Studios A, Sound Cottage (Nashville, Tennessee), 2006

Single Releases
CD single, US, September 10, 2007—BMRTS0103
7-inch vinyl, 45 rpm, limited 4,000-copy hand-numbered edition, white vinyl, November 22, 2019—BMRTS0103V
Best Rankings: Hot Country: 1; Hot 100: 16

Technical Team
Producer: Nathan Chapman
Executive Producer: Scott Borchetta
Mixing: Chuck Ainlay, Jeff Balding
Sound Engineers: Nathan Chapman, Chad Carlson
Mastering: Hank Williams

Genesis

Taylor Swift wrote "Our Song" for her high school talent show. Given the success of this performance, she was keen to have the song featured on her debut album and released as a single. In her opinion, the song's natural "bounce" made it extremely radio-friendly. The singer was not mistaken: "Our Song" was to become the album's biggest hit, selling over four million copies (it was certified quadruple platinum).

Production

One of the series of tracks that start with an instrumental intro: Rob Hajacos's fiddle, which opens the festivities, is joined by Eric Darken's cajón rhythm along with syncopated acoustic guitar and banjo picking, both played by Nathan Chapman. Apart from Tim Marks's minimalist, groovy bass playing and Chapman's electric guitar, the song retains its acoustic, "grain-fed" country-pop flavor right to the end. The moderate tempo (90 bpm) makes you want to tap your toes alone in your room, daydreaming instead of doing your homework, or get out on the dance floor. The sober (but tremendously effective) arrangement, the clarity of the mix, and the conversational lyrics and impeccable phrasing of young Taylor Swift exude an infectious energy, an irresistible, unifying adolescent candor in a Western world still imbued with a certain insouciance.

Hidden Message

Live in love.

Taylor Swift at the 2009 V Festival in Stafford, her first major performance in the UK.

I'M ONLY ME WHEN I'M WITH YOU

Taylor Swift, Robert Ellis Orrall, Angelo Petraglia / 3:33

Musicians

Taylor Swift: vocals, backing vocals
Mike Brignardello, Tim Marks: bass
Nick Buda, Shannon Forrest: drums
Gary Brunette: electric guitar
Eric Darken: percussion
Dan Dugmore: pedal steel
Rob Hajacos, Wanda Vick: fiddle
Tony Harrell: keyboards
Andy Leftwich: fiddle, mandolin
Liana Manis, Robert Ellis Orrall: backing vocals
Lex Price: mandolin
Joshua Whitmore: dobro, pedal steel
Ilya Toshinsky: acoustic guitar
John Willis: banjo, mandolin, high-strung acoustic guitar

Recorded

January 15, 2004

Technical Team

Producers: Robert Ellis Orrall, Angelo Petraglia

Genesis

The first bonus track on the Deluxe Edition, this is also the first song co-written with singer, songwriter, and producer Robert Ellis Orrall toward the end of 2003, when Taylor Swift was still living in Pennsylvania. In it, the singer enjoys the company of her friends, with whom she can express herself freely and be fully herself. This recording is part of the January 15, 2004, session with producers Robert Ellis Orrall, Angelo Petraglia, and Jamie Tate, during which the tracks "A Place in This World" and "What Do You Say" were also recorded. "I'm Only Me When I'm with You" appears as the bonus twelfth track on the Deluxe reissue of the first album, released in 2007.

Production

The resolutely pop-rock sound and the lack of density in the low-midrange mix show that the production of "I'm Only Me When I'm with You" took place before the album's official production, with fewer resources and outside the criteria set by producers Scott Borchetta and Nathan Chapman. The bass drums' pulse and the overdriven electric guitars form the hard core of the orchestra, while the fiddle, pedal steel, and mandolin remain in the background (except on the instrumental bridges at 1:06, 2:16, and in the intro when the fiddle takes the lead), but true to form, as proud representatives of the Nashville sound of the 2000s. In fact, it is likely that these three instruments were recorded after the event, as an overdub, to better suit the album's country-pop aesthetic. Whatever the case, Robert Ellis Orrall and Angelo Petraglia have achieved an arrangement that is straight to the point, tight, and with no weak moments.

During her live shows, Taylor Swift sometimes performs "Invisible" on acoustic guitar, to emphasize the song's gentleness and introspective character.

INVISIBLE

Taylor Swift, Robert Ellis Orrall / 3:23

Musicians
Taylor Swift: vocals, backing vocals
Mike Brignardello: bass
Nick Buda: drums
Gary Brunette: electric guitar
Eric Darken: percussion
Dan Dugmore: pedal steel
Shannon Forrest: drums
Rob Hajacos, Wanda Vick: fiddle
Tony Harrell: keyboards
Andy Leftwich: fiddle
Liana Manis: backing vocals
Tim Marks: bass
Robert Ellis Orrall: backing vocals
Joshua Whitmore: dobro, pedal steel
Ilya Toshinsky: acoustic guitar
John Willis: high-strung acoustic guitar

Recorded
November 2005

Technical Team
Producer: Robert Ellis Orrall
Executive Producer: Scott Borchetta

Genesis

It's possible that the boy Taylor evokes in "Invisible" could be none other than the famous Drew Hardwick featured in "Teardrops on My Guitar." The feeling seems similar: The young man has his heart set on someone else; Taylor is invisible to him but knows that only she can see the true inner and outer beauty of the man she loves. "She can't see the way your eyes / Light up when you smile." This is the second bonus track on the Deluxe Edition.

Production

The piano returns to the center of the arrangement. As on "Cold as You," Tony Harrell's score and touch establish the melancholy, dreamy tone of this subtly orchestrated ballad. Pedal steel and airy playing for the dreamy aspect; the piano is in symbiosis with guitar arpeggios for the melancholy aspect. The piano sound is doubled from beginning to end by a layer of synthesizers, discreet but adding a certain depth to the whole, a 3D feel to the mix. Without overdoing it, the fiddle and electric guitar arpeggios tug at the heartstrings and, from the second chorus onward, the backing vocals reinforce the emotional range of Taylor Swift's voice. Will her plea be heard? The bass and drums frame the whole in a sober, precise performance, perfect for the last-chance slow dance.

"A Perfectly Good Heart" was written when Taylor Swift was fourteen years old. Heralding the young woman's future albums, the song is about love, breakups, and the cruelty of feelings.

A PERFECTLY GOOD HEART

Taylor Swift, Brett James, Troy Verges / 3:40

Musicians
Taylor Swift: vocals, backing vocals
Mike Brignardello, Tim Marks: bass
Nick Buda, Shannon Forrest: drums
Gary Brunette: electric guitar
Eric Darken: percussion
Tony Harrell: keyboards, mandolin
Liana Manis: backing vocals
Lex Price: mandolin
Ilya Toshinsky: acoustic guitar

Recorded
Abtrax Recording (Nashville, Tennessee), The Engine Room (Nashville, Tennessee), 2003

Technical Team
Producers: Brett James, Troy Verges
Executive Producer: Scott Borchetta
Mixing: Chuck Ainlay, Jeff Balding
Sound Engineer: Chad Carlson
Mastering: Hank Williams

Genesis

The third bonus track on the Deluxe Edition, "A Perfectly Good Heart" tells the story of a breakup in love, or, more precisely, of the day when our hearts break for the first time. Written by Taylor Swift the year she turned fourteen, this song expresses the innocence of first love, absolute trust in others, and incomprehension when faced with the cruelty of feelings.

Production

After a short Hammond organ fade-out as an introduction, the song launches straight into a chorus of guitars and vocals. From the very first phrase, Taylor harmonizes her own voice, overdubbing a third below. The piano comes in at 0:15, then bass and drums introduce the verse at 0:27. The most striking production detail of this arrangement is the effect applied to the sound of the electric piano (on the left in the stereo field). Very elaborate, and easy to mistake for an electric guitar, it passes through a Uni-Vibe pedal to create a rotating effect that adds density and movement to the whole. From 1:47 onward, on the instrumental bridge, the double-note electric guitar part inevitably evokes the playing of the famous The Edge (the guitarist from the rock band U2), followed by a highly melodic mandolin solo. The track ends with a very gradual fade-out to a long instrumental ad lib, which can be interpreted as both a tribute and a farewell to teenage romance.

NEW 1

BEAUTIFUL EYES

Taylor Swift / 2:59

1. Beautiful Eyes
2. Should've Said No (alternate version)
3. Teardrops On My Guitar (acoustic version)
4. Picture To Burn (Radio edit)
5. I'm Only Me When I'm with You
6. I Heart?

Release Dates
United States: July 15, 2008 (ref. Big Machine Records)

Musicians
Taylor Swift: vocals, backing vocals
Gary Burnette: bass, guitar
Rusty Danmyer: pedal steel
Robert Ellis Orrall: chorus
Ken Lewis: drums
Chris Rowe: shaker

Recorded
The Tracking Room (Nashville), 2005–2008

Technical Team
Producer: Robert Ellis Orrall
Mixing: Chris Rowe
Sound Engineers: Eric Richardson, Robert Ellis Orrall
Mastering: Ken Love
Best Ranking: 9

EPs (extended plays), or releases with more songs than singles but fewer than albums, often allow rising artists to attain or retain musical relevance while waiting to offer a new LP (long play). That was precisely what Taylor did when she released *Beautiful Eyes* on July 15, 2008, especially as her growing popularity in the country world needed to be consolidated. It mainly contains acoustic or alternative versions of several previously released titles, but it also offers two new tracks, "Beautiful Eyes" and "I Heart?" (detailed below). It also includes a DVD of clips produced at the time, a video specially made for *Beautiful Eyes* of sequences filmed during the singer's eighteenth birthday, excerpts from interviews, and behind-the-scenes moments.

The disc was sold for a limited time only in Walmart stores and on the retail chain's website in MP3 version. It has become a collector's item for her biggest fans—further proof that, from her very first years in the music industry, the young woman has used her keen sense of marketing to maintain a privileged link with the hard core of her audience.

Genesis

Presumably written to appear on Taylor Swift's debut album, released on October 24, 2006, "Beautiful Eyes" is a spirited and sentimental romp. Taylor expresses her exaltation at the idea of losing herself in the gaze of her loved one, her heart pounding, letting herself be transported by the force of such emotions. In the song she dreams of living the perfect romance without any downside.

Production

The intro of this country pop ballad at a moderate tempo (95 bpm) gives pride of place to acoustic instruments: The arpeggios of acoustic guitar and mandolin (played by Chris Row or Gary Burnette—the credits do not specify) steal the show until the vocals begin and the bass drum pulses on beats 2 and 4. The rest of the group enters on the first chorus, bringing with them their electric arsenal: guitar, pedal steel, bass, and keyboards. The second verse highlights the playing of Gary Burnette and his mixture of arpeggios, well-felt turnarounds and melodic double-string gimmicks, all delivered with a sound that is both crunchy and detailed, reminiscent of a Fender Telecaster guitar passed through an ODR1 overdrive pedal from the Nobles brand (a typical combination of the Nashville sound from the 2000s). On the Hammond organ, Chris Row, a multi-instrumentalist and producer of the title, also plays particularly shimmering music, a perfect complement to Burnette's guitar and the pedal steel provided by Rusty Danmyer.

The six-track EP *Beautiful Eyes* (2008) includes previously unreleased songs as well as rerecorded versions, such as "Teardrops on My Guitar."

NEW 2

I HEART?

Taylor Swift / 3:21

Musicians
Shannon Forrest: drums
Tony Harrell: keyboard
Mike Brignardello: bass
Wanda Vick: banjo, mandoline
Liana Manis, Robert Ellis Orrall: backing vocals
Gary Burnette: electric guitar
Dan Dugmore: pedal steel

Recorded
The Tracking Room (Nashville), 2005–2008

Technical Team
Producer: Robert Ellis Orrall
Mixing: Ben Fowler
Sound Engineers: Clarke Schleicher, Allen Ditto
Mastering: Ken Love

Genesis

Taylor Swift wrote this song in 2003, at the age of thirteen. She recorded the demo version in 2004 for one of her demo albums, with the songs "Your Face" and "The Outside" (the latter appears on her first album). "I Heart?" deals with romantic confusion during a breakup that occurs without Taylor understanding the reason. From this confusion arises a questioning, the young woman not knowing who she should love, hence the question mark in the title.

Production

The arrangement and production of this track immediately recall the bounding energy of Taylor Swift onstage in her early days. The country bluegrass instrumentation counts for a lot—banjo, mandolin, and pedal steel going all out. The composition itself, simple and rhythmic, is designed to establish a direct connection between Taylor and her fans during a live concert, though she's not yet performing in prestigious venues, least of all enormous tours in stadiums around the world. Like a wink from keyboardist Tony Harrell, the first notes of the Hammond organ inevitably evoke the organ played by Al Kooper on "Like a Rolling Stone," Bob Dylan's classic from 1965. To reinforce its impact, the sound of the snare drum seems to have been doubled by a sample. Although "I Heart?" is an early work, it already has the traditional structure inherent to Taylor Swift's songs: intro / verse / pre-chorus / chorus and, above all, the famous bridge at the end of the second chorus. This way of writing, common in mainstream pop and almost systematic in country in the 2000s, is the mark of a surprising maturity for such a young songwriter.

RELEASE DATES
United States: November 11, 2008
(ref.: Big Machine Records BMRATS0200)
***Deluxe reissue, Fearless Platinum Edition: October 26, 2009**
(ref.: Big Machine Records BMRBTS0250)
Best Ranking: 1

ALBUM

Fearless

Jump Then Fall* · Untouchable* · Come in with the Rain* · Superstar* · The Other Side of the Door* · Fearless · Fifteen · Love Story · Hey Stephen · White Horse · You Belong with Me · Breathe (feat. Colbie Caillat) · Tell Me Why · You're Not Sorry · The Way I Loved You · Forever & Always · The Best Day · Change

In December 2009, dazzling in her silver-sequined fringe outfit, Taylor Swift shines at KIIS FM's Jingle Ball in Los Angeles.

FOR DISCERNING SWIFTIES

While under a publishing contract with Sony/ATV as a songwriter, Taylor composed more than 250 songs, alone or in collaboration. She later admitted that she refused to cede a number of them to other artists, preferring to reserve them for her future albums. *Taylor Swift*, *Fearless*, and *Speak Now* also contain songs written before her singing career took off.

THE SUPERHIGHWAY TO SUCCESS

Taylor Swift had not yet turned eighteen when she learned that she had been nominated for Best New Artist at the 2008 Grammy Awards. Amy Winehouse won the award in the end, but Taylor, catapulted from the country scene into the mainstream, knew that she was now major league. That same year, she picked up a number of other awards, including the Country Music Association Television Award for Video of the Year (for "Our Song") and the Academy of Country Music Awards' Top New Female Vocalist, a major accolade in the country music world. By the end of 2008, her debut album had sold over three million copies. Her home videos, which she edited herself and posted on MySpace, had now passed the fifty-million-streams mark. Even so, Taylor continued to respond directly to her fans, sometimes individually, on this platform.

Media Curiosity

For Scott Borchetta, it was essential to strike while the iron was hot. So, before the release of her second album in November, he had Taylor record an EP, *Beautiful Eyes*, released on July 15, 2008, and distributed exclusively by Walmart. Within the first week of its release, the EP climbed to ninth place on the Billboard 200 and to number one on Top Country. On the media front, interest grew. *Billboard* and *Seventeen* magazines devoted their front pages to her in 2008. But it was undoubtedly her brief romance that same year with Joe Jonas of the Jonas Brothers, and above all their breakup, which Taylor recounted in no uncertain terms on *The Ellen DeGeneres Show*—the young man allegedly broke up with her during a phone call lasting just a few minutes—that made her a household name. She also became the youngest musician ever to appear on *Saturday Night Live*.

Critical Recognition

From an artistic point of view, *Fearless* was a first turning point for Taylor, primarily because she wrote seven songs on her own for it, including two singles ("Love Story" and "White Horse"), and co-wrote the other six with Liz Rose and country artists Colbie Caillat, John Rich, and Hillary Lindsey. As with *Taylor Swift*, *Fearless* finds the young singer expressing her adolescent state of mind, susceptible to the whims of first love, but she has sharpened her pen over the past two years. In a short review of the album, the *New York Times* described her as "one of pop's finest songwriters, country's foremost pragmatist and more in touch with her inner life than most adults." And while *Rolling Stone* magazine is critical of her "almost impersonal professionalism," it praises her lyrics for their "confessions that are squirmingly intimate and true." On the production side, Nathan Chapman, who previously worked on *Taylor Swift*, is once again at the helm. But this time Taylor is making her debut as a producer. The two of them venture a little further into pop and rock, although country remains the backbone of the record. *Rolling Stone* goes on to say, "[*Fearless* is] so rigorously crafted it sounds like it has been scientifically engineered in a hit factory."

Opposite: **Taylor Swift shares the stage with Faith Hill at the 2010 CMT Music Awards, symbolizing the collaboration between two influential women in country music.**

Next page spread: By the end of 2008, *Taylor Swift* had sold 3 million copies. Here the artist and her contemporaries are photographed that same year by Austin Hargrave.

At the 2008 American Music Awards, eighteen-year-old Taylor Swift wins Favorite Female Country Artist.

First Records

"Love Story," the first single released in September 2008, two months before the album's release, broke the record for paid downloads for a country song in less than a year, with over three million purchases. It also became the first country song to reach number one on the Mainstream Top 40. It even made headway internationally, with over eighteen million paid downloads worldwide.

The whole album was a huge success, even bigger than *Taylor Swift*. In the week following its release, it sold over 590,000 copies, becoming the best-selling album by a female artist in seven days in the United States. It immediately entered the Billboard 200 chart, where it held the top spot for eleven consecutive weeks, a feat not achieved by any album in the prior decade. In total, *Fearless*—also supported by the single "You Belong with Me," which enjoyed strong radio and TV rotation—sold seven million copies in the United States and almost twelve million worldwide, making it one of the best-selling albums of the 2000s, alongside Linkin Park's *Hybrid Theory* (2000), Norah Jones's *Come Away with Me* (2002), Coldplay's *A Rush of Blood to the Head* (2002), and Eminem's *The Eminem Show* (2002).

Numerous Collaborations

Taylor's first headlining tour, the "Fearless Tour," ran from April 2009 to June 2010 in six countries (she performed ninety times in the United States, seven times in Australia, six times in Europe, and once in Japan). The concerts sold out within minutes of tickets going on sale. Katy Perry, John Mayer, and Faith Hill, whom she had admired so much as a child, joined her onstage for duets. Taylor Swift collaborated with many artists during the *Fearless* years. She co-wrote Kellie Pickler's single "Best Days of Your Life" (2008), contributed backing vocals to "Half of My Heart" on John Mayer's fourth album, *Battle Studies* (2010), and took part in the soundtracks to the films *Hannah Montana: The Movie* (Peter Chelsom, 2009) and *Valentine's Day* (Garry Marshall, 2010), a romantic comedy with a large cast (Jessica Alba, Bradley Cooper, and Julia Roberts, to name a few).

Kanye West Spoils the Party

The end of 2009 was marked by a crucial event in Taylor Swift's career that suddenly raised her global profile. Nominated at the MTV Video Music Awards in the Best Female Video category for "You Belong with Me," on the

evening of September 13 she took the prize against superstars Beyoncé, Pink, Lady Gaga, and Katy Perry. As she launched into her acceptance speech with a smile, rapper Kanye West took to the stage, snatched the microphone from her hand, and claimed that Beyoncé deserved to win the award instead of Taylor, for her song "Single Ladies (Put a Ring on It)." After being booed by the audience, the rapper left the auditorium, leaving the young singer flushed and dazed. This brutal interruption by a personality as influential as Kanye West was repeated on a loop on screens the world over, becoming one of the most controversial moments in the history of music television. However, while the incident remains a difficult moment in Taylor Swift's life, it had the benefit of generating a wave of sympathy for her, not only from the artistic community but also from the general public. In the media and on social networks, it emphasized her humility and the dignity she showed following this mortifying moment. In the aftermath of this incident, few people in the United States or abroad did not know who Taylor Swift was, then aged twenty and already much more than a country-pop phenomenon.

A Flurry of Awards

In early 2010, Taylor seemed unstoppable. She won four Grammy Awards for *Fearless*, including Best Country Album, Best Country Song (for "White Horse"), Best Female Country Vocal Performance, and above all, Album of the Year, the ceremony's most coveted award. She became the youngest artist in Grammy Awards history to win this title. The crowning night also brought her first negative reviews: Her live performances—two duets with Stevie Nicks of the rock band Fleetwood Mac—were described as vocally disastrous. Taylor would have to get used to it: The more a star is adored, the less she is forgiven for her faux pas.

JUMP THEN FALL

Taylor Swift / 3:57

Musicians
Taylor Swift: vocals, backing vocals
Nathan Chapman: acoustic guitar, banjo, bass, drums, electric guitar, backing vocals, mandolin, keyboards
Nick Buda, John Keefe: drums
Eric Darken, Al Wilson: percussion
Rob Hajacos: fiddle
Tony Harrell, Tim Lauer: keyboards
Tim Marks, Amos Heller: bass
Ilya Toshinsky: banjo
Caitlin Evanson, Sammie Allan: backing vocals
Kenny Greenberg, Grant Mickelson: electric guitar
Bryan Sutton: acoustic guitar, mandolin

Recorded
Blackbird Studio (Nashville), 2008

Technical Team
Producers: Nathan Chapman, Taylor Swift
Executive Producer: Scott Borchetta
Mixing: Justin Niebank, Nathan Chapman, Chad Carlson
Sound Engineers: Nathan Chapman, Chad Carlson, Brian David Willis, Jed Hackett
Programming: Nathan Chapman
Mastering: Hank Williams
Best Rankings: Hot Country: 59; Hot 100: 10

2008

Genesis

According to Taylor Swift, this love song evokes a magical, wonderfully pleasant summer during which we jump, then fall, letting go and abandoning ourselves completely. It was a way of opening this second album on a positive, bright, and carefree note.

Production

From the outset, Nathan Chapman's very clean production is reminiscent of the first album. There is an exclusively acoustic intro, with the bouncy banjo ritornello (subtly passed through an envelope filter effect) that Taylor loves so much, followed by the explosion of the first chorus with the entrance of the full band—bass, drums, fiddle, electric and acoustic guitar rhythms—and a third chorus. The last third of the song follows the traditional pattern: electric guitar leading out of the second chorus, bridge, third verse, final chorus, and ad lib ending with the lyrics "Jump then fall, / Jump then fall into me."

Hidden Message

Last summer was magical.

At the Sound Relief concert in Sydney, Australia, March 2009.

FOR DISCERNING SWIFTIES

Taylor Swift first performed "Jump Then Fall" onstage in the broadcast *Dancing with the Stars*, on October 27, 2009. During the "Eras Tour," she performed the acoustic version of it as the first surprise song on the evening of the third concert in Arlington, Texas, on April 2, 2023.

UNTOUCHABLE

Taylor Swift, Cary Barlowe, Nathan Barlowe, Tommy Lee James / 5:11

Musicians

Taylor Swift: vocals, backing vocals
Nathan Chapman: acoustic guitar, banjo, bass, drums, electric guitar, backing vocals, mandolin, keyboards
Nick Buda, John Keefe: drums
Eric Darken, Al Wilson: percussion
Dan Dugmore: pedal steel
Tony Harrell, Tim Lauer: keyboards
Tim Marks, Amos Heller: bass
Ilya Toshinsky: banjo
Caitlin Evanson: backing vocals
Kenny Greenberg, Grant Mickelson: electric guitar
Claire Indie: cello
Bryan Sutton: acoustic guitar, mandolin

Recorded

Blackbird Studio, 2008

Technical Team

Producer: Nathan Chapman
Executive Producer: Scott Borchetta
Mixing: Justin Niebank, Nathan Chapman, Chad Carlson
Sound Engineers: Nathan Chapman, Chad Carlson, Brian David Willis, Jed Hackett
Mastering: Hank Williams
Best Ranking: Hot 100: 19

Genesis

"Untouchable" is a cover of the song by the rock band Luna Halo, composed by Cary Barlowe, Nathan Barlowe, and Tommy Lee James and released in 2007. Produced by Rick Rubin and Neil Avron, the original up-tempo rock version is transformed into a romantic ballad. Taylor's version brings the lyricism of the lyrics to the fore, taking the listener into the bittersweet dream of impossible love.

Production

All the ingredients of the country-pop ballad are here: Acoustic instruments dominate the arrangement—acoustic guitar played with fingers, melodic counterpoints and mandolin rhythm, drum toms played with mallets—enveloped in swirls of pedal steel and airy electric guitars (a long delay on the right guitar and tremolo effect on the left). The musicians' nuanced playing keeps the listener in a hushed atmosphere, in a waking dream, where the hope of being loved in return still seems possible: "In the middle of the night when I'm in this dream / It's like a million little stars spelling out your name."

Hidden Message

We always want what we can't reach.

SCOTT BORCHETTA AND BIG MACHINE RECORDS

Scott Borchetta, born on July 3, 1962, in Burbank, California, came to meet Taylor Swift having followed in the footsteps of his father, Mike, who left home when Scott was a child. After a career in music promotion with Mercury Records, Capitol Records, and RCA Records in Los Angeles, Mike moved permanently to Nashville to set up his own independent record promotion company. As a teenager, Scott stayed with his mother in the San Fernando Valley, where he spent his time practicing motocross and skateboarding in empty swimming pools with his friends. Sensing that college was not for him, he decided, at the age of nineteen, to reconnect with his father, over 1,800 miles away, and left California with only a bass guitar and some clothes.

Genesis of the Big Machine Records Label

In Nashville, Scott worked during the day in the mail room of his father's company. He dreamed of being a rock star, but, aware that he lacked the talent to break through, he chose to focus his energy where he felt he could succeed, namely backstage. Scott wrote in the *New York Times* that "I wasn't that great of a musician myself, but I knew the business and could explain it to others, especially the artists." In 1985, he joined MTM Records, the label of actress and producer Mary Tyler Moore, and stayed for three years. This was followed by two years of independent promotion and many more at MCA Records Nashville, DreamWorks Nashville, and Universal Music Group Nashville, where he held senior positions in artist promotion and development.

In 2005, convinced that he could run a label more efficiently than others, he founded Big Machine Records—named after a song by the hard rock band Velvet Revolver. Taylor Swift was the very first artist to join his label, after meeting him in 2004 at Nashville's Bluebird Cafe. He listened to her demo, which blew him away. As Taylor was only fourteen years old at the time, Scott knew he was taking a risk in signing such a young artist, but he sensed an untapped market: teenage girls who loved country music. At the same time, he was producing other country artists, such as Jack Ingram and Danielle Peck, but Taylor quickly became his biggest hit.

The End of a Collaboration and the Beginning of a War

Scott and Taylor worked together for thirteen long years, during which they released six albums. In October 2018, after Taylor informed him of her desire to leave the label (her contract expired after the *Reputation* album), he put Big Machine up for sale; it was valued at an estimated $300 million. Macquarie Group, Evan Spiegel, and Universal Music Group made bids, but it was Ithaca Holdings, a media and entertainment company founded by American entrepreneur Scooter Braun, that won the sale and became owner of the rights to Taylor's original discography. Because the singer had not had the opportunity to buy back her own master recordings, the acquisition sparked a public controversy. It was also the start of the war over her master recordings and the end of the long collaboration between Taylor and Scott, which previously had been professional and friendly. Scott, a racing car enthusiast, was involved in a road accident during a competition on March 26, 2023, from which he fortunately emerged unscathed.

Scott Borchetta and Taylor Swift would go on to work together for thirteen years, on six albums.

COME IN WITH THE RAIN

Taylor Swift, Liz Rose / 3:58

Musicians
Taylor Swift: vocals, backing vocals
Nathan Chapman: acoustic guitar, banjo, bass, drums, electric guitar, backing vocals, mandolin, keyboards
Nick Buda, John Keefe: drums
Eric Darken, Al Wilson: percussion
Rob Hajacos: fiddle
Tony Harrell, Tim Lauer: keyboards
Tim Marks, Amos Heller: bass
Ilya Toshinsky: banjo
Caitlin Evanson, Sammie Allan: backing vocals
Kenny Greenberg, Grant Mickelson: electric guitar
Bryan Sutton: acoustic guitar, mandolin
Jonathan Yudkin: cello, strings arrangements, strings

Recorded
Blackbird Studio (Nashville), 2008

Technical Team
Producers: Nathan Chapman, Taylor Swift
Executive Producer: Scott Borchetta
Mixing: Justin Niebank, Nathan Chapman, Chad Carlson
Sound Engineers: Nathan Chapman, Chad Carlson, Brian David Willis, Jed Hackett
Programming: Nathan Chapman
Mastering: Hank Williams
Best Ranking: Hot 100: 19

Genesis

In "Come in with the Rain," Taylor Swift describes that singular mixture of weariness and hope we feel when a story seems to be coming to an end, but we would nevertheless like to see it resolved—to witness the miraculous return of the loved one through a window on a rainy evening: "I'll leave my window open / [...] / Just know I'm right here hoping / That you'll come in with the rain."

Production

This is a slow-tempo acoustic ballad (70 bpm). All the elements of the genre are present. The nuanced strumming of the acoustic guitar is complemented by the arpeggios of the banjo, the arrangement of the fiddle that echoes the swirls of the pedal steel, the ascetic playing of the bass drums, and the contrasts in intensity between the verses and the choruses. The climax comes with the entry of the third chorus, at 3:20.

Hidden Message

Won't admit that I wish you'd come back.

"Superstar" is one of the songs that Taylor Swift previewed at concerts prior to the official release of *Speak Now.*

SUPERSTAR

Taylor Swift / 4:21

Musicians

Taylor Swift: vocals, backing vocals
Nathan Chapman: acoustic guitar, banjo, bass, drums, electric guitar, backing vocals, mandolin, keyboards, programming
Nick Buda, John Keefe: drums
Eric Darken: percussion, vibraphone
Rob Hajacos: fiddle
Tony Harrell, Tim Lauer: keyboards
Tim Marks, Amos Heller: bass
Ilya Toshinsky: banjo
Caitlin Evanson, Sammie Allan: backing vocals
Kenny Greenberg, Grant Mickelson: electric guitar
Bryan Sutton: acoustic guitar, mandolin
Al Wilson: percussion
Jonathan Yudkin: cello, strings arrangements, strings

Recorded

Blackbird Studio (Nashville), 2008

Technical Team

Producers: Nathan Chapman, Taylor Swift
Executive Producer: Scott Borchetta
Mixing: Justin Niebank, Nathan Chapman, Chad Carlson
Sound Engineers: Nathan Chapman, Chad Carlson, Brian David Willis, Jed Hackett
Mastering: Hank Williams

2008

Genesis

Taylor Swift wrote "Superstar" as an admiration-filled declaration of love to a music star whose name she decided not to reveal. As the hidden message in the lyrics indicates, she will never reveal it.

Production

This is a midtempo, restrained ballad: The arrangement is essentially a balance created by the dialogue between banjo (right), mandolin (left), acoustic guitar (slightly to the left), and electric guitar (right). Eric Darken's vibraphone wraps everything in a few resonant, dreamy notes. Bass and drums unwind and effortlessly support the delicate architecture of a supple, confident groove. In the distance, the male backing vocals and the layer of synthesizers, mimicking a discreet string arrangement, give this intimate space a depth of field conducive to reverie.

Hidden Message

I'll never tell.

"The Other Side of the Door," from the deluxe edition of *Fearless* (2008), has rarely been sung in concert. Taylor Swift performed it live for the first time in 2009.

THE OTHER SIDE OF THE DOOR

Taylor Swift / 3:57

Musicians
Taylor Swift: vocals, backing vocals
Nathan Chapman: acoustic guitar, banjo, bass, drums, electric guitar, backing vocals, mandolin, keyboards, programming, dobro
Nick Buda, John Keefe: drums
Eric Darken, Al Wilson: percussion
Rob Hajacos: fiddle
Tony Harrell, Tim Lauer: keyboards
Tim Marks, Amos Heller: bass
Ilya Toshinsky: banjo
Caitlin Evanson, Sammie Allan: backing vocals
Kenny Greenberg: electric guitar
Grant Mickelson: electric guitar
Bryan Sutton: acoustic guitar, mandolin
Recorded
Blackbird Studio (Nashville), 2008
Technical Team
Producers: Nathan Chapman, Taylor Swift
Executive Producer: Scott Borchetta
Mixing: Justin Niebank, Nathan Chapman, Chad Carlson
Sound Engineers: Nathan Chapman, Chad Carlson, Brian David Willis, Jed Hackett
Mastering: Hank Williams
Best Ranking: Hot 100: 22

Genesis

In "The Other Side of the Door," Taylor Swift has fun painting a picture of a conflicted relationship. In this song, written in 2007, she describes those moments when you become belligerent, when words come out without you wanting them to, when all you really want is to make up. Some speculate that she drew inspiration for the song from her tumultuous relationship with Sam Armstrong, one of her high school classmates. With a touch of humor, in a 2009 interview with iTunes, Taylor confided about the song: "[...] and you're like [acts dramatic], 'Leave me alone, I never wanna talk to you again, I hate you!' But what you really mean is, 'Please go buy me flowers and beg that I forgive you and stand at the door and don't leave for three days.'"

The four other songs that Taylor Swift seems to have drawn inspiration from her relationship with Sam Armstrong are "Should've Said No," "White Horse," "You're Not Sorry," and "Come in with the Rain."

Production

This moderate-tempo (80 bpm) country-pop ballad features the dobro and mandolin driving the arrangement with its heady rhythm, hand in hand with the banjo played with a clawhammer technique. At 2:21, at the end of the second chorus, the electric guitar solo passed through a wah-wah pedal adds an unexpected classic rock dimension, despite the omnipresence of electric guitars at the end of the first verse. The Hammond organ and pedal steel are confined to the role of a harmonic layer, very much at the back of the mix, but crucial to the overall effect. The drums, for their part, allow themselves a few liberties—this time for a change—gradually increasing the density of the drum breaks as the song progresses, right up to the climax of the final chorus.

Hidden Message

What I was really thinking when I slammed the door.

Taylor Swift performs "Fearless" at Madison Square Garden, August 2009, wearing a feathered hat and a white military jacket to symbolize strength and glamor.

FOR DISCERNING SWIFTIES

During the "Speak Now World Tour" (2011–2012), Taylor Swift performed "Fearless" as a medley with the songs "I'm Yours" by singer-songwriter Jason Mraz and "Hey, Soul Sister" by Californian rock band Train. A version of this mash-up was later recorded during a live BBC broadcast on March 23, 2011.

SINGLE

FEARLESS

Taylor Swift, Hillary Lindsey, Liz Rose / 4:02

Musicians

Taylor Swift: vocals, backing vocals
Nathan Chapman: acoustic guitar, banjo, bass, drums, electric guitar, backing vocals, mandolin, keyboards, programming
Nick Buda, John Keefe: drums
Eric Darken, Al Wilson: percussion
Rob Hajacos: fiddle
Tony Harrell, Tim Lauer: keyboards
Tim Marks, Amos Heller: bass
Ilya Toshinsky: banjo
Caitlin Evanson, Sammie Allan: backing vocals
Kenny Greenberg, Grant Mickelson: electric guitar
Bryan Sutton: acoustic guitar, mandolin

Recorded

Blackbird Studio (Nashville), 2008

Technical Team

Producers: Nathan Chapman, Taylor Swift
Executive Producer: Scott Borchetta
Mixing: Justin Niebank, Nathan Chapman, Chad Carlson
Sound Engineers: Nathan Chapman, Chad Carlson, Brian David Willis, Jed Hackett
Mastering: Hank Williams

Single Release

CD single, US, 2009—BMRTS0209
Best Rankings: Hot Country: 10; Hot 100: 9

Genesis

Taylor Swift wrote "Fearless" while on tour promoting her debut album *Taylor Swift*. At the time, she was not in a relationship nor at the beginning or at the end of a romantic affair. She reflects on the courage it takes to reach out and take the risk of falling in love, even after having had her heart broken a thousand times. For Taylor, the word *fearless* does not mean "without fear," but rather being petrified by fear and launching into a new relationship in spite of it. She also evokes the adolescent fantasy of the "best first date," the one that, as a young teenager, she had yet to experience.

Production

For the fifth and final single from the album, Nathan Chapman and Taylor Swift take the listener to the land of 100 bpm country-rock ballads. Tailored for the road, this arrangement features electric guitar and mandolin. The Hammond organ (right) and the sophisticated playing (a combination of arpeggios, melodic counterpoints, and strumming) of the twelve-string acoustic guitar (left) widen the stereo field, while the bass and drums keep the whole band at cruising speed. Taylor Swift's voice accentuates the contrasts, covering more than two octaves, from *F3* to *C5*, in the key of *F* major, which suits her perfectly.

Hidden Message

I loved you before I met you.

Taylor Swift performs "Fifteen," a song about youth and first experiences, at the 2009 CMA Awards.

SINGLE

FIFTEEN

Taylor Swift / 4:54

Musicians
Taylor Swift: vocals, backing vocals
Nathan Chapman: acoustic guitar, banjo, bass, drums, electric guitar, backing vocals, mandolin, keyboards, programming
Nick Buda, John Keefe: drums
Eric Darken, Al Wilson: percussion
Tim Marks, Amos Heller: bass
Ilya Toshinsky: banjo
Kenny Greenberg, Grant Mickelson: electric guitar
Bryan Sutton: acoustic guitar, mandolin
Sammie Allan: backing vocals
Claire Indie: cello

Recorded
Blackbird Studio (Nashville), 2008

Technical Team
Producers: Nathan Chapman, Taylor Swift
Executive Producer: Scott Borchetta
Mixing: Justin Niebank, Nathan Chapman, Chad Carlson
Sound Engineers: Nathan Chapman, Chad Carlson, Brian David Willis, Jed Hackett
Mastering: Hank Williams

Single Release
CD single, US, August 30, 2009—BMRTS0208
Best Rankings: Hot Country: 7; Hot 100: 23

Genesis

In "Fifteen," Taylor Swift speaks directly to her best friend in her first year of high school, Abigail Anderson. In the midst of a romantic breakup, Abigail is struggling to recover from this terrible disillusionment—her first teenage heartbreak. Her story leaves its mark on young Taylor, who supports her with sisterhood and empathy. So she decided to turn her friend's story into a song, starting with the line that would become the text of the bridge: "Abigail gave everything she had to a boy / Who changed his mind." From this framework, Taylor Swift begins a kind of reverse songwriting process: She develops the verses and choruses, eventually painting a strikingly realistic picture of coming of age. Taylor says she cried during the recording of "Fifteen," so much so that the song resonates with her, as if taken directly from her private diary.

Production

This moderate-tempo ballad (96 bpm) opens with a duet of acoustic guitar and mandolin, played in rapid strumming, oscillating between sixteenth and eighth notes. Supported from the intro by a bass melody performed at the top of the neck and a counterpoint electric guitar in the treble, the folk guitar-mandolin duo drives the ethereal orchestration in "Fifteen" from start to finish. Right from the first verse, as the bass leaves the field clear for Taylor Swift's voice, two electric guitars with highly complementary playing gradually widen the panoramic field before the bass returns, this time supported by drums played with brushes. From the first chorus onward, Claire Indie's cello adds a touch of melancholy, first with the grace of a few held notes, then distilling melodic leads to flesh out the transitions. At almost five minutes long, it is the longest song on the album, just edged out by "Untouchable" (5:11) on the Platinum reissue.

Hidden Message

I cried while recording this.

SINGLE

LOVE STORY

Taylor Swift / 3:55

Musicians

Taylor Swift: vocals, backing vocals
Nathan Chapman: acoustic guitar, banjo, bass, drums, electric guitar, backing vocals, mandolin, keyboards, programming
Nick Buda, John Keefe: drums
Eric Darken: percussion
Rob Hajacos: fiddle
Tony Harrell, Tim Lauer: keyboards
Tim Marks, Amos Heller: bass
Ilya Toshinsky: banjo
Caitlin Evanson, Sammie Allan: backing vocals
Kenny Greenberg, Grant Mickelson: electric guitar
Bryan Sutton: acoustic guitar, mandolin
Al Wilson: percussion
Tim Van Der Kuil: electric guitar

Recorded

Blackbird Studio (Nashville), March 2008

Technical Team

Producers: Nathan Chapman, Taylor Swift
Executive Producer: Scott Borchetta
Mixing: Justin Niebank, Jeremy "Jim Bob" Wheatley
Sound Engineers: Chad Carlson, Jeremy "Jim Bob" Wheatley
Mastering: Hank Williams

Single Release

CD single, US, September 12, 2008—BMRTS0201
Best Rankings: Hot Country: 1; Hot 100: 4; Mainstream Top 40: 1

Genesis

For the album's first single, Taylor Swift and her team chose "Love Story," a song loosely based on William Shakespeare's *Romeo and Juliet*. Taylor wrote the lyrics in her notebook over a period of twenty minutes, lying on the floor of her bedroom. The inspiration came shortly after her parents had forbidden her to see the young man she was dating at the time, as he seemed to be going through a difficult phase. Also, the parents of the two families did not get along. Unlike *Romeo and Juliet*, however, "Love Story" is not a tragic tale of impossible love, since here everything has a happy ending. The lyrics also allude directly to Nathaniel Hawthorne's 1850 novel *The Scarlet Letter*: "'Cause you were Romeo, / I was a scarlet letter." "Love Story" was so successful that it changed the course of Taylor Swift's career, becoming the first country song to reach number one on the Billboard Mainstream Top 40. The song also went platinum ten times in Australia and eight times in the United States. With over eighteen million copies sold worldwide, it set a new record that officially marked Taylor Swift's entry into the vast world of mainstream pop music. Taylor's Version of "Love Story," on the album *Fearless (Taylor's Version)* released in 2021, also reached number one on the US Hot Country Songs chart, making the singer the second artist (after Dolly Parton) to reach number one on the chart with both the original and rerecorded versions of the same song.

Production

Launched at a brisk tempo (120 bpm in 4/4 time), the rhythmic backbone in "Love Story" is based on the acoustic guitar played in eighth-note palm mute and the banjo arpeggio that runs an ostinato through the whole song, with the exception of a short pause on the bridge. In the key of *D* major, the harmonic structure consists of three chords sequenced as follows: *D* major, *A* major, *G* major, *A* major, without ever departing from the perfect cadence *I-V-IV-V*. To rekindle attention, at 3:17, the key of the final chorus rises a tone from *D* major to *E* major. It pushes Taylor's voice to the top of its register, maintaining her chest voice and pushing the sense of intensity to its maximum. Rob Hajacos's fiddle plays an important role, taking

At the 2008 CMA Awards in Nashville, Taylor Swift performs "Love Story" in a spectacular production, creating a magical and romantic atmosphere.

the lead on the instrumental parts at the end of the chorus. The electric guitar, immersed in delay and reverb, plays an atmospheric role, accentuated by the violining effect of a volume pedal that softens the attacks and sounds like an instrument played with a bow or a synthesizer pad. Another electric guitar provides rhythmic support, reinforcing or replacing the acoustic guitar, depending on the moment. Thanks to the straight, highly compressed drums, the no-frills bass playing, and the dynamics compressed by the aggressive—but mastered—mastering of engineer Hank Williams (the aim being to have the track able to sound as loud as possible from any type of listening system: hi-fi, laptop, portable speakers, headphones, etc.), the listener plunges into an emo rock (punk) atmosphere that exalts adolescent passions and romanticism.

Hidden Message

Someday, I'll find this.

FOR DISCERNING SWIFTIES

It seems the boy evoked in the song "White Horse" may have also inspired "Love Story."

Taylor Swift during a photo shoot for *Us Weekly* in Los Angeles, September 2008. Her natural charm and image as a young star on the rise reinforce her appeal to the public.

HEY STEPHEN

Taylor Swift / 4:14

Musicians

Taylor Swift: vocals, backing vocals
Nathan Chapman: acoustic guitar, bass, drums, electric guitar, backing vocals, keyboards
Nick Buda, John Keefe: drums
Eric Darken, Al Wilson: percussion
Tony Harrell, Tim Lauer: keyboards
Tim Marks, Amos Heller: bass
Caitlin Evanson, Sammie Allan: backing vocals
Bryan Sutton: acoustic guitar

Recorded

Blackbird Studio (Nashville), 2008

Technical Team

Producers: Nathan Chapman, Taylor Swift
Executive Producer: Scott Borchetta
Mixing: Justin Niebank, Jeremy "Jim Bob" Wheatley
Sound Engineers: Chad Carlson, Jeremy "Jim Bob" Wheatley
Mastering: Hank Williams
Best Ranking: Hot 100: 94

Eric Gunderson of Love and Theft performed with Taylor Swift at the Kicker Country Stampede, June 2015.

Genesis

For Taylor Swift, writing "Hey Stephen" was an outlet. In the song, Taylor has no hesitation in revealing her feelings for Stephen Barker Liles, one of the two singers of the country duo Love and Theft (now Stephen Barker Liles and Eric Gunderson, active since 2006), who opened for her for a number of gigs. A virtuoso of communication, Taylor first revealed the band's identity to her fans via the hidden message, a Swiftian tradition firmly established since her first album. At the time, the singer decided not to divulge her feelings to Stephen, fearing that this love would not be shared and knowing that life on tour is hardly conducive to developing lasting relationships. According to a 2009 article in the *New York Times*, Taylor did, however, send him a text message alerting him to the track when the album was released. A surprised Stephen replied with a long email beginning "Oh my God!"

Production

For once, the nylon string guitar, strummed with the fingers, takes pride of place here. Its syncopated playing perfectly complements the straight, minimalist groove of the drums. The orchestration, surprisingly sober and uncluttered, brings Taylor Swift's narration and warm timbre to the fore. The bass part sounds as if it were played on a fretless instrument (a nonfretted electric bass), the timbred sound rich and warm, almost reminiscent of a double bass. From the first chorus onward, Tony Harrell's Hammond B3 organ lends the necessary relief and extra soul to this type of stripped-down arrangement. A true master of the electric organ, the musician's supple, nuanced playing superbly enhances the storytelling and Taylor Swift's voice. The humming melody and finger snaps on the closing ad lib underline the intimate atmosphere of this open-letter track. Somewhere between country pop and teen pop, Taylor Swift takes listeners by the hand and lets them identify with this unrequited love story. Who has never loved someone in secret?

Hidden Message

Love and theft. (Could the band's name be an allusion to the album of the same name by Bob Dylan, released in 2001?)

2008 American Music Awards, Nokia Theatre, Los Angeles: Taylor Swift sings "White Horse."

SINGLE

WHITE HORSE

Taylor Swift, Liz Rose / 3:54

Musicians

Taylor Swift: vocals, backing vocals
Nathan Chapman: acoustic guitar, bass, drums, electric guitar, backing vocals, keyboards, piano
Nick Buda, John Keefe: drums
Eric Darken, Al Wilson: percussion
Tony Harrell, Tim Lauer: keyboards, piano
Tim Marks, Amos Heller: bass
Caitlin Evanson, Sammie Allan: backing vocals
Kenny Greenberg, Grant Mickelson: electric guitar
Bryan Sutton: acoustic guitar

Recorded

Blackbird Studio (Nashville), March 2008

Technical Team

Producers: Nathan Chapman, Taylor Swift
Executive Producer: Scott Borchetta
Mixing: Justin Niebank, Jeremy "Jim Bob" Wheatley
Sound Engineers: Chad Carlson, Jeremy "Jim Bob" Wheatley
Mastering: Hank Williams

Single Release

CD single, US, 2008—BMRTS0203
Best Rankings: Hot Country: 2; Hot 100: 13

Genesis

"White Horse" is the disenchanted sequel to "Love Story." Written a few weeks after "Love Story," and logically chosen as the album's second single, it deals with the same love affair as "Love Story," but this time it is love coming to an end. Here, it is not Shakespeare's *Romeo and Juliet* or Nathaniel Hawthorne's *The Scarlet Letter* that Taylor takes as a reference, but rather the Disney Hollywood version of the fairy tales she grew up with. Taylor realizes that she was never the princess imprisoned at the top of the tower and that Prince Charming will never come to rescue her and take her away on his beautiful white horse.

Production

We return to the fundamentals of the acoustic country-pop ballad for brokenhearted teenagers for this arrangement. In a key of *C* major and a moderate 4/4 tempo, the delicate acoustic guitar intertwines with piano arpeggios, and Claire Indie's cello adds its share of gravity, right from the first chorus. The male backing vocals in thirds (sung by Nathan Chapman or Sammie Allan), the round bass, and the drums played with brushes add to the dramatic, almost solemn intensity of this orchestration. Despite the small number of instruments used, Nathan Chapman's arrangement succeeds in enveloping the listener in a pocket symphony where the disillusionment is palpable: This is the moment when the scenery falls away and reality takes over from the fairy tale.

Hidden Message

All I ever wanted was the truth.

"You Belong With Me," performed at the 2009 CMT Music Awards, reflects Taylor Swift's evolution toward a more pop sound while remaining rooted in country.

SINGLE

YOU BELONG WITH ME

Taylor Swift, Liz Rose / 3:51

Musicians

Taylor Swift: vocals, backing vocals
Nathan Chapman: acoustic guitar, banjo, bass, drums, electric guitar, backing vocals, mandolin, keyboards, programming
Nick Buda, John Keefe: drums
Eric Darken, Al Wilson: percussion
Rob Hajacos: fiddle
Tony Harrell, Tim Lauer: keyboards
Tim Marks, Amos Heller: bass
Ilya Toshinsky: banjo
Caitlin Evanson, Sammie Allan: backing vocals
Kenny Greenberg: electric guitar
Grant Mickelson: electric guitar
Bryan Sutton: acoustic guitar, mandolin
Tim Van Der Kuil: electric guitar

Recorded

Blackbird Studio (Nashville), 2008

Technical Team

Producers: Nathan Chapman, Taylor Swift
Executive Producer: Scott Borchetta
Mixing: Justin Niebank, Jeremy "Jim Bob" Wheatley
Sound Engineers: Chad Carlson, Jeremy "Jim Bob" Wheatley
Mastering: Hank Williams

Single Release

CD single, US, April 21, 2009—BMRTS0204
Best Rankings: Hot Country: 1; Hot 100: 2; Mainstream Top 40: 2

Genesis

The framework for "You Belong with Me" came to her when Taylor Swift overheard a friend arguing on the phone with his girlfriend, a sexy, popular girl, always in a short skirt and high heels, captain of the high school cheerleading squad, who clearly did not appreciate the young man at all. Taylor, who had feelings for this friend and felt that she understood him better than anyone, immediately decided to rush over to Liz Rose's house and ask her to help her write this song as a personal message. Together with Liz, Taylor drew up a list of comparisons—"She wears short skirts, I wear T-shirts" and "She wears high heels, I wear sneakers"—to prove to his friend that he is meant to be with her, and that he has nothing in common with the popular girl who only dates him for appearances' sake.

Production

"You Belong with Me" begins with minimalist, binary drum machine programming, over which a banjo and acoustic guitar duo weave their arpeggios. At a faster-than-usual tempo (130 bpm), the electric guitar's palm mute, eighth note on the verses and open on the choruses, helps shift this arrangement from country pop to power pop, or even twee indie pop (a subgenre of the indie pop category that emerged in 1986 with the release of a compilation published by *NME* magazine, characterized by simple, catchy melodies and sentimental lyrics about innocence, femininity, friendship, and love). The distorted sound of the electric guitars is reminiscent of 1990s mainstream rock (the diatonic chord sequence *I-V-II-IV* employed is also typical of the genre), and the tense interplay between the bass drum and drum machine would almost recall new wave and 1980s pop. The banjo, mandolin, and fiddle are present, albeit slightly in the background, but this time their playing, modeled on that of the electric guitar, has nothing country about it. There is also a filter effect on the banjo, which sometimes makes it hard to distinguish from the electric guitar. The flow of the lyrics, the theme, and Taylor's energetic vocals completely justify the decision to leave the well-trodden paths of country pop, from which little will remain on the following album. "You Belong with Me" remains one of Taylor's most popular songs today, and the music video for the song has exceeded one billion views on YouTube.

FOR DISCERNING SWIFTIES

In Taylor's Version, the words "I'm in the room" were changed to "I'm in my room," which does seem more appropriate.

Hidden Message

Love is blind, so you couldn't see me.

In 2010 Taylor Swift receives the Grammy for Album of the Year with "Breathe" cowriter Colbie Caillat in the background.

BREATHE

(FEAT. COLBIE CAILLAT)

Taylor Swift, Colbie Caillat / 4:23

Musicians

Taylor Swift: vocals, backing vocals
Colbie Caillat: vocals, backing vocals
Nathan Chapman: acoustic guitar, banjo, bass, drums, electric guitar, mandolin, keyboards
Nick Buda, John Keefe: drums
Eric Darken, Al Wilson: percussion
Rob Hajacos: fiddle
Tony Harrell, Tim Lauer: keyboards
Tim Marks, Amos Heller: bass
Ilya Toshinsky: banjo
Bryan Sutton: acoustic guitar, mandolin
Jonathan Yudkin: cello, strings arrangements, strings

Recorded

Blackbird Studio (Nashville), Starstruck (Nashville), 2008

Technical Team

Producers: Nathan Chapman, Taylor Swift
Executive Producer: Scott Borchetta
Mixing: Justin Niebank, Jeremy "Jim Bob" Wheatley
Sound Engineers: Chad Carlson, Jeremy "Jim Bob" Wheatley
Mastering: Hank Williams
Best Ranking: Hot 100: 87

2008

Genesis

Taylor Swift was a great admirer of Colbie Caillat's work and voice and decided to invite her to co-write a song for her second album. Pop-folk singer Colbie is four years Taylor's senior. Her career only really began in 2007, with the huge success of her song "Bubbly" on the MySpace platform. The two singers wrote "Breathe" in one day, and Taylor invited Colbie to sing the vocal harmonies on the day of recording. The text describes the difficulty and sadness of ending a fading love affair, without anger or resentment. As Taylor and Colbie so aptly sing: "But I have to / Breathe without you."

Production

With its 72 bpm tempo, this 4/4 country-pop ballad puts acoustic instruments and vocals in the spotlight. The duo of Taylor Swift and Colbie Caillat works wonderfully, due in particular to the latter's timbre, slightly richer in the alto register and ideal for singing harmonies one-third below. However, her voice briefly rises above Taylor's on the second half of the bridge. In addition to the fundamentals (banjo, mandolin, acoustic guitar, piano, bass, drums), Jonathan Yudkin's string arrangement adds a cinematic dimension and a certain solemnity to the whole.

Hidden Message

I'm sorry I'm sorry I'm sorry.

Taylor Swift sings at New York City's Madison Square Garden, August 2009.

TELL ME WHY

Taylor Swift, Liz Rose / 3:20

Musicians

Taylor Swift: vocals, backing vocals
Nathan Chapman: acoustic guitar, bass, drums, electric guitar, backing vocals, keyboards
Nick Buda, John Keefe: drums
Eric Darken, Al Wilson: percussion
Tim Marks, Amos Heller: bass
Caitlin Evanson, Sammie Allan: backing vocals
Kenny Greenberg, Grant Mickelson: electric guitar
Bryan Sutton: acoustic guitar

Recorded

Blackbird Studio (Nashville), 2008

Technical Team

Producers: Nathan Chapman, Taylor Swift
Executive Producer: Scott Borchetta
Mixing: Justin Niebank, Jeremy "Jim Bob" Wheatley
Sound Engineers: Chad Carlson, Jeremy "Jim Bob" Wheatley
Mastering: Hank Williams

Genesis

Exasperated by the behavior of a boy who could not make up his mind when she had the courage to make the first move, Taylor Swift asked Liz Rose to help her write "Tell Me Why." The young man runs hot and cold and belittles her, but Taylor, though enamored, sees his mean streak. As fans already know, when she does not feel respected, Taylor settles the score in song.

Production

"Tell Me Why" opens with drum machine programming that sounds like a hip-hop sample straight out of the late 1980s. The recurring melodic gimmick, first set out by the fiddle, is immediately superimposed on the boom-bap rhythm (hip-hop from the 1980s and '90s) of the intro, over a fast tempo (100 bpm). On the first verse, it fades away to make way for vocals and acoustic guitar, then bass and acoustic drums make their entrance before the tutti of the first chorus with its dense orchestration: banjo, electric guitars, fiddle, mandolin, pedal steel, backing vocals—everyone is in. From halfway through the second verse, the bass playing, more rocking and loquacious than usual, leads to a palpable excitement. Although largely supported by the presence of traditional country instruments, Nathan Chapman and Taylor have fun blurring the lines of this arrangement by including elements usually associated with hip-hop and rock—a great success.

Hidden Message

Guess I was fooled by your smile.

At the 2009 CMA Awards in Nashville, Taylor Swift strengthened her position in country music and showed the evolution of her style through popular songs from *Fearless*.

Taylor Swift
Love
Taylor

KANYE WEST VERSUS TAYLOR SWIFT: THE INCIDENT

On September 13, 2009, the twenty-sixth MTV Video Music Awards took place at Radio City Music Hall in New York City. The ceremony had been underway for less than an hour when the very young Taylor Swift learned that she had just won Best Female Video for "You Belong with Me," up against the world's biggest pop and R'n'B stars of the moment: Beyoncé, Kelly Clarkson, Lady Gaga, Katy Perry, and Pink. Taylor let out a "Wow!" of surprise and began her acceptance speech onstage, all smiles and disbelief. No more than twenty seconds passed before the rapper Kanye West, whose success and influence were immense at the time, abruptly appeared and took the microphone out of her hands. "Yo, Taylor, I'm really happy for you. I'ma let you finish. But Beyoncé had one of the best videos [the one for "Single Ladies (Put a Ring on It)"] of all time!" he interjected before returning to his seat accompanied by the booing of the audience. Beyoncé, who was present in the auditorium, could not contain her discomfort in front of the camera: "Oh, Kanye..." we read on her lips. Taylor, bewildered in front of millions of viewers, silently left the stage. Later in the evening, Beyoncé, who did, in turn, receive an award, graciously invited her back into the spotlight to finish her speech. But the damage had been done: In an instant, Kanye West had not only humiliated the young singer but also linked their respective careers forever.

A Costly Faux Pas for Kanye West

The incident triggered an immediate wave of reactions from the public and celebrities present that evening, most of whom expressed not only their support but also their admiration for Taylor's great maturity and professionalism. Interviewed by a journalist after the ceremony, Taylor chose not to stir up controversy, even though she shared her surprise and disappointment at West's behavior: "I was standing onstage, and I was really excited because I had just won the award, and then I was really excited because Kanye West was on the stage," she said. "And then...I wasn't so excited anymore," she declared. Asked if she had a grudge against him, she replied: "I don't know him, and I've never met him, so..." The interviewer concluded by asking her if she had been a fan of the rapper before the incident. With an almost childlike demeanor, she was unable to suppress a small, admiring smile: "Yeah...It's Kanye West."

After a few days, Kanye publicly apologized to Taylor via his blog—in a post that was later deleted—and in several interviews. But this mea culpa failed to restore his image in public opinion. Even Barack Obama, president of the United States at the time, made a comment, although it was intended to be off the record. In the minutes before an interview with CNBC, he called Kanye a "jackass," thinking his microphone was switched off. The remark was recorded and widely broadcast. Kanye's behavior also had a direct impact on the singer's career, with performance cancellations and a drop in popularity in the months following the incident.

A Shared Bitterness

Taylor and Kanye attempted to publicly defuse the situation, without seeking to make it disappear. Kanye regularly addressed the incident in interviews, repeating that he regretted his behavior. He also makes reference to it in his music, choosing to make guilt and redemption the main themes of his album released in November 2010, *My Beautiful Dark Twisted Fantasy*. For her part, Taylor also dedicated a song to the episode, "Innocent," featured on her album *Speak Now*. In a direct response to Kanye, she unveiled the song at the 2010 MTV Video Music Awards, almost a year to the day after the incident. The lyrics, on the theme of forgiveness, are unequivocal: "It's okay, life is a tough crowd / Thirty-two and still growin' up now," she sang onstage in a gentle voice. Thirty-two was the rapper's

Kanye West interrupts Taylor Swift at the 2009 MTV Video Music Awards in New York.

age at the time. This time, the media saw it as a low blow from Taylor, who seemed unable to turn the page and no longer showed the same magnanimity as before. Kanye withdrew his apology and insisted that interrupting her speech was in no way arrogant, as she did not deserve the award. He added that, despite his apology, Taylor had never once defended him in an interview, preferring to exploit Kanyegate for her own publicity. The hatchet has yet to be buried.

Between Publicity Stunt and Manipulation

In 2015, more than five years after the event, a thaw seemed to be setting in. Taylor and Kanye, both present at the Grammy Awards, were spotted backstage in the midst of a friendly exchange. That same year, at the MTV Video Music Awards, the scene of the inciting incident, Taylor went so far as to present the rapper with the Video Vanguard Award, the ceremony's highest honor, which honors artists for lifetime achievement in music and music videos. Taylor referred to him as a "friend" and joked about the incident that drove them apart; Kanye smiled and hugged her. But the lull was short-lived.

In February 2016, Kanye unveiled the track "Famous," from his album *The Life of Pablo*. In it, he chants, "I feel like me and Taylor might still have sex / Why? I made that bitch famous." The phrase, which immediately attracted media and fan attention, naturally displeased Taylor, who expressed her unhappiness the day after the track's release during her acceptance speech for the Grammy Award for Album of the Year (*1989*). The rapper defended himself: Taylor was alleged to have approved these lyrics, which she supposedly considered amusing, during a long telephone conversation several months earlier. Taylor denied this. She claims that, while she was indeed warned of a lyric whose turn of phrase was still under discussion during their exchange, she was never aware of the second part in which she is branded a bitch. She also claimed that Kanye's main aim in making the call was to convince her to share his latest track on her Twitter account on the day of its release.

Taylor in Disgrace

The clash became a full-blown scandal when Kim Kardashian, who was married to Kanye at the time, got

Beyoncé, uncomfortable after the rapper's intervention, invites Taylor Swift to come onstage with her.

Taylor Swift speaks after being interrupted by Kanye West. This moment reveals the grace and professionalism of the young woman and marks a turning point in her career.

involved as well. In an interview with *GQ* magazine in June 2016, following the release of the "Famous" video (in which we see a naked Kanye sharing a huge bed with equally naked look-alikes of Taylor Swift, Kim Kardashian, and Donald Trump), she declared that Taylor had indeed given her consent for the entirety of the lyrics and accused her of playing the victim to serve her image. She also pointed out that she had a recording of the telephone conversation that proved her version of events. She ended up posting this audio testimony, which later was revealed to have been heavily edited, on Snapchat.

Taylor, plagued on social networks and by the media, was forced to formulate a final response in an Instagram post. In this message, published on July 17, 2016, she reaffirmed that she had never been informed of the exact content of the song "Famous," that she believed in Kanye's good faith, and that she wanted once and for all "to be excluded from this narrative, one that I have never asked to be a part of, since 2009," a phrase that has become emblematic of this controversy. Kim did not stop there, however. On her social networks, she compared Taylor to a snake, encouraging her own fans to flood the singer with hate messages containing snake emojis. This was all too much for Taylor, who significantly reduced her public appearances and activities on social networks between 2016 and 2017.

Back with a Vengeance

It was not until August 2017 that the singer decided to return to the spotlight, as part of a cleverly orchestrated promotional campaign. In total silence, she deleted all photos from her Instagram account and posted, without further explanation, a photo of a snake on a black background. This gesture, a symbol of a new beginning, marked the release of her single "Look What You Made Me Do" and her sixth studio album, *Reputation*. The album is a real break with her musical and aesthetic universe: The sounds are more rock-like, and the palette of colors that characterizes it, in contrast to the blue, pink, and mauve of previous albums, shifts to darker tones.

The latest notable twist in the Taylor Swift–Kanye West feud came more than ten years after it began. In March 2020, an anonymous source leaked the entire telephone conversation between Taylor and Kanye, proving that Taylor had indeed not been informed of the controversial lyrics in their entirety. For fans and observers alike, this revelation is irrefutable proof that Taylor has been the victim of an injustice. Undoubtedly, the confrontation between the two artists has left a lasting imprint on popular culture. At the very least, it has had the merit of prompting the media to reflect on celebrity behavior, how to handle public disagreements, and the often-blinding influence of social networks.

During the music program *TRL*, February 2008, at MTV studios in New York.

YOU'RE NOT SORRY

Taylor Swift / 4:21

Musicians

Taylor Swift: vocals, backing vocals
Nathan Chapman: bass, drums, electric guitar, keyboards
Nick Buda, John Keefe: drums
Eric Darken, Al Wilson: percussion
Rob Hajacos: fiddle
Tony Harrell, Amos Heller: keyboards
Tim Marks: bass
Tim Lauer: keyboards
Sammie Allan: backing vocals
Jonathan Yudkin: cello, strings arrangements, strings

Recorded

Blackbird Studio (Nashville), 2008

Technical Team

Producers: Nathan Chapman, Taylor Swift
Executive Producer: Scott Borchetta
Mixing: Justin Niebank, Jeremy "Jim Bob" Wheatley
Sound Engineers: Chad Carlson, Jeremy "Jim Bob" Wheatley
Mastering: Hank Williams
Best Rankings: Hot 100: 11; Pop 100: 21

Genesis

"You're Not Sorry" could have been written about the same boy as the one in "Tell Me Why," as a logical sequel to that story full of bitterness. Taylor discovers that the real face of the young man she has fallen for is the exact opposite of the Prince Charming she had imagined. At the very moment she realizes that she has let herself be bullied, she decides to break off all communication without waiting for an explanation or apology. Deep down, she knew that the young man felt no remorse, and the last thing she wanted was to let him think that he could continue to make her suffer. She will never plead with him again. "Don't wanna hurt anymore, / And you can tell me that you're sorry, / But I don't believe you, baby / Like I did before."

Production

Neither the form of this composition, nor Nathan Chapman's production, nor Jonathan Yudkin's string arrangement would place "You're Not Sorry" in the country-pop category. Not the shadow of a banjo, not a note of mandolin or dobro, not a quiver of pedal steel to sow doubt. As Todd Martens put it in a *Los Angeles Times* review published on April 5, 2009 (in which he compared, among others, the albums of Taylor Swift, Miley Cyrus, and Miranda Lambert), this song is more akin to an old-fashioned power ballad, or "metal ballad." With its 66 bpm tempo, *E*-flat minor key, heavy piano chords, heavy drums marked by the tambourine on each snare hit (on the chorus), thick electric guitar grain, and amped-up string arrangement, "You're Not Sorry" lacks nothing in its arsenal to bring a tear to the eye. The bass allows itself some interesting liberties, notably on the instrumental part that precedes the second verse, with its particularly shimmering double-stopped playing (on the tonic and the upper third), or on the solo, with its arpeggiated playing in the upper part of the neck. The theme, Taylor's flow, and the singer's range—covering more than two octaves here—give this track a very special place on the album, that of the orchestral rebel ballad. On March 5, 2009, to coincide with Taylor's appearance on *CSI: Crime Scene Investigation* (the "Turn, Turn, Turn" episode), Big Machine released a remix of "You're Not Sorry," which appears on the soundtrack of the episode.

Hidden Message

She can have you.

Taylor Swift sings "The Way I Loved You" at Wembley Arena in London, November 2009. This concert marks her entry onto the European music scene.

THE WAY I LOVED YOU

Taylor Swift, John Rich / 4:04

Musicians

Taylor Swift: vocals, backing vocals
Nathan Chapman: acoustic guitar, bass, drums, electric guitar, backing vocals, keyboards
Nick Buda, John Keefe: drums
Eric Darken, Al Wilson: percussion
Tony Harrell, Tim Lauer: keyboards
Tim Marks, Amos Heller: bass
Caitlin Evanson, Sammie Allan: backing vocals
Kenny Greenberg, Grant Mickelson: electric guitar
Bryan Sutton: acoustic guitar

Recorded

Blackbird Studio (Nashville), 2008

Technical Team

Producers: Nathan Chapman, Taylor Swift
Executive Producer: Scott Borchetta
Mixing: Justin Niebank, Jeremy "Jim Bob" Wheatley Sound Engineers: Chad Carlson, Jeremy "Jim Bob" Wheatley
Mastering: Hank Williams
Best Rankings: Hot Country: 72; Hot 100: 94

Genesis

Taylor Swift wrote this song with the help of John Rich, country music singer and songwriter since 1992, member of the bands Lonestar and Big & Rich, and successful entrepreneur. Taylor and John came up with the idea of creating a song in which the verses radically contrasted with the choruses. The verses glorify the perfect boyfriend, always on time, considerate, sensitive, and kind, while the choruses express Taylor's frustration with a relationship that feels routine. She misses the craziness of the early days: the 2 a.m. declarations of love, the fights, and the adrenaline rush of falling in love. Taylor wants to recapture that intensity, but boredom has definitely set in, and she no longer feels anything.

Production

With its 80 bpm andantino tempo, country-pop radio-calibrated choruses, and American brass band rhythms in the verses, the instrumentation on "The Way I Loved You" goes back to basics. Jonathan Yudkin's string arrangement, harpsichord chords, and tubular bells (from the end of the bridge) recall the baroque pop of the 1960s, while banjo, mandolin, and electric and acoustic guitars hold high the banner of the Nashville sound and country music.

Hidden Message

We can't go back.

Taylor Swift and Joe Jonas at the 2008 MTV Video Music Awards in Los Angeles. Their short relationship was widely covered by the media.

FOREVER & ALWAYS

Taylor Swift / 3:45

Musicians

Taylor Swift: vocals, backing vocals
Nathan Chapman: acoustic guitar, bass, drums, electric guitar, backing vocals, keyboards
Nick Buda, John Keefe: drums
Eric Darken, Al Wilson: percussion
Dan Dugmore: pedal steel
Rob Hajacos: fiddle
Tony Harrell, Tim Lauer: keyboards
Tim Marks, Amos Heller: bass
Caitlin Evanson, Sammie Allan: backing vocals
Kenny Greenberg, Grant Mickelson: electric guitar
Bryan Sutton: acoustic guitar, mandolin

Recorded

October 2008

Technical Team

Producers: Nathan Chapman, Taylor Swift
Executive Producer: Scott Borchetta
Mixing: Justin Niebank, Jeremy "Jim Bob" Wheatley
Sound Engineers: Chad Carlson, Jeremy "Jim Bob" Wheatley
Mastering: Hank Williams
Best Rankings: Hot 100: 34; Canadian Hot 100: 37

Genesis

Taylor Swift wrote "Forever & Always" toward the end of the recording process for the *Fearless* album. She convinced Scott Borchetta to include this ultra-dramatic and crazy song (in his own words) on this second album, because it reflected the reality of her daily life. Largely inspired by her breakup with singer Joe Jonas of the pop-rock group Jonas Brothers, Taylor describes a relationship that slowly falls apart as she continues to show her feelings, as well as the difficulty of having to face misunderstanding and frustration that results from it.

Production

Placed in the seventeenth position of the Platinum Edition and in eleventh position of the standard version, the initial arrangement of "Forever & Always" focuses on energy and growth in power. At a tempo of 127 bpm, the rhythm guitars (both acoustic and electric) drive the orchestration, synthesizers enhance the harmonic spectrum, either through discreet layers, or by providing some counterpoints with shimmering pop colors. Rob's fiddle Hajacos crowns it all by reinforcing the dramatic notes achieved with great bow strokes. Nathan Chapman and Taylor voluntarily opt for busy production, a little emphatic but completely assumed by the singer, who takes the opportunity to deliver a particularly intense vocal performance, not hesitating to seek out her voice chest within the limits of its high register.

A piano version of the song appears on the Platinum Edition of the album and it evokes a completely different

emotion from the original version. At first very pure, this new arrangement is based on a dialogue between the expressive playing of Tim Lauer on keyboards and Taylor Swift's contrasting vocals. From 1:53, the duo gradually expands thanks to the arrangement of solemn, even grandiloquent strings, composed and conducted by Jonathan Yudkin, who himself plays one of the cello parts, the first section being provided by the cellist Claire Indie.

Hidden Message

If you play these games, we're both going to lose.

2015 Academy of Country Music Awards in Arlington, Texas: Taylor Swift receives the Anniversary Milestone Award. Her mother, Andrea, the inspiration for "The Best Day," is by her side.

FOR DISCERNING SWIFTIES

In 2010, for Mother's Day, Taylor Swift released a limited edition of "The Best Day" as a CD single, via her line of greeting cards.

THE BEST DAY

Taylor Swift / 4:05

Musicians

Taylor Swift: vocals, backing vocals
Nathan Chapman: acoustic guitar, bass, drums, electric guitar, backing vocals, keyboards
Nick Buda, John Keefe: drums
Eric Darken, Al Wilson: percussion
Tony Harrell, Tim Lauer: keyboards
Tim Marks, Amos Heller: bass
Caitlin Evanson, Sammie Allan: backing vocals
Kenny Greenberg, Grant Mickelson: electric guitar
Bryan Sutton: acoustic guitar

Recorded

Blackbird Studio (Nashville), 2008

Technical Team

Producers: Nathan Chapman, Taylor Swift
Executive Producer: Scott Borchetta
Mixing: Justin Niebank
Sound Engineers: Chad Carlson, Jeremy "Jim Bob" Wheatley
Mastering: Hank Williams
Best Ranking: Hot Country: 56

Genesis

Taylor Swift wrote "The Best Day" as a tribute to her mother, Andrea Swift. It was her way of giving her the most beautiful gift for Mother's Day. The singer recounts how much fun and how complicated it was to prepare this text in secret—she was seventeen at the time—because her mother was always around. In it, she compiles her best childhood memories; the music video for this song shows a selection of old family videos, filmed with a camcorder. Andrea, who would never have imagined such a surprise, burst into tears when she heard this tender and loving dedication.

Production

The rounded arrangement and hushed touch of the musicians are perfectly suited to the theme of this song. Drums with brushes, delicate strumming, harmonics, arpeggios on acoustic guitar, a coarse shaker, the warm sound of the bass...It takes no more than this to transport the listener into a cozy atmosphere, inviting them to sit comfortably by the fire, immersed in the family cocoon. Welcome to the Swift home.

Hidden Message

God bless Andrea Swift.

Taylor Swift in concert in Texas, June 2008.

CHANGE

Taylor Swift / 4:41

Musicians

Taylor Swift: vocals, backing vocals
Nathan Chapman: acoustic guitar, bass, drums, electric guitar, backing vocals, keyboards
Nick Buda, John Keefe: drums
Eric Darken, Al Wilson: percussion
Tony Harrell, Tim Lauer: keyboards
Tim Marks, Amos Heller: bass
Caitlin Evanson, Sammie Allan: backing vocals
Kenny Greenberg, Grant Mickelson: electric guitar
Bryan Sutton: acoustic guitar

Recorded

Blackbird Studio (Nashville), 2008

Technical Team

Producers: Nathan Chapman, Taylor Swift
Executive Producer: Scott Borchetta
Mixing: Justin Niebank
Sound Engineer: Chad Carlson
Mastering: Hank Williams
Best Rankings: Hot 100: 10; Hot Country: 57; Pop 100: 21

Genesis

Knowing that she would have to fight to compete with the big labels and become the star she had always dreamed of being, Taylor began writing "Change" to give herself courage. At the time, Big Machine was still a small independent label trying to break into the big leagues. While she had been waiting for an epiphany, a landmark event to help her finish the song, it was not until the day after the 2007 Country Music Association Awards ceremony, where the singer received the Horizon Award, that Taylor found inspiration and managed to add the final stone to the edifice. "Change" is a hymn to the challengers, a tribute to all those who fight to get what they want, but for Taylor, it is also an opportunity to publicly affirm her desire to change the rules of the game in the country music business, which is still very conservative in many respects. "Change" was selected to be part of the official set list for the 2008 Beijing Olympics.

Production

The arrangements here are a fireworks display. Nathan Chapman and Taylor Swift do not hesitate to employ the production tricks necessary to achieve the "big sound"—it is all about living up to this epic theme. Ultracompressed bass and drums, superimpositions of saturated electric guitars, muted acoustic guitar strumming on the verses and full strumming on the choruses, and vocals immersed in reverb and long delay all help to build up to a particularly intense climax at 3:36 and keep the tension at its peak on the instrumental part from 3:45 to the end. This galvanizing orchestration makes you want to excel and break records.

Hidden Message

You made things change for me. (This message is addressed to the fans.)

RELEASE DATE
United States: April 9, 2021
(ref.: Republic Records B0033581-02)
Best Ranking: 1

ALBUM

Fearless (Taylor's Version)

Today Was a Fairytale · You All Over Me* (feat. Maren Morris) · Mr. Perfectly Fine* · We Were Happy* · That's When* · Don't You* · Bye Bye Baby*

**From the Vault*

Advertisement in Times Square, New York City.

A FIRST IN MUSIC HISTORY

Fearless (Taylor's Version) marks the beginning of Taylor Swift's attempts to regain control of her discography following the controversial sale of her original masters. It is the first of the Taylor's Versions albums. Released on April 9, 2021, the tracks were completely rerecorded in the studio, but also slightly rearranged. While it faithfully reproduces the nineteen tracks that appeared on this second album, including the hits "Fifteen" and "You Belong with Me," and the 2010 single "Today Was a Fairytale," it also contains six previously unreleased tracks referred to as "From the Vault." These are tracks that had originally been composed for the 2008 album but, for various reasons, were not recorded. And that is the strength of Taylor's Versions: In addition to breathing new life into Taylor's already well-known tracks, they offer fans previously unreleased compositions imagined at different periods in the singer's career, giving them an insight into her creative process. This was a major selling point when it comes to getting the public to listen to and buy the rerecorded versions rather than the originals, the rights to which were held by a private investment fund.

On the production side, alongside Taylor herself, is Christopher Rowe, a sound engineer and guitarist who would work on subsequent Taylor's Versions. Also collaborating are those she had already surrounded herself with for a number of years: Jack Antonoff, producer, songwriter, and sought-after musician, and Aaron Dessner, founding member of rock band the National. While country singer Colbie Caillat agreed to rerecord her voice on the featuring song "Breathe," other artists agreed to add their touch to the From the Vault tracks, including Keith Urban, who sings and plays guitar on "That's When" and "We Were Happy," and Maren Morris, who provides backing vocals on "You All Over Me."

This critically acclaimed first Taylor's Version was also warmly received by the public: It topped the Billboard 200 in the United States, becoming the first rerecorded album in history to do so. It also topped the charts in Australia, Canada, Ireland, New Zealand, Scotland, and the UK.

SINGLE

TODAY WAS A FAIRYTALE

Taylor Swift / 4:01

Musicians
Taylor Swift: vocals
Max Bernstein: midi banjo, synthesizer strings, glockenspiel, synthesizer programming
Matt Billingslea: drums, drum programming
Dan Burns: drum machine programming
Amos Heller: bass
Mike Meadows: acoustic guitar, mandolin, banjo
Christopher Rowe: backing vocals
Paul Sidoti: electric and acoustic guitars

Recorded
Blackbird Studio and Prime Recording (Nashville)

Technical Team
Producers: Christopher Rowe, Taylor Swift
Mixing: Serban Ghenea
Sound Engineers: Christopher Rowe, David Payne, Lowell Reynolds, Derek Garten, John Hanes
Mastering: Randy Merrill

Single Release
CD single, US, January 19, 2010—(ref. ?)
Best Rankings: Hot 100: 2; Hot Country: 41; Mainstream Top 40: 20

2021

Genesis

"Today Was a Fairytale" is a genuine bonus track on this 2021 edition: It was not included on either the original *Fearless* (2008) or the *Platinum Edition* (2009) versions of the album. At the time of the latter's conception, Taylor Swift felt that the theme and musical style of the track did not fit in with the others. However, after being cast in the film *Valentine's Day*, she suggested the track to the team, as its theme and lighthearted mood might suit this romantic comedy. The producers agreed, and the song was included on the film's soundtrack, released in 2010. As with many of the lyrics written around the time of *Fearless*, "Today Was a Fairytale" recycles the fairy-tale trope. There are a prince and a damsel in distress, but they're both immersed in real life: The prince's dark gray T-shirt marks the hour of a new kind of romantic rendezvous.

Production

Largely dominated by the presence of acoustic instruments, the country-pop arrangement and its ballad-like tempo (80 bpm) perfectly highlight the positivity and innocence evoked by Taylor Swift in this ode to teenage love. The combined high notes of banjo, mandolin, and acoustic guitar strumming give the orchestration a glittering, dreamy sheen. This "magical" effect is reinforced by the stratospheric string arrangement, the saturated, delay-laden electric guitars, and the snare drum triggered (doubled) by a glittering sample. The infectious energy of "Today Was a Fairytale" plunges listeners into a firework display of major chords (except for *E* minor in third position: *G*, *C*, *E* minor, *D*) and shimmering harmonies. The backing vocals and melodic gimmick played in unison by the electric guitar and strings sublimate the main melody, here masterfully interpreted by Taylor Swift, who seems to have put her Southern intonations aside. Another step toward mainstream pop.

SINGLE

YOU ALL OVER ME

(FEAT. MAREN MORRIS)

Taylor Swift, Scooter Carusoe / 3:40

Musicians

Taylor Swift: vocals, backing vocals
Maren Morris: backing vocals
Aaron Dessner: acoustic guitar, bass, drum machine programming, electric guitar, high-strung guitar, percussion, piano, keyboards, synthesizers
Eric Slick: drums
Josh Kaufman: electric guitar, harmonica

Recorded

Kitty Committee (London), Long Pond (Hudson Valley, NY), 2020

Technical Team

Producers: Aaron Dessner, Taylor Swift
Mixing: Jonathan Low
Sound Engineers: Aaron Dessner, Bella Blasko, Jonathan Low, Christopher Rowe
Mastering: Randy Merrill

Single Release

Digital release, March 26, 2021
Best Rankings: Hot 100: 51; Hot Country: 6

Genesis

In April 2021, a rumor had already been circulating for a few months among Swifties: the legendary demo "You All Over Me" would be included in Taylor Swift's identically rerecorded debut album: *Fearless (Taylor's Version)*. This demo version had leaked in 2017 via the notorious Taylor's Inner Circle, a controversial circle of fans active since 2004 and known for collecting unreleased tracks, demos, and other rare recordings. Often described as pretentious and egotistical, its unofficial members have a reputation for neither sharing nor selling their prized possessions. The singer herself came forward and revealed the news two days before the release of her album on March 24, 2021. "You All Over Me" recounts the painful experience of mourning for one's lover, a theme echoed later, in 2014, in "Clean" on the album *1989*. The acoustic guitar chord progression foreshadows "All Too Well," released in 2012 on *Red*. A great admirer of Maren Morris, Taylor asked this country singer, songwriter, and producer since 2005 to sing backing vocals on the official recording. Just as Taylor had imagined, their two vocal timbres were a perfect match.

Production

To embellish this moderate-tempo country-pop ballad (70 bpm in 4/4), Aaron Dessner devised a relatively minimalist country-pop arrangement, in harmony with all the tracks on *Fearless (Taylor's Version)*. The major originality of the orchestration lies in the rhythm: The three sixteenth-note bass drums played in a row on the opening beats of each bar (by drummer Eric Slick and the drum machine programming) create an atypical yet modern pulse, like a heartbeat that is constantly restarted and interrupted. After the second chorus, Josh Kaufman's electric guitar solo is particularly heartfelt, a far cry from the Nashville sound clichés of the 2000s.

Taylor Swift and Maren Morris at the 2019 iHeartRadio Music Awards in Los Angeles.

SINGLE

MR. PERFECTLY FINE

Taylor Swift / 4:37

Musicians
Taylor Swift: vocals, backing vocals
Jack Antonoff: acoustic guitar, backing vocals, bass, electric guitar, keyboard, modular synthesizer, percussion, programming
Mikey Freedom Hart: electric guitar, Hammond B3, pedal steel, twelve-string guitar
Sean Hutchinson: drums
Michael Riddleberger: percussion
Evan Smith: saxophone, synthesizers

Recorded
Conway Recording (Los Angeles), Electric Lady (New York), Kitty Committee (London), Rough Customer (Brooklyn, NY), 2020

Technical Team
Producers: Jack Antonoff, Taylor Swift
Mixing: Serban Ghenea
Sound Engineers: Jack Antonoff, John Hanes, Laura Sisk, Christopher Rowe
Mastering: Randy Merrill
Best Rankings: Hot 100: 30; Hot Country: 2

Genesis

Taylor Swift wrote "Mr. Perfectly Fine" in 2009, with the intention of including it on the Platinum version of *Fearless*, but in the end, the song failed to make the cut. The lyrics seem to evoke her relationship with Joe Jonas. As in "Forever and Always," the portrait of this "Mr. Perfect" could indeed correspond in every way to that of the young singer.

Production

In terms of arrangements, "Mr. Perfectly Fine" is somewhat at odds with the rest of the album. Ten years had passed. Jack Antonoff's signature pop style is back, oscillating elegantly between electro and acoustic. The velvety, organic timbre of the synthesizers blends perfectly with Sean Hutchinson's acoustic guitar and drums, which are at once restrained, precise, and energetic. Only a few discreet notes of pedal steel recall the Nashville sound of the 2000s, of which Nathan Chapman mastered all the subtleties. Naturally, Taylor Swift's voice is transfigured, her timbre is fuller, and her singing style is very different, more detailed and expressive, and her Southern intonations have completely disappeared.

2021

WE WERE HAPPY

Taylor Swift, Liz Rose / 4:04

Musicians
Taylor Swift: vocals, backing vocals
Keith Urban: electric guitar, backing vocals
Aaron Dessner: acoustic guitar, bass, drum machine programming, electric guitar, high-strung guitar, keyboards, percussion, synthesizers
Eric Slick: drums
Josh Kaufman: acoustic guitar, lap steel guitar
Clarice Jensen: cello
Yuki Numata Resnick: violin

Recorded
Kitty Committee (London), Long Pond (Hudson Valley, NY), 2020

Technical Team
Producers: Aaron Dessner, Taylor Swift
Mixing: Jonathan Low
Sound Engineers: Aaron Dessner, Bella Blasko, Jonathan Low, Christopher Rowe
Mastering: Randy Merrill

Genesis

Written with Liz Rose for the original version of *Fearless*, "We Were Happy" is a nostalgic song with a bittersweet tone. Taylor and Liz enjoy enumerating some evocative and remarkably cinematic romantic sketches, invoking memories of a perfect idyll whose magic has faded with time. To help her retrieve this song out of her vault, Taylor asked famous country music singer Keith Urban to sing backing vocals.

Production

Aaron Dessner and Taylor Swift offer a sensitive orchestration, a play of light that relies essentially on the contrast between the acoustic guitar (the main instrument, doubled on the right and left), the deliciously three-dimensional string arrangement, and the drum pulse played with mallets, like the coming and going of a heady, percussive surf. The depth of field is further enhanced by the addition of a delay set to sixteenth notes on the right acoustic guitar, and bass playing at the top of the neck that does not confine itself to the tonic. The voices of Taylor Swift and Keith Urban blend perfectly. The two singers' sober yet vibrant and emotional interpretation transcends this tender, nostalgic ballad.

For "We Were Happy," Taylor Swift asked Keith Urban to sing the backing vocals. Keith had supported Taylor's career since her debut.

THAT'S WHEN

Taylor Swift, Brad Warren, Brett Warren / 3:09

Musicians
Taylor Swift: vocals, backing vocals
Keith Urban: vocals, twelve-string guitar
Jack Antonoff: acoustic guitar, backing vocals, bass, electric guitar, keyboard, percussion, programming, synthesizers
Mikey Freedom Hart: bass, celesta, drums, electric guitars, Hammond B3, keys, pedal steel, piano
Sean Hutchinson: drums
Michael Riddleberger: percussion
Evan Smith: saxophones, flutes

Recorded
Conway Recording (Los Angeles), Electric Lady (New York), Kitty Committee (London), Rough Customer (Brooklyn, NY), 2020

Technical Team
Producers: Jack Antonoff, Taylor Swift
Mixing: Serban Ghenea
Sound Engineers: Jack Antonoff, John Hanes, Laura Sisk, David Hart, Christopher Rowe, Nick Rowse
Mastering: Randy Merrill
Best Ranking: Hot Country: 30

2021

Genesis

Taylor Swift wrote the song at the age of fourteen, with the help of brothers Brad and Brett Warren, members of country music duo the Warren Brothers (active since 1998). Keith Urban is once again involved, but this time he not only records the vocal harmonies; he also sings lead vocals on the second verse and the first cycle of the second chorus, in a true duet with Taylor. The singer also takes on the twelve-string guitar part. "That's When" and "We Were Happy" are not Taylor Swift's first collaborations with Keith Urban. The singer recorded the acoustic guitar part on "Highway Don't Care" (a duet by Tim McGraw and Taylor Swift) on Tim McGraw's first album for Big Machine, *Two Lanes of Freedom*, which was released on March 25, 2013. "That's When" is a story of reconciliation in love, a dialogue between two lovers who still have feelings for each other and are trying to find each other again.

Production

The production of this moderate-tempo (90 bpm) country-pop ballad was provided by producer Jack Antonoff. Elements specific to the genre are present (pedal steel, acoustic guitar, drums played with brushes) but are blended with more modern sounds (synthesizer layers, drum machine programming), and a great deal of textural work has gone into the backing vocals. Jack Antonoff and Taylor Swift are at the cutting edge of the new Nashville sound of the 2020s here, more pop and resolutely in tune with the times.

DON'T YOU

Taylor Swift, Tommy Lee James / 3:28

Musicians

Taylor Swift: vocals, backing vocals
Jack Antonoff: backing vocals, drums, electric guitars, keys, programming, synthesizers, vocoder
Mikey Freedom Hart: bass, electric guitar, percussion, Rhodes
Evan Smith: electric guitars, flutes, percussion, synthesizers
Bobby Hawk: violin

Recorded

Conway Recording (Los Angeles), Electric Lady (New York), Kitty Committee (London), Rough Customer (Brooklyn, NY), 2020

Technical Team

Producers: Jack Antonoff, Taylor Swift
Mixing: Serban Ghenea
Sound Engineers: Jack Antonoff, John Hanes, Laura Sisk, Christopher Rowe
Mastering: Randy Merrill

Genesis

According to Taylor's Inner Circle, a piano and vocal demo of "Don't You," probably recorded in 2005 and intended for Taylor Swift's debut album, is the source of this Taylor's Version. Written in collaboration with Tommy Lee James (American songwriter and producer of country music for Still Working Music Group and Capitol Records since the early 1990s), "Don't You" describes the painful moment when Taylor stumbles across an ex-boyfriend for whom she still has feelings. She knows that he is seeing another woman, very different from her. This chance encounter triggers strong, contradictory emotions within her.

Production

The arrangement of this mid-tempo ballad (100 bpm) begins with chords played on the "flutes" sound of a mellotron (a keyboard instrument where each key corresponds to the note of an acoustic or electric instrument). Jack Antonoff often enjoys slipping vintage sounds and retro references into his productions—in this case, the sound used on the Beatles' song "Strawberry Fields Forever." In the confrontation between instruments from the analog era and modern sounds (layering, strings, synthesizer bass sequences, and programmed electronic rhythms), which are less organic and warm, the arrangement acquires greater relief. The sophistication of the vocal harmonies, all sung in overdub by Taylor Swift herself to create this choral effect, lends a certain dynamic to this intentionally hybrid orchestration.

BYE BYE BABY

Taylor Swift, Liz Rose / 4:02

Musicians

Taylor Swift: vocals, backing vocals
Jack Antonoff: backing vocals, bass, electric guitar, percussion, piano, programming
Mikey Freedom Hart: electric guitar, Hammond B3, pedal steel, piano, Wurlitzer
Sean Hutchinson: drums
Michael Riddleberger: percussion
Evan Smith: saxophones, flutes
Bobby Hawk: violin

Recorded

Conway Recording (Los Angeles), Electric Lady (New York), Kitty Committee (London), Rough Customer (Brooklyn, NY), 2020

Technical Team

Producers: Jack Antonoff, Taylor Swift
Mixing: Serban Ghenea
Sound Engineers: Jack Antonoff, John Hanes, Laura Sisk, Christopher Rowe
Mastering: Randy Merrill
Best Ranking: Hot Country: 49

Genesis

As its title suggests, "Bye Bye Baby" is a breakup song, where Taylor reluctantly says goodbye to a lover whose feelings have faded. It was co-written with Liz Rose for the original version of *Fearless*, but the track was not chosen. Rumor has it that this decision was made because of its strong similarities to Michelle Branch's 2002 hit "Goodbye to You." Taylor decided to change the lyrics—a demo had been leaked on the internet without her knowledge, under the original title "The One Thing." Thus "And all you have is to walk away / From the one thing I thought would never leave me" became "'Cause you took me home but you just couldn't keep me."

Production

As for production, there is no doubt that Jack Antonoff and Taylor Swift are in 2020 with this mix of acoustic drums and 1980s-style programming; pedal steel; electric organ; textural strings; a low-filtered piano gimmick; a deep, muffled double-note bass; and subtle electric guitar sounds. Similarly, the backing vocals are enveloping, the lead vocal is treated very dryly (without delay or reverb) on the verses, and the whole piece is sprinkled with sound design elements to serve up a modern pop sound that is both intimate and shimmering. Perhaps the most striking element of this arrangement is the treatment of the slightly detuned electric guitar arpeggio sound, typical of the chill pop of the late 2010s.

RELEASE DATES
United States: October 25, 2010
(ref.: Big Machine Records—BTMSR0300A)
*** Deluxe Edition (exclusive to Target): October 25, 2010**
(ref.: Big Machine Records—BTMSR0300B)
Best Ranking: 1

ALBUM

Speak Now

Mine* (Pop Mix) · Sparks Fly · Back to December* · Speak Now · Dear John · Mean · The Story of Us · Never Grow Up · Enchanted · Better Than Revenge · Innocent · Haunted* (Acoustic) · Last Kiss · Long Live (We Will Be Remembered) · Ours* · If This Was a Movie* · Superman* · Ronan (non-album single)

New Orleans, 2010: Performing songs from *Speak Now* as Taylor Swift's sound veers more overtly toward rock.

In July 2011, Taylor Swift played four consecutive sold-out concerts in the New York metropolitan area, captivating more than 52,000 fans.

THE ALBUM OF MATURITY, IN THE REAL SENSE OF THE WORD

2010

Downtime is definitely not part of Taylor Swift's life. *Fearless* had not even been released twenty-four hours before the singer began work on her third studio album, *Speak Now*. This time, the album was written entirely by her; there were no official collaborations. The album took two years to complete, from the time the singer wrote the first lines until its release. At the time her schedule was overloaded: Between 2008 and 2010, she performed one concert after another as part of the "Fearless Tour." Like *Fearless*, *Speak Now* was recorded and arranged by Nathan Chapman in the Big Machine Nashville studio. There was no question of changing a winning team, especially as the young artist still felt confident with the discreet producer. She was also more confident than ever before, taking an active role in all aspects of production. As well as writing and composing each track, she was involved in the musical arrangements and, more generally, was in charge, along with Chapman, of the album's artistic direction.

A New Independence

While the very pop-sounding *Fearless* had already ventured a little into rock, *Speak Now* took this even further. Playful electric guitars mixed with acoustic guitars; drum rolls and breaks; lyrical, grandiloquent strings...Taylor's country music becomes less identifiable, suggesting that the singer was moving away from her first love. She was, in fact, growing up. In 2009, at the age of twenty, she bought herself a flat, a penthouse on Nashville's Music Row, for nearly $2 million. In this very first place of her own, she enjoyed composing more freely than on tour, where she was always surrounded by people. "Living alone, you can do so many fantastic things," she told *People* magazine. "You can walk around and have conversations with yourself and, like, sing your thoughts. I think I'm the only one who does that."

Performing "Innocent" at the 2010 MTV Video Music Awards, Nokia Theatre, Los Angeles.

2010

Coming of Age

This change, which undeniably corresponds to the passage from adolescence to adulthood, is also felt in the singer's lyrics. Whereas *Fearless* tackled the themes of teenage love affairs, which are often sentimental, conveying hope for the future and self-affirmation, *Speak Now* is less optimistic and more tinged with disillusionment. Having been in the spotlight for several years now, the young woman had accumulated many experiences, both happy and painful, which her celebrity status certainly intensified. Top of the list was her clash with Kanye West, which brought her to the attention of the world's media. She returns to this in the "Innocent" track, in which she suggests that she forgives the rapper and that a person's mistakes do not define them forever. But disappointment in love and regret are indeed the main themes of the album—as evidenced by its title, which is a direct reference to the famous phrase uttered at wedding ceremonies: "If anyone objects to this union, let them speak now or forever hold their peace." Taylor is reminding us that it is better to share what is on our minds before it is too late.

Conquests and Heartbreaks, Creative Drivers

Speak Now also confirms Taylor's cherished tradition of "Easter eggs," the cryptic messages she distills, from the lyrics of her songs to the music videos and clothes she wears at interviews. Many of these clues, which take the form of innuendo, typographical nuances, or visual symbols, subtly inform fans about the identity of the conquests in which she is engaged. In "Dear John," she settles scores with singer John Mayer, with whom she had a painful relationship between late 2009 and early 2010; she loved him so much, while he only played with her. In "Back to December," she is probably speaking tenderly to actor Taylor Lautner, whom she ended up spurning a few weeks after their meeting on the set of the romantic comedy *Valentine's Day*. In 2010, she also began a romance with the *Glee* series actor Cory Monteith, and with Hollywood star Jake Gyllenhaal, nine years her senior,

Taylor Swift is named Artist of the Year at the 2011 American Music Awards in Los Angeles, a confirmation of her enormous success.

whom she met backstage at *Saturday Night Live*. When asked by MTV about the relationship she had been forming with Jake for several months, she explained that she could indeed confide details of her personal life in writing, but that she did not wish to talk about them in person. Fans who follow her intense love life were delighted. Love, which is by no means anecdotal in the star's work, is and would remain her number one source of inspiration. More than her previous albums, *Speak Now* is crystal clear: If a man makes an impression, for good or ill, there is a good chance that he will inspire her to write a song and end up on one of her albums. They have been warned...

New Records Set, and Confirmation of a Talent

The *Speak Now* album finally enabled Taylor Swift to set new records. In the United States, it sold over a million copies in the first week of its release. It went platinum six times and spent six weeks at the top of the charts, supported by six singles ("Mine," "Back to December," "Mean," "The Story of Us," "Sparks Fly," and "Ours"), four of which broke into the top 10 of the Hot 100. The singer's international success was also confirmed, with more than one single breaking into the top 10 in several countries, including Australia, Canada, and the UK.

As far as the critics are concerned, Taylor continues to impress. The *New York Times* described the album as "a bravura work of nontransparent transparency. [...] Ms. Swift is at her most musically adventurous when she's most incensed." According to *Rolling Stone*, "Swift's third album, Speak Now, is roughly twice as good as 2008's Fearless, which was roughly twice as good as her 2006 debut." The magazine goes as far as to wonder where all the older artists are, supposedly making better pop records than Taylor Swift, before concluding that there are none.

In 2011, Taylor hit the road again for a world tour. The "Speak Now World Tour" included 111 concerts on four continents and brought together 1.5 million fans, earning $150 million.

SINGLE

MINE

(POP MIX)

Taylor Swift / 3:50

Musicians

Taylor Swift: vocals, backing vocals
Nathan Chapman: acoustic guitar, bass, drums, electric guitar, backing vocals, keyboard, programming
Nick Buda, John Gardner, Shannon Forrest: drums
Eric Darken, Al Wilson: percussion
Tony Harrell, Tim Lauer: keyboard
Tim Marks, Amos Heller, Michael Rhodes, Tommy Sims: bass
Caitlin Evanson, Liz Huett: backing vocals
Kenny Greenberg, Grant Mickelson, Mike Meadows, Paul Sidoti, Tom Bukovac: electric guitar
Bryan Sutton: acoustic guitar
Smith Curry: lap steel guitar

Recorded

Aimeeland, Blackbird, Pain in the Art, and Starstruck (Nashville); Capitol (Hollywood); Stonehurst (Bowling Green)

Technical Team

Producers: Nathan Chapman, Taylor Swift, Matt Ward, Dean Gillard
Mixing: Justin Niebank, Nathan Chapman, Chad Carlson, Mark Crew, Matt Ward, Dean Gillard
Sound Engineers: Nathan Chapman, Chuck Ainlay, Chad Carlson, Steve Churchyard, Jeremy Hunter, Jed Hackett, Steve Marcantonio, Joel Quillen, Lowell Reynolds, Brian David Willis
Mastering: Hank Williams

Single Releases

Digital and radio release: August 4, 2010; CD single, US: October 25, 2010—BMRTS0301
Best Rankings: Hot Country: 2; Hot 100: 3; US Pop Songs: 12

2010

Genesis

Recorded in a day in Nathan Chapman's basement, Taylor Swift and her team had no hesitation in choosing "Mine" as the first single to launch *Speak Now*, the singer's third album, so eagerly awaited by the fans. With her usual shrewdness, she evokes her recent tendency to run away from love. All her past relationships having ended in breakups, Taylor writes "Mine" as an outlet, in which she describes the exception that, in her opinion, proves the rule: meeting a young man so stable and robust that she would not be afraid to make a full commitment to him.

Production

On streaming platforms, the Deluxe Edition of *Speak Now* begins with the Pop Mix version of "Mine," more pared down than the original; the lap steel, acoustic guitar, and electric guitar overtones (arpeggios and melodic counterpoints) have disappeared. However, both versions feature a very pop-sounding arrangement, tailor-made for mainstream radio. With its fast tempo (120 bpm), its vocal gimmick right from the intro, its palm mute guitars on the verses and open play on the choruses, its judiciously placed vocal harmonies, and its traditional bridge after the second chorus, "Mine" has a formidably effective arrangement. Its triple platinum certification (over three million units based on sales and streaming) confirmed that Taylor Swift and Nathan Chapman had chosen the ideal first single to propel *Speak Now* straight to the top of the pop and country charts.

Hidden Message

Toby ("Toby").

SINGLE

SPARKS FLY

Taylor Swift / 4:20

Musicians

Taylor Swift: vocals, backing vocals, acoustic guitar
Nathan Chapman: acoustic guitar, bass, drums, electric guitar, backing vocals, keyboard, programming
Nick Buda, John Gardner, Shannon Forrest: drums
Eric Darken, Al Wilson: percussion
Rob Hajacos: fiddle
Tony Harrell, Tim Lauer: keyboard
Tim Marks, Amos Heller, Michael Rhodes, Tommy Sims: bass
Caitlin Evanson, Liz Huett: backing vocals
Kenny Greenberg, Grant Mickelson, Mike Meadows, Paul Sidoti, Tom Bukovac: electric guitar
Bryan Sutton: acoustic guitar, twelve-string guitar, ukulele
Smith Curry: pedal steel

Recorded

Aimeeland, Blackbird, Pain in the Art, and Starstruck (Nashville); Capitol (Hollywood); Stonehurst (Bowling Green)

Technical Team

Producers: Nathan Chapman, Taylor Swift
Mixing: Justin Niebank, Nathan Chapman, Chad Carlson, Mark Crew, Matt Ward, Dean Gillard
Sound Engineers: Nathan Chapman, Chuck Ainlay, Chad Carlson, Steve Churchyard, Jeremy Hunter, Jed Hackett, Steve Marcantonio, Joel Quillen, Lowell Reynolds, Brian David Willis
Mastering: Hank Williams

Single Release

CD single, US, July 18, 2011—BMRTS0305
Best Rankings: Hot Country: 1; Hot 100: 17

Genesis

Taylor Swift wrote the first version of "Sparks Fly" the year she turned sixteen, shortly before the release of her first single, "Tim McGraw." A live version recorded in 2007 circulated on the internet and quickly went viral as fans demanded an official version of the song. Taylor Swift continued to rework her copy until 2010, when she decided it was time to record "Sparks Fly" in the studio for inclusion on *Speak Now.* Taylor and her team chose to make it the fifth single from the album. It features a number of elements that the singer is particularly fond of: the theme of forbidden love, fairy-tale imagery, and the metaphor of a rendezvous in the rain, already present in "Hey Stephen" and "Forever and Always" on her previous album, *Fearless.*

Production

Nathan Chapman's dense, flashy production pushes "Sparks Fly" into the mainstream power pop territory that Taylor Swift felt particularly comfortable with since *Fearless.* All the elements are there: the 115 bpm tempo, the flawless acoustic guitar rhythm that oscillates between energetic strumming and delicate arpeggios, the successive layers of electric guitar (palm mute rhythm, ostinato gimmick, tremolo effects, melodic counterpoints in the form of questions and answers placed face-to-face right and left in the stereo field), the bass played in eighth notes, and the distant-sounding organ layer. At 2:38, placed on the right in the stereo field, the electric guitar's mini-solo passed through an octave pedal particularly stands out. As for the drums, to take the intensity up a notch, the bass drum switches from playing beats 1 and 3 on the verses to the constant, hammered quarter note on the choruses. Taylor Swift's voice, which is supple and energetic, seems to float effortlessly above this busy but dynamic arrangement, because of its structure and Justin Niebank's perfectly clear, well-balanced mixing, which contributes greatly to the legibility of the whole production.

Hidden Message

Portland, Oregon.

Wearing a fairytale dress at the 2010 CMA Awards, Taylor Swift performs "Back to December" on the piano.

SINGLE

BACK TO DECEMBER

Taylor Swift / 4:53

Musicians

Taylor Swift: vocals, backing vocals, acoustic guitar
Nathan Chapman: acoustic guitar, banjo, bass, drums, electric guitar, backing vocals, mandolin, keyboard, programming
Nick Buda, John Gardner, Shannon Forrest: drums
Eric Darken, Al Wilson: percussion
Rob Hajacos: fiddle
Tony Harrell, Tim Lauer: keyboard
Tim Marks, Amos Heller, Michael Rhodes, Tommy: bass
Caitlin Evanson, Liz Huett: backing vocals
Kenny Greenberg, Grant Mickelson, Mike Meadows, Paul Sidoti, Tom Bukovac: electric guitar
Bryan Sutton: acoustic guitar, twelve-string guitar, ukulele
Smith Curry: pedal steel
Paul Buckmaster: conductor, orchestral arrangements
Chris Carmichael: composer, string arrangements

Recorded

Aimeeland, Blackbird, Pain in the Art, and Starstruck (Nashville); Capitol (Hollywood); Stonehurst (Bowling Green)

Technical Team

Producers: Nathan Chapman, Taylor Swift, Matt Ward, Dean Gillard
Mixing: Justin Niebank, Nathan Chapman, Chad Carlson, Mark Crew, Matt Ward, Dean Gillard
Sound Engineers: Nathan Chapman, Chuck Ainlay, Chad Carlson, Steve Churchyard, Jeremy Hunter, Jed Hackett, Steve Marcantonio, Joel Quillen, Lowell Reynolds, Brian David Willis
Mastering: Hank Williams

Single Release

CD single, US, November 15, 2010—(ref. ?)
Best Rankings: Hot Country: 3; Hot 100: 6; US Pop Songs: 19

Genesis

"Back to December" is the album's second single and Taylor Swift's first song motivated by the need to apologize to an ex-boyfriend: *Twilight* actor Taylor Lautner—his identity is confirmed by the song's hidden message ("Tay") and by the actor himself. Usually, when Taylor Swift decides to address one of her ex-boyfriends directly in song, it is in the form of a bittersweet assessment or a frontal and assertive settling of scores, but in this case the singer realizes that she has been inconsiderate toward her loved one, that she needs to learn from her past experiences and issue a mea culpa with dignity. Another step toward maturity.

Production

What better way to express regret than with an orchestral ballad? In "Back to December," the strings take center stage, and the arrangements by Paul Buckmaster and Chris Carmichael add a solemn dimension to the clean lines of this country-pop composition. The acoustic version (at number eighteen on the Deluxe version of *Speak Now*) leaves out the electric instruments and drums to highlight the strings, mandolin, acoustic guitars, and Taylor Swift's sensitive interpretation. Although this version is stripped of much of its instrumentation, a similar emotion to the original mix emanates from it, and the message gains in clarity without losing any of its power.

Hidden Message

Tay.

The dreamlike world of *Speak Now* is symbolized on tour by a large, colorful tree.

SINGLE

SPEAK NOW

Taylor Swift / 4:00

Musicians

Taylor Swift: vocals, backing vocals, acoustic guitar
Nathan Chapman: acoustic guitar, banjo, bass, drums, electric guitar, backing vocals, mandolin, keyboard, programming
Nick Buda, John Gardner, Shannon Forrest: drums
Eric Darken, Al Wilson: percussion
Rob Hajacos: fiddle
Tony Harrell, Tim Lauer: keyboard
Tim Marks, Amos Heller, Michael Rhodes: bass
Caitlin Evanson, Liz Huett: backing vocals
Kenny Greenberg, Grant Mickelson, Mike Meadows, Paul Sidoti, Tom Bukovac: electric guitar
Bryan Sutton: acoustic guitar, twelve-string guitar, ukulele
Smith Curry: pedal steel
Paul Buckmaster: conductor, orchestral arrangements
Chris Carmichael: composer, string arrangements

Recorded

Aimeeland, Blackbird, Pain in the Art, and Starstruck (Nashville); Capitol (Hollywood); Stonehurst (Bowling Green)

Technical Team

Producers: Nathan Chapman, Matt Ward
Mixing: Justin Niebank, Nathan Chapman, Chad Carlson, Mark Crew, Matt Ward, Dean Gillard
Sound Engineers: Nathan Chapman, Chuck Ainlay, Chad Carlson, Steve Churchyard, Jeremy Hunter, Jed Hackett, Steve Marcantonio, Joel Quillen, Lowell Reynolds, Brian David Willis
Mastering: Hank Williams

Single Release

Digital promotional single, US, October 5, 2010
Best Rankings: Hot Country: 58; Hot 100: 8

2010

Genesis

Even when it was barely sketched out, the song "Speak Now" gave Taylor Swift the idea of building her third album around a concept perfectly in tune with a new way of approaching her songwriting: seeing each song as an avowal, a confession addressed to a specific person. Far from being a stylistic exercise, this approach is a natural development of Taylor Swift's style, a way of writing that is often direct and diary-like. "Speak Now" gives its name to Taylor's first album as sole songwriter, like an ode to self-assertion. She got the idea for the theme from a friend's story about her childhood sweetheart getting married to a woman with a bad attitude, who cut the young man off from his friends and all contact with his family. The two of them have fun imagining how they might turn up in the middle of a wedding—Taylor with guitar in hand—to oppose this union.

Production

Introduced by a duo of acoustic guitars playing the same rhythmic sequence in unison, one with a pick (right) and the other with fingers (center), "Speak Now" inevitably evokes the doo-wop hits of the late 1950s. The swaying binary rhythm in a 120 bpm tempo (the snare drum bounce on the eighth note of the second beat of each bar is typical of the genre), the harmonic progression, the backing vocals that flirt with close harmony, and the arrangement bursting with zesty details (orchestral bells and glockenspiel in counterpoint, Hammond organ strings, lead parts, and twelve-string electric guitar arpeggios) all bear witness to this. From the very first verse, Taylor Swift sings at the top end of her range, with pop intonations with which we are still unfamiliar coming from her (the pitch correction software can be heard quite extensively at the end of certain phrases), but which serve this colorful text marvelously well.

Hidden Message

You always regret what you don't say.

13

Taylor Swift in New York, November 2011.

FOR DISCERNING SWIFTIES

Before the release of the song "All Too Well" (10-minute version) in 2021 on the album *Red (Taylor's Version)*, "Dear John" was the longest song at 6:43.

DEAR JOHN

Taylor Swift / 6:43

Musicians

Taylor Swift: vocals, backing vocals, acoustic guitar
Nathan Chapman: acoustic guitar, bass, drums, electric guitar, backing vocals, mandolin, keyboard, programming
Nick Buda, John Gardner, Shannon Forrest: drums
Eric Darken, Al Wilson: percussion
Tony Harrell, Tim Lauer: keyboard
Tim Marks, Amos Heller, Michael Rhodes: bass
Caitlin Evanson, Liz Huett: backing vocals
Kenny Greenberg, Grant Mickelson, Mike Meadows, Paul Sidoti, Tom Bukovac: electric guitar
Bryan Sutton: acoustic guitar, twelve-string guitar, ukulele
Smith Curry: pedal steel

Recorded

Aimeeland, Blackbird, Pain in the Art, and Starstruck (Nashville); Capitol (Hollywood); Stonehurst (Bowling Green)

Technical Team

Producers: Nathan Chapman, Taylor Swift, Matt Ward, Dean Gillard
Mixing: Justin Niebank, Nathan Chapman, Chad Carlson, Mark Crew, Matt Ward, Dean Gillard
Sound Engineers: Nathan Chapman, Chuck Ainlay, Chad Carlson, Steve Churchyard, Jeremy Hunter, Jed Hackett, Steve Marcantonio, Joel Quillen, Lowell Reynolds, Brian David Willis
Mastering: Hank Williams

2010

Genesis

"Dear John" is the transposition of a breakup email, the kind in which you settle scores point by point and that never gets sent. Taylor Swift chose to include the song on her *Speak Now* album, and given her celebrity status, it seems somewhat like her having decided to click "send" after all. The song is addressed to her ex-boyfriend John Mayer.

Production

With its slow tempo and three-beat rhythm, this country-pop waltz joins the ranks of maudlin power ballads, rare but already recurrent in Taylor Swift's work, and systematically positioned at number five in the track listing of every album, from "Cold as You" on *Taylor Swift* to "White Horse" on *Fearless*. The arrangement is peppered with electric guitar licks, reminiscent of the southern rock sound of the Allman Brothers Band, Lynyrd Skynyrd, or, more recently, John Mayer—has John Mayer's presence in Taylor Swift's life had a conscious or unconscious influence on the musical direction of this album? The acoustic guitar strumming carries the arrangement. The Hammond organ can be heard in the distance, the piano melody on the right hand. After the rigorous, minimalist playing of the bass and drums section, the climax is reached on a tutti at 5:19, then revived by a few notes of orchestral bells to maintain the tension until 6:01, before the final descent. "You should have known," Taylor Swift repeats to her beloved John.

Hidden Message

Loved you from the very first day.

At the 2011 Academy of Country Music Awards in Las Vegas, Taylor Swift is recognized for her impact on the country music scene.

SINGLE

MEAN

Taylor Swift / 3:57

Musicians
Taylor Swift: vocals, backing vocals, acoustic guitar
Nathan Chapman: acoustic guitar, banjo, bass, drums, electric guitar, backing vocals, mandolin, keyboard, programming
Nick Buda, John Gardner, Shannon Forrest: drums
Eric Darken, Al Wilson: percussion
Rob Hajacos: fiddle
Tony Harrell, Tim Lauer: keyboard
Tim Marks, Amos Heller, Michael Rhodes, Tommy Sims: bass
Caitlin Evanson, Liz Huett: backing vocals
Kenny Greenberg, Grant Mickelson, Mike Meadows, Paul Sidoti, Tom Bukovac: electric guitar
Bryan Sutton: acoustic guitar, twelve-string guitar, ukulele
Recorded
Aimeeland, Blackbird, Pain in the Art, and Starstruck (Nashville); Capitol (Hollywood); Stonehurst (Bowling Green)
Technical Team
Producers: Nathan Chapman, Taylor Swift, Matt Ward, Dean Gillard
Mixing: Justin Niebank, Nathan Chapman, Chad Carlson, Mark Crew, Matt Ward, Dean Gillard
Sound Engineers: Nathan Chapman, Chuck Ainlay, Chad Carlson, Steve Churchyard, Jeremy Hunter, Jed Hackett, Steve Marcantonio, Joel Quillen, Lowell Reynolds, Brian David Willis
Mastering: Hank Williams
Single Release
Promotional CD single, US, October 19, 2010—BMRTS0303
Best Rankings: Hot Country: 2; Hot 100: 11

Genesis

"Mean" takes aim at the sometimes gratuitous nastiness of certain journalists and influencers. The song deals more generally with the way in which certain criticisms, especially abrasive and non-constructive ones, can damage self-esteem. Taylor Swift herself says she does not have a thick skin. Over time, these repeated attacks, these "knife wounds" ("with your words like knives") led her to stop paying attention to prevailing rumors. It seems that "Mean" is targeting music critic Bob Lefsetz in particular, who, after Taylor Swift's performance alongside Stevie Nicks at the 2010 Grammy Awards, declared that Taylor could not sing, that she had just sunk her career and that she was simply too young and stupid to realize it. One of Taylor Swift's great strengths is that she has always been able to settle scores in song. And this is yet another proof of that—clear, crisp, direct, and to the point.

Production

In terms of production, "Mean" marks a return to the country pop–bluegrass of her early days. A fast tempo (160 bpm), banjo, fiddle, mandolin, strumming acoustic guitar, drums played with brushes—everything is there. This 100 percent acoustic orchestration (with the exception of the electric bass) is a good way to support Taylor Swift's rebellion, and she has no hesitation in pointing the finger at her detractors, in the manner of Woody Guthrie (figurehead of the American folk protest movement, influenced by the anarchist Joe Hill, and model for the young Bob Dylan) and the folk singers of the 1930s–1950s who put their demands against employers into song.

Hidden Message

I thought you got me.

2010

September 2010: Taylor Swift attends the Roberto Cavalli fashion show during Milan Fashion Week.

SINGLE

THE STORY OF US

Taylor Swift / 4:25

Musicians

Taylor Swift: vocals, backing vocals, acoustic guitar
Nathan Chapman: acoustic guitar, banjo, bass, drums, electric guitar, backing vocals, mandolin, keyboard, programming
Nick Buda, John Gardner, Shannon Forrest: drums
Eric Darken, Al Wilson: percussion
Rob Hajacos: fiddle
Tony Harrell, Tim Lauer: keyboard
Tim Marks, Amos Heller, Michael Rhodes, Tommy Sims: bass
Caitlin Evanson, Liz Huett: backing vocals
Kenny Greenberg, Grant Mickelson, Mike Meadows, Paul Sidoti, Tom Bukovac: electric guitar
Bryan Sutton: acoustic guitar, twelve-string guitar, ukulele

Recorded

Aimeeland, Blackbird, Pain in the Art, and Starstruck (Nashville); Capitol (Hollywood); Stonehurst (Bowling Green)

Technical Team

Producers: Nathan Chapman, Taylor Swift, Matt Ward, Dean Gillard
Mixing: Justin Niebank, Nathan Chapman, Chad Carlson, Mark Crew, Matt Ward, Dean Gillard
Sound Engineers: Nathan Chapman, Chuck Ainlay, Chad Carlson, Steve Churchyard, Jeremy Hunter, Jed Hackett, Steve Marcantonio, Joel Quillen, Lowell Reynolds, Brian David Willis
Mastering: Hank Williams

Single Release

Promotional CD single, US, April 19, 2011—(ref. ?)
Best Ranking: Hot 100: 41

Genesis

Like "Dear John," "The Story of Us" tackles the John Mayer case. This time, however, it is not an indictment of the musician, as Taylor Swift expresses her regrets, tinged with a certain bitterness. In the very first chorus, she alludes to the Country Music Television awards ceremony, where the two musicians were seated just a few seats apart. She wonders if her ex-lover feels as embarrassed as she does, despite the indifference they display toward each other, in a game of deception that is inevitable in such a situation. Taylor conceives the song as a short story in two chapters. After the first chorus, she clearly announces "Next chapter," then "The end" to close the song. The Mayer page has definitely been turned.

Production

For the album's fourth single, the supercharged production on "The Story of Us" attacks hard from the outset, with two bars of ultra-compressed disco drums, clearly doubled by snare and bass drum samples borrowed from a Linn-LM1 or Roland TR-808 drum machine. The power pop register, underpinned by eighth-note bass and the rhythmic palm mute of saturated electric guitars, is as reminiscent of new wave and the new romantics as it is of the rock sound of the 1980s. Taylor Swift's harmony, melody, and interpretation, on the other hand, are very much of their time, blending in a little with the mainstream pop of the early 2010s. In the twenty-second and final position on the Deluxe Edition is the original interpretation of the song, released on the first version of *Speak Now* in 2010, similar in every way but without the above-mentioned artifacts borrowed from electronic music.

Hidden Message

CMT Awards.

Taylor Swift fans fill the stands of Minute Maid Park in Houston, November 2011.

NEVER GROW UP

Taylor Swift / 4:50

Musicians

Taylor Swift: vocals, backing vocals, acoustic guitar
Nathan Chapman: acoustic guitar, backing vocals

Recorded

Aimeeland, Blackbird, Pain in the Art, and Starstruck (Nashville); Capitol (Hollywood); Stonehurst (Bowling Green)

Technical Team

Producers: Nathan Chapman, Taylor Swift, Matt Ward, Dean Gillard
Mixing: Justin Niebank, Nathan Chapman, Chad Carlson, Mark Crew, Matt Ward, Dean Gillard
Sound Engineers: Nathan Chapman, Chuck Ainlay, Chad Carlson, Steve Churchyard, Jeremy Hunter, Jed Hackett, Steve Marcantonio, Joel Quillen, Lowell Reynolds, Brian David Willis
Mastering: Hank Williams

2010

Genesis

"Never Grow Up" is a message full of tenderness and wisdom addressed to the little girl that Taylor was and to all seven- and eight-year-old girls. It's an ode to candor and knowing how to stay simple, even if growing up is inevitable.

Production

This is the most stripped-down arrangement on the album: a folk lullaby with two acoustic guitars and two voices. The guitar playing, very complementary, oscillates between delicate arpeggios and open but always light strumming. The production of "Never Grow Up" is a model of sobriety, without added reverb or excessive compression, which preserves dynamics. Nathan Chapman's voice harmonizes in a third, in perfect harmony with the warm tone of Taylor Swift. From 3:57, the singer's backing vocals, recorded in overdub and placed at both ends of the stereo field, bring an additional dimension to this arrangement, which smells like a fireside.

Hidden Message

I moved out in July.

ENCHANTED

Taylor Swift / 5:52

Musicians

Taylor Swift: vocals, backing vocals, acoustic guitar
Nathan Chapman: acoustic guitar, banjo, bass, drums, electric guitar, backing vocals, mandolin, keyboard, programming
Nick Buda, John Gardner, Shannon Forrest: drums
Eric Darken, Al Wilson: percussion
Tony Harrell, Tim Lauer: keyboard
Tim Marks, Amos Heller, Michael Rhodes, Tommy Sims: bass
Caitlin Evanson, Liz Huett: backing vocals
Kenny Greenberg, Grant Mickelson, Mike Meadows, Paul Sidoti, Tom Bukovac: electric guitar
Bryan Sutton: acoustic guitar, twelve-string guitar, ukulele
Smith Curry: pedal steel
Paul Buckmaster: conductor, orchestral arrangements
Chris Carmichael: composer, string arrangements

Recorded

Aimeeland, Blackbird, Pain in the Art, and Starstruck (Nashville); Capitol (Hollywood); Stonehurst (Bowling Green)

Technical Team

Producers: Nathan Chapman, Taylor Swift, Matt Ward, Dean Gillard
Mixing: Justin Niebank, Nathan Chapman, Chad Carlson, Mark Crew, Matt Ward, Dean Gillard
Sound Engineers: Nathan Chapman, Chuck Ainlay, Chad Carlson, Steve Churchyard, Jeremy Hunter, Jed Hackett, Steve Marcantonio, Joel Quillen, Lowell Reynolds, Brian David Willis

FOR DISCERNING SWIFTIES

Originally, Taylor Swift wanted the album to be called *Enchanted*, but her label decided otherwise, finding the title immature and out of step with the evolution of her career.

Genesis

"Enchanted" tells the story of Taylor Swift's meeting with singer Adam Young (originally known under the pseudonym Owl City for his synthpop rock project). Taylor describes the fluidity of their exchanges and the happiness brought by this unexpected encounter. Adam Young responded by recording his own version of "Enchanted," in which he took the liberty of changing a few lyrics, including in the outro: "Please don't have somebody waiting on you" becomes "I was never in love with someone else / [...] Because you were all of my dreams come true / And I just wish you knew / Taylor, I was so in love with you."

Production

The exact opposite of "Never Grow Up," the arrangement of "Enchanted" quickly drifts into the realms of the orchestral power ballad to create a strong contrast in a linear album listening experience. Nathan Chapman and Taylor Swift stop at nothing to transform this romantic ballad into a mainstream pop hit. Layers of synthesizers, superimposed electric guitar tracks, acoustic guitar in palm mute on the verses and open strumming on the choruses, martial bass drums, and the inevitable epic electric guitar solo at 3:37. Chris Carmichael and Paul Buckmaster have no hesitation in bringing out the heavy artillery; the string arrangement juggles skillfully between marcato, energetic staccato, and long holds. The orchestral timpani take the intensity up a notch from the bridge, at 4:00. Precise and dynamic, Taylor Swift's vocal performance is equal to the challenge. Her mastery of her chest voice enables her to soar over the instrumental density of the choruses without a hitch.

Hidden Message

Adam (for Adam Young).

Taylor Swift at the 2010 CMT Music Awards at the Bridgestone Arena in Nashville.

BETTER THAN REVENGE

Taylor Swift / 3:37

Musicians

Taylor Swift: vocals, backing vocals, acoustic guitar
Nathan Chapman: acoustic guitar, banjo, bass, drums, electric guitar, backing vocals, mandolin, keyboard, programming
Nick Buda, John Gardner, Shannon Forrest: drums
Eric Darken, Al Wilson: percussion
Tony Harrell, Tim Lauer: keyboard
Tim Marks, Amos Heller, Michael Rhodes, Tommy Sims: bass
Caitlin Evanson, Liz Huett: backing vocals
Kenny Greenberg, Grant Mickelson, Mike Meadows, Paul Sidoti, Tom Bukovac: electric guitar
Bryan Sutton: acoustic guitar

Recorded

Aimeeland, Blackbird, Pain in the Art, and Starstruck (Nashville); Capitol (Hollywood); Stonehurst (Bowling Green)

Technical Team

Producers: Nathan Chapman, Taylor Swift
Mixing: Justin Niebank, Nathan Chapman, Chad Carlson, Mark Crew, Matt Ward, Dean Gillard
Sound Engineers: Nathan Chapman, Chuck Ainlay, Chad Carlson, Steve Churchyard, Jeremy Hunter, Jed Hackett, Steve Marcantonio, Joel Quillen, Lowell Reynolds, Brian David Willis

2010

Genesis

Taylor Swift wrote this song at the age of eighteen, when she learned that her then-current boyfriend had left her for another woman. She felt that he had been stolen from her, and experienced this episode as a betrayal. Later, she would come to understand that no one leaves against their will, and that no one can steal a person from another. According to a persistent rumor, "Better Than Revenge" deals with her breakup with singer Joe Jonas and her romantic rival, actress Camilla Belle. The hidden message is addressed to the latter: "You thought I was going to forget." But Taylor does not forget; she settles the score in song.

Production

Continuing the trend of strong contrasts, "Better Than Revenge" hits hard. Nathan Chapman and Taylor Swift conceive an unbridled pop-punk arrangement reminiscent of singer Avril Lavigne's music in the early 2000s (her fourth album was released in 2011, shortly after *Speak Now*). With its fast tempo (145 bpm), the all-guitar production, ultra-compressed drums, slamming snare drum, and eighth-note bass played in a one-way pick, the song presents us with a Taylor Swift who is not afraid to show that she can do what she wants, when she wants. Melodic leads and layers of saturated rhythmic electric guitars are the backbone of this rock orchestration, effective and without excessive frills. Once again, Taylor Swift is having fun surprising her fans and the sometimes rather staid world of the music industry, despite being perfectly at ease in an unexpected register. The new tour de force is a success.

Hidden Message

You thought I would forget.

A memorable Taylor Swift performance of "Innocent" at the 2010 MTV Video Music Awards in Los Angeles.

INNOCENT

Taylor Swift / 5:02

Musicians

Taylor Swift: vocals, backing vocals, acoustic guitar
Nathan Chapman: acoustic guitar, banjo, bass, drums, electric guitar, backing vocals, mandolin, keyboard, programming
Nick Buda, John Gardner, Shannon Forrest: drums
Eric Darken, Al Wilson: percussion
Rob Hajacos: fiddle
Tony Harrell, Tim Lauer: keyboard
Tim Marks, Amos Heller, Michael Rhodes, Tommy Sims: bass
Caitlin Evanson, Liz Huett: backing vocals
Kenny Greenberg, Grant Mickelson, Mike Meadows, Paul Sidoti, Tom Bukovac: electric guitar
Bryan Sutton: acoustic guitar, twelve-string guitar, ukulele
Smith Curry: pedal steel
Paul Buckmaster: conductor, orchestral arrangements
Chris Carmichael: composer, string arrangements

Recorded

Aimeeland, Blackbird, Pain in the Art, and Starstruck (Nashville); Capitol (Hollywood); Stonehurst (Bowling Green)

Technical Team

Producers: Nathan Chapman, Taylor Swift, Matt Ward, Dean Gillard
Mixing: Justin Niebank, Nathan Chapman, Chad Carlson, Mark Crew, Matt Ward, Dean Gillard
Sound Engineers: Nathan Chapman, Chuck Ainlay, Chad Carlson, Steve Churchyard, Jeremy Hunter, Jed Hackett, Steve Marcantonio, Joel Quillen, Lowell Reynolds, Brian David Willis
Best Ranking: Hot 100: 27

Genesis

"Innocent" is the first song in which Taylor Swift addresses the Kanye West incident. Emotionally shaken by the American rapper's damning intervention, she wrote the first lines of "Innocent" around a year after the incident and did not put the finishing touches on it until six months later. This was quite unusual for someone who is typically not afraid to express herself. Following the thread of this open letter with *Speak Now*, she decided to address Kanye West directly in an attempt to calm their relationship. However, the tone may seem slightly condescending and self-righteous. Is this approach intentional, or did she write the text in complete candor?

Production

Set to a tempo of 67 bmp, this slow ballad gradually shifts from an intimate pop-folk sound to an amped-up, somewhat solemn orchestral form. The arrangement begins with acoustic guitar picking, supported by drums that are largely filtered in both bass and treble (as if only the ambient mics positioned at the back of the room were open) and electric guitar, also filtered, to expose the recurring melodic theme for the first time. A few ghostly backing vocals complete the picture, seeming to herald the entrance of the main protagonist: Taylor Swift's voice, in a restrained, whisper-like interpretation. Discreetly, the piano and strings make their entrance on the first verse, the filters gradually open up on the pre-chorus and chorus (while the drums suddenly stop until 1:25), then the track gradually takes off from the second verse onward. As a preamble to the second chorus, the bass provides some melodic shots to great effect (between 2:27 and 2:30, this is particularly shimmering). The bridge brings the tension down before the climax of the third and final chorus. As an outro, two acoustic guitars and a piano suffice to embellish the final verse cycle, conveying a message of hope and reconciliation: When you lose your balance, it is never too late to catch yourself.

Hidden Message

Life is full of little interruptions.

In front of a packed crowd of more than 51,000 people, Lincoln Financial Field, Philadelphia, August 2011.

HAUNTED

Taylor Swift / 4:02

Musicians

Taylor Swift: vocals, backing vocals, acoustic guitar
Nathan Chapman: acoustic guitar, banjo, bass, drums, electric guitar, backing vocals, mandolin, keyboard, programming
Nick Buda, John Gardner, Shannon Forrest: drums
Eric Darken, Al Wilson: percussion
Rob Hajacos: fiddle
Tony Harrell, Tim Lauer: keyboard
Tim Marks, Amos Heller, Michael Rhodes, Tommy Sims: bass
Caitlin Evanson, Liz Huett: backing vocals
Kenny Greenberg, Grant Mickelson, Mike Meadows, Paul Sidoti, Tom Bukovac: electric guitar
Bryan Sutton: acoustic guitar, twelve-string guitar, ukulele
Smith Curry: pedal steel
Paul Buckmaster: conductor, orchestral arrangements
Chris Carmichael: composer, string arrangements

Recorded

Aimeeland, Blackbird, Pain in the Art, and Starstruck (Nashville); Capitol (Hollywood); Stonehurst (Bowling Green)

Technical Team

Producers: Nathan Chapman, Taylor Swift, Matt Ward, Dean Gillard
Mixing: Justin Niebank, Nathan Chapman, Chad Carlson, Mark Crew, Matt Ward, Dean Gillard
Sound Engineers: Nathan Chapman, Chuck Ainlay, Chad Carlson, Steve Churchyard, Jeremy Hunter, Jed Hackett, Steve Marcantonio, Joel Quillen, Lowell Reynolds, Brian David Willis

Genesis

Taylor Swift wrote “Haunted” in the midst of a breakup, undoubtedly to exorcise her pain. In it she dissects her emotions, moving from denial to painful acceptance, immersed in a melancholy that time seems to stretch endlessly. With its unequivocally somber lexical field—“haunted,” “dark,” “cold,” “terribly wrong,” “pain”—this is one of her most gothic texts. “Haunted” can be seen as the disenchanted side of the Swiftian fairy tale. The coming-of-age steamroller spares no one, and breeds many disillusions. Fans who grew up with the singer are well aware of this. Taylor is here to reach out and show them they are not alone.

Production

For the production of "Haunted," Taylor Swift and her team could perfectly well have applied the traditional pop-rock recipe of guitars, bass, drums, and keyboards. But that would be a misunderstanding of the singer, who had no hesitation in asking Paul Buckmaster to concoct an orchestral arrangement that flirted with excess. The song was recorded at the legendary Capitol Studios in Los Angeles. Buckmaster himself conducted the epic session, with string ensemble, grand piano, orchestral bells, and timpani, and Taylor Swift and Nathan Chapman took no prisoners. To best illustrate the emotional roller coaster described in "Haunted," the cinematic decor is accentuated by the overdrive of saturated guitars and the power of bass drums, which do not give way under the cascades of strings or the pounding of the orchestral percussion. To rise to the challenge, Taylor Swift delivers a vocal performance of an intensity rarely achieved during her recording sessions. Everything is done to leave the listener breathless, and at the same time exhausted and satisfied.

At number nineteen on the Deluxe Edition, the acoustic version loses none of its dramatic intensity. The lush sonorities produced by the grand piano and symphonic orchestra combination are sufficient to support Taylor Swift's voice and her army of overdubbed backing vocals.

Hidden Message

Still to this day.

At the opening of the exhibition *American Woman: Shaping a National Identity*, Metropolitan Museum of Art, New York, May 2010.

FOR DISCERNING SWIFTIES

The unusually long intro to "Last Kiss" lasts 27 seconds, exactly the same length as the telephone conversation in which Joe Jonas told Taylor Swift that he was breaking up with her.

LAST KISS

Taylor Swift / 6:07

Musicians

Taylor Swift: vocals, backing vocals
Nathan Chapman: acoustic guitar, bass, drums, electric guitar, keyboard, programming
Nick Buda, John Gardner, Shannon Forrest: drums
Eric Darken, Al Wilson: percussion
Tim Marks, Amos Heller, Michael Rhodes, Tommy Sims: bass
Caitlin Evanson, Liz Huett: backing vocals
Bryan Sutton: acoustic guitar
Smith Curry: pedal steel

Recorded

Aimeeland, Blackbird, Pain in the Art, and Starstruck (Nashville); Capitol (Hollywood); Stonehurst (Bowling Green)

Technical Team

Producers: Nathan Chapman, Taylor Swift, Matt Ward, Dean Gillard
Mixing: Justin Niebank, Nathan Chapman, Chad Carlson, Mark Crew, Matt Ward, Dean Gillard
Sound Engineers: Nathan Chapman, Chuck Ainlay, Chad Carlson, Steve Churchyard, Jeremy Hunter, Jed Hackett, Steve Marcantonio, Joel Quillen, Lowell Reynolds, Brian David Willis

2010

Genesis

After the gothic storm of "Haunted," Taylor Swift delivers a sweet, sad song. "Forever and always" is the hidden message contained in the lyrics of "Last Kiss," which enables fans to understand that this nostalgic composition is once again addressed to her ex-boyfriend Joe Jonas. "Forever and Always," released on *Fearless*, had already been dedicated to the young singer.

Production

The contrast with "Haunted" is also felt in the pared-down production of "Last Kiss." Delicately arpeggiated on the verses and softly strummed on the choruses, the acoustic guitar is at the heart of the arrangement. The atmosphere is created by the filtered sound of the drum programming and the snare sample, immersed in a long reverb and a delay effect set to sixteenth notes. The piano notes, crystalline and sparse, recall the bright, percussive sound of an una corda (a piano in which each key actuates a single string), or that of a toy piano whose keys operate thin metal strips. The distant sound of the pedal steel blends elegantly with the soft roundness of the vibraphone and the tinkling of the chimes. The resulting orchestration, as delicate as stardust, weaves an ethereal backdrop conducive to melancholy reverie.

Hidden Message

Forever and always.

At the All for the Hall charity concert, organized by the Country Music Hall of Fame in 2010.

LONG LIVE

Taylor Swift / 5:17

Musicians
Taylor Swift: vocals, backing vocals
Nathan Chapman: acoustic guitar, bass, drums, electric guitar, backing vocals, keyboard, programming
Nick Buda, John Gardner, Shannon Forrest: drums
Eric Darken, Al Wilson: percussion
Tony Harrell, Tim Lauer: keyboard
Tim Marks, Amos Heller, Michael Rhodes, Tommy Sims: bass
Caitlin Evanson, Liz Huett: backing vocals
Kenny Greenberg, Grant Mickelson, Mike Meadows, Paul Sidoti, Tom Bukovac: electric guitar
Bryan Sutton: acoustic guitar
Smith Curry: pedal steel guitar

Recorded
Aimeeland, Blackbird, Pain in the Art, and Starstruck (Nashville); Capitol (Hollywood); Stonehurst (Bowling Green)

Technical Team
Producers: Nathan Chapman, Taylor Swift, Matt Ward, Dean Gillard
Mixing: Justin Niebank, Nathan Chapman, Chad Carlson, Mark Crew, Matt Ward, Dean Gillard
Sound Engineers: Nathan Chapman, Chuck Ainlay, Chad Carlson, Steve Churchyard, Jeremy Hunter, Jed Hackett, Steve Marcantonio, Joel Quillen, Lowell Reynolds, Brian David Willis

Genesis

"Long Live" is the first song in which Taylor Swift addresses her band, her producer Nathan Chapman, and her entire team. Conceived as a series of snapshots, the song is an ode to the joys and tears shared onstage and on the road. Taylor paints these sketches of everyday life on tour with the intention of paying a vibrant tribute to the perseverance, courage, and slightly mad enthusiasm of her faithful traveling companions. A remix of "Long Live," on which Brazilian country singer Paula Fernandes performs verses she wrote in her native Portuguese, was released as a single on January 3, 2012, to promote the live album *Speak Now World Tour—Live.*

Production

Launched at a cruising tempo of 100 bpm, the song "Long Live" revisits the traditional country-pop ballad. The arrangement and production by Nathan Chapman and Taylor Swift are based on the fundamentals of the genre: palm mute and acoustic guitar strumming, superimposed tracks of saturated electric guitars immersed in delay, aerial pedal steel, piano and synthesizer layers, all supported by a solid, disciplined rhythm section. In an unusual coquetry, a few notes of glockenspiel add a touch of glittery gloss to the whole. The Nashville sound arsenal of the 2010s is employed to full effect, with Justin Niebank's flashy, abundantly compressed mixing preserving a certain dynamic that Hank Williams's highly competitive mastering does not totally overwhelm, which is, in itself, a technical feat. Completely in her element, Taylor Swift exploits the full range of her vocal register and delivers, as usual, an impeccable performance, both powerful and nuanced.

Hidden Message

For you (Taylor addressing her team).

Taylor Swift captivates the audience during her performance of "Ours" at the 2011 CMA Awards in Nashville.

SINGLE

OURS

Taylor Swift / 3:58

Musicians

Taylor Swift: vocals, backing vocals, acoustic guitar
Nathan Chapman: acoustic guitar, bass, drums, electric guitar, backing vocals, mandolin, keyboard, programming
Nick Buda, John Gardner, Shannon Forrest: drums
Eric Darken, Al Wilson: percussion
Tony Harrell, Tim Lauer: keyboard
Tim Marks, Amos Heller, Michael Rhodes, Tommy Sims: bass
Caitlin Evanson, Liz Huett: backing vocals
Kenny Greenberg, Grant Mickelson, Mike Meadows, Paul Sidoti, Tom Bukovac: electric guitar
Bryan Sutton: acoustic guitar, twelve-string guitar, ukulele

Recorded

Aimeeland, Blackbird, Pain in the Art, and Starstruck (Nashville); Capitol (Hollywood); Stonehurst (Bowling Green)

Technical Team

Producers: Nathan Chapman, Taylor Swift, Matt Ward, Dean Gillard
Mixing: Justin Niebank, Nathan Chapman, Chad Carlson, Mark Crew, Matt Ward, Dean Gillard
Sound Engineers: Nathan Chapman, Chuck Ainlay, Chad Carlson, Steve Churchyard, Jeremy Hunter, Jed Hackett, Steve Marcantonio, Joel Quillen, Lowell Reynolds, Brian David Willis

Single Release

CD single, US, November 21, 2011—BMRTS0306A
Best Rankings: Hot Country: 1; Hot 100: 13

Genesis

"Ours" is the sixth single from the *Speak Now* era. Included as a bonus track on the Deluxe Edition of the *Speak Now* album, a live version of the song was released simultaneously on the *Speak Now World Tour—Live* album. The CD single was released exclusively in Walmart shops to accompany the release of the live album. In "Ours," Taylor Swift talks about the sometimes unkind way in which people can view couples, judging whether they are a good match without knowing the quality or strength of the bond that brings them together. At the time, Taylor was dating a guy whom some people thought was a bad match for her, based solely on his looks, height, attractiveness, and the like. This irritated the singer and prompted her to write a song to set the record straight, denouncing this type of inquisitive, hasty, and unfounded judgment. "Ours" urges fans not to worry about what people will say.

Production

This is, without doubt, the most typically country-folk arrangement of the *Speak Now* era. Fender Rhodes aside, the all-acoustic, driving instrumentation takes the listener back to the candor of the early days, when Taylor Swift was still a teenager and much more carefree. The sound of the acoustic guitar strumming is surprisingly deep in the midrange, probably to enable the ingenious Rhodes part to express itself fully. The drums, played with brushes, twirl lightly and Taylor Swift's voice hovers gracefully over the whole sound, supported by the third harmony sung by Nathan Chapman on the choruses. The instrumental bridge (at 2:12) is particularly well orchestrated, showcasing the precision of Bryan Sutton's playing and the rich timbre of his twelve-string guitar.

Hidden Message

Mayor (or could this be the name of the young man in question? A name that bears a strange resemblance to John Mayer's).

Taylor Swift and Martin Johnson of Boys Like Girls perform together at the 2009 Z100 Jingle Ball at Madison Square Garden to sing "If This Was a Movie."

IF THIS WAS A MOVIE

Taylor Swift, Martin Johnson / 3:54

Musicians

Taylor Swift: vocals, backing vocals, acoustic guitar
Nathan Chapman: acoustic guitar, banjo, bass, drums, electric guitar, backing vocals, mandolin, keyboard, programming
Nick Buda, John Gardner, Shannon Forrest: drums
Eric Darken, Al Wilson: percussion
Rob Hajacos: fiddle
Tony Harrell, Tim Lauer: keyboard
Tim Marks, Amos Heller, Michael Rhodes, Tommy Sims: bass
Caitlin Evanson, Liz Huett: backing vocals
Kenny Greenberg, Grant Mickelson, Mike Meadows, Paul Sidoti, Tom Bukovac: electric guitar
Bryan Sutton: acoustic guitar, twelve-string guitar, ukulele
Smith Curry: pedal steel
Paul Buckmaster: conductor, orchestral arrangements
Chris Carmichael: composer, string arrangements

Recorded

Aimeeland, Blackbird, Pain in the Art, and Starstruck (Nashville); Capitol (Hollywood); Stonehurst (Bowling Green)

Technical Team

Producers: Nathan Chapman, Taylor Swift, Matt Ward, Dean Gillard
Mixing: Justin Niebank, Nathan Chapman, Chad Carlson, Mark Crew, Matt Ward, Dean Gillard
Sound Engineers: Nathan Chapman, Chuck Ainlay, Chad Carlson, Steve Churchyard, Jeremy Hunter, Jed Hackett, Steve Marcantonio, Joel Quillen, Lowell Reynolds, Brian David Willis
Best Ranking: Hot 100: 10

2010

Genesis

"If This Was a Movie" is the only song from the *Speak Now* era not to have been written entirely by Taylor Swift, which may explain why it was not chosen for the first version of the album. Co-written with Martin Johnson, it appeared for the first time on the Deluxe version, on October 25, 2010, at number six. On March 16, 2023, to celebrate the start of the "Eras Tour," Taylor Swift announced the release of Taylor's Version of "If This Was a Movie" ahead of the release of the album *Speak Now (Taylor's Version)* on July 7, 2023. The song is about lost love and the hope that things will magically work out. Taylor knows this is impossible, but she cannot help hoping and imagines a scenario in which her wish might come true, because in a film, nothing is impossible.

Production

Back to the epic power ballad for Taylor Swift and Nathan Chapman, who are careful not to leave out any of the ingredients in this five-tiered musical showpiece. Ostinato arpeggios on twelve-string guitar (on the intro and verses), mandolin rhythm, strumming and acoustic guitar arpeggios, successive layers of saturated electric guitars, ultra-compressed bass drums, and deliberately emphatic string arrangements, all set to a 73 bpm tempo, driven on the eighth notes. That is all it takes to make "If This Was a Movie" the perfect theme song for a Hollywood-style sentimental drama.

Hidden Message

Let's press rewind.

Taylor Swift ready for an Oscars party, 2011.

SUPERMAN

Taylor Swift / 4:36

Musicians

Taylor Swift: vocals, backing vocals, acoustic guitar
Nathan Chapman: acoustic guitar, bass, drums, electric guitar, backing vocals, mandolin, programming
Nick Buda, John Gardner, Shannon Forrest: drums
Eric Darken, Al Wilson: percussion
Tim Marks, Amos Heller, Michael Rhodes, Tommy Sims: bass
Caitlin Evanson, Liz Huett: backing vocals
Kenny Greenberg, Grant Mickelson, Mike Meadows, Paul Sidoti, Tom Bukovac: electric guitar
Bryan Sutton: acoustic guitar

Recorded

Aimeeland, Blackbird, Pain in the Art, and Starstruck (Nashville); Capitol (Hollywood); Stonehurst (Bowling Green)

Technical Team

Producers: Nathan Chapman, Taylor Swift, Matt Ward, Dean Gillard
Mixing: Justin Niebank, Nathan Chapman, Chad Carlson, Mark Crew, Matt Ward, Dean Gillard
Sound Engineers: Nathan Chapman, Chuck Ainlay, Chad Carlson, Steve Churchyard, Jeremy Hunter, Jed Hackett, Steve Marcantonio, Joel Quillen, Lowell Reynolds, Brian David Willis
Best Ranking: Hot 100: 26

2010

Genesis

During her concerts, Taylor sometimes explains that the idea for the song "Superman" came to her during a night out with friends. When she saw her then-boyfriend leaving the room, she said instinctively: "It's like watching Superman fly away." This little phrase amused her enough to make her want to turn it into a song. "Superman" is the seventeenth song on the Deluxe version of the *Speak Now* album, as the track was not included on the original version of the album. There is a rumor among Swifties that the Superman boyfriend is none other than John Mayer.

Production

With its lightly saturated electric guitars, eighth-note bass, energetic acoustic guitar strumming, and 130 bpm tempo, Nathan Chapman and Taylor Swift's production fits perfectly into the American pop rock sound of the early 2010s. Right from the intro, an envelope filter effect, set on a slow cycle, gives a rotating feel to the rhythmic electric guitar, played as a palm mute. A few programmed percussive samples reinforce the acoustic drums at the top of the spectrum, and the profusion of backing vocals generously processed through the auto-tune mill (or Melodyne, a software program designed to artificially adjust vocal tone and timbre) immediately evoke the production artifices of mainstream pop at the time. However, on the bridge outro at 3:23, the mandolin licks played by Nathan Chapman in response to the acoustic guitar arpeggios furtively mark the track's affiliation with the extended realm of country music.

Hidden Message

Today I am saved.

Taylor Swift has sung "Ronan" live only twice: first at the Stand Up to Cancer telethon (September 2012) and during the *1989* world tour in Glendale, Arizona (August 2015).

SINGLE

RONAN

Taylor Swift, Maya Thompson / 4:25

Musicians
Taylor Swift: vocals, songwriting, electric guitar, piano (?)
Nick Buda: drums (?)

Recorded
Kitty Committee (Belfast), Blackbird (Nashville), 2012

Technical Team
Producer: Taylor Swift
Mixing: Justin Niebank (?)
Sound Engineers: Brian David Willis, Chad Carlson, Matt Rausch (?)
Mastering: Hank Williams (?)

Single Release
Digital Release: September 8, 2012
Best Rankings: Hot Country: 34; Hot 100: 16

Genesis

Few Taylor Swift songs are as dramatic as "Ronan." This soft rock ballad is dedicated to a little boy who died on the eve of his fourth birthday from neuroblastoma, an aggressive brain tumor. In 2011, the singer discovered the blog of the mother, Maya Thompson, who recounted her son's painful journey and proclaimed her love for him. Maya Thompson began writing in August 2010, when her child was diagnosed with incurable cancer, and continued to write after their nine-month battle, both to cope with her grief and to raise awareness of the symptoms of childhood cancer. In October 2011, Taylor Swift contacted Maya Thompson to tell her that her story had inspired a song she would like to perform on the telethon *Stand Up to Cancer*. She also announced that she had credited Maya as the song's co-author, with some phrases from her blog having been included in the lyrics. All proceeds from the track are donated to associations fighting the disease.

Although the track was released on September 8, 2012, as an exclusive download on iTunes, it was not included on any album at the time, and was one of the isolated singles in Taylor Swift's repertoire. The singer only performed it live twice: the first time on the show, and the second on August 17, 2015, during the "1989 World Tour" stopover in Glendale, Arizona, because Maya Thompson and her family were in the audience. In 2021, she chose to include a rerecorded version of *Ronan* on Taylor's Version of *Red*. She asked Maya Thompson for permission to make this addition, which was granted.

Production

"Ronan" is the first song to be produced entirely by Taylor Swift. The singer plays all the instruments (electric guitar and piano) except the drums, in a slow, poignant ballad set to a 58 bpm tempo. The finger-style electric guitar, played mainly in arpeggios, is the backbone of the sober, delicate arrangement. To achieve a slightly crunchy, warm sound, the guitar is run through a tube amp pushed to the breaking point of clean tone, then through a reverb and long delay. From 1:26 onward, subdued drums—resonant bass drum and snare drum played with brushes only—and minimalist piano—with the loud pedal permanently engaged—are sufficient to create an atmosphere conducive to contemplation. Ronan's melody line and harmonic construction are reminiscent of "Papa Was a Rodeo," the classic by indie pop folk band the Magnetic Fields, released in 1999.

An identically recorded version of "Ronan" (as with the vast majority of Taylor's Versions) was released in 2021 on the album *Red (Taylor's Version)*. However, the electric guitar sound has neither the density nor the grain of the original version, and Taylor Swift's voice trembles less—everything is smoother.

2012

Andrea Swift speaks at the 2015 CMA Awards in Arlington, Texas.

ANDREA SWIFT, MOM AND ALLY

Taylor Swift has never hidden the love and affection she feels for her family members. But she often shows the most gratitude in her music and public statements to her mother. Andrea Gardner Swift, née Finlay, born January 10, 1958, in Pennsylvania, is a pillar in both her daughter's personal and professional life. She supported Taylor right from the start, never hesitating to travel back and forth to Nashville to canvass record labels, while Taylor's father stayed at home to look after her brother. Her mother was her confidante and was the one who often wiped away her daughter's tears after a breakup.

Origins

If we assume that a love of music is in the genes, Taylor Swift undoubtedly owes this to her maternal grandmother, Marjorie Finlay. Andrea's mother was an opera singer known for her ability to hit high notes. Taylor Swift dedicated a song to her, "Marjorie," on the album *Evermore*. Andrea, on the other hand, opted for a career as a marketing manager in mutual funds. In 1988, she married Scott Kingsley Swift, a financial advisor at Merrill Lynch in Houston, Texas. They gave birth to Taylor the following year, and then to her brother, Austin, in 1992. Andrea chose to pause her career to become a stay-at-home mother.

Challenges

In 2012, Andrea and Scott's divorce was made public, after twenty-four years together. The couple had in fact broken up several years earlier but had delayed signing the divorce papers. Taylor Swift has never made a clear reference to her parents' separation, although she does hint at the difficulties they faced as a couple in the song "Mine," featured on *Speak Now* ("You say we'll never make my parents' mistakes," she sings). On the other hand, she did speak more directly about the health problems faced by her mother, who was diagnosed with breast cancer in 2015. After going into remission, the disease returned in 2019. This ordeal inspired the singer to write "Soon You'll Get Better," a duet with country trio the Chicks, which is featured on *Lover*. "The Best Day," a track from *Fearless* that details happy childhood memories and has the feel of a love letter, is also dedicated to her. "Mom is calculated, logical, business-minded; kind but very, very direct. Makes you better by giving you these little pointers but doesn't baby you," she told *Vogue* magazine in 2012.

Taylor Swift receives the Hal David Starlight Award at the Songwriters Hall of Fame, New York, June 17, 2010.

SONGWRITING THAT STANDS OUT

In a career spanning almost twenty years (and counting), Taylor Swift has made changes to her style, sound, atmosphere, and sometimes even personality. However, there is one element of her music that never changes: the power and rawness of her lyrics. They are one of her greatest strengths, and undoubtedly one of the keys to her success. Never "pretexts"—unlike many pop hit lyrics, which are designed primarily to serve the rhythm and melody—her lyrics are deep and, with each new album, the subject of a great deal of scrutiny by her fans. The (main) reason for their interest is simple: The artist has never hesitated to confide the slightest detail of her states of mind. She has an uncanny ability to put words together that are effective both musically and narratively.

Stories That Speak to Everyone

After eleven studio albums, it can be said that Taylor Swift enjoys telling stories. Her own, of course, but also those of her audience: One of her talents lies in the fact that she almost always gives her listeners the feeling that it could be their own story. What Swiftie has not thought of their most disappointing ex while screaming the chorus of "We Are Never Ever Getting Back Together"? How many fans must have identified with the simple yet touching lyrics of "Delicate" at the feverish start of an affair? Taylor Swift also loves not only the art of pure storytelling, with a beginning and an end ("Love Story," "All Too Well," "Champagne Problems," etc.), but also using the characters themselves as narrators ("The Lucky One," "Betty," "August, "The Last Great American Dynasty," "Dorothea," "Seven," etc.).

Hit Songs

Hit songs tend to be less interesting from a harmonic point of view. They are generally constructed around classic pop chord progressions and arrangements in the same standard style of any given time period. But Taylor Swift's talent lies elsewhere, in her ability to combine verbal outbursts of a rare authenticity in today's music industry with melodic ideas that are often pleasing, even brilliant.

Since 2023, several American universities, including Stanford and Berkeley, have been offering courses on the "Taylor Swift style" of songwriting and its influence on today's music. In early 2024, the website Hit Songs Deconstructed, which provides songwriting analyses of the top 10 hits on the Billboard Hot 100, organized a master class to examine her discography, from *Fearless* to *Midnights*. On April 2, 2024, the site published a 93-page report: *The Taylor Swift Evolution*, which is available for free online.

RELEASE DATE
United States: July 7, 2023
(ref.: Republic Records—2455678249)
Best Ranking: 1

ALBUM

Speak Now (Taylor's Version)

Electric Touch* (feat. Fall Out Boy) · When Emma Falls in Love* · I Can See You* · Castles Crumbling* (feat. Hayley Williams) · Foolish One* · Timeless*

**From the Vault*

Taylor Swift wins the Global Icon Award at the 2021 BRIT Awards in London.

2023

CONFESSIONS AND MELANCHOLY

Although *Speak Now* is Taylor Swift's third album, her Taylor's Version is the third rerecorded album to see the light of day after *Fearless (Taylor's Version)*, released on April 9, 2021, and *Red (Taylor's Version)*, on November 12, 2021. Highly anticipated by fans, particularly for its previously unreleased From the Vault songs, the album was released on July 7, 2023, by Republic Records, thirteen years after the original version. Its release date had been the subject of much speculation since 2021.

It is not surprising that Taylor Swift had to wait until 2023 to put it online: In the course of 2022, she recorded Taylor's Version of *1989*, as well as *Midnights*, her tenth studio album. At the same time, she was also hard at work preparing her "Eras Tour," a monumental worldwide tour, with each performance lasting over three hours. In May 2023, onstage in Nashville, she finally announced the release of Taylor's Version, commenting on Instagram, "The songs that came from this time in my life were marked by their brutal honesty, unfiltered diaristic confessions and wild wistfulness." Mischievously, in an Instagram post on the eve of the album's release, she states that the record is timed for July 9, without saying more. This date, mentioned in the lyrics of "Last Kiss," a ballad evoking the pain of a breakup, has become emblematic for fans ("That July ninth, the beat of your heart / It jumps through your shirt / I can still feel your arms"). On July 9, 2023, performing in Kansas City as part of the "Eras Tour," she played "Last Kiss" live.

Backstage, the Taylor's Version team remained unchanged: Christopher Rowe is still in charge of production for the 2010 tracks, while Jack Antonoff and Aaron Dessner piloted From the Vault tracks. Of the six tracks written by Taylor between the ages of eighteen and twenty and left out at the time, two are recorded as featuring tracks: "Electric Touch" with the emo-oriented rock band Fall Out Boy, and "Castles Crumbling" with Hayley Williams of the pop-rock band Paramore.

Patrick Stump, frontman of Fall Out Boy, is a guest performer on "Electric Touch."

FOR DISCERNING SWIFTIES

Taylor Swift performed "Electric Touch" for the first time, alone at the piano, as a surprise song at the February 8, 2024, concert in Tokyo.

ELECTRIC TOUCH (FEAT. FALL OUT BOY)

Taylor Swift / 4:26

Musicians
Taylor Swift: vocals
Patrick Stump: voice, electric guitar
Aaron Dessner: acoustic guitar, bass, electric guitar, synthesizer, percussion
Benjamin Lanz: synthesizer
James McAlister: synthesizer
Joe Russo: drums, percussion
Josh Kaufman: acoustic guitar, electric guitar, piano, electric organ
Thomas Bartlett: keyboards, piano, synthesizer

Recorded
2023

Technical Team
Producers: Taylor Swift, Aaron Dessner
Mixing: Jonathan Low
Sound Engineers: Aaron Dessner, Christopher Rowe, Jonathan Low
Mastering: Randy Merrill

2023

Genesis

Taylor Swift wrote "Electric Touch" in 2010, with the intention of including it on her new album *Speak Now*, but the song did not make the cut. It was in 2023, during the recording of Taylor's Version, that Electric Touch was recorded for the first time in the studio as part of the From the Vault unreleased tracks. Taylor Swift asked guitarist and singer Patrick Stump to back her, transforming the song into a pop-rock duet with an emo edge. She describes the mixture of anxiety and excitement triggered by a new encounter. Her burgeoning feelings are fraught with contradictions: The promise of shared happiness and the fear of having her heart broken once again inspire this edgy lyric, ideal for a duet with the leader of pop-punk band Fall Out Boy, who is a master of the art of singing about emotional urgency.

Production

With Aaron Dessner at the helm, "Electric Touch" assumes a dramatic dimension, while avoiding the trap of bloated production. The sound of the electric guitars remains organic and does not succumb to the temptation of overdrive turned right up to ten; the synthesizers bring a depth of field conducive to reverie; and the rhythm section manages to maintain the tension from beginning to end with its nuanced and always well-judged playing. The judicious division of the vocal parts (verse 1: Taylor / chorus 1: Taylor / verse 2: Patrick Stump / chorus 2: Taylor + Patrick Stump / bridge: Taylor + Patrick Stump / chorus 3: Taylor + Patrick Stump) also contributes to keeping the listener on the edge of their seat right up to the last second, highlighting the timbre and respective performances of the two artists.

S60-D

WHEN EMMA FALLS IN LOVE

Taylor Swift / 4:12

Musicians

Taylor Swift: vocals
Aaron Dessner: acoustic guitar, bass, electric guitar, synthesizer, percussion
Benjamin Lanz: synthesizer
James McAlister: synthesizer, drums, percussion
James Krivchenia: drums, percussion
Josh Kaufman: electric guitar, banjo, electric organ
Thomas Bartlett: keyboards, piano, synthesizer
Mike Meadows: backing vocals

Recorded

2023

Technical Team

Producers: Taylor Swift, Aaron Dessner
Mixing: Jonathan Low
Sound Engineers: Aaron Dessner, Christopher Rowe, Jonathan Low
Mastering: Randy Merrill
Best Ranking: Hot 100: 34

2023

Genesis

Also written to feature on the original version of *Speak Now*, "When Emma Falls in Love" would ultimately become part of the unreleased From the Vault tracks, recorded for Taylor's Version of the album. As a keen observer, Taylor Swift watches Emma, her best friend, navigate her life through an emotional roller coaster. Full of empathy and admiration for the young woman, she admits that she learns a lot from her and would like to be like her. According to a persistent rumor, this intimate is none other than actress Emma Stone, who became very close to Taylor Swift during the genesis of *Speak Now*.

Production

To embellish this 78 bpm country-pop ballad, Taylor Swift and Aaron Dessner created a highly contrasting arrangement. The intro and first verse rely entirely on piano and voice, while two acoustic guitars (one with light strumming and the other with arpeggios) and a banjo discreetly enter the scene to announce the band's massive entrance on the first chorus. At 0:55, the synthesizer strings, electric organ, electric guitars, banjo, piano, bass, drums, and Mike Meadows's backing vocals on the third interval—whose timbre is reminiscent of R.E.M. singer Michael Stipe—harmonize perfectly with the singer's voice. The gentle piano-voice chord does not return until the third and final verse, after the bridge. Here, the two instruments are backed by a bass part played in the upper part of the neck, a distant organ, the gentle arpeggios of the acoustic guitar, and a banjo, before the climax of the final chorus.

SINGLE

I CAN SEE YOU

Taylor Swift / 4:33

Musicians
Taylor Swift: vocals
Jack Antonoff: programming, acoustic guitar, bass, electric guitar, twelve-string acoustic guitar, synthesizer, clavier, backing vocals, percussion
Evan Smith: saxophone
Mikey Freedom Hart: electric guitar, synthesizer, Wurlitzer
James McAlister: synthesizer
Sean Hutchinson: drums, percussion

Recorded
2023

Technical Team
Producers: Taylor Swift, Jack Antonoff
Mixing: Serban Ghenea, Bryce Bordone
Sound Engineers: Jack Antonoff, David Hart, Evan Smith, Laura Sisk, Christopher Rowe
Mastering: Randy Merrill
Best Rankings: Hot Country: 3; Hot 100: 5

Genesis

Written in 2010, "I Can See You" is Taylor Swift's first sexually suggestive song; it expresses her unfulfilled desire and the resulting sexual tension. Because of this adult content, which did not fit in with the star's image at the time, Big Machine reportedly advised the songwriter not to include it on the original version of *Speak Now*.

The identity of the man involved has never been revealed, but Taylor has made no secret of the fact that it was one of her close collaborators. A hint is given in the first sentence of the second verse: "And we kept everything professional."

Production

Right from the intro, Jack Antonoff's touch is recognizable. The main guitar riff sets the retro-hybrid tone of this production, which skillfully combines references to late-1960s pop with the icy sounds of the 1980s. Indeed, the tape-delay–style slap-back echo applied to the guitar riff, the twelve-string acoustic guitar, the saxophone played staccato on the verses and in unison with the voice melody on the choruses, as well as the Wurlitzer part and spring reverb explosions, seem to have come straight out of 1960s garage pop and surf productions. The drums, synthesizer leads, bass, and sound design elements—resembling the sounds of Commodore 64 video games—are direct references to 1980s pop culture. Yet the way all these elements coexist and are brought together, the treatment of the voice lead and backing vocals, and the clarity of the mix make "I Can See You" a pop song with a resolutely modern sound.

CASTLES CRUMBLING
(FEAT. HAYLEY WILLIAMS)

Taylor Swift / 5:06

Musicians
Taylor Swift: vocals
Hayley Williams: vocals
Jack Antonoff: programming, acoustic guitar, bass, electric guitar, synthesizer, piano
Bobby Hawk: violin
Eric Byers: cello
Evan Smith: flute, saxophone
Mikey Freedom Hart: synthesizer
Sean Hutchinson: drums, percussion
Recorded
2023
Technical Team
Producers: Taylor Swift, Jack Antonoff
Mixing: Serban Ghenea, Bryce Bordone
Sound Engineers: Jack Antonoff, David Hart, Evan Smith, Laura Sisk, Christopher Rowe, Taylor York
Mastering: Randy Merrill
Best Rankings: Hot Country: 13; Hot 100: 31

2023

Genesis

To enable "Castles Crumbling" to join the prestigious ranks of From the Vault tracks, Taylor Swift called upon Hayley Williams. During the genesis of *Speak Now*, this singer, co-founder of the American rock band Paramore, was one of the few artists whose songwriting influenced Swift's. So it was only natural that Taylor invited her to lend her voice to a duet on "Castles Crumbling." She wrote the lyrics in 2010, evoking the pangs of celebrity, the constant pressure and the fear that everything could fall apart in an instant—all themes with which Hayley is (all too) familiar. Some critics suggest an interpretation of these lyrics as a reference to the Kanye West incident. This would be the second track to evoke it, after "Innocent," written the same year and released on the original version of *Speak Now* in 2010.

Production

For this 74 bpm indie-folk ballad, Taylor Swift and Jack Antonoff weave a nuanced arrangement in which everything is played out gently: To begin with, the piano lightly touched by Jack Antonoff with the damper pedal engaged, then the micro-tonal variations of the electric guitar arpeggios plunge into a rapid vibrato effect, along with the delicate strumming of the acoustic guitar, the harmonic richness of the bass line, Sean Hutchinson's drums, and his high hat playing on the sixteenth note blending with the programmed percussion. The violin and cello lines, played by Bobby Hawk and Eric Byers, respectively, add their dose of brilliance and depth to the synthesizer layers laid down by Mikey Freedom Hart in the background. After the second chorus, from 2:51 onward, Taylor Swift and Hayley Williams take the time to develop a skillfully interwoven voice part, creating a spellbinding choral effect, like a meditative pause before the third verse and the climax of the final chorus.

ON YOUR HEADPHONES

On the intro, as well as on the outro, a Hayley Williams whisper can be heard: "Once, I had an empire." Guitarist Taylor York, co-founder of Paramore and current romantic partner of almost twenty years, recorded the whisper.

FOOLISH ONE

Taylor Swift / 5:11

Musicians

Taylor Swift: vocals
Aaron Dessner: acoustic guitar, bass, electric guitar, synthesizer, programming, percussion
Benjamin Lanz: synthesizer
James McAlister: drums, synthesizer, programming, percussion
Josh Kaufman: acoustic guitar, electric guitar, electric organ, pedal steel

Recorded

2023

Technical Team

Producers: Taylor Swift, Aaron Dessner
Mixing: Jonathan Low
Sound Engineers: Aaron Dessner, Christopher Rowe, Jonathan Low
Mastering: Randy Merrill
Best Ranking: Hot 100: 40

Genesis

Written in 2009, "Foolish One" is a poignant tale of disillusionment in love. Taylor Swift realizes that the boy she is dating will never commit, despite his gentle looks and promises. She knows that he will end up marrying someone else. Taylor writes this song like a memorandum—maybe she will finally learn a lesson?

Production

Aaron Dessner returns to produce this moderate-tempo (97 bpm) country-pop ballad. Despite its relative length (5:11), this track gets straight to the heart of the matter, with Taylor Swift's voice, acoustic guitar strumming swept to the sixteenth note, and pedal steel picking out notes in the distance, immersed in a long reverb. From the second cycle of the first verse, the combination of programmed percussion and acoustic drums played with brushes makes itself heard, as does the bass. From the first chorus onward, all the instruments are there—ethereal synthesizer layers, drums switched to drumsticks for a more percussive sound—and the orchestration unfolds in a linear fashion right up to the end of the bridge, pausing for a sparse third verse: acoustic guitar / voice / pedal steel. The full arrangement resumes its course from the third chorus, so that the listener is taken quietly by the hand to the end of the track.

Taylor Swift performed "Foolish One" in a mash-up with "Tell Me Why" for the first time as a surprise song at the "Eras Tour" concert in Singapore on March 4, 2024.

TIMELESS

Taylor Swift / 5:21

Musicians

Taylor Swift: vocals
Jack Antonoff: programming, acoustic guitar, bass, electric guitar, acoustic guitar, synthesizer, keyboard, mellotron
Evan Smith: flute, saxophone, synthesizer, electric organ, ukulele
Sean Hutchinson: drums, percussion
Christopher Rowe: backing vocals

Recorded

2023

Technical Team

Producers: Taylor Swift, Jack Antonoff
Mixing: Serban Ghenea, Bryce Bordone
Sound Engineers: Jack Antonoff, Evan Smith, Laura Sisk, Christopher Rowe, Sean Hutchinson
Mastering: Randy Merrill
Best Ranking: Hot 100: 48

Genesis

For the writing of "Timeless," considered by many fans to be a classic of the *Speak Now* era, Taylor was inspired by the story of her grandmother, Marjorie Finlay. Turning the yellowed pages of a photo album found in an antique shop, she imagines how her grandmother met her first love. She immerses herself in her character and has fun developing her story, from the 1930s through 1944 to 1958. With a reference to the tragedy of Shakespeare's Romeo and Juliet in the second pre-chorus—which inevitably evokes "Love Story" from *Fearless*—this ballad traces the timelessness of a very strong love. Later, in December 2020, Taylor Swift pays a further tribute to her grandmother with "Marjorie" (*Evermore*). A few months earlier, in July, she recalled her grandfather, Robert Finlay, in "Epiphany" (*Folklore*).

Production

The honor of concluding this From the Vault six-song cycle falls to Jack Antonoff. The backbone of this arrangement rests on two strumming acoustic guitars, mixed far forward and distributed to the right and left of the stereo field. Over a 72 bpm tempo, Sean Hutchinson's drums seem to build on the pulse of the acoustic guitars, as if they had been recorded beforehand. Antonoff's bass rolls freely over this elegant rhythmic carpet, rewarding the listener with a few turnarounds along the way. Christopher Rowe's chorus adds an extra touch of emotion to Taylor Swift's storytelling-infused performance. Electric organ, mellotron, horns, ukulele arpeggios, and synthesizer layers wrap everything up without overloading the indie-folk instrumentation, taking the listener on a journey through the ages.

RELEASE DATE
United States: October 22, 2012
(ref.: Big Machine Records—BMR310450A)
Best Ranking: 1

ALBUM

Red

State of Grace · Red · Treacherous · I Knew You Were Trouble · All Too Well · 22 · I Almost Do · We Are Never Ever Getting Back Together · Stay Stay Stay · The Last Time (feat. Gary Lightbody) · Holy Ground · Sad Beautiful Tragic · The Lucky One · Everything Has Changed (feat. Ed Sheeran) · Starlight · Begin Again · The Moment I Knew* · Come Back...Be Here* · Girl at Home*

** Deluxe Edition*

Opposite: During the 2012 MTV Video Music Awards in Los Angeles, September 2012.

Left: The stage of Z100's Jingle Ball 2012, in New York, surrounded by festive lights and a spectacular backdrop.

2012

FOR DISCERNING SWIFTIES

For *Red*, Taylor Swift confided that she was inspired by Joni Mitchell's album *Blue*—her favorite—which, she says in a 2016 *Rolling Stone* article, "explores somebody's soul so deeply," including "her deepest pains and most haunting demons."

A BIG LEAP INTO POP

Red, Taylor Swift's big leap into pop, was released on October 22, 2012, almost two years to the day after the release of *Speak Now*. After six years in the music business, Taylor Swift no longer sought to reproduce the recipes that had made her a success, but pursued a real stylistic change of direction. As with her previous album, she wrote most of the album on tour, but this time she decided to surround herself with a number of collaborators who would bring a new breath of fresh air to her music. Alongside Nathan Chapman, the main producer, she also called on several production heavyweights: Sweden's Max Martin, an internationally renowned hitmaker responsible for Britney Spears's legendary *...Baby One More Time* and numerous chart toppers over the past two decades (Katy Perry's "I Kissed a Girl," The Weeknd's "Blinding Lights," Ariana Grande's "Problem" and "Into You," etc.); Karl Johan Schuster, aka "Shellback," another Swede and collaborator with Martin, behind tracks by Pink, Usher, Maroon 5, and Muse; American Jeff Bhasker, partner of Jay-Z, Beyoncé, Kid Cudi, and Kanye West; Dan Wilson, American singer and guitarist who a year before the release of *Red* was praised for his co-writing work on Adele's "Someone Like You"; and Irish sound engineer Jacknife Lee, who has worked with U2, R.E.M., Bloc Party, and Weezer. Even though Big Machine Records made the astonishing commercial choice of presenting *Red* as a country album, Taylor Swift undeniably pulled out the big guns to distance herself as never before from her roots. "When you're making album 4, you have two choices: You can either do things the way that you have always done them [...], or you can switch it up and go outside your comfort zone," the star confided to Yahoo when promoting the album.

2012

Taylor Swift's Gibson Les Paul guitar and her lucky number (corresponding to her birthday), 13.

A Real Breakup Album

The first single from the album, "We Are Never Ever Getting Back Together" sets the tone. Mainstream pop was now Taylor Swift's genre of choice, and she no longer hesitated to make use of synths and drum machines. She remained in this mode, at least until the album *Folklore*. *Red* nevertheless ventures into new territory, flirting with arena rock, dance, and even dubstep, some of which can be heard on the chorus of "I Knew You Were Trouble." This song is one of seven singles on the album along with "Begin Again," "22," "Red," "Everything Has Changed" (a duet with Ed Sheeran), and "The Last Time" (with Gary Lightbody of British rock band Snow Patrol). This eclecticism is largely embraced by Taylor Swift, who insists that she wants to focus on the diversity of emotions she felt in each track. With her numerous producers, she employed a new working method, which consists of first orally describing to them the feelings that motivated her at the time of writing this or that track, then playing the tracks on guitar and finally giving them rein with their ideas.

Deep down, *Red* is once again a cathartic album with a diary feel. Indeed, its title is a reference to the tumultuous emotions the young woman was prey to in 2011 and 2012, "red" feelings ("intense love, intense frustration, jealousy, confusion," as she explained in an interview with Yahoo in 2012). Her difficult separation from actor Jake Gyllenhaal inspired her to write the first of thirty songs for the album (not all of which made the cut). And so "All Too Well" was born, an emotionally intense ballad acclaimed by critics and fans alike, which Taylor's longtime songwriting coach Liz Rose helped reduce its length from twenty (!) to around five minutes (currently, Taylor Swift plays it live in a ten-minute version). But the whole album swims in the troubled waters of disappointment in love. The singer, who places a quotation from Chilean poet Pablo Neruda ("Love is so short, forgetting is so long") at the beginning of her liner notes, explains that this is her only real breakup album. She may have become one of the most listened-to and financially successful singers of her generation, but she was still a young woman of twenty-two, struggling with the most ordinary heartaches and upsets, similar to those of her fans. She knew that this universality strengthened her bond with the public, and that this emotional storytelling, her trademark since the beginning, is also her most powerful weapon.

An Intense Promotional Campaign

Commercially, *Red* was a smash hit. In the week of its release, it climbed to number one on the Billboard 200,

Taylor Swift performs her hit song "Red" at BBC Radio 1's Teen Awards in London, October 2012.

selling over 1.2 million copies in the United States alone. It stayed at the top of the chart for seven weeks in a row, making Taylor Swift the first female artist and the second artist of any gender, after the Beatles, to have three consecutive albums stay at number one for at least six weeks. It also became the best-selling first-week album in the US in a decade and broke an iTunes download record on its first day, with 262,000 copies purchased. This represents more sales in a single day than most number one albums had achieved in a single week in previous years. International success also continued to grow, with multiplatinum certification obtained in many countries.

The effectiveness of the tracks is indisputable, but it has to be said that the marketing strategy implemented by the singer and her team had gained in strength. On September 22, on the *Good Morning America* show, Taylor Swift launched a four-week countdown to the staggered release of four of her singles ("Begin Again," "Red," "I Knew You Were Trouble," and "State of Grace"), which would be played successively on the airwaves before the album's release. Fans were also offered various options the day after the album's release: a twenty-two-track Deluxe Edition was sold exclusively at Target; a limited-edition pair of "Red" sneakers was launched by the Keds brand; a special "Taylor Swift" package was offered by the Papa John's pizza chain (a free album with the purchase of a giant pizza in a box bearing the star's image). Taylor Swift wanted and needed to be everywhere—including, of course, in the media. The day after the album's release, she made TV and radio appearances one after another. In a single day of promotion, she gave an interview to seventy-two different stations. She even suggested to her Twitter followers that they call radio stations and ask them nicely (but repeatedly) to play her latest single, "Begin Again." Although some journalists and commentators criticized her definitive move away from country and a lack of homogeneity, *Red* was favorably received by critics. It has been featured in lists of the best albums of the 2010 decade and ranks ninety-ninth in *Rolling Stone* magazine's 2023 review of the five hundred greatest albums of all time. The Grammys and the Country Music Association Awards, on the other hand, shunned it, even though it was nominated in several categories (Album of the Year and Best Country Album for the 2014 Grammys, and Album of the Year at the 2013 Country Music Association Awards). *1989*, the album the singer released two years later, would more than pay back for that.

Taylor Swift opens the festivities of the 2012 Jingle Ball with "State of Grace."

SINGLE

STATE OF GRACE

Taylor Swift / 4:55

Musicians
Taylor Swift: vocals, songwriting
Nathan Chapman: electric guitar, bass
Nick Buda: drums
Eric Darken: percussion

Recorded
Blackbird Studio (Nashville), 2012

Technical Team
Producers: Nathan Chapman, Taylor Swift
Mixing: Justin Niebank
Sound Engineers: Brian David Willis, Chad Carlson, Matt Rausch
Mastering: Hank Williams

Single Release
Digital Release: October 16, 2012
Best Ranking: Hot 100: 13

2012

Genesis

"State of Grace" sets the tone for the album: it is characterized by passion in love, sometimes sublime, but often all-consuming and dangerous. As Taylor Swift herself explains in "Stories behind the *Red* Songs," this song was written at the beginning of the album's creation process. Its lyrics sum it up in a single phrase, like a warning: "Love is a ruthless game / Unless you play it good and right." The singer describes a state of grace with a fragile balance, always walking a tightrope. Sometimes you have to fight to live love to the fullest.

Production

On the production side, Nathan Chapman and Taylor Swift decided to play the U2 stadium rock card. Everything here recalls the sound of the Irish band led by singer Bono and guitarist The Edge. First, the main electric guitar is duly saturated and passed through a pair of delay units, each set differently to create a stereo rhythmic effect (most frequently in triplets, as on U2's 1987 song "Where the Streets Have No Name"). Nick Buda's powerful playing then hammers out the eighth note on the tom bass, the rim shot snare on beats 2 and 4, and the bass drum on beats 1 and 3. A terrifically effective formula, all the more so when coupled with constant eighth-note bass playing at 130 bpm. Finally, ambient sounds are created by layering electric guitars. The staccato string arrangement reinforces the pulse of the bridge. Taylor Swift's stellar performance is to be commended as much for the quality of her lead vocals as for the profusion of backing vocals recorded in overdub and heavily processed (distortion, delay, long reverb). The result is as epic as this exercise was perilous.

Hidden Message

"I love you" doesn't count after "goodbye."

At the 2013 CMT Music Awards in Nashville, Taylor Swift sets the tone for the evening with a masterful performance of "Red."

SINGLE

RED

Taylor Swift / 3:43

2012

Musicians
Taylor Swift: vocals, backing vocals
Nathan Chapman: acoustic guitar, percussion
Dann Huff: electric guitar, bouzouki
Aaron Sterling: drums
Jimmie Sloas: bass
Tom Bukovac: electric guitar
Paul Franklin: pedal steel
Ilya Toshinsky: ganjo
Jonathan Yudkin: cello, fiddle
Charlie Judge: upright piano, Hammond B3 organ, synthesizer

Recorded
Pain in the Art (Nashville), Instrument Landing (Minneapolis), The Village (Los Angeles), The Garage (Topanga Canyon), Ruby Red (Atlanta), 2012

Technical Team
Producers: Nathan Chapman, Dann Huff, Taylor Swift
Mixing: Justin Niebank
Sound Engineer: Steve Marcantonio
Mastering: Hank Williams

Single Release
Digital Release: October 2, 2012, July 3, 2013 for the limited edition CD (Big Machine Records—BMRTS0405)
Best Rankings: Hot Country: 2; Hot 100: 6

Genesis

In "Red," Taylor Swift compares the emotions her ex-boyfriend evokes to different colors: red for passionate love, blue for separation, and gray for loneliness. The song reflects the emotional whirlwind she was sucked into and the intensity of contradictory feelings: love, jealousy, frustration, and turmoil. Rumor has it that the ex-boyfriend featured here—as in most of the songs on the album—is American actor Jake Gyllenhaal, whom she dated from October to December 2010. Some Swiftologists theorize that the abbreviation "SAG" in the hidden message could refer to the first three letters of Gyllenhaal's astrological sign, Sagittarius, or to the acronym of the Screen Actor's Guild.

Production

On the production side, this is a festival of strings of all kinds. The most unusual are the bouzouki of Dann Huff (a producer, studio musician, and songwriter who has collaborated with Keith Urban, Kenny Rogers, Shania Twain, Céline Dion, etc.), who co-produced the song, and the galloping (bordering on frailing) ganjo (or guitar banjo) of Ilya Toshinsky. Jonathan Yudkin's fiddle and cello accentuate the epic quality of this country-pop arrangement with sweeping bow strokes. As for the guitars, these take pride of place: Nathan Chapman's straightforward acoustic guitar strumming, faithful session musician Tom Bukovac's precise and incisive electric guitar playing, and Paul Franklin's steel guitar strokes give density to this mix, which was destined to conquer American radio stations. The solid playing of drummer Aaron Sterling and bassist Jimmie Sloas benefits from a limpid and particularly flashy mix (pushed by the aggressive and forward parallel compression) and propels Taylor Swift's performance, more expressive and energetic than ever, to new heights. The onomatopoeic backing vocals (cut, sampled, edited, and autotuned to the extreme) that accompany the phrase "Loving him was red" bring mainstream pop color to this intentionally

outrageous orchestration. All the meters are in the red, but for the title track of "Red," Swift, Chapman, and Huff have no reason to be half-hearted. An acoustic version of "Red," recorded at the 2013 Country Music Association Awards, was released as a single on November 8, 2013. For the occasion, Taylor Swift is joined by two legends of the country bluegrass revival, Alison Krauss and Vince Gill, on vocal harmonies.

Hidden Message

SAG (for Sagittarius or Screen Actors Guild).

Taylor Swift performing at London's Westfield in 2012.

TREACHEROUS

Taylor Swift, Dan Wilson / 4:02

Musicians
Taylor Swift: vocals, backing vocals, acoustic guitar
Dan Wilson: backing vocals, electric guitar, bass, piano
Andy Thompson: electronic piano, synth strings, guitar
Aaron Sterling: drums

Recorded
Ballroom West (Los Angeles), Marlay Studio (North Hollywood), Instrument Landing (Minneapolis), 2012

Technical Team
Producer: Dan Wilson
Mixing: Manny Marroquin
Sound Engineers: Andy Thompson, John Rausch, Eric Robinson
Mastering: Hank Williams
Best Rankings: Hot Country: 26; Bubbling Under Hot 100: 2

2012

Genesis

"Treacherous" is the chronicle of a disaster foretold. Taylor Swift knows at first sight that the man she has noticed is going to get her into trouble, yet she runs straight into the ambush, driven by an irrepressible attraction. Seeking to learn something new, she ventured into uncharted territory, asking Dan Wilson to co-write and produce the song with her. She admired the work of the musician, songwriter, and producer, who had his first success in 1998 with the indie pop hit "Closing Time" (by his band Semisonic).

Production

Recorded at Ballroom West (Los Angeles), Dan Wilson's personal studio, this track reveals the American producer's indie pop rock style. The sober production gives pride of place to the guitars: acoustic guitar strumming passed through a light phasing effect is superimposed on the eighth-note palm mute (played first by two stereo acoustics, then discreetly joined by two electrics to thicken the sound). From 1:31 onward, electric guitar arpeggios passed through a chorus effect and copiously reverberated open up the horizon, before the bridge explosion at 2:06, with its army of saturated guitars. The intensity subsides on the third chorus, then swells again to climax on the bridge reprise at 3:00, before falling back one last time on the chorus coda. The addition of the tambourine on the fourth beat (and then on beats 2 and 4 on the bridges) proves to be an aesthetically pleasing addition to the unadorned bass and drums, focused on low frequencies (bass drum and toms, essentially). Andy Thompson's contribution on electronic piano and synth strings expands the sonic palette of this guitar-centric arrangement. The structure is rather unusual, but works perfectly. For Taylor Swift, who had been trying to break out of her comfort zone (her creative bubble with Nathan Chapman since her first album), this collaboration with Dan Wilson is a success.

Hidden Message

Won't stop till it's over.

SWIFT

"I Knew You Were Trouble" captures the confusion and pain of a toxic relationship.

SINGLE

I KNEW YOU WERE TROUBLE

Taylor Swift, Max Martin, Shellback / 3:39

Musicians
Taylor Swift: vocals, backing vocals
Max Martin: keyboards
Shellback: acoustic and electric guitars, bass, keyboards, programming
Recorded
MXM (Stockholm), Conway Recording (Los Angeles), 2012
Technical Team
Producers: Max Martin, Shellback
Mixing: Serban Ghenea
Sound Engineers: John Hanes, Sam Holland, Michael Ilbert
Mastering: Tom Coyne
Single Releases
Digital Release: October 9, 2012
CD single release, numbered, limited edition: December 13, 2012—BMR310414
Best Rankings: Hot 100: 2; Mainstream Top 40: 1

Taylor Swift and Harry Styles stroll through Central Park in New York, December 2012.

2012

Genesis

Like "Treacherous," "I Knew You Were Trouble" speaks of an irresistible attraction, the kind that renders all resistance useless, when all the signs are ominous. After her performance at the Brit Awards, and in answer to a reporter's question about the difficulty of performing such a song, Taylor Swift assures us that it is easy to access this emotion when the person concerned is standing at the side of the stage. The young woman wrote this song to talk about her relationship with actor, musician, and singer Harry Styles. A remix version featuring American rapper Sammy Adams was released in November 2012.

Production

For the production of "I Knew You Were Trouble," Taylor Swift once again took the risk of trying out a new register, enlisting the help of two hitmakers specializing in dance pop: producers and successful songwriters Max Martin and Shellback. The former produced Britney Spears's "...Baby One More Time" in 1998, the Backstreet Boys' "I Want It That Way" in 1999, Céline Dion's "That's the Way It Is" in 1999, and NSYNC's "It's Gonna Be Me" in 2000. The latter was responsible for numerous hits for Pink, Britney Spears, Avril Lavigne, Ariana Grande, and Adele. It was a successfully controlled risk for Taylor Swift, who can now call on the services of some of the world's top producers. It should be said that "I Knew You Were Trouble" has all the ingredients of the genre: abrasive synthesizers, sidechain compression techniques, massive distorted bass, multiple distortion, reverb, and delay effects on lead and backing vocals, drop effects, hyper-edited instruments (in this case, acoustic and electric guitars), all enhanced by Serban Ghenea's highly compressed mixing and Tom Coyne's perfectly calibrated mastering. This is a transformed experience for Taylor Swift, taking her first steps into the huge world of dance-floor music. With "I Knew You Were Trouble," the singer knew that a new, wider, international audience was within her grasp. Her ascent continues and will not stop here.

Hidden Message

When you saw me dancing...

The 2012 Jingle Ball on December 1 at the Nokia Theatre, Los Angeles.

FOR DISCERNING SWIFTIES

The hidden message "maple latte" refers to the Thanksgiving Day when Taylor Swift and Jake Gyllenhaal ordered the same autumnal beverage in a Brooklyn coffee shop.

ALL TOO WELL

Taylor Swift, Liz Rose / 5:29

2012

Musicians
Taylor Swift: vocals
Nathan Chapman: electric and acoustic guitars, bass, drums, keyboards, backing vocals
Recorded
Pain in the Art (Nashville), 2012
Technical Team
Producers: Nathan Chapman, Taylor Swift
Mixing: Justin Niebank
Sound Engineer: Nathan Chapman
Mastering: Hank Williams
Best Ranking: Hot Country Songs: 17

Genesis

Taylor Swift wrote a first draft of "All Too Well" during the "Speak Now World Tour" in February 2011, which she continued shortly after her breakup with actor Jake Gyllenhaal. This was the first song written for the *Red* album, before "State of Grace." The tone is set: The theme of this breakup will be the common thread running through the album. Overwhelmed by her emotions, Taylor Swift was unable to write a lyric short enough to keep the song under ten minutes to make the record's cut. So she decided to ask Liz Rose, her loyal songwriting partner, to help her sort through her ideas. However, this first version left her wanting more, and she decided to make up for it almost ten years later by releasing "All Too Well (10 Minute Version)" on the From the Vault section of *Red (Taylor's Version)*, released in 2021. This version contains three long extra verses, which she likes to sing in a moment of communion with her fans at her concerts. The lines "And I left my scarf there at your sister's house / And you've still got it in your drawer, even now" in the first verse and "But you keep my old scarf from that very first week / Cause it reminds you of innocence" in the penultimate verse have given rise to much speculation about the fate of the scarf. (Many fans believe it is the blue, gray, and red striped Gucci scarf she was wearing when a paparazzi took a photo of her walking with Gyllenhaal in 2010.) The reappearance of the scarf in the final verse is a remarkable narrative pirouette, proof of rigorous, masterful songwriting.

Production

With a 93 bpm tempo, the ballad "All Too Well" returns to the fundamentals of country-pop and stadium-rock production. Taylor Swift and Nathan Chapman are alone at the controls, and he alone, the one-man band, handles the parts for each instrument: acoustic guitar strumming up front, electric guitar ramping up from subtle turnaround to full chord playing, punctuated by melodic gimmicks and heartfelt arpeggios. To highlight his expressive, dynamic touch, Chapman opts for a crunch sound (passed through a Nobles ODR-1-type overdrive pedal, the famous secret weapon of Nashville session guitarists) that pushes the amp's tubes to their limits as the attack of his playing intensifies. A discreet piano serves to enhance the top end of the spectrum with a few notes perched at the top of the keyboard (essentially octaves of C played ostinato), and the indispensable synthesizer layer provides binding and depth of field. The bass is confined to an eighth-note roll-out over a straight, sober drum part that includes a mix of programming and elements played on an acoustic kit. Taylor Swift makes perfect use of her tight vibrato and delivers a performance that leaves the listener in no doubt: phrase after phrase, this is a lived experience.

Hidden Message

Maple latte.

Taylor Swift sings "22" at the Billboard Music Awards, 2023.

2012

SINGLE

22

Taylor Swift, Max Martin, Shellback / 3:52

Musicians
Taylor Swift: vocals, backing vocals, acoustic guitar
Max Martin: keyboards
Shellback: acoustic and electric guitars, bass, keyboards, programming
Recorded
MXM (Stockholm), Conway Recording (Los Angeles), 2012
Technical Team
Producers: Max Martin, Shellback
Mixing: Serban Ghenea
Sound Engineers: John Hanes, Sam Holland, Michael Ilbert
Mastering: Tom Coyne
Single Release
Digital and CD single release, numbered, limited edition: March 13, 2013—BMR310404
Best Rankings: Hot 100: 20; US Mainstream Top 40: 12

Genesis

For the album's fourth single, Taylor Swift chose a light, danceable, recreational track. In contrast to the song "Fifteen," written for *Fearless* (2008), "22" represents the age of recklessness. When Taylor Swift refers to her fifteenth birthday as the age of all vulnerabilities, she is keen to tell her fans that at twenty-two she is feeling good about herself, despite the many heartbreaks and disappointments she has been through. She celebrates with her best friends (Ashley, Dianna, Claire, and Selena, quoted in the hidden message), experiences magical moments, even though they can be miserable ("It's miserable and magical, oh yeah"), and always remains resilient, full of dreams and energy.

Production

For the production of this upbeat, festive song, Taylor Swift once again called upon Max Martin and Shellback. Over a tempo of 104 bpm, the acoustic guitar strumming in sixteenth notes blends with electric guitar's unstoppable chops and synthesizer chords pulsed in sidechain by the electronic bass drum. The small chords on the pre-chorus sound exactly like an Omnichord OM-27. The electronic snare drum slams like never before, doubled by stinging claps, and the tambourine played on sixteenth notes reinforces the high hat at the end of each chorus (when Taylor sings "22" in ad lib) and remains until the end, from the bridge onward. From 2:41 to 2:50, it is time for the famous filtered drop to prepare the restart of the last chorus, for everyone to raise their arms and get ready to jump to the rhythm. Taylor Swift seems to be having a lot of fun interpreting this ode to celebration, recording a cascade of backing vocals in overdub. The backing vocals in the chorus are given an extensive treatment (Melodyne, perfect alignment, pitch harmonies), typical of dance pop in the early 2010s. The conquest of the dance floor continues.

Hidden Message

Ashley, Dianna, Claire, Selena.

HATERS GONNA HATE

Taylor Swift is photographed in London, January 2012.

I ALMOST DO

Taylor Swift / 4:04

Musicians
Taylor Swift: vocals
Nathan Chapman: acoustic guitar, bass, drums
Recorded
Pain in the Art (Nashville), 2012
Technical Team
Producers: Nathan Chapman, Taylor Swift
Mixing: Justin Niebank
Sound Engineer: Nathan Chapman
Mastering: Hank Williams
Best Ranking: Hot Country Songs: 13

FOR DISCERNING SWIFTIES

Although she did not include this song in the regular "Red Tour" playlist, Taylor Swift performed it twice as a surprise acoustic track. First at the first concert of the tour, on March 13, 2013, in Omaha, Nebraska, then on April 20, 2013, in Tampa, Florida. She would not perform it again onstage until ten years later, during the "Eras Tour," as a second surprise track, on the evening of June 9, 2023, in Detroit, Michigan, alone at the piano.

Genesis

With "I Almost Do," judiciously positioned after the upbeat, catchy break of "22," Taylor Swift picks up the breakup thread running through *Red*. As revealed in the hidden message, "Wrote this instead of calling," she decides to put her emotions down on paper to resist the temptation of calling her ex back or answering his calls. "I Almost Do" contains all the words she wishes to express: however difficult, she does not want to suffer yet—it is more than she has strength for.

Production

"I Almost Do" is a country-pop folk ballad in the Taylor Swift and Nathan Chapman style. Set to a 73 bpm tempo, the acoustic guitars drive the song with a combination of heavy, groovy strumming (sometimes reminiscent of Neil Young's binary rhythmic touch and syncopation), melodic solos, and delicate arpeggios. Even though Chapman can play a dozen instruments, one should not overlook his immense talent as a guitarist and arranger, and the quality of his precise, versatile playing. The bass and drums are formidably effective, and the snare drum sound, both nuanced and clattering, passes through a chain of compression and reverb that is on the edge of what is reasonable for such a restrained, intimate arrangement. In Taylor's Version of the song, the snare treatment is less pronounced, which seems more in keeping with the arrangement and the choice of relatively dry, natural mixing (especially in the original version). As always, Taylor Swift's performance is impeccable, as much for the presence and emotion she manages to convey in her lead vocals as for the quality of her vocal harmonies and her particularly inspired descants.

Hidden Message

Wrote this instead of calling.

The song "We Are Never Ever Getting Back Together" sums up the theme of *Red*: breakup and resilience.

SINGLE

WE ARE NEVER EVER GETTING BACK TOGETHER

Taylor Swift, Max Martin, Shellback / 3:13

Musicians
Taylor Swift: vocals, backing vocals, acoustic guitar
Max Martin: keyboards
Shellback: acoustic and electric guitars, bass, keyboards, programming
Recorded
MXM (Stockholm), Conway Recording (Los Angeles), 2012
Technical Team
Producers: Max Martin, Shellback
Mixing: Serban Ghenea
Sound Engineers: John Hanes, Sam Holland, Michael Ilbert
Mastering: Tom Coyne
Single Releases
Digital Release: August 14, 2012
CD single, numbered, limited edition: September 4, 2012—BMR310401A
Best Rankings: Hot 100: 1; US Mainstream Top 40: 2; Hot Country Songs: 1

2012

Genesis

Judiciously chosen as the album's first single, "We Are Never Ever Getting Back Together" combines two of the most specific elements of this *Red* era: the breakup theme and the upbeat dance pop production of Max Martin and Shellback. The song is most likely addressed to Taylor Swift's ex-boyfriend Jake Gyllenhaal, although this has never been confirmed. In it, the young woman denounces a certain masculine or male gaze and a form of mansplaining. When she talks about her ex's taste in music ("with some indie record that's much cooler than mine"), she shows how he tries to belittle her, more or less consciously. For her, "We Are Never Ever Getting Back Together" is a song of empowerment, a way of regaining full confidence in herself. As the hidden message says ("When I stopped caring what you thought"), the *Red* era is one of resilience. Taylor will not be taken for a fool again.

Production

From the very first bars of "We Are Never Ever Getting Back Together," the hyper-cut acoustic guitar is reminiscent of Mirwais's productions of the 2000s—Mirwais, co-founder of the band Taxi Girl, also produced four Madonna albums. The arrangement of this track, a future global dance-pop hit for Taylor Swift and her team, evolves over a moderate tempo (86 bpm) and features pulsating synthesizer sequences and synthesized strings. The electronic drums sound both massive in the low end (kick) and slamming in the high mids (snare). As on "22" and "I Knew You Were Trouble," tracks also produced by Max Martin and Shellback, Taylor Swift's lead vocals, relatively dynamic and natural on the verses, plunge into a series of marked treatments on the pre-refrains and backing vocals—Martin and Shellback played a major role in creating the codes of dance and electro-pop folk music of the 2000s and 2010s. At the end of the third chorus, treated as a long drop before the climactic reprise of the last chorus, Taylor Swift includes a recording of a conversation in which she expresses herself sarcastically about her ex-boyfriend. Between 2:20 and 2:25 precisely, she utters the phrase "We are never getting back together, like ever," which Martin, Shellback, and Taylor are sure to seize upon as the basis of their next hit. "We Are Never Ever Getting Back Together" broke the record for nine consecutive weeks at the top of the Hot Country Songs charts. This record had been held for forty-seven years by "Once a Day," the first single by American singer Connie Smith, released in 1965 with the help of the legendary Bob Ferguson, who also produced Dolly Parton.

Hidden Message

When I stopped caring what you thought.

STAY STAY STAY

Taylor Swift / 3:25

Musicians
Taylor Swift: vocals, backing vocals
Nathan Chapman: acoustic and electric guitars, keyboards, mandolin, bass, backing vocals
Nick Buda: drums
Eric Darken: percussion

Recorded
Pain in the Art (Nashville), 2012

Technical Team
Producers: Nathan Chapman, Taylor Swift
Mixing: Justin Niebank
Sound Engineer: Chad Carlson
Mastering: Hank Williams
Best Ranking: Hot Country Songs: 13

Genesis

For once, Taylor Swift does not approach the writing of "Stay Stay Stay" as a way of settling scores with the pangs of reality or sublimating her own experiences. This song, in the form of a daydream, is an ode to true love, a love that she imagines to be anchored in reality and capable of being long-term: imperfect, but rich in companionship and capable of bringing out the poetry of everyday life. While it is hard to imagine a superstar like Taylor Swift living a "normal" love story, "Stay Stay Stay" enables her to project herself into a healthy, stable relationship for the duration of a song.

Production

Nathan Chapman opens the festivities with a mandolin rhythm set to 100 bpm. The melody played on the keyboard seems to emulate two instruments in unison: a small string ensemble played in pizzicato and a percussive instrument such as a toy piano or glockenspiel. The joyous sound produced is perfectly suited to the song's light, carefree atmosphere. Simple, bouncy drums (this is probably mostly programming); a round bass with lively, melodic playing; and electric guitar play as a perfect complement to the mandolin, tambourine, claps, and backing vocals... Everything sparkles. Taylor Swift is having the time of her life performing this folk-pop "bluette" (a short, brilliant, playful piece of music) as the infectious laughter at the end of the song proves. "That's so fun!" she concludes, hilariously, in the vocal sound booth.

Hidden Message

Daydreaming about real love.

SINGLE

THE LAST TIME (FEAT. GARY LIGHTBODY)

Taylor Swift, Gary Lightbody, Jacknife Lee / 4:59

Musicians

Taylor Swift: vocals
Gary Lightbody: vocals
Jacknife Lee: guitars, bass, keyboards, programming
Owen Pallett: conductor
Bill Rieflin: drums
Marcia Dickstein: harp
Jamie Muhoberac: piano

Recorded

The Village (Los Angeles), The Garage (Topanga Canyon), 2012

Technical Team

Producer: Jacknife Lee
Mixing: Mark "Spike" Stent
Sound Engineers: Matt Bishop, Sam Bell
Mastering: Hank Williams
Best Ranking: Bubbling Under Hot 100: 3

Genesis

Yet another musical adventure for Taylor Swift, who this time decided to call on two talented Irishmen: Gary Lightbody, best known as leader of the indie rock and pop band Snow Patrol, and Jacknife Lee, producer and sound mixer, known for his work with U2, R.E.M., Robbie Williams, and Snow Patrol. She co-wrote "The Last Time" with them and asked Lightbody to sing a duet with her and Lee to produce the track. Canadian multi-instrumentalist, singer-songwriter, and arranger Owen Pallett wrote the string arrangement and conducted the orchestra. After the lightness of "Stay Stay Stay," "The Last Time" returns to the theme of breaking up in love, tracing a relationship in decline where the two protagonists tear each other apart, forgive each other, and never manage to leave each other.

Production

Rather than just a guest-featuring-artist number, "The Last Time" is a true duet, written six-handed and poignantly sung by two accomplished performers. After the first piano chords, Gary Lightbody takes the lead on this first verse with its solemn atmosphere (something unheard of in Taylor Swift's discography, who until then had always attacked first on the duets or guest feature numbers included on her own albums). Taylor Swift enters in thirds on the pre-chorus, continues to harmonize on the chorus, and finally sings the lead on the second verse, soon joined by Lightbody's chorus. As he knows how to do so well, Lee pushes the song's production into pop-rock territory fashioned for stadiums, with electric guitars and bass and drums to the fore, aided by Owen Pallett's sumptuous string arrangement. Between 2:43 and 3:03, on the instrumental bridge, the combination of an electric guitar immersed in a suite of effects (distortion, chorus, tremolo, etc.) and an acid synthesizer lead produces a phenomenal sound. The power that emanates from this lead part, a melodic unison with a complex texture, is totally consistent with the cinematic dimension of this orchestral and epic power ballad.

Hidden Message

L.A. on your break.

At the 2012 Grammy Awards, the singer received the award for Best Country Song for "Mean."

2012

HOLY GROUND

Taylor Swift / 3:22

Musicians

Taylor Swift: vocals
Jeff Bhasker: programming, bass, keyboards, piano, backing vocals
Tyler Johnson: backing vocals
Anders Mouridsen: acoustic and electric guitars

Recorded

Enormous (Los Angeles), 2012

Technical Team

Producer: Jeff Bhasker
Mixing: Serban Ghenea
Sound Engineers: Pawel Sek, Tyler Johnson, John Hanes
Mastering: Tom Coyne
Best Ranking: Hot Country Songs: 37

Genesis

Red is an album of experimentation for Taylor, and it gave her the opportunity to be involved in many exciting musical collaborations. On "Holy Ground," the singer calls upon Jeff Bhasker, an American producer known for his work with Kanye West, Mark Ronson, Harry Styles, and Jay-Z, to name but a few. Recalling the good times of a past relationship, she pays tribute to her ex-companion, whom she describes as her "Holy Land." According to the hidden message ("When you came to the show in S.D."), this is Joe Jonas, who came to see her in concert in San Diego on October 20, 2011. This meeting was an opportunity for the two artists to reconcile and begin a friendly relationship. In addition, the lyrics "But I don't want to dance if I'm not dancing with you" are very reminiscent of the "Last Kiss" song on the *Fearless* album ("I'm not much for dancing but for you I did"), which was clearly dedicated to Joe Jonas.

Production

Jeff Bhasker's energetic, up-tempo production fits into the very American category of heartland rock, a type of rock born in the USA in the 1970s, characterized by a straight rhythm and simple harmonic structure and generally associated with the spirit of struggle and the social conscience of the working class, spearheaded by Bruce Springsteen, Tom Petty, and Jackson Browne. After four bars of eighth-note strummed acoustic guitar, the bass and drums and the palm mute of the electric guitar begin a one-way trip to ecstasy, set to the beat of a 157 bpm tempo. A grainy synthesizer (Moog-like for the deep bass, and Juno for the high-mid-range arpeggio), a discreet overlay, and a few orchestral bells lend a hand to the army of guitars, all played and orchestrated by Anders Mouridsen. Taylor Swift's intensity and unusually rapid delivery impress. The ensemble of backing vocals (thirds and discants) plays a major part in creating the hook of the chorus, which stays on the same heady rhythmic pulse.

Hidden Message

When you came to the show in S.D. [San Diego].

SAD BEAUTIFUL TRAGIC

Taylor Swift / 4:44

Musicians

Taylor Swift: vocals, background vocals
Nathan Chapman: acoustic and electric guitars, ukulele, bass, keyboards, drums, percussion, programming

Recorded

Pain in the Art (Nashville), 2012

Technical Team

Producers: Nathan Chapman, Taylor Swift
Mixing: Justin Niebank
Sound Engineer: Nathan Chapman
Mastering: Hank Williams

Genesis

Written in the midst of the "Speak Now World Tour," this is, as it were, a positive reading of the breakup theme. "Sad Beautiful Tragic" is Taylor Swift's way of expressing the fact that, despite its tragic, sad, and painful ending, this story, like so many others, was worth experiencing.

Production

This song begins with the sound of a stylized train, created via sound design with an electric guitar immersed in delay and reverb effects. Right from the intro, the notion of distance and the metaphor of the train that separates as much as it brings the loved one closer are evoked: "When you're a little too late / I stood right by the tracks"; "Distance, timing, breakdown, fighting / Silence, the train runs off its tracks." Nathan Chapman is back at the controls to produce this arrangement, which seems directly influenced by the sound and atmosphere of alternative folk band Mazzy Star and rooted in the California Paisley Underground movement of the 1980s and 1990s. Witness the three-beat rhythm, the addition of the shaker resonating on the first beat of every second bar (and dipped in Phil Spector–style tambourine reverb) and the chord progression, albeit a tone lower, very similar to that of "Fade into You" (1994), the California band's flagship song ("Sad Beautiful Tragic": *I-V-II- IV,* i.e. *G-D-Am-C;* "Fade Into You": *I-V-II-II,* i.e. *A-E-Bm-Bm,* minus the resolution of the fourth degree). Taylor Swift's whispery vocals are reminiscent of Hope Sandoval's gentle nonchalance, and Nathan Chapman's melodious wanderings on nylon guitar contribute to the nostalgic yet delightfully casual atmosphere. On the final chorus, a distant cello (most probably MIDI programming) reinforces this minimalist orchestration, conducive to melancholy and solitary reverie. A fine tribute to nineties alternative folk music.

Hidden Message

While you were on a train.

Taylor Swift throws herself into the audience at the 2012 MTV Video Music Awards at the Staples Center in Los Angeles.

THE LUCKY ONE

Taylor Swift / 4:00

Musicians
Taylor Swift: vocals
Jeff Bhasker: programming, bass, keyboards, piano, backing vocals
Anders Mouridsen: acoustic and electric guitars

Recorded
Enormous (Los Angeles), 2012

Technical Team
Producer: Jeff Bhasker
Mixing: Serban Ghenea
Sound Engineers: Pawel Sek, Tyler Johnson, John Hanes
Mastering: Tom Coyne

2012

Genesis

Written between concerts on her Australian tour, "The Lucky One" describes the trials and tribulations of celebrity and the preconceived notions of what it means to be a popular icon. A veritable catalyst for fantasy, star status is often envied or coveted, yet people rarely know the other side of the coin. The song shares harmonic and melodic similarities with the verses of Kim Wilde's 1988 hit "Four Letter Word." The resemblance is probably intentional, since the lyrics "Chose the rose garden over Madison Square" seem to refer to the life of the English singer, who voluntarily abandoned fame for the simpler life of gardener and landscaper. The luckiest people are not always those one thinks of.

Production

Taylor Swift returned to Los Angeles to produce this mid-tempo (118 bpm) soft rock pop track, with Jeff Bhasker, in the den of Enormous Studio. Driven by acoustic guitar strumming and a heady drum pattern reminiscent of 1960s pop (snare drum played on beat 2, eighth note on every bar and, in addition, the little roll of four eighth notes for the boost effect every two bars). For "The Lucky One," Swift and Bhasker rely on an organic production style, where the instruments sound dynamic and expressive: the grainy bass played on a synthesizer (Moog type), the electric guitar (passed through a strong tremolo effect), and the synthesizer layers play in concert to open up the stereo field. All this keeps the attention intact and enhances the very natural treatment of Taylor Swift's voice, whose performance makes it difficult not to think it was captured in a single take. The multiple layers of backing vocals, which become increasingly busy as the chorus progresses, round off this sober orchestration with a rich, shimmering palette of sounds.

Hidden Message

Wouldn't you like to know.

At the Radio 1 Teen Awards in London, October 2012.

SINGLE

EVERYTHING HAS CHANGED (FEAT. ED SHEERAN)

2012

Taylor Swift, Ed Sheeran / 4:05

Musicians
Taylor Swift: vocals
Ed Sheeran: vocals, acoustic guitar, backing vocals
Butch Walker: guitars, keyboards, drums, backing vocals, percussion
Gary Lightbody: backing vocals
Patrick Warren: string arrangements, composition

Recorded
Ruby Red Productions (Santa Monica), 2012

Technical Team
Producer: Butch Walker
Mixing: Justin Niebank
Sound Engineer: Jake Sinclair
Mastering: Hank Williams

Single Release
Digital Release: July 14, 2013
Best Rankings: Hot 100: 32; Mainstream Top 40: 14; Adult Top 40: 8

Genesis

It seemed inevitable that the paths of Taylor Swift and Ed Sheeran, two of the most acclaimed artists in the world of pop and folk music at the time, would eventually cross. This was now the case with "Everything Has Changed," written together while playing on a trampoline in Taylor Swift's backyard. The two musicians had expressed their desire to work together, and their respective agents contacted each other at the same time. The planets aligned, and the song became the sixth single from *Red*. Its lyrics tell the story of how the world seems to change after a meeting that creates butterflies in the stomach and stars in the eyes. Taylor Swift and Ed Sheeran reunited in 2017 to write (with the help of Max Martin, Shellback, and Future) and record the song "End Game" from the album *Reputation*, then reunited in 2021 to record "Run" (a song from their 2012 songwriting).

Production

To follow Ed Sheeran's lead and respect his organic approach, Taylor Swift had the idea of calling on an artist whose emotionally charged productions she loved: Butch Walker, songwriter, performer, and producer of rock, glam metal, and pop-punk music, who has notably collaborated with Pink, Fall Out Boy, Green Day, and Weezer as composer and/or producer. But for this folk ballad, she takes Butch Walker's talents in the opposite

direction, with an intimate, pared-down arrangement that relies on acoustic instrumentation (apart from the chords played on mellotron flutes from 1:26 onward on the second verse, for which Ed Sheeran sings the first three lines in lead vocals). However, the acoustic guitar sounds rootsier than usual, the drums with brushes slap and remain very dry, the lead vocals are treated in a natural way, and the deep sound of the electric bass set up with flatwound strings almost evokes that of a double bass. Butch Walker manages to bring a punchy, slightly abrasive, emo edge to this folk duet. The result is surely exactly what Taylor Swift must have had in mind when she invited this producer from the rock scene.

Hidden Message

Hyannis Port.

Awaiting the CMA Awards at the Bridgestone Arena, Nashville, 2012.

STARLIGHT

Taylor Swift / 3:40

Musicians
Taylor Swift: vocals, backing vocals
Nathan Chapman: acoustic and electric guitars, piano, synthesizer
Dann Huff: electric guitar
J Bonilla: acoustic drums, percussion programming
Jimmie Sloas: bass
Charlie Judge: synthesizers, strings

Recorded
Blackbird Studio (Nashville), 2012

Technical Team
Producers: Nathan Chapman, Dann Huff, Taylor Swift
Mixing: Serban Ghenea
Sound Engineers: Joe Baldridge, John Hanes
Mastering: Tom Coyne

2012

FOR DISCERNING SWIFTIES

Taylor Swift adds the phrase "Made of starlight," taken from the line "Like we're made of starlight" in her song "Starlight," to the name of the new version of her fragrance Taylor by Taylor Swift: Made of Starlight, commercially released in February 2014.

Genesis

The song "Starlight" is a tribute to Ethel Kennedy, the wife of Bobby Kennedy. As she explains in an interview with the *Wall Street Journal*, Taylor Swift, who likes to look to the 1960s and old black-and-white photos for her sartorial inspiration, one day came across a photo of a young couple dancing at a ball in the late 1940s. The joy that emanated from the photo appealed to her. The image of the young dancers—seventeen-year-old Ethel and a slightly older Bobby Kennedy—and its context prompted her to extrapolate. She decided to write the script for this extraordinary evening. By a twist of fate, a few weeks later, Ethel's daughter Rory, who had come to see her in concert, invited her to meet her mother (Ethel and Bobby are the grandparents of Conor Kennedy, whom Taylor Swift dated while writing the album *Red*). So, on their first meeting, Taylor played "Starlight" for Ethel, who was very appreciative. The two women became close friends.

Production

"Starlight" benefits from a flashy production, straddling mainstream pop, arena rock, and dance pop. By infusing a skillful blend of saturated electric guitars, piano notes plunged into a rapid delay effect, accompanied by a long reverb and synthesizers with certain sounds bursting from all sides, as if to evoke a sky covered in shooting stars, Taylor Swift, Dann Huff, and Nathan Chapman create a very upbeat atmosphere, conducive to both dance and reverie. The drums, doubled by snare and bass drum samples, propel this hybrid arrangement to a 126 bpm tempo that renders futile any resistance to tapping one's foot or moving one's head in cadence. From 2:32 to 2:48, the electric guitar solo is more reminiscent of the great guitar heroes era, with its melodic bends rather than its technicality. It helps kick-start the climax of the final chorus. The end of the chorus and the outro bring a final variation full of hope, as if inviting the listener to dream and wish for the impossible.

Hidden Message

For Ethel.

At the 2012 CMA Awards, Taylor Swift performs "Begin Again."

2012

SINGLE

BEGIN AGAIN

Taylor Swift / 3:59

Musicians

Taylor Swift: vocals, backing vocals
Nathan Chapman: acoustic, high-strung acoustic and electric guitars
Dann Huff: electric and acoustic guitars
Aaron Sterling: drums
Jimmie Sloas: bass
Tom Bukovac: electric guitar
Charlie Judge: piano, synthesizers, Hammond B3 organ, strings, accordion
Caitlin Evanson: backing vocals
Ilya Toshinsky: mandolin
Paul Franklin: pedal steel
Jonathan Yudkin: violin, strings

Recorded

Blackbird Studio (Nashville), 2012

Technical Team

Producers: Nathan Chapman, Dann Huff, Taylor Swift
Mixing: Justin Niebank
Sound Engineer: Steve Marcantonio
Mastering: Hank Williams

Single Releases

Digital Release: September 25, 2012
CD single, numbered, limited edition: October 25, 2012—BMR310402B
Best Rankings: Hot 100: 7; US Country: 10; US Digital: 1

Genesis

"Begin Again" exposes the state of vulnerability one can find oneself in on a first date, shortly after a painful breakup: Taylor Swift feels the young man's benevolent gaze settling in, in contrast to the one focused on her by her ex-boyfriend. She gradually regains her confidence, allows herself to be talked to and enjoys the moment, like a breath of fresh air, the promise of a new beginning. This song probably refers to her date with Will Anderson from the band Parachute, with whom Taylor was spotted in early December 2011.

Production

This is the third and final track co-produced by Taylor Swift, Nathan Chapman, and Dann Huff. It was chosen as the second single from the album. Set to a tempo of 79 bpm, acoustic instruments dominate the arrangement of this bittersweet ballad. Arpeggios on acoustic guitar, strumming doubled with acoustic guitar high-strung and standard range, piano, accordion, violin, drums with brushes (then with drumsticks to raise the intensity), mandolin—the essentials of the early country-pop sound are present. The seventies soft rock folk sound of James Taylor's albums is not far away. The loose chords, played on electric guitar, the depth of sound of the bass, the soaring pedal steel, and the discreet layer of synthesizers open up the stereo field and add an extra dimension to the orchestration, as if to evoke the shadow of a recent past, like a veil. The restrained vocal performance, often close to a whisper, supports this view: determined to move forward, Taylor Swift remains cautious.

Hidden Message

I wear heels now.

Taylor Swift at Madison Square Garden during Z100's Jingle Ball 2012.

THE MOMENT I KNEW

Taylor Swift / 4:46

Musicians
Taylor Swift: vocals, backing vocals
Nathan Chapman: acoustic and electric guitars, bass, drums, keyboards
Liz Huett: backing vocals
Recorded
Pain in the Art (Nashville), 2012
Technical Team
Producers: Nathan Chapman, Taylor Swift
Mixing: Justin Niebank
Sound Engineer: Nathan Chapman
Mastering: Hank Williams

Genesis

"The Moment I Knew" is one of three original tracks included as bonus tracks on the Deluxe version of *Red*, released on October 22, 2012. In it, Taylor Swift describes her twenty-first birthday party, which Jake Gyllenhaal, her boyfriend at the time, did not attend (Taylor Swift has confirmed that this song is about him). This was a profound disappointment for the young woman who was expecting him. She tries to put on a brave face in her party dress, despite the passing hours and the presence of Jake's friends. Between sadness, tears, and frustration, she experiences this interminable wait in slow motion, with no real way out. She knows that this absence speaks volumes about their relationship. The singer also refers to this evening in "All Too Well (10 Minute Version)," released nine years later on *Red (Taylor's Version)*.

Production

Nathan Chapman and Taylor Swift decided to treat the song like a pocket symphony. The orchestral dimension of this arrangement relies not only on the cello part and the synthetic strings, with each instrument playing a specific role: the ultra-compressed drums and snare doubled by a sample immersed in outrageous reverb, the piano chords caressed on the verses and hammered on the choruses, the dynamic, expressive playing of the acoustic guitar, the percussion programmed in crescendo (as if to evoke the ticking of time), the bass lines, and layers played on synthesizers, all set to an adagio tempo of 63 bpm, all contribute to making the song a piece of chamber pop goldsmithery. The intensity of the performance is not outweighed by the singer's former stage backing vocalist, her friend Liz Huett (former member of the Agency).

COME BACK... BE HERE

Taylor Swift, Dan Wilson / 3:43

Musicians
Taylor Swift: vocals, backing vocals, acoustic guitar
Dan Wilson: electric guitar, bass, piano
Dave Stone: bass
Andy Thompson: synthesizer bass, mellotron, music box, synthesizers
David Campbell: strings arrangement and conductor
Aaron Sterling: drums

Recorded
Ballroom West (Los Angeles), Marlay Studio (West Hollywood), Instrument Landing (Minneapolis), 2012

Technical Team
Producer: Dan Wilson
Mixing: Justin Niebank
Sound Engineers: Andy Thompson, John Rausch, Eric Robinson
Strings Recording: Steve Churchyard
Mastering: Hank Williams

Genesis

"Come Back...Be Here" is the second song co-written with Dan Wilson and was included as a bonus track on the *Red* Deluxe Edition album. It depicts the difficulty of maintaining a long-distance relationship. How does one manage the incessant coming and going between two cities separated by an ocean, as well as the separation and inevitable exhaustion that comes with it?

Production

Here we encounter Dan Wilson's pop simplicity: songwriting that never sacrifices its honesty for pompous stylistic devices, and a straightforward sense of melody that perfectly matches Taylor Swift's direct style. On the production side, Dan Wilson does not beat about the bush either. The acoustic guitar strumming (doubled left and right) is played in a straightforward, syncopated manner by the singer herself. This guitar introduces the song and drives the arrangement right up to the smooth entry of the string ensemble on the pre-chorus. Dave Stone and Aaron Sterling attack on the first chorus, with their fearsomely effective bass and drums, programmed percussion takes over on the second verse, and Dan Wilson lays down his first melodic electric guitar counterpoints on the bottleneck, echoing Taylor Swift's vocals and the strings. David Campbell's orchestration gradually swells, playing on tension (staccato) and release (long holds) until the climax of the final chorus. The symphonic dimension creates the sense of space needed for this song about distance and separation of two people missing each other.

Taylor Swift rocks Gillette Stadium in Foxboro, Massachusetts, at a sold-out concert.

GIRL AT HOME

Taylor Swift / 3:40

Musicians
Taylor Swift: vocals, backing vocals
Nathan Chapman: acoustic and electric guitars, bass, drums, keyboards
Recorded
Pain in the Art (Nashville), 2012
Technical Team
Producers: Nathan Chapman, Taylor Swift
Mixing: Justin Niebank
Sound Engineer: Nathan Chapman
Mastering: Hank Williams

Genesis

"Girl at Home" is the third and final unreleased number included as a bonus track on the Deluxe version of the *Red* album. In it, Taylor Swift observes, describes, and points the finger at the behavior of a young man who has no hesitation in cheating on his girlfriend while she waits for him at home. In the song, the young man in question, without showing the slightest hint of remorse, tries to seduce her. Taylor Swift does not fall for this, explaining that he represents everything that makes her sad in a man: "You're the kind of man who makes me sad." According to a persistent rumor, the young man targeted here is none other than actor Zac Efron, whom the singer met during the filming of *The Lorax*, released on March 2, 2012, by Universal Pictures. To this day, Taylor Swift has never performed the song live, no longer accepting responsibility for the lyrics "It would be a fine proposition, / If I was a stupid girl," which places part of the blame on the woman, whereas the lying, unfaithful man is solely responsible.

Production

"Girl at Home" is a country-pop track produced by Taylor Swift and Nathan Chapman, who once again dons his one-man-band hat, playing and recording all the instruments himself. With his acoustic guitar strumming to the fore, the arrangement unfolds at a tempo of 125 bpm and kicks off with a chorus of lead vocals, backing vocals, acoustic guitar, and synthesizers, plunging the listener straight into the heart of the matter. The programmed drums make their entrance on the first verse, and the acoustic guitar switches to an eighth-note palm mute (doubled on the right and left of the stereo field). The pre-chorus is fleshed out with a round bass and a small arpeggiator synth (on the right), but the orchestration only comes into its own on the first chorus (excluding the intro): The bass switches to eighth-note as soon as the acoustic drums enter, and the electric guitar arpeggios, immersed in delay and long reverb, blend with the synthesizer layer. The only new element, from the second chorus onward, is a synthesizer sound that expands the sonic palette, creating melodic discants with a shimmering, high-pitched sound that borders on lo-fi. After that, it is all a matter of relaunching and nuancing to keep the listener's attention right to the end.

RELEASE DATE
United States: November 12, 2021
(ref.: Republic Records—B0034504-02)
Best Ranking: 1

ALBUM

Red (Taylor's Version)

Better Man* · Nothing New* (feat. Phoebe Bridgers) · Babe* · Message in a Bottle* · I Bet You Think about Me* (feat. Chris Stapleton) · Forever Winter* · Run* (feat. Ed Sheeran) · The Very First Night* · All Too Well (10 Minute Version)*

** From the Vault*

A POP MOMENT

Red (Taylor's Version) is the second full-length rerecording of the six albums released by Big Machine Records. It was released on November 12, 2021, just seven months after *Fearless (Taylor's Version)*, which was released on April 9, 2021. In 2012, *Red* was one of the best-selling albums of the decade, selling nearly seven million copies worldwide. The fans eagerly awaited her Taylor's Version, and they were certainly not disappointed. Taylor Swift announced in a lengthy message posted on June 18, 2021, that the new version of *Red* includes no fewer than thirty tracks, including nine previously unreleased tracks, known as From the Vault, which were written at the time the original album was conceived but were not selected for inclusion. In an introductory text to this 2021 reissue, Taylor Swift explains that she preferred to save them for her next album. But *1989* turned out to be very different from the other albums, so she left them out in the end. Three of the nine new tracks are collaborations: the first with Ed Sheeran ("Run"), with whom the singer had already recorded the duet "Everything Has Changed," featured on the 2012 album; the second with country artist Chris Stapleton ("I Bet You Think about Me"); and the third with indie folk singer Phoebe Bridgers ("Nothing New").

Ten Long-Awaited Minutes

The star was also taking advantage of this reissue to finally deliver to her fans one of the songs that has been the subject of the most rumor and speculation: the ballad "All Too Well" in its extended version. Ten years earlier, Liz Rose had helped the young singer rewrite this intense song, reducing it from twenty minutes to five minutes. This time, in a ten-minute format, Taylor Swift reveals previously unknown moments in her story.

Long-Term Collaborations

The remaining twenty tracks are all re-orchestrations of the sixteen original tracks, the three bonus tracks from the Deluxe Edition, and an acoustic version of "State of Grace," produced by Christopher Rowe. For this producer, the main aim was to recapture the sound of the 2012 album, while making some improvements. He was assisted from time to time by Swedish producers Max Martin and Shellback, who had already worked on several of the original tracks on *Red*, and by Nathan Chapman, who was responsible for ensuring some continuity in the overall sound. Jack Antonoff and Aaron Dessner continued to pilot the From the Vault tracks, as they would on all Taylor's Versions.

Dimensions of Genius

This new version of *Red* was particularly well received, both by the public and the critics, who hailed the production as less compressed and, in fact, more elegant than that of 2012. Taylor Swift's voice, warmer and more poised—years of experience notwithstanding—also contributed to the enthusiastic reception of this rerecording, if "enthusiastic" is the right word. On the day of its release, the album broke several streaming records, including that of the most-listened-to album by a female artist in one day on Spotify, with over 90.8 million streams, surpassing the previous record of 80.6 million set by Taylor herself. That day, Taylor Swift quite simply became the most-listened-to woman in a single day, with over 122.9 million streams, for her entire discography at the time. Once again, she proved that as crazy as rerecording six albums in their entirety seemed, her projects are successes every time. In the specific case of Taylor's Version of *Red*, she demonstrated above all that rerecorded songs are capable of arousing even more enthusiasm than their original versions.

At the 2012 American Music Awards in Los Angeles, Taylor Swift performs "I Knew You Were Trouble." Nine years later she would rerelease the song as part of *Red (Taylor's Version)*.

BETTER MAN

Taylor Swift / 4:57

Musicians

Taylor Swift: vocals
Aaron Dessner: acoustic and electric guitars, bass, synthesizers, keyboards, piano, drums programming
Josh Kaufman: acoustic and electric guitars, electric lap steel guitar, mandolin
James Krivchenia: drums, percussion
Bryce Dessner: orchestral arrangements
London Contemporary Orchestra: orchestra
Robert Ames: conductor
Galya Bisengalieva: first violin
Caitlin Evanson: backing vocals
Liz Huett: backing vocals

Recorded

Kitty Committee (Belfast), Prime Recording (Nashville), Long Pond (Hudson Valley, NY), 2021

Technical Team

Producers: Taylor Swift, Aaron Dessner
Mixing: Jonathan Low
Sound Engineers: Christopher Rowe, Jonathan Low, Jeremy Murphy, Aaron Dessner, Derek Garten
Mastering: Randy Merrill

Genesis

Taylor Swift, who wrote the song with the intention of including it on her fourth album, *Red*, did not include it in the final track listing. The songwriter thought of her friends in the country band Little Big Town to sing and sublimate her track because of the quality of their vocal harmony. She sent them the song, and the band, then in the middle of a tour, listened to it over and over again. After a few weeks, the band unanimously replied that they would be honored to record "Better Man" in the studio. Their version was released on October 20, 2016, and ended up at the top of the country charts. Taylor Swift recorded her own version in 2021 for inclusion on her album *Red (Taylor's Version)*, as track 22, the first previously unreleased track.

Production

Aaron Dessner took on the production of this first From the Vault track. His light touch is perfectly suited to this 74-bpm country-pop ballad, both romantic and bittersweet. As usual, he plays most of the instruments. He is, however, ably supported by Josh Kaufman, who drives the arrangement on six-string and mandolin. The delicate vocal harmonies, echoing the Little Big Town version, are sung by Taylor Swift's two good friends: Caitlin Evanson and Liz Huett. The London Contemporary Orchestra, conducted by Robert Ames, brings a cinematic dimension to the song, and the power of Taylor Swift's interpretation never wavers.

NOTHING NEW (FEAT. PHOEBE BRIDGERS)

Taylor Swift / 4:18

Musicians

Taylor Swift: vocals
Phoebe Bridgers: vocals
Aaron Dessner: acoustic and electric guitars, bass, synthesizer, keyboards, piano
Bryce Dessner: orchestral arrangements
Clarice Jensen: cello
Yuki Numata Resnick: violin

Recorded

Kitty Committee (Belfast), Long Pond (Hudson Valley, NY), Sound City (Los Angeles), 2021

Technical Team

Producers: Taylor Swift, Aaron Dessner
Mixing: Jonathan Low
Sound Engineers: Aaron Dessner, Bella Blasko, Jonathan Low, Christopher Rowe, Will Maclellan, Kyle Resnick, Clarice Jensen, Tony Berg
Mastering: Randy Merrill

Genesis

Like most of the nine From the Vault tracks released on Taylor's Version of *Red*, this song was written to be part of the original version of the album, released in 2012. To create the event on this first studio version, Taylor Swift called upon her friend and new star of American indie pop folk music: Phoebe Bridgers. Inspired by Joni Mitchell's song "A Case of You," "Nothing New" deals with the singer's fear of one day lapsing back into anonymity, of growing old and ending up alone.

Production

Taylor Swift and Aaron Dessner remain in delicate mode, without reaching the epic dimension of "Better Man," with this padded, acoustic production. The string arrangement by Aaron's twin brother, Bryce Dessner, is pure and airy. Overdubbed on several tracks to create a veritable small orchestra feel, the cello and violin swirl gracefully around the acoustic guitar, with the gentle piano and the voices of Taylor Swift and Phoebe Bridgers, often close to a whisper. The timbres of the two singers and friends blend perfectly, the anxiety is palpable, everything is on the surface. What better than a timeless folk ballad to evoke the inexorable passing of time?

BABE

Taylor Swift, Patrick Monahan / 3:44

Musicians

Taylor Swift: vocals
Jack Antonoff: programming, bass, drums, electric and acoustic guitars, synthesizer, keyboard, mellotron, percussion
Evan Smith: flute, saxophone
Mikey Freedom Hart: slide, electric and acoustic guitars; synthesizers; celesta; Hammond B3 organ
Sean Hutchinson: drums, percussion
Michael Riddleberger: percussion
Cole Kamen-Green: trumpet, mellophone

Recorded

Kitty Committee (Belfast), Electric Lady (New York), Rough Customer (Brooklyn, NY), Conway Recording (Los Angeles)

Technical Team

Producers: Taylor Swift, Jack Antonoff
Mixing: Serban Ghenea
Sound Engineers: Jack Antonoff, David Hart, Evan Smith, Cole Kamen-Green, Laura Sisk, Christopher Rowe, Michael Riddleberger, Mikey Freedom Hart, Sean Hutchinson, John Rooney, Bryce Bordone
Mastering: Randy Merrill

2021

Genesis

This song was first co-written in 2012 by Taylor Swift and Patrick Monahan (an American singer and songwriter, and the only permanent member of the pop-rock band Train) for the original version of *Red*. As with "Better Man" (which was first recorded by the band Little Big Town), the singer did not record her version of "Babe" until three years after the country music duo Sugarland's version, released in 2018, to include it on Taylor's Version of *Red*. This break-up-themed song would not have been out of place on *Red*, but Taylor Swift, always extremely prolific, had to make choices. The From the Vault versions, scattered throughout Taylor's Versions, are there to do justice to these songs, which were sometimes unfairly left out.

Production

Back at the helm for this very upbeat folk-pop production, Jack Antonoff, a master in the subtle art of mixing genres, returns to his favorite arrangement tricks. The sounds of the 1980s (high woodblock percussion, brilliant brass staccato, slamming snare drum, backing vocal treatment) coexist with textures reminiscent of 1960s music (mellotron, slightly crunchy electric guitar arpeggios, celesta, Hammond B3 organ). Finally, the modern pop color is provided by the deep bass and bass drum, the acoustic guitar treatment, the brass, and the drum programming, all with very little reverberation in contrast to the atmospheric synthesizer layers. Between Antonoff's programming, Cole Kamen-Green's trumpet, and Evan Smith's saxophone, the collective effort on the brass arrangement is remarkable, as much for the richness of the rhythmic syncopations as for its textural complexity. Taylor Swift, in top form as ever, delivers an energetic performance, both as lead vocalist and overdubbing backing vocals, which holds its own against the abundant, percussive orchestration.

SINGLE

MESSAGE IN A BOTTLE

Taylor Swift, Max Martin, Shellback / 3:45

Musicians

Taylor Swift: vocals
Shellback: guitar, keyboards, programming
Elvira Anderfjärd: programming, keyboards, drums, bass, backing vocals

Recorded

Kitty Committee (Belfast), House Mouse (Stockholm), Kallbachen Studios (Stockholm), 2021

Technical Team

Producers: Elvira Anderfjärd, Shellback
Mixing: Serban Ghenea
Sound Engineers: Christopher Rowe, Bryce Bordone
Mastering: Randy Merrill

Release Date

Digital Release: November 12, 2021
Best Rankings: Hot 100: 45; Mainstream Top 40: 17

Genesis

This first song, which came from Taylor Swift's songwriting sessions with Max Martin and Shellback in 2012, was not recorded until 2021. In it, Taylor Swift confides her fear of falling in love and her inability to suppress this burgeoning feeling. Although not confirmed, "Message in a Bottle" is probably about her relationship with singer Harry Styles.

Production

Unlike the three tracks that Taylor Swift co-wrote with Max Martin and Shellback for the original version of *Red* ("I Knew You Were Trouble," "22," and "We Are Never Ever Getting Back Together"), this song is co-produced with Elvira Anderfjärd, who takes Max Martin's place. This Swedish producer and songwriter, better known as Elvira, notably remixed "Willow" in 2020 and "Love Story" in 2021. The effective dance pop style of Martin's and Shellback's productions is here, with a hint of modernity in the choice of synthesizer sounds and rhythmic programming. Over a tempo of 116 bpm, arpeggiators mingle with chiming DX7 chords and the bass bounces to the disco house beat. As well as programming and playing the keyboards, bass and drums, Elvira Anderfjärd harmonizes Taylor Swift's voice. The guitar, other keyboards, and programming are left to Shellback, for whom this kind of production has become an exact science. A remix of "Message in a Bottle" by Fat Max G was released on January 20, 2022.

I BET YOU THINK ABOUT ME (FEAT. CHRIS STAPLETON)

Taylor Swift, Lori McKenna / 4:45

Musicians
Taylor Swift: vocals
Chris Stapleton: vocals
Aaron Dessner: acoustic guitar, bass, high-strung guitar, piano
Josh Kaufman: electric guitar, lap steel guitar, harmonica
James Krivchenia: drums, percussion
London Contemporary Orchestra: strings
Robert Ames: conductor
Bryce Dessner: orchestral arrangements
Galya Bisengalieva: first violin

Recorded
Hoffman Streets and Long Pond (Hudson Valley, NY), Kitty Committee (Belfast), Sputnik Sound (Nashville), EBC (London), 2021

Technical Team
Producers: Taylor Swift, Aaron Dessner
Mixing: Jonathan Low
Sound Engineers: Aaron Dessner, Jonathan Low, Christopher Rowe, Jeremy Murphy, Vance Powell
Mastering: Randy Merrill
Best Rankings: Hot 100: 45; Mainstream Top 40: 17

Genesis

In 2011, Taylor Swift called upon Lori McKenna, the famous American songwriter and singer, to co-write this song. In the end, "I Bet You Think about Me" was not chosen for *Red* but was picked up again in 2021 for the From the Vault tracks on Taylor's Version. For the recording, Taylor Swift asked guitarist, singer, and songwriter Chris Stapleton to back her on backing vocals. She knew that the country, soul, and Southern rock inflections of the singer's voice would enhance the track. In "I Bet You Think about Me," she compares the way she grew up to the way her partner was born with a silver spoon in his mouth ("You grew up in a silver spoon gated community"), whereas she was brought up on a farm. These clues suggest that "he" might be Jake Gyllenhaal. The next two lines leave little doubt as to the young man's identity: "I bet you think about me when you're out / At your cool indie music concerts every week."

Production

Aaron Dessner is at the helm of this country-folk-pop production, reminiscent of the heyday of Americana folk and rock in the 1970s. Over a three-beat rhythm flirting with the 6/8 shuffle, the arrangement, driven by acoustic guitar strumming and James Krivchenia's drums, unfolds at a tempo of 150 bpm. All the ingredients of American folk music are there: pedal steel and harmonica embroider the voices of Taylor Swift and Chris Stapleton, and the piano played by Aaron Dessner contributes a lovely breeze. To top it all off, Bryce Dessner's arrangement of strings transcends this heady waltz, carrying the listener away in a dizzying musical whirlwind.

In "I Bet You Think About Me" there is the same allusion to his discerning musical tastes and snobbery as in the song "We Are Never Ever Getting Back Together," released on *Red* in 2012: "And you would hide away and find your peace of mind / with some indie record that's much cooler than mine."

Mark Foster, frontman of Foster the People, joins Taylor Swift at Nashville's Nissan Stadium to perform "Forever Winter" on May 6, 2023.

2021

FOREVER WINTER

Taylor Swift, Mark Foster / 4:23

Musicians

Taylor Swift: vocals
Jack Antonoff: programming; bass; drums; electric, acoustic, and acoustic twelve-string guitars; keyboards; mellotron; percussion
Evan Smith: flute, saxophones
Mikey Freedom Hart: electric guitar, bass, pedal steel, synthesizers
Sean Hutchinson: drums, percussion
Mark Foster: backing vocals
Michael Riddleberger: percussion
Cole Kamen-Green: trumpet, mellophone

Recorded

Kitty Committee (Belfast), Conway Recording (Los Angeles), Electric Lady (New York), Rough Customer (Brooklyn, NY), 2021

Technical Team

Producers: Taylor Swift, Jack Antonoff
Mixing: Serban Ghenea
Sound Engineers: Jack Antonoff, David Hart, Evan Smith, Cole Kamen-Green, Laura Sisk, Christopher Rowe, Michael Riddleberger, Mikey Freedom Hart, Sean Hutchinson, John Rooney, Bryce Bordone
Mastering: Randy Merrill

Genesis

Co-written in 2012 with Mark Foster, leader of the group Foster the People, this song was not part of the original version of the *Red* album. Its demo version leaked onto the internet on February 26, 2023, two years after the singer recorded the official version From the Vault for *Red (Taylor's Version)*. In it, Taylor Swift talks to a friend who is suffering from a mental illness, probably depression. There is little doubt as to the identity of this person: It is probably her childhood friend Jeff Lang, who died at the age of twenty-one. To thank him and pay tribute to him—she used to play her songs for the first time in front of him—Taylor Swift sang at his funeral.

Production

Jack Antonoff takes over from Aaron Dessner to produce this emotionally charged alternative folk-pop track. Apart from the presence of Mark Foster on vocal harmonies, the team is identical to that of "Babe," minus the playfulness. The composition, arrangements, and mood may be different, but the energy is there, and apart from a few details, the ingredients are the same: an elaborate brass arrangement (though much less focused on rhythm and syncopation), acoustic guitar strumming up front, synthesizer layers, round bass, and solid drums (with its snare drum pattern on the second beat and the eighth note on the third beat of each bar). This rhythm is enhanced by a tambourine that accentuates the fourth beat on the verses, beats 2 and 4 on the choruses, and the sixteenth note on the bridge. Blending with the chiming sounds of the keyboards and synthesizers, the arpeggios of the twelve-string acoustic guitar played by Antonoff help to create an ethereal atmosphere, full of sparkles, as if to suggest to the listener that there is always hope, even in the most tragic moments.

At the 2016 Grammy Awards, Taylor Swift is crowned for Album of the Year for *1989* and Ed Sheeran wins the award for Song of the Year for "Thinking Out Loud." Their musical friendship is later reflected in the song "Run."

RUN
(FEAT. ED SHEERAN)

Taylor Swift, Ed Sheeran / 4:00

Musicians

Taylor Swift: vocals
Ed Sheeran: vocals, acoustic guitar, backing vocals
Aaron Dessner: drum machine programming, synthesizers, keyboards, acoustic and high-strung guitars, bass
Josh Kaufman: electric guitar
London Contemporary Orchestra: orchestra
Robert Ames: conductor
Galya Bisengalieva: first violin
James Krivchenia: drums, percussion
Thomas Bartlett: keyboards, synthesizers
Bryce Dessner: orchestral arrangements

Recorded

Kitty Committee (Belfast), Long Pond (Hudson Valley, NY), 2021

Technical Team

Producers: Taylor Swift, Aaron Dessner
Mixing: Jonathan Low
Sound Engineers: Aaron Dessner, Bella Blasko, Jonathan Low, Christopher Rowe, Robert Sellens
Mastering: Randy Merrill

Genesis

This was the first song Taylor Swift wrote with Ed Sheeran in 2012. But it was "Everything Has Changed" that was chosen for the original version of *Red*. A catch-up session for "Run," a song about the desire to escape, the need to get away from the daily grind, to leave together, in the momentum of a new love encounter.

Production

This ballad duet is driven by Ed Sheeran's guitar. Sheeran is a master in the art of delicate picking accompaniment. With a tempo of 125 bpm, Dessner and Taylor Swift's production strikes a chord. The subtle changes in texture are brought about, on the one hand, by the London Contemporary Orchestra's gentle, sometimes *sul ponticello*–like playing and, on the other, by the percussion and backing vocals that gently break up the apparent linearity of this atmospheric orchestration. The Fender Rhodes–style keyboard played by Aaron Dessner enhances the harmony, and the throbbing bass synth adds its share of dramatic tension. "Run" benefits from an edgy folk-pop arrangement, where everything is done to enhance the narrative carried by Taylor Swift and Ed Sheeran's soulful vocals.

Freddy Holm, one of Taylor Swift's studio musicians on "The Very First Night," plays numerous instruments, including the violin.

THE VERY FIRST NIGHT

Taylor Swift, Amund Bjørklund, Espen Lind / 4:00

Musicians
Taylor Swift: vocals
Espen Lind: guitars, bass, keyboards
Freddy Holm: dobro
Torstein Lofthus: drums
Amund Bjørklund: keyboards

Recorded
Kitty Committee (Belfast), Propeller and Norsk Innspillingsbyrå (Oslo), 2021

Technical Team
Producers: Tim Blacksmith, Danny D., Espionage
Mixing: Serban Ghenea, Bryce Bordone
Sound Engineers: John Hanes, Espen Lind, Mike Hartung, Christopher Rowe
Mastering: Randy Merrill

Genesis

In 2012, Taylor Swift co-wrote this song with Amund Bjørklund and Espen Lind, a Norwegian production duo based in New York and known as Espionage. The pair are responsible for numerous hits, notably for artists such as Beyoncé, Chris Brown, and the group Train. In "The Very First Night," Taylor Swift reminisces nostalgically about a past relationship. She wishes she could go back in time and relive the thrill of their first night together, even though it broke her heart.

Production

Powered by Freddy Holm's sixteenth-note acoustic guitar strumming, this dance-pop track is reminiscent of Max Martin and Shellback productions. The sound palette is much the same: drums doubled by dance-floor-friendly samples, arpeggiators, synthesizer sequences and layers, and a round bass on the eighth note or in symbiosis with the bass drum, all set to a tempo of 121 bpm. The work on Taylor Swift's voice and the superimposition of backing vocals on the pre-choruses, choruses, and bridge are particularly catchy.

During her "Red Tour" at the Prudential Center (Newark, New Jersey), March 2013.

ALL TOO WELL
(10 MINUTE VERSION)

Taylor Swift, Liz Rose / 10:13

2021

Musicians
Taylor Swift: vocals
Jack Antonoff: programming; bass; drums; slide, electric and acoustic guitars; keyboards; mellotron; percussion
Evan Smith: flute, saxophone, synthesizers
Mikey Freedom Hart: celesta, Hammond B3 organ, piano, reed organ, baritone guitar, Wurlitzer
Sean Hutchinson: drums, percussion
Michael Riddleberger: percussion
Bobby Hawk: strings
Recorded
Kitty Committee (Belfast), Conway Recording (Los Angeles), Electric Lady and Rough Customer (Brooklyn, NY), 2021
Technical Team
Producers: Taylor Swift, Jack Antonoff
Mixing: Serban Ghenea
Sound Engineers: Jack Antonoff, David Hart, Evan Smith, John Gautier, Laura Sisk, Christopher Rowe, Michael Riddleberger, Mikey Freedom Hart, Sean Hutchinson, John Rooney, Bryce Bordone
Mastering: Randy Merrill
Best Rankings: Hot Country Songs: 1; Hot 100: 1

Genesis

With the recording of this ten-minute version, Taylor Swift was able to express all the condescension and lack of consideration she suffered in her relationship with actor Jake Gyllenhaal. Interesting detail: the only phrase that belongs directly to the feminist lexicon is associated with her ex-boyfriend and includes one of the rare f-bombs in the singer's discography to this point: "fuck the patriarchy" is written on the keychain of the car keys he tosses on the ground when he's upset. The listener will detect as much of the sarcasm as they want to hear. Note also the rich rhyme between "patriarchy" and "car keys." For fans, this version is a must-see live. The Swifties sing all six verses, the bridge, and the chorus by heart, in one voice. In this version, the verse in which the scarf is mentioned for the second and last time is not in third or last position—as might have been expected—but in fifth and penultimate position, with the singer preferring to end with a new verse that means even more to her.

Production

Traditionally, the rerecordings made for Taylor's Versions are produced as faithfully as possible to the original versions so that fans could recapture their initial emotions and choose, without hesitation, to listen to these new adaptations of their favorite songs or albums. Unlike the rerecording of "All Too Well," co-produced by Christopher Rowe and modeled on the version Nathan Chapman and Taylor Swift recorded in 2012, the ten-minute version, produced by Jack Antonoff, is very different from the original. The guitars are less prominent and more atmospheric, the synthesizers and keyboards play a major role, the orchestral elements border on dissonance (between 3:59 and 4:04), and Taylor Swift's backing vocals take on a dimension reminiscent of the role of the chorus in ancient Greek theater. From 7:13 onward, the arrangement begins a long decrescendo packed with musical events as evocative as they are remarkable: orchestra timpani, ghostly backing vocals, synth arpeggiators, and trumpets (akin to mariachi playing). The surge continues with distant violins and a few acoustic guitar arpeggios in successive waves. The deep synth bass and the superimposition of synthesizer layers mix with played and programmed percussion and brushes on the snare drum passed through a long delay set to sixteenth notes. The atmosphere is positively spectral.

RIDDLES AND EASTER EGGS: A TAYLOR TRADEMARK

There is one aspect of Taylor Swift's artistic and marketing universe that captivates her public as much as it intrigues those who only know her by name: the many hidden messages, or "Easter eggs," that she deploys wherever she can. Lyrics, album booklets, video clip decorations, interviews, promotional photos, outfits—nothing is ever left to chance with the star, to the delight of fans who meticulously study tracks and videos for clues relating to her forthcoming albums, current projects, or private life. On TikTok in particular, speculation and theories about the meaning of the slightest symbol, number, or color scheme abound, helping to strengthen the bonds of a community that has for many years shared a pronounced taste for investigation. Taylor Swift knows this only too well, having declared in a 2019 *Entertainment Weekly* interview that she has "trained [her fans] to be that way." And she is very happy about this: "I love that they like the cryptic hint-dropping. Because as long as they like it, I'll keep doing it."

From *Taylor Swift* to *1989*: Typographical Games

Taylor Swift's cryptic messages were born with her music. From the age of fifteen, when she was writing her first songs, the singer enjoyed slipping them into her lyrics. In the lyric booklet for her first album, *Taylor Swift*, she uses capital letters to form a code for each track. For example, in the lyrics to "Should've Said No," she reveals the name of the cheating boyfriend she knew in high school by capitalizing the letters *S*, *A*, and *M* in the lyrics ("Sam Sam Sam Sam Sam Sam"). In "Fifteen," she offers her audience an intimate anecdote by hiding the message "I cried while recording this," while in "All Too Well," she encrypts the words *maple latte*, the drink she shared with Jake Gyllenhaal on their dates in cafés in New York and Nashville. The purpose of these little riddles is to deliver to fans a personal piece of information, often revealing the identity of the person evoked in the song (when it is not their first name that is directly given). Taylor Swift reproduces this pattern of capital letters right up to her *Red* album. In the first part of the singer's career, this playfulness was an ideal way of encouraging her audience to focus on her lyrics, a central element of her music, which she confesses, in numerous interviews, to being particularly proud of.

On *1989*, she did the opposite: it was now the lowercase letters that had to be aligned to obtain a message of one or more sentences. Thus, when the album was released in 2014, all the messages placed end to end were interpreted as a summary of her relationship with singer Harry Styles, who is said to have inspired the whole album. After *1989*, Taylor Swift put an end to this tradition of coded messages in liner notes. But Swifties know they have to keep an eye on the track credits. In the technical notes of sister albums *Folklore* and *Evermore*, for example, they have the opportunity to read the name of a mysterious co-writer, William Bowery, pseudonym of the singer's then companion, British actor Joe Alwyn, with whom she would share six years of her life (fans were able to discover that Joe's great-grandfather was named William Alwyn and that the Bowery Hotel was where the couple met in 2016).

Reputation and *Lover*: Time for the Visual Clues

Reputation is perhaps the album with the most hidden messages, but it is also the one that takes them to a new dimension. Hint after hint, Taylor Swift seems to be settling scores with the personalities who led her to withdraw from public life for almost a year, breaking with her image as a romantic young woman and an expert in the art of singing about separation. This time, she uses images rather than text to get her message across. The video for "Look What You Made Me Do," which launched the album, was conceived as a treasure hunt for fans. Among the countless cryptic references it contains, the figure of the snake is symbolic of the attacks she suffered online as part of the conflict that pitted her against Kanye West and Kim Kardashian, but also of her resilience in the face of adversity; the dollar bill seen on the edge of the bathtub in which she is lying corresponds to the symbolic amount she used to sue DJ David Mueller for sexual assault; the name on the gravestone that appears in the opening seconds, Nils Sjöberg, is the pseudonym she used to co-write "This Is What You Came For" with her ex-partner, British DJ Calvin Harris (the track, performed by Rihanna, was one of the biggest hits of 2016).

Lover is no exception. The video for "ME!," the first promotional single, is also full of Easter eggs. The singer hides the name of the album, due for release several weeks later, in the form of a neon sign that says "Lover" perched on a building in the background. Similarly, she reveals the name of the next single, "You Need to Calm Down," when Brendon Urie says the line "Calme-toi, s'il te plait," essentially a translation of the phrase in a French-language scene.

With *Folklore*, New Types of Games

Social networks remain the medium Taylor Swift seems to cherish most when it comes to concocting real puzzles. On Instagram, her favorite playground, she no longer hesitates to take on the role of gamemaster. In 2021, she unveiled Taylor's Version of *Fearless* in a video featuring anagrams of the album's From the Vault tracks. Among her other most notable enigmas is the famous black-and-white photo where she poses on a sofa in what appears to be a cabin or cottage. Posted during the pandemic, when the whole world saw itself locked down, its caption—"Not a lot going on at the moment"—did not arouse the Swifties' suspicions. And yet, three months later, in July 2020, she announced the release of *Folklore*, taking her fans and the music industry by surprise. Just four months after the release of this eighth album, she did it again with a photo bearing the same caption. This time, it was a way of hinting at the even more surprising release of *Evermore*, her ninth studio album, in December 2020.

With *Midnights* and *The Tortured Poets Department*, Taylor Swift continues to play by her own rules. She still managed to catch the public off guard when announcing the release of the former at the MTV Video Music Awards 2022, when everyone expected the release of a new Taylor's Version. In the two months leading up to its release, she also slips the word *midnight* several times, in an innocuous way, into posts when the video clip for "Anti-Hero," the album's first promotional single, is obviously riddled with cryptic references. Finally, she chose the "Bejeweled" clip to announce the forthcoming release of *Speak Now (Taylor's Version)* by pressing the purple button on an elevator to go up to the third floor—*Speak Now* was her third album, and purple is its dominant color.

Taylor Swift's passion for cryptic messages shows no signs of abating. To promote *The Tortured Poets Department—TTPD* for short—she went so far as to set up an ephemeral library in Los Angeles, scattered with clues to the album's titles and lyrics. Fans could visit the library—provided they were not afraid to stand in line to investigate. This is what it means to be a Taylor Swift fan: always carrying a magnifying glass.

RELEASE DATES
United States: October 27, 2014
(ref.: Big Machine Records—BMRBD0500A)
***Deluxe Edition: October 27, 2014**
(ref.: Big Machine Records—BMRBD0550A)
Best Ranking: 1

ALBUM

1989

Welcome to New York · Blank Space · Style · Out of the Woods · All You Had to Do Was Stay · Shake It Off · I Wish You Would · Bad Blood · Wildest Dreams · How You Get the Girl · This Love · I Know Places · Clean · Wonderland* · You Are in Love* · New Romantics*

At the 2014 American Music Awards, Taylor Swift is voted Artist of the Year and performs "Blank Space."

A commercial for Diet Coke, released before the official release of the *1989* album, uses an extract from "How You Get the Girl." Taylor Swift humorously introduces her cat, Olivia Benson (named after the detective in the TV series *Law & Order: Special Victims Unit*), as the star of the video.

POWER AND INDEPENDENCE

With the eclectic *Red*, Taylor Swift had jumped into the pop genre with both feet. With *1989*, she dives in even more boldly, and headfirst. Written in 2013, during the "Red Tour," the album leaves no room for doubt or debate: The star is no longer a country artist, the genre that was so decisive in her career. This radical change of direction is the result of the failed experiment of her previous album. Nominated for Album of the Year at the 2014 Grammy Awards, *Red*, which blended several styles, failed to win the prize. In *1989*, she fully embraces the electro-pop she had already tried her hand at in 2012 with "We Are Never Ever Getting Back Together" and "I Knew You Were Trouble," and goes in a new direction by drawing inspiration from the synthpop that made the 1980s so great. The album's name, *1989*—the year of Taylor Swift's birth, to be understood also as the year of her artistic renaissance—sets the new opus squarely in that era. This was the first Taylor Swift album not to be promoted on country radio at the time of its release.

Taylor Swift called back the successful producers and songwriters Max Martin and Shellback, who had proved the effectiveness of their electro-pop sound on *Red*, and hired them this time as main producers. As for Nathan Chapman, he now seemed to belong to that bygone country era. Although he contributed his own touch to *1989*, he never worked on a Taylor Swift album again. This was also the very first album to feature Jack Antonoff, who was to become the singer's most loyal collaborator, assuming the role of main producer on all subsequent albums. He co-wrote and co-produced two tracks on this album, "Out of the Woods" and "I Wish You Would." Ryan Tedder, leader of the pop-rock band OneRepublic, contributed to "Welcome to New York" and "I Know Places," while British singer Imogen Heap co-wrote the final track, "Clean."

Empowerment

Gone are the acoustic elements of previous albums: *1989* is a grand symphony of electronic instruments, including vintage and contemporary synths, drum machines, and backing vocals generously adorned with effects. Lyrically, Taylor Swift continues her reflections on relationships, both current and past, and adds a relatively fresh dose of self-mockery. In "Blank Space," for example, she ironizes her multiple conquests ("Got a long list of ex-lovers / They'll tell you I'm insane / But I've got a blank space, baby / And I'll write your name"), a fact that the press has not failed to pick up on, not always in a benevolent way. Some commentators have accused her of having affairs

In September 2015, Taylor Swift's world tour fleet of trucks arrives in Houston, Texas.

In the United States alone, the "1989 Tour" grossed $181.5 million, making it the most lucrative tour ever by a woman. This record was broken in 2018 by Taylor herself, with the "Reputation Stadium Tour."

with celebrities for the sole purpose of drawing inspiration for catchy songs. There is also in *1989*, more than in any other album, a joyful feminism, a kind of celebration of freedom and independence. Taylor Swift shows herself to be a resilient and, above all, self-assured twenty-five-year-old, who does not care about the many criticisms to which her celebrity status constantly exposes her ("And the haters gonna hate, hate, hate, hate, hate / Baby, I'm just gonna shake, shake, shake, shake, shake"). A personal event also seems to have helped her gain mental strength: the purchase of a double penthouse in New York's Tribeca district, a city that had long intimidated her and to which she dedicates the album's first track, "Welcome to New York." Opening the album with this song is significant. Her move from Nashville (although Taylor Swift retains her apartment there as a pied-à-terre), the capital of country music, to the electric metropolis can also be construed as a metaphor for her artistic turnaround.

A Mammoth Promotion

With Big Machine Records, Taylor Swift put together a massive marketing plan for *1989*. She made more public appearances than ever before in the weeks leading up to and following the album's release, appearing on magazine covers, TV shows, and award ceremonies. She even went so far as to broadcast a message in the sky by plane over Central Park—"Taylor Swift 8/18 5 p.m. Yahoo"—to announce the livestream where she revealed the album title and unveiled the single "Shake It Off." The livestream took place from the top of the Empire State Building! For the first time, Taylor Swift also decided not to appear from head to toe on the album cover. She appears, truncated at eye level, in an intriguing Polaroid shot scrawled on with a felt-tip marker. She explained in an interview in *Amateur Photographer* that, like her eyes, the overall tone of the album retained an air of mystery. With its retro aesthetic, already in its heyday in 2014, the cover of *1989* would become the most emblematic of her entire discography and would be ranked by *Billboard* in 2022 among the 50 greatest album covers of all time. Taylor Swift did not stop there. To create the collector's effect, she slipped a series of 13 other shots of herself into each copy of the album—with 5 five different sets being randomly distributed. In all, 65 different snapshots are in circulation, which is sure to arouse the envy of fans. Taylor Swift also launched a new concept with this album designed to strengthen the commitment and loyalty of her fans. She organized several private listening sessions of the album—the "*1989* Secret Sessions"—for a handful of fans in reward for their high level of engagement on her social networks. The singer

The *1989* world tour showcases Taylor Swift's retro style, with looks inspired by the 1980s: sequined jackets, glittering outfits, and vintage sunglasses.

invited them directly, in small groups, to her various American properties and in London throughout September 2014. Ultra-popular for their unique and intimate nature, these Secret Sessions were to be repeated before the release of her next two albums, *Reputation* and *Lover*.

Raining Records

While several tracks, such as "Out of the Woods" and "Welcome to New York," were chosen as promotional singles, almost all the tracks on *1989* became not only hits, but also the artist's biggest successes. However, in the days leading up to the album's release, music industry professionals—at a time heavily impacted by the rise of free streaming platforms—were predicting lower sales figures than for previous albums. Taylor Swift quickly proved them wrong: In the first week after its release, *1989* sold nearly 1.3 million copies, almost double the low estimates. She became the first artist to sell three albums in excess of a million copies in the first week, and *1989* was the first album of 2014 to surpass this famous million mark. It remained at the top of the Billboard 200 for eleven consecutive weeks and occupied the top 10 for a full year. The album set so many records that we can only keep in mind one of them: In 2019, with 6.215 million copies sold worldwide, it became the third-best-selling album of the decade in the United States. Ahead of it are Adele's *21* and *25*, which sold around 12 and 9.5 million copies, respectively. However, according to *Billboard*, in 2023, nine years after *1989*'s release, the music data analysis company Luminate updated its figures and estimated that the album had now sold 12.3 million units, taking it to the top of Taylor Swift's discography from a commercial point of view, and surpassing *Fearless*, with its 12 million copies sold.

Open Warfare Against Streaming Platforms

The *1989* era begins Taylor Swift's assumption of power. On November 3, 2014, just a few days after the album's release, the singer decided to withdraw her entire music catalog from Spotify. According to her, the platform did not sufficiently remunerate authors, composers, performers, and producers for their work, and conveyed a consumption model that was worrying for the future of the music market. Spotify, which at the time was still largely communicating its free offer to attract new users (in return for ad breaks between tracks), notably failed to compensate artists for listens within the first three months of its offer. In the summer of 2014, Taylor Swift had already voiced her concerns in an op-ed published in the columns of the *Wall Street Journal*: "The value of an album is, and will continue to be, based on the amount

2014

Taylor Swift in Manhattan, May 2015.

Taylor Swift sweeps the 2016 Grammy Awards, winning Album of the Year and Best Pop Album for *1989* and Best Music Video for "Bad Blood."

FOR DISCERNING SWIFTIES

The term *poptimism* was coined in critical and cultural circles in the early 2000s to describe a benevolent and inclusive attitude toward pop music, often neglected or denigrated in favor of other genres.

of heart and soul an artist has bled into a body of work, and the financial value that artists (and their labels) place on their music when it goes out into the marketplace," she wrote. Her decision to remove her music from Spotify was such a thunderclap that the company's CEO, Daniel Ek, made several trips to Nashville to meet the singer and convince her to return to the platform. She would not return to it until June 2017. In June 2015, she addressed an open letter directly to Apple and its boss, Tim Cook, whose music-dedicated streaming service had just been launched. In her missive, she deplored, once again, the lack of remuneration for artists during users' free trial period. Apple Music immediately backpedaled, anxious not to upset the great Taylor Swift. In a response letter, Apple announced that the company would pay artists during the free trial period after all.

An Underlying Darkness

1989 may have been one of her most powerful, glorious, and "poptimist" albums, but it was also the one that led the singer through a difficult phase on a personal level. Constantly hounded by the paparazzi and scrutinized by the media, she did not allow herself any slack and began to suffer in silence over her body image. In the documentary *Miss Americana* (2020), she talks about the serious eating disorders she suffered during this period.

On February 15, 2016, *1989* won her three major Grammy Awards: Album of the Year, Best Pop Vocal Album, and Best Music Video for "Bad Blood." She became the first female solo artist to win Album of the Year twice—her revenge after the disappointment of *Red*. But that evening, she was still unaware that she was about to experience the worst year of her career.

Taylor appears on *Good Morning America* in Times Square, October 30, 2014.

2014

FOR DISCERNING SWIFTIES

"Welcome to New York" and "Shake It Off" (performed by Reese Witherspoon and Nick Kroll) were used, respectively, for the soundtracks of the films *The Secret Life of Pets* (2016) and *Sing* (2016). "Ready for It" and "Look What You Made Me Do," derived from *Reputation* (2017), are also included in the soundtrack of *Sing 2* (2021).

WELCOME TO NEW YORK

Taylor Swift, Ryan Tedder / 3:32

Musicians
Taylor Swift: vocals
Noel Zancanella: synthesizers, drum programming
Ryan Tedder: piano, synthesizers [Juno], backing vocals

Recorded
Conway Recording (Los Angeles), 2014

Technical Team
Producers: Taylor Swift, Noel Zancanella, Ryan Tedder
Mixing: Serban Ghenea
Sound Engineers: John Hanes, Ryan Tedder, Smith Carlson
Mastering: Tom Coyne

Genesis

To open *1989*, her first 100 percent pop album, Taylor Swift chose the song "Welcome to New York," her declaration of love for the Big Apple. She had been dreaming of moving there for several years, attracted by the energy and sense of creative bubbling that emanate from this multicultural hothouse. In 2014, she officially became a New Yorker, free as a bird and ready to take on new challenges. This song can be seen as the final piece in a trilogy inaugurated in 2006 with "A Place in This World" on her first album (her tribute to Nashville, her adopted hometown at the time), followed by "Mean," on *Speak Now* (2010), in which she expresses her wish to live in a good old-fashioned metropolis ("Someday, I'll be livin' in a big ole city"). Growing up on a farm in Pennsylvania, her three successive moves were decisive

steps in her rise to success. In addition, the lines "And you can want who you want / Boys and boys and girls and girls" were seen as a gesture of support for the LGBTQIA+ community.

Production

Taylor Swift called on Ryan Tedder, producer and prolific songwriter, as well as lead singer of American pop rock band OneRepublic, to co-write and co-produce "Welcome to New York." In response to the singer's request to recapture elements of the 1980s sound, Ryan Tedder decided to acquire an iconic synthesizer of the era: the Juno 106. The effect is immediate: From the very first chords, the listener is plunged into eighties pop music. On the intro, the claps and bass drum of the rudimentary Roland TR-808 or Linn Drum LM-1 drum machine accentuate this nostalgic effect. Noel Zancanella, a producer who has collaborated with OneRepublic, Maroon 5, and Colbie Caillat, adds the modern touch. From the very first chorus, the sound thickens: The richness of the bass and the grain of the synth bass, the compression of the synthesizer layer in sidechain with the bass drum, the sophistication of the programming, the dry cuts, the drops, and the treatment of the vocals and backing vocals indicate that this is indeed a synthpop production from the 2010s. "It's a new soundtrack / I could dance to this beat," proclaims Taylor Swift in the choruses.

Hidden Message

We begin our story in New York.

In "Blank Space," about chaotic romantic relationships, Taylor Swift embodies the bad girl. Seen here at the Golden Globe Awards.

SINGLE

BLANK SPACE

Taylor Swift, Max Martin, Shellback / 3:51

Musicians
Taylor Swift: vocals
Shellback: acoustic and electric guitars, bass, keyboards, programming, percussion, sounds [stomps], voices [shouts]
Max Martin: keyboards, programming

Recorded
MXM (Stockholm), Conway Recording (Los Angeles), 2014

Technical Team
Producers: Max Martin, Shellback
Mixing: Serban Ghenea
Sound Engineers: John Hanes, Michael Ilbert, Sam Holland
Mastering: Tom Coyne

Single Release
Digital Release: November 10, 2014
Best Rankings: Hot 100: 1; Mainstream Top 40: 1; Adult Pop Airplay: 1

Genesis

In "Blank Space," Taylor Swift has fun donning the "serial dater" costume created from scratch by a certain fringe of the celebrity press. Tired of being caricatured as a vindictive man-eater, she fully embraces this glamorous predatory persona, the exact opposite of her real-life personality and behavior. This is a thumbing of the nose at the media, which she will become an expert at doing, through both playfulness and an instinct for media survival.

Production

Taylor Swift reunites with her comrades Max Martin and Shellback, already involved in *Red*, to produce this jewel of electro-pop at the cutting edge of mainstream music in the 2010s. "Blank Space" begins with two bars of minimalist drum machine, accompanied by a three-note musical gimmick (*C / F / A / F*), played ostinato. The harmonic percussion sound used is reminiscent of a marimba (probably modeled using a synthesizer or simply taken from a sampler) and becomes the track's main instrumental gimmick. Set to a tempo of 96 bpm, the arrangement gradually fleshes out, right from the entrance of the vocals. The bass drum rolls out its bouncing pattern, and the chord progression, revealed by a lo-fi organ sound, remains the same throughout: *F / D* minor (7) / *B* flat / *C*. The programmed percussion intensifies, the grainy bass synth broadens the sound spectrum, and the acoustic guitar strumming plays both a rhythmic and textural role. The multiple effects of stomps (percussive sounds, often struck with the foot), played then sampled and programmed by Shellback, contribute to diversifying the relaunches and creating this particular atmosphere, where the icy splendor of synthesizer layers rubs shoulders with the roughness of urban music and the fascination of a tribal pulsation. It is easy to imagine Taylor Swift as a glamorous Amazon, just like the exuberant seductress she portrays in the video directed by Joseph Kahn.

Hidden Message

There once was a girl known by everyone and no one.

With its bewitching rhythms and sensual atmosphere, "Style" captures the intensity of a passionate relationship.

During the late 1970s and early 1980s, three great electronic-music pioneers marked the musical and cinematographic landscape with their compositions. They are Vangelis, John Carpenter, and Giorgio Moroder.

2014

SINGLE

STYLE

Taylor Swift, Max Martin, Shellback, Ali Payami / 3:51

Musicians
Taylor Swift: vocals
Shellback: acoustic and electric guitars, bass, keyboards, programming, percussion, sounds [stomps], voice [shouts]
Niklas Ljungfelt: guitar
Max Martin, Ali Payami: keyboards, programming

Recorded
MXM (Stockholm), Conway Recording (Los Angeles), 2014

Technical Team
Producers: Taylor Swift, Max Martin, Shellback, Ali Payami
Mixing: Serban Ghenea
Sound Engineers: John Hanes, Michael Ilbert, Sam Holland
Mastering: Tom Coyne

Single Release
Digital Release: February 9, 2015
Best Rankings: Hot 100: 6; Mainstream Top 40: 1

ON YOUR HEADPHONES

In electronic music, certain sounds in the riser category play according to the principle of the infinite scale. This is an auditory illusion based on the repetition of the same sound motif, which initiates the sensation of an infinite ascending scale. However, if you listen carefully, the illusion is perceptible.

Genesis

In "Style," Taylor Swift portrays an unstable and addictive relationship motivated primarily by a shared physical attraction. Several clues seem to indicate that the singer is describing, at least in part, her romance with Harry Styles: the disjointed nature of the relationship, the appearance of the "paper airplane" pendant in the video (Taylor and Styles wore the same one during their relationship), and the title of the track, which can be interpreted as a reference to the ex–One Direction singer's surname. "Style" and "Shake It Off" were the last two songs written for the *1989* album.

Production

Iranian-born Swedish producer Ali Payami, whose credits include the Weeknd, Demi Lovato, Ariana Grande, and Katy Perry, lends a hand to the trio of Swift, Martin, and Shellback on this lush synthpop track. Inspired by the synthwave that emerged in the early 2010s with the likes of Kavinsky, Com Truise, and Daft Punk, Taylor Swift and her team take full advantage of the analog charm of vintage machines such as the Roland Juno-6 and Jupiter-8, Yamaha DX7, and Memorymoog. The listener is immersed in a deluge of oscillators: fluctuating arpeggiators, icy strings, and risers, all carried by a grainy-sounding bass sequence compressed in sidechain on the bass drum played on the quarter notes, disco-style. The ultra-compressed electric guitar chops played by Shellback creates the link between the drum machine programming (such as Roland TR-707 or LinnDrum) and the synthesizers.

Hidden Message

Her heart belonged to someone who couldn't stay.

At the 2016 Grammy Awards, Taylor Swift performs "Out of the Woods," emphasizing vocal emotion over dance.

FOR DISCERNING SWIFTIES

In an interview with *Rolling Stone* magazine in 2021, Jack Antonoff says he put his heart and soul into producing the track. A tribute to Taylor Swift, who was the first artist to give him his chance as a producer.

2014

SINGLE

OUT OF THE WOODS

Taylor Swift, Jack Antonoff / 3:55

Musicians
Taylor Swift: vocals
Jack Antonoff: acoustic and electric guitars, bass, keyboards, drums, backing vocals, programming

Recorded
Conway Recording (Los Angeles), Jungle City (New York), 2014

Technical Team
Producers: Taylor Swift, Jack Antonoff, Max Martin
Mixing: Serban Ghenea
Sound Engineers: John Hanes, Sam Holland, Laura Sisk
Mastering: Tom Coyne

Single Release
Digital Release and CD Single Promo (for radio): October 14, 2014

Genesis

Co-written with Jack Antonoff, "Out of the Woods" invokes the mixed feelings of excitement and constant anxiety that can be experienced during a tumultuous relationship, under the almost omnipresent gaze of the media. In it, Taylor Swift talks openly about the fragility of her relationship with Harry Styles, and wonders whether her relationship will be able to overcome the hurdle of fame or truly move on. How does one recover from a breakup announced live to the world? When she mentions their snowmobile accident—serious enough to land them in hospital—it is to express the tragic aspect of their story. Yet the famous "paper airplane" pendant resurfaces as a testament to the sincerity of their love. Taylor Swift knew the relationship was doomed, but she has no regrets.

Production

Taylor Swift knew Jack Antonoff's penchant for 1980s sounds, having collaborated with him on the song "Sweeter than Fiction," written especially for the soundtrack of the 2013 film *One Chance*. It was only natural that she turned to him, along with Max Martin, to produce the track "Out of the Woods." Indeed, the tone of *1989* is established and the guidelines clear: a course set for flamboyant, uninhibited synthpop. Arpeggiators, Yamaha DX7 strings, and risers hover over the abundantly distorted bass sequence, and the Minimoog Voyager adds its modern touch to the choruses. All drum machines aside, Jack Antonoff massively edits his backing vocals and those of Taylor Swift for a heady result, echoing the programmed percussion. A few acoustic guitar arpeggios discreetly color the verses, as if to illuminate the lulls before the electronic storm returns. The electric guitar performs a few neck effects bursting with chorus and delays to add to the sense of urgency that emanates from this intense, colorful orchestration. Max Martin handles the production of the lead vocals, a crucial step in enabling Serban Ghenea to enhance Taylor Swift's performance in the mix. "Out of the Woods" is one of Taylor Swift's favorite tracks on the album as a whole, as she feels it best represents the spirit of *1989*.

Hidden Message

They loved each other recklessly.

Taylor Swift's 2015 concert at the Mercedes-Benz Arena in Shanghai, China, features futuristic sets of LED screens, dynamic projections, and other lighting effects.

ALL YOU HAD TO DO WAS STAY

Taylor Swift, Max Martin / 3:13

Musicians
Taylor Swift: vocals
Mattman & Robin: drums, bass, guitar, keyboards, percussion
Shellback: guitar, keyboards, programming
Max Martin: keyboards, programming

Recorded
MXM (Stockholm), Conway Recording (Los Angeles), 2014

Technical Team
Producers: Mattman & Robin, Max Martin, Shellback
Mixing: Serban Ghenea
Sound Engineers: John Hanes, Sam Holland
Mastering: Tom Coyne

Genesis

In an interview with *Time* magazine in November 2014, Taylor Swift explained that the idea for this song came to her in a dream that was as strange as it was uncomfortable: As her ex-boyfriend rang her doorbell, she couldn't help but sing, as she opened the door, "Stay!" at the top of her lungs, in a high-pitched, almost operatic voice, instead of listening to what he might have had to say. "All You Had to Do Was Stay" is no exception to the Swiftian tradition of placing the album's saddest, most cathartic song at number five. Originally written as a piano-vocal ballad, it was one of the first songs Taylor Swift and Max Martin composed for *1989*.

Production

Taylor Swift enlisted the help of Swedish synthpop duo Mattman & Robin, producers and songwriters, to support her loyal Shellback and Max Martin. "All You Had to Do Was Stay" fits perfectly into the artistic line of *1989*. It features the same elements as "Out of the Woods" and "Style": drum machine programming, a pulsating sidechain bass synth sequence, and a festival of analog synthesizers. The moderate tempo of this arrangement is typical of the synthpop style, itself derived from disco music ("Out of the Woods": 92 bpm; "Style": 95 bpm; and "All You Had to Do Was Stay": 97 bpm). However, even though it blends perfectly between the programmed percussion and synthesizer sequences, the acoustic guitar strumming plays a more important rhythmic role than in most of the album's productions. Like all the songs selected for *1989*, "All You Had to Do Was Stay" could easily have become a single.

Hidden Message

They paid the price.

During the iHeartRadio Music Festival in Las Vegas, September 2014.

"Shake It Off," the big hit from *1989*, invites listeners to disregard the critics and free themselves from judgment.

SINGLE

SHAKE IT OFF

Taylor Swift, Max Martin, Shellback / 3:39

2014

Musicians
Taylor Swift: vocals, backing vocals, claps, voice [shouts]
Shellback: acoustic and bass guitars, keyboards, drums, programming, percussion, backing vocals, claps, voice [shouts]
Max Martin: keyboards, programming, backing vocals, claps, voice [shouts]
Jonas Thander: saxophone
Magnus Wiklund: trombone
Jonas Lindeborg: trumpet

Recorded
MXM (Stockholm), Conway Recording (Los Angeles), 2014

Technical Team
Producers: Max Martin, Shellback
Mixing: Serban Ghenea
Sound Engineers: John Hanes, Michael Ilbert, Sam Holland
Mastering: Tom Coyne

Single Release
Digital Release: August 19, 2014
Best Rankings: Hot 100: 1; Mainstream Top 40: 1; Adult Pop Airplay: 1

Genesis

In "Mean," released in 2010 on the *Speak Now* album, Taylor Swift had already dealt with the trials and tribulations of celebrity, and for the first time assumed the position of victim. Now, in October 2014, during a discussion about her new album on US radio station network NPR, she explained that "Shake It Off" marked a turning point in the way she deals with attacks from certain journalists, and haters in general. Taylor Swift, who has gained in maturity, refuses to let her feelings get the better of her, and now knows how to respond to her detractors with humor. Criticism is inevitable, and while she may not be able to control rumors, she has learned to control her reactions. The popular adage "Haters gonna hate," which was inscribed on the T-shirt she wore during her performance at the 2013 Billboard Music Awards, became her new motto. "Shake It Off" remains one of Taylor Swift's biggest commercial successes to date.

Production

"Shake It Off" begins with a drum and clap pattern whose heady groove is reminiscent of hip-hop group Outkast's hit "Hey Ya!" (2003). The rhythmic pattern, tempo (159 bpm for "Hey Ya!" and 160 bpm for "Shake It Off") and sound treatment are very similar indeed. The dynamic arrangement of "Shake It Off" is based on two main elements: the unstoppable beat created by Shellback and the syncopated playing of the brass trio (saxophone, trumpet, trombone). From 2:18 to 2:42, in a caustic tone halfway between the girl-power energy of the Spice Girls and a more modern flow, Taylor Swift delivers the first spoken-word verse of her career. The bass only enters on the first chorus, where the sustained notes of the brass section finally reveal the track's (already largely suggested) harmony. From start to finish, the chord progression *A* minor / *C* / *G* x 2 remains unchanged. A cascade of backing vocals fleshes out the choruses: counterpoint melodies, harmonies mingling with the brass, interjections, echoed responses to the lead vocals...The listener is not short of stimuli. "Shake It Off" is minimalist in every respect, but fiendishly effective.

Hidden Message

She danced to forget him.

Taylor Swift performing on *Good Morning America*, October 30, 2014.

2014

I WISH YOU WOULD

Taylor Swift, Jack Antonoff / 3:27

Musicians
Taylor Swift: vocals
Jack Antonoff: acoustic and electric guitars, bass, keyboards, drums, backing vocals, programming
Greg Kurstin: keyboards

Recorded
Conway Recording (Los Angeles), Lamby's House Studios (Brooklyn, NY), 2014

Technical Team
Producers: Taylor Swift, Jack Antonoff, Max Martin, Greg Kurstin
Mixing: Serban Ghenea
Sound Engineers: John Hanes, Sam Holland, Jack Antonoff
Mastering: Tom Coyne

Genesis

"I Wish You Would" is the first song Taylor Swift co-wrote with her friend Jack Antonoff. Its origins date back to 2012, when Antonoff created his instrumental part alone at his parents' home in New Jersey. Proud of the result, the musician decided to play his creation for Taylor Swift, who immediately recognized the arrangement's potential. The singer asked if she could make it her own. Antonoff agreed and sent her the track, which she listened to at length on her laptop (despite being in the middle of a tour), recording her vocal ideas on her phone. For the text, Taylor Swift drew inspiration from John Hughes films—depictions of suburban teenagers and their passage to adulthood—which she watched over and over again during her first months in New York, where she felt serene because she was single, but full of new creative energy. In the song, she talks about her relationship with Harry Styles, who bought a house on a street adjacent to hers shortly after they broke up. After becoming friends—the first time that Taylor Swift managed to create a bond of friendship with one of her ex-boyfriends—Styles confesses that he has often passed down her street behind the wheel of his car, and that each time he felt like stopping and ringing her doorbell. But thinking she hated him, he never dared. Taylor Swift, on the other hand, was just waiting for him to do exactly that.

Production

Present right from the intro, the electric guitar duo, played like a chop by Jack Antonoff, is the backbone of the arrangement. The compressed sound passes through a short delay set to the sixteenth note. The effect is reminiscent of the rhythmic vivacity of U2 guitarist The Edge. The rhythm of the drums and programmed percussion seems to split into two on the chorus, with the bass drum syncopated and the snare drum played only on the third beat of each bar. The resulting sound is massive, producing a feeling of openness and orchestral power that contrasts with

the driving linearity of the verses. Greg Kurstin supports Antonoff's keyboards and programming with a sequence of bass synths, swirling arpeggiators, shimmering synthesizer leads and layers, and an explosive mix of drum machine and acoustic drums. Bordering on overkill, the superimposition of backing vocal tracks and the highly reverberated treatment of the lead vocals help to establish the modern synthpop and dance aesthetic so dear to Max Martin.

Hidden Message

He drove past her street every night.

A remix version of "Bad Blood" was released on May 17, 2015 with rapper Kendrick Lamar.

2014

SINGLE

BAD BLOOD

Taylor Swift, Max Martin, Shellback / 3:31

Musicians
Taylor Swift: vocals
Shellback: acoustic guitar, bass, keyboards, programming, percussion, sounds [body percussion effects, stomps, sound effects], backing vocals
Max Martin: piano, keyboards, programming
Ilya Salmanzadeh: backing vocals, programming (remix version)

Recorded
MXM (Stockholm), Conway Recording (Los Angeles), 2014
Best Rankings: Hot 100: 1; Mainstream Top 40: 1; Adult Pop Airplay: 1

Technical Team
Producers: Taylor Swift, Max Martin, Shellback, Ilya Salmanzadeh (remix version)
Mixing: Serban Ghenea
Sound Engineers: John Hanes, Michael Ilbert, Sam Holland, Peter Carlsson
Mastering: Tom Coyne

Single Release
Digital Release, remix version "Bad Blood" (feat. Kendrick Lamar): May 17, 2015

Genesis

"Bad Blood" denounces friendly betrayal, a painful subject. Shortly after the track's release and due to persistent rumors, the song was quickly associated with singer Katy Perry, who allegedly had no hesitation in poaching three dancers from Taylor Swift, who was then in the middle of a tour. In reality, the story is not so simple, and the two rivals made peace in 2018, when Katy Perry sent an olive branch to Taylor Swift to wish her good luck on the opening day of the "Reputation Stadium Tour" and to symbolize their reconciliation.

Subsequently, the two singers were seen together in the clip for "You Need to Calm Down," shot in 2019. Taylor Swift appears in a French fry cone costume and Katy Perry as a hamburger. The remix version of "Bad Blood" featuring special guest rapper Kendrick Lamar was released on May 17, 2015, as the fourth single of the *1989* era. This version is co-produced by Ilya Salmanzadeh, a Swedish producer, songwriter, and singer who has collaborated with Ariana Grande and Jennifer Lopez, among others.

Production

The arrangement begins with a chorus sung a capella in unison by an army of Taylor Swifts. The chanted, almost warlike tone sets the mood. With its martial groove and simulated tribal air, the percussion ensemble played and programmed by Shellback perfectly underscores the theme. Slightly less retro than on the rest of the album, the synthesizers are not to be outdone: rumbling synth bass, airy arpeggiators, weightless strings and risers. Tambourine and eighth-note acoustic guitar strumming create the rhythmic and harmonic link between vocals and massive percussion. "Bad Blood" benefits from stadium-caliber production.

In the "Bad Blood" version featuring Kendrick Lamar—the remix chosen for release as a single—producer Ilya Salmanzadeh and artist Kendrick Lamar enhance the arrangement with Roland TR-808-style elements of trap and hip-hop: high hat, and clap sounds with fluctuating timing; high-pitched, blistering snare, shifting bass, and resonant kick drum. Lamar lays down his vocals on two self-penned verses, intervenes on the bridge, and infuses the final ad lib of the chorus with hip-hop interjections.

Hidden Message

She made friends and enemies.

The onstage props used during the performance of "Wildest Dreams" symbolize Taylor Swift's memories and the golden age of cinema.

2014

SINGLE

WILDEST DREAMS

Taylor Swift, Max Martin, Shellback / 3:40

Musicians
Taylor Swift: vocals, sounds [heartbeat]
Shellback: acoustic and electric guitars, percussion, keyboards, programming
Max Martin: piano, keyboards, programming
Mattias Bylund: strings arrangement

Recorded
MXM (Stockholm), Conway Recording (Los Angeles), 2014

Technical Team
Producers: Taylor Swift, Max Martin, Shellback
Mixing: Serban Ghenea
Sound Engineers: John Hanes, Michael Ilbert, Sam Holland, Peter Carlsson, Mattias Bylund
Mastering: Tom Coyne

Single Release
Digital Release: August 31, 2015
Digital Release, remix by R3hab: October 15, 2015
Best Rankings: Hot 100: 5; Mainstream Top 40: 1; Adult Pop Airplay: 1

Genesis

In "Wildest Dreams," Taylor Swift describes a budding love affair whose end she already predicts. An idealist by nature, she has always invested a great deal in her relationships, but experience and the accumulation of disillusionment have changed her vision of love. Today, she knows that you have to live in the moment to engrave the best moments in your memory.

Production

The arrangement of "Wildest Dreams" begins with an authentic recording of a series of Taylor Swift's heartbeats. Edited to create a rhythmic loop, the sequence is laid over an icy, sophisticated synthesizer layer. The three chords exposed in the intro remain the same for the verses and are repeated in a different order for the choruses (to which a single resolution chord is added: *C#*). Couplets: *F* minor / *A♭* / *E♭*. Refrains: *A♭* / *E♭* / *F#* minor / *C#*. Max Martin is no stranger to compositional tricks of this kind, which keep the listener in an optimum state of auditory comfort. The song modulates, and the transition to the chorus makes itself felt, but the tonal change is barely perceptible, and the harmonic atmosphere is preserved from start to finish. The orchestration is based on the same principle of subtle evolution, using Mattias Bylund's staccato string arrangement, the textural contribution of synthesizers, and percussion that gradually reinforces the singer's heartbeat. Taylor Swift's performance spans exactly two octaves. In perfect harmony with the varying intensity of the orchestration, her voice moves from the nonchalant low midrange at the start of the verses, to the high midrange for a more energetic, resonant vocal on the choruses.

Hidden Message

He only saw her in his dreams.

In Taylor Swift's repertoire, it is often the young girl who is waiting for love or struggling to win it. This is not the case in "How You Get the Girl."

2014

HOW YOU GET THE GIRL

Taylor Swift, Max Martin, Shellback / 4:07

Musicians
Taylor Swift: vocals, backing vocals
Shellback: acoustic guitar, bass, drums, keyboards, programming
Max Martin: keyboards, programming

Recorded
MXM (Stockholm), Conway Recording (Los Angeles), 2014

Technical Team
Producers: Max Martin, Shellback
Mixing: Serban Ghenea
Sound Engineers: John Hanes, Michael Ilbert, Sam Holland
Mastering: Tom Coyne

Genesis

"How You Get the Girl" is a veritable tutorial, showing step by step what a man must do to get back the girl he let down for six months, before he feels her absence and realizes he must make amends. Everything is there, listed point by point. This is Taylor Swift's gift to anyone who wants to make amends the hard way—the only hope of regaining a place in their loved one's heart.

Production

Vocals edited in a modern pop dance style and three acoustic guitar chords dropped: This is all it takes to introduce this very upbeat production by Shellback and Max Martin. Over a 120 bpm tempo, the arrangement evolves over a 100 percent major chord progression (*F / C / B♭* x 2), which lasts right to the end of the track. Played by Shellback, the sixteenth-note strumming of the acoustic guitar energizes the programmed drums and percussion. The resolutely modern use of synthesizers plays a slightly more anecdotal role than on other *1989* productions, especially on the verses, but gives the choruses their full scope. Taylor Swift's lead and backing vocals complement and reinforce each other in a joyful, disciplined, and skillfully composed chorus.

Hidden Message

Then one day, he came back.

THIS LOVE

Taylor Swift / 4:10

Musicians
Taylor Swift: vocals, acoustic guitar, backing vocals
Nathan Chapman: electric guitar, bass, drums, keyboards

Recorded
Pain in the Art (Nashville), 2014

Technical Team
Producers: Nathan Chapman, Taylor Swift
Mixing: Serban Ghenea
Sound Engineers: John Hanes, Nathan Chapman
Mastering: Tom Coyne

Genesis

The chorus of "This Love" comes from a short poem Taylor Swift wrote on the fly in her diary in October 2012. It did not take long for these few lines to turn into a melody and a song in their own right. In this track, Taylor Swift takes a tender and yet detached look at the complexity of love relationships, the duality and cyclical aspect inherent in human feelings. It is the only song on *1989* that Taylor Swift composed entirely on her own.

Production

"This Love" marks the unexpected return of longtime collaborator Nathan Chapman. It is the only track he co-produced with Taylor Swift on this album. It is also the album's most atmospheric track. Taylor Swift plays acoustic guitar herself, and Chapman, as usual, records and plays all the other instruments. In keeping with the aesthetic of *1989*, Taylor Swift does not hesitate to set the tone: synthesizers in the foreground, guitars in the background. This does not frighten Chapman, who does nevertheless have to step out of his comfort zone. The meditative quality of the arrangement rests essentially on the synthesizer layers and sequences, Taylor Swift's restrained interpretation, and the mantra-like text of the chorus. The drums, distant and reverberant, only make their entrance in the second third of the track. To suit the spirit of the album, Chapman's straight, mechanical playing sounds like drum machine programming.

Hidden Message

Timing is a funny thing.

Ryan Tedder, musician and songwriter, who co-wrote "I Know Places."

I KNOW PLACES

Taylor Swift, Ryan Tedder / 3:15

Musicians
Taylor Swift: vocals
Ryan Tedder: acoustic and electric guitars, piano, backing vocals, synthesizers, programming
Noel Zancanella: bass, synthesizers, programming

Recorded
Conway Recording (Los Angeles), 2014

Technical Team
Producers: Taylor Swift, Noel Zancanella, Ryan Tedder
Mixing: Serban Ghenea
Sound Engineers: John Hanes, Ryan Tedder, Smith Carlson
Mastering: Tom Coyne

Genesis

In "I Know Places," Taylor Swift once again deals with the need to escape the constant glare of the media to live life fully and serenely in a budding relationship. She knows places where she can hide, where her relationship can be sheltered from a not always benevolent entourage. In her song, she makes brilliant use of the lexical field of urgency and stalking—bad sign, vultures, dark clouds, cages, guns, lights flash, run, hunters, hide, shots, bulletproof—to immerse the listener in an oppressive, anxiety-inducing world that puts all the senses on alert. With its verses in the key of *A* minor—*A* minor / *F* / *D* minor / *F* (maj7)—and its tense chorus—*C* / *D* minor / *F* x 2—it is undoubtedly the darkest track on the album.

Production

"I Know Places" is the second track on *1989* co-written and co-produced by Ryan Tedder. As on "Welcome to New York," the opening track, Noel Zancanella is also involved. Tedder and Zancanella's rhythmic programming is more modern than the rest of the album. There are elements borrowed from contemporary hip-hop and electro-pop music: the scathing cross-stick snare drum, the tambourine and high-hat mix, the syncopated rhythmic pattern, and the various percussive elements distance "I Know Places" from the retro-eighties synthwave productions of *1989*. On the verses, the four piano notes (*A* / *F* / *D* / *E*), the bass sound played with a plectrum with plenty of attack, and the synthesizer sounds evoke a dark, trip-hop-like atmosphere, while the hyper-edited "I, I, I, I…" and the almost chanted, reggaeton-style vocals foreshadow the urban sounds of the *Reputation* era. The choruses, meanwhile, are firmly rooted in the electro-pop sound of the 2010s.

Hidden Message

And everyone was watching.

When Imogen Heap was absent for the performance of "Clean," Taylor Swift delivered an intimate and cathartic performance in a minimalist setting.

CLEAN

Taylor Swift, Imogen Heap / 4:31

Musicians
Taylor Swift: vocals
Imogen Heap: vibraphone, drums, mbira, percussion, programming, keyboards, backing vocals

Recorded
The Hideaway (London), 2014

Technical Team
Producers: Taylor Swift, Imogen Heap
Mixing: Serban Ghenea
Sound Engineers: John Hanes, Imogen Heap
Mastering: Tom Coyne

Imogen Heap a cappella at the London Without Limits festival, London, July 30, 2015.

Genesis

Taylor Swift co-wrote and co-produced this song with one of her heroines, Englishwoman Imogen Heap. In the London home studio of this singer, songwriter, and producer of folktronica, the two musicians laid the foundations for the track and recorded their two voices in just one day. Imogen Heap mixed the track the following day and sent it to her partner. In this song, Taylor Swift describes a love relationship as an addiction, and metaphorically recounts how she manages to detoxify herself overnight by letting the (emotional) storm wash over her. When she woke up, she felt liberated, soothed, and weaned. "Clean" and "Shake It Off" were the last two songs Taylor Swift composed for *1989*. Although not written with this intention, "Clean" would become an opportunity for the singer, when she performs the song live, to make a speech about mental illness, addiction, and victims of abuse.

Production

With its metallic, almost childlike tones (mbira, vibraphone, small percussion, glitch sounds), and its grainy, almost lo-fi sounding keyboards (the discreet organ sound and the eighth-note bass sequence), Imogen Heap's singular touch radiates from this arrangement that is as organic and precise as Swiss clockwork. Taylor Swift's and Imogen Heap's voices blend perfectly, illuminating this folktronica production with a softness bordering on ambient music. For the last song on the original version of *1989*, the palpable 100 percent female touch is a far cry from the synthwave sounds that dominate the album, but consistent with the electronica pop line. A fine way to conclude this emotionally charged album, like a rite of passage.

Hidden Message

She lost him, but she found herself, and somehow, that was everything.

2014

In 2015, Taylor Swift opted for a shorter, tapered haircut, symbolizing her evolution into a new musical and personal era.

Taylor Swift and Calvin Harris in Manhattan, May 2015.

WONDERLAND

Taylor Swift, Max Martin, Shellback / 4:05

Musicians
Taylor Swift: vocals, backing vocals
Shellback: guitar, bass, keyboards, programming
Max Martin: keyboards, programming
Recorded
MXM (Stockholm), Conway Recording (Los Angeles), 2014
Technical Team
Producers: Max Martin, Shellback
Mixing: Serban Ghenea
Sound Engineers: John Hanes, Sam Holland
Mastering: Tom Coyne

Genesis

The first of three bonus tracks on the Deluxe Edition of *1989*, "Wonderland" draws a parallel between a love affair too good to be true and the hallucinatory world of *Alice's Adventures in Wonderland* (1869) by English writer Lewis Carroll. Taylor Swift knows that this story is doomed to failure but does not hesitate to dive in headfirst and live it as intensely as possible, until the illusion is shattered.

Production

The winning trio of Max Martin, Shellback, and Taylor Swift return for this electro-pop production with its epic choruses. There is no question of half-measures here: a riot of synthesizers, syncopated percussion, programmed drums with a thick, slamming sound, all crisscrossed by abundantly distorted, filtered, and sidechain-compressed synth bass. The lead vocal and its cascade of backing vocals in hyper-edited interjections ("ey-ey-ey-ey") do much to nourish the impression of warlike power being exuded. At the back of the mix, other backing vocals sing "aaaah" to double the lead of acid-sounding, outrageously portamento synthesizers. The verses, meanwhile, are more evolving and nuanced. With their two high-pitched piano notes (B♭ / E♭), muted percussion that suddenly transforms into a marching band snare drum, muffled keyboard chords, and energetic yet restrained lead vocals, they enable the choruses to explode and assume their full dimension.

The *1989* world tour is a visual and sound journey marking a transition to electro-pop.

2014

YOU ARE IN LOVE

Taylor Swift, Jack Antonoff / 4:27

Musicians
Taylor Swift: vocals
Jack Antonoff: acoustic and electric guitars, bass, keyboards, drums, backing vocals
Recorded
Conway Recording (Los Angeles), Jungle City (New York), 2014
Technical Team
Producers: Taylor Swift, Jack Antonoff, Max Martin
Mixing: Serban Ghenea
Sound Engineers: John Hanes, Sam Holland, Brendan Morawski
Mastering: Tom Coyne

Genesis

The third track co-written by Taylor Swift and Jack Antonoff on *1989*, "You Are in Love" depicts the relationship Antonoff forms with his friend Lena Dunham. As with "I Wish You Would," Taylor Swift wrote her lyrics and melody directly onto the instrumental track sent to her by her partner. Inspired and moved by the music, which for her perfectly represents the "sound of love," she immediately knew the direction she wanted the song to take. "I Wish You Would" is a tribute to Jack and Lena, whose purity and strength of bond Taylor Swift admires, and which corresponds in every way to her idea of true love.

Production

What jumps out instantly is the deeply nostalgic sound of the synthesizer played by Jack Antonoff. Filtered highs, unstable oscillators, choruses, and successive waves of arpeggios sound like distant echoes of 1980s music. The rhythm is initially marked by small finger percussion and filtered drums played with the brushes, to match the synthesizer's padded aesthetic. On the second half of the first verse, a little electric guitar riff played in double note and palm mute reinforces the harmony with a kind of sophisticated ostinato. From the very first chorus, the high notes of the drums come to life again, and the drum kit is immersed in a long reverb. The electric guitar embellishes the tonic with a retro twang sound played in the bass, and a layer of synthesizers opens up the upper spectrum with a rich, shimmering swell sound. The orchestration then plays with the appearance and disappearance of these various elements, with masterful work on sound textures flirting with sound design and the intensity of the drumming. Taylor Swift's interpretation and the proportioning of backing vocals are in perfect symbiosis with this light-and-shadow arrangement.

The dance moves reinforce the retro aesthetic of "New Romantics," in the style of 1980s pop videos.

2014

SINGLE

NEW ROMANTICS

Taylor Swift, Max Martin, Shellback / 3:50

Musicians
Taylor Swift: vocals, backing vocals
Shellback: guitar, bass, keyboards, drums, backing vocals, programming
Max Martin: keyboards, programming
Recorded
MXM (Stockholm), Conway Recording (Los Angeles), 2014
Technical Team
Producers: Max Martin, Shellback
Mixing: Serban Ghenea
Sound Engineers: John Hanes, Sam Holland
Mastering: Tom Coyne
Single Release
Digital Release: February 23, 2016
Best Rankings: Hot 100: 46; Mainstream Top 40: 18; Adult Pop Airplay: 9

Genesis

The third and final bonus track on the Deluxe Edition of *1989*, "New Romantics" refers to the 1980s cultural movement generally associated with the new wave music of the time, which Taylor Swift and her collaborators quote extensively throughout the album. The seventh and final single from the *1989* era is an ode to resilience, freedom, audacity, and change. Taylor Swift is determined to live life to the fullest and to enjoy her youth. She is no longer afraid to take risks or to say no—nothing will ever be the same again.

Production

The trio of Max Martin, Shellback, and Taylor Swift have the honor of rounding off the track list of the Deluxe version of *1989* with this flamboyant synthwave production, a veritable hymn to hedonism. With its 122 bpm tempo, the supercharged disco pop rhythm gains in urgency. The bass drum embellishes its quarter-note beat with percussive, groovy sixteenth notes, and the snare drum slams to the max. The layers, risers, and synthesizer sequences seem to glow, and the pick bass rolls over the creeping, grainy synth bass. Backed by her army of overdubbed backing vocals, Taylor Swift invites everyone to the party: Now is the time to celebrate broken hearts and embrace celibacy. At this stage of her career, "New Romantics" is probably her most dance-floor-friendly track. Many reviewers, journalists, and Swifties are still wondering why this track was not included on the original version of *1989*, released on October 27, 2014.

RELEASE DATE
United States (and worldwide): October 27, 2023
(ref.: Republic Records—0245554214)
Best Ranking: 1

ALBUM

1989 (Taylor's Version)

Slut!* · Say Don't Go* · Now That We Don't Talk* ·
Suburban Legends* · Is It Over Now?*

**From the Vault*

THE BLUE WAVE SURGES ONCE MORE

The rerecorded version of *1989* was released on October 27, 2023, exactly nine years after the release of the original. Taylor Swift announced the release a few weeks earlier, on August 9, 2023, at an "Eras Tour" concert in Los Angeles. Seasoned fans had guessed that evening that the singer was preparing a surprise for them: Throughout the show, she wore a succession of blue outfits, the reference color of *1989*, and repeatedly flashed the spectators' wristbands in the same color. Toward the end of the concert, the new version of the cover appeared on the giant screens, drawing jubilant applause from the audience. The following day, in a message posted on Instagram, Taylor Swift made it known that this reissue was her favorite of all, in particular for its five From the Vault tracks: "Slut!," "Say Don't Go," "Now That We Don't Talk," "Suburban Legends," and "Is It Over Now?" Unlike the From the Vault tracks on previous Taylor's Versions, which featured numerous duets, the tracks on *1989* are all performed by Taylor Swift solo.

As Close as Possible to the Original Version

The rerecorded tracks were produced by Taylor Swift and Christopher Rowe, except those originally co-produced by Jack Antonoff, Ryan Tedder, Noel Zancanella, and Imogen Heap, all of whom are present on the reissue. Swedish producer Shellback, at the helm on several tracks in 2014, came to add his touch on "Wildest Dreams (Taylor's Version)," at the time co-produced with Max Martin. The latter was not involved in the album's production, perhaps for reasons of availability (Martin was then—and still remains—one of the most in-demand producers on the planet). For their part, the From the Vault tracks were composed and produced by Taylor Swift and Jack Antonoff, with the exception of "Say Don't Go," co-written with American singer-songwriter Diane Warren. Sonically, *1989* is perhaps the closest Taylor's Version comes to her original album, so much so that it is difficult for the untrained ear to distinguish one from the other. Only Taylor Swift's voice, warmer, more controlled, and particularly punchy on this album, brings a subtle nuance at times.

Records, Again and Again

As *1989* was the singer's best-selling album, this Taylor's Version was the most eagerly awaited of all. But did the pop star imagine the tsunami it would create? Probably not. Once again, the release was accompanied by a flurry of records of all kinds. "Is It Over Now?" topped the Hot 100 for the most streams for a song on Spotify in a single day, which in turn led to another: the most streams for an artist, once again in a single day, with over 260 million plays of tracks from her entire discography. It also broke two records set by *Midnights* (her 2022 opus), becoming the best-selling album of 2023 and recording the biggest vinyl sales week since tracking of these figures began in 1991, with 580,000 copies sold in six days. According to figures released by Republic Records, *1989 (Taylor's Version)* had sold 3.5 million units within seven days of its release.

Taylor Swift onstage at the Mercedes-Benz venue in Shanghai, 2015.

SINGLE

"SLUT!"

Taylor Swift, Patrik Berger, Jack Antonoff / 3:00

Musicians
Taylor Swift: vocals
Patrik Berger: bass, guitar, synthesizers, programming
Jack Antonoff: synthesizers, programming, backing vocals

Recorded
Electric Lady (New York), Rough Customer (Brooklyn, NY), Conway Recording and Sharp Sonics Studios (Los Angeles)

Technical Team
Producers: Jack Antonoff, Patrik Berger, Taylor Swift
Mixing: Serban Ghenea, Bryce Bordone
Sound Engineers: Jack Antonoff, Laura Sisk
Mastering: Randy Merrill
Vinyl Mastering: Ryan Smith

Single Release
Digital Release: October 27, 2023
Best Ranking: Hot 100: 3

Genesis

For Taylor Swift, the song "Slut!" is a way of appropriating the insulting term often used against her on the social networks and by a whole fringe of the media. It is her response to the taunts and her way of mocking the relentlessness of "haters," whose numbers are growing in proportion to her popularity. Taylor Swift tries to have the healthiest and most "normal" social, friendship, and love life possible for a girl her age, and given her star status, she is doing just fine. Perhaps she is being criticized for not hiding away to live her life? Whatever the case, between unfair reproaches and unfounded rumors, Taylor responds with intelligence: in song and with an increasingly sharp sense of humor.

Production

"Slut!" is the first From the Vault track on *1989 (Taylor's Version)*, an unreleased track with an almost surreal synth-wave orchestration produced by Jack Antonoff, Taylor Swift, and Patrik Berger (a Swedish producer who has worked with the likes of Ariel Pink, Robyn, Charli XCX, and Icona Pop). This haunting musical atmosphere enables Taylor to interpret her lyrics with an appropriate nonchalance. This detachment matches the ironic, gently provocative tone of the lyrics. Synthesizers twirl lazily over a 78 bpm tempo; backward-passed sounds and grainy-textured analog sequences mingle with the digital charm of arpeggiators, strings, and risers. The arrangement of "Slut!" skillfully plays on the juxtaposition of timbres. The random sequence of sound events, akin to sound design, plunges the listener into a slow-motion road trip, floating between dream and reality, where the neon lights are still flashing as the night draws to a close.

Las Vegas 2014, nine years before the release of *1989 (Taylor's Version)*.

SAY DON'T GO

Taylor Swift, Diane Warren / 4:39

Musicians

Taylor Swift: vocals
Mikey Freedom Hart: bass, electric guitar, synthesizer [guitar synth], electric piano [Rhodes], synthesizer [Moog], synthesizer [OB-Xa], synthesizer [modular]
Michael Riddleberger and Sean Hutchinson: drums, percussion
Evan Smith: saxophone, synthesizers, programming
Zem Audu: synthesizers
Jack Antonoff: synthesizers, mellotron, percussion, acoustic and electric guitars, programming, backing vocals

Recorded

Electric Lady (New York), Rough Customer (Brooklyn, NY), Conway Recording and Sharp Sonics Studios (Los Angeles)

Technical Team

Producers: Jack Antonoff, Taylor Swift
Mixing: Serban Ghenea, Bryce Bordone
Sound Engineers: Jack Antonoff, Laura Sisk, David Hart, Evan Smith, Sean Hutchinson, Mikey Freedom Hart, Michael Riddleberger, Zem Audu
Mastering: Randy Merrill
Vinyl Mastering: Ryan Smith

Genesis

Taylor Swift wrote "Say Don't Go" with Diane Warren in 2013, with the intention of including it on the original version of *1989*. Diane Warren has had a successful career as an American songwriter since 1983. She has written hits for Cher, Céline Dion, LeAnn Rimes, and Aerosmith. In the tradition of "All You Had to Do Was Stay" and "I Wish You Would," the lyrics of "Say Don't Go" describe an unbalanced, virtually one-sided, doomed love affair.

Production

Like the five From the Vault tracks on Taylor's Version of *1989*, "Say Don't Go" was produced by Jack Antonoff and Taylor Swift. This 110 bpm power ballad verges on an exercise in style, with its strong, assertive homage to the sounds of the 1980s. The treatment of Taylor Swift's voice is one of the most striking elements of this musical journey back in time. Indeed, the reverb applied here is very reminiscent of the sound of the iconic Lexicon 224, a digital reverb unit used to excess by studios the world over since 1978. The same applies to the gated snare drum. Mikey Freedom Hart, Antonoff, and Zem Audu have no qualms about exploiting the plethora of synthesizers at their disposal: bass synthesizer played on a Moog, high-pitched sequence programmed on a modular system, use of a guitar synth (guitar / MIDI controller, such as SynthAxe or the GK range developed by Roland). For the strings sounds, the Oberheim OB-Xa blends gracefully with mellotron strings and chords from Juno 6, DX100, and Korg M1; the listener is in the middle of a synthetic dream.

2023

NOW THAT WE DON'T TALK

Taylor Swift, Jack Antonoff / 2:26

Musicians
Taylor Swift: vocals
Mikey Freedom Hart: bass, electric guitar, synthesizer [guitar synth], electric piano [Rhodes], synthesizer [Moog], synthesizer [OB-Xa], synthesizer [modular]
Michael Riddleberger and Sean Hutchinson: drums, percussion
Evan Smith: saxophone, synthesizers, programming
Zem Audu: synthesizers
Jack Antonoff: synthesizers, mellotron, percussion, guitar [Ebow], programming, backing vocals

Recorded
Electric Lady (New York), Rough Customer (Brooklyn, NY), Conway Recording and Sharp Sonics Studios (Los Angeles)

Technical Team
Producers: Jack Antonoff, Taylor Swift
Mixing: Serban Ghenea, Bryce Bordone
Sound Engineers: Jack Antonoff, Laura Sisk, David Hart, Evan Smith, Sean Hutchinson, Mikey Freedom Hart, Michael Riddleberger, Zem Audu
Mastering: Randy Merrill
Vinyl Mastering: Ryan Smith
Best Rankings: Hot 100: 2

Genesis

"Now That We Don't Talk" tells the story of the difficulty of dealing with the aftermath of a passionate relationship that ended badly. Taylor Swift understands that in such cases, it is best not to pursue a friendship, and her mother, who is always on hand with good advice, helps her to come to terms with this state of affairs. In an acerbic, caustic tone, Taylor lists a number of situations in which she felt uncomfortable and often left out. Once again, she seems to draw inspiration from her romance with singer Harry Styles, although some elements also recall her story with actor Jake Gyllenhaal ("I don't have to pretend I like acid rock"), or her song "Dear John" (*Speak Now*, 2010) about musician John Mayer.

Production

The production of "Now That We Don't Talk" uses the same elements and the same team as "Say Don't Go," but with a much more modern, less eighties sound. While the surge of synthesizers and their heady sequences are still present, Jack Antonoff and Taylor Swift's synth-pop arrangement is very much of its time. Set against a linear orchestration punctuated by discreet, effective relaunches, the vocal melody is inventive and concise. Taylor Swift sprinkles her performance with a few heartfelt falsettos and embellishes her lead vocals with backing vocals recorded in overdubs (harmonies, textural unisons, and choral responses), like so many highlighter pen strokes on the key words of this vitriolic critique.

SUBURBAN LEGENDS

Taylor Swift, Jack Antonoff / 2:51

Musicians
Taylor Swift: vocals
Mikey Freedom Hart: guitar, synthesizer, electric organ [Farfisa]
Michael Riddleberger and Sean Hutchinson: drums, percussion
Evan Smith: saxophone, synthesizer, guitar
Zem Audu: synthesizers
Jack Antonoff: synthesizers, programming, backing vocals

Recorded
Electric Lady (New York), Rough Customer (Brooklyn, NY), Conway Recording and Sharp Sonics Studios (Los Angeles)

Technical Team
Producers: Jack Antonoff, Taylor Swift
Mixing: Serban Ghenea, Bryce Bordone
Sound Engineers: Jack Antonoff, Laura Sisk, David Hart, Evan Smith, Sean Hutchinson, Mikey Freedom Hart, Michael Riddleberger, Zem Audu
Mastering: Randy Merrill
Vinyl Mastering: Ryan Smith
Best Ranking: Hot 100: 10

Genesis

In "Suburban Legends," Taylor Swift sets to song a provincial girl's dream of emancipation through a romantic encounter with a popular young man. The strength of their bond would silence the school's bad mouths, and together they would set out to conquer the world. The story, however, ends before the escape, just as Taylor predicted: "You don't knock anymore, and I always knew it / That my life would be ruined."

Production

The third From the Vault track to feature the same team, the "Suburban Legends" synth-pop production is very similar to that of "Now That We Don't Talk." Over a 118 bpm binary rhythm, acoustic drums blend with programmed percussion to propel the teeming synthesizer sequences, bursting with filter effects. The layering of strings, risers, arpeggiators, and discreet leads elegantly underpins Taylor Swift's vocal performance, without ever taking precedence over the narrative or her warm timbre.

SINGLE

IS IT OVER NOW?

Taylor Swift, Jack Antonoff / 3:49

Musicians

Taylor Swift: vocals
Mikey Freedom Hart: synthesizers
Michael Riddleberger and Sean Hutchinson: drums, percussion
Evan Smith: saxophone, synthesizer
Zem Audu: saxophone
Jack Antonoff: synthesizers, programming, backing vocals

Recorded

Electric Lady (New York), Rough Customer (Brooklyn, NY), Conway Recording and Sharp Sonics Studios (Los Angeles)

Technical Team

Producers: Jack Antonoff, Taylor Swift
Mixing: Serban Ghenea, Bryce Bordone
Sound Engineers: Jack Antonoff, Laura Sisk, David Hart, Evan Smith, Sean Hutchinson, Mikey Freedom Hart, Michael Riddleberger, Zem Audu
Mastering: Randy Merrill
Vinyl Mastering: Ryan Smith

Single Release

Digital Release: October 31, 2023
Best Rankings: Hot 100: 1; Mainstream Top 40: 1

Genesis

The final track From the Vault, "Is It Over Now?" is a humorous nod from Taylor Swift to her fans. She hopes the listener will wonder if the album is already finished, as time flies when one is immersed in music. It is a chronicle of an aftermath, an introspective song made up of a series of memories and confessions in which Taylor does not hesitate to reveal the state of distress into which a love affair—most likely with singer Harry Styles—had plunged her, or to acknowledge her mistakes and point out those of her partner. Taylor sees "Is It Over Now?" as a sister song to "Out of the Woods" and "I Wish You Would." So it is easy to understand the singer's dilemma when she had to choose to exclude "Is It Over Now?" from the final track listing of the original album version.

Production

Written and co-produced by Taylor Swift and Jack Antonoff, "Is It Over Now?" begins with a sound montage of superimposed vocals played backward over a background of arpeggiator, creeping bass synth, and programmed (clave-like) percussion. The mood is calm, intriguing, almost mysterious. Carried by the same team of musicians and producers as on the three previous tracks, the synthesizers reign supreme. This is the track From the Vault where the synthwave color is most pronounced. The choice of textures, the nostalgic chord progression (*C / F / A* minor */ F*), the long reverb applied to the vocals and most of the instruments, and the meticulous work on all the percussive elements make "Is It Over Now?" the track most faithful to the original spirit of *1989*. In fact, it was the only From the Vault single from the album to reach number one on the US charts.

Does the emancipation dream of the young girl from "Suburban Legends" echo the songwriter's?

RELEASE DATES
United States: November 10, 2017
(ref.: Big Machine Records—BMRCO0600A)
Deluxe Edition: November 10, 2017 (double CD),
(ref.: Big Machine Records—BMRCO0600B and BMRCO0600C)
Best Ranking: 1

ALBUM

Reputation

...Ready for It? · End Game (feat. Ed Sheeran and Future) · I Did Something Bad · Don't Blame Me · Delicate · Look What You Made Me Do · So It Goes... · Gorgeous · Getaway Car · King of My Heart · Dancing with Our Hands Tied · Dress · This Is Why We Can't Have Nice Things · Call It What You Want · New Year's Day

In the *Reputation* era, Taylor Swift asserts herself as a "bad girl" ready for revenge.

FOR DISCERNING SWIFTIES

It was during the *Reputation* era, on August 14, 2017, that Taylor Swift won her case for the sexual assault committed against her in 2013 by a local radio host, David Mueller. During a photo shoot session, the man had slipped his hand up her skirt and touched her buttocks. The jury found in favor of the young woman, and Mueller was ordered to pay the symbolic amount of one dollar requested by the singer.

THE TASTE OF REVENGE

In 2014 and 2015, *1989* propelled Taylor Swift into the stratosphere. For more than a year and a half, singles from the synthpop album—including three number one singles on the Billboard Hot 100 ("Shake It Off," "Blank Space," "Bad Blood")—dominated radio waves and music channels. At the start of 2016, the singer also swept up the most prestigious Grammy Awards. Could this ubiquity explain the disgrace she would experience over the following months? No doubt in part. Taylor Swift's reign was beginning to annoy more than a few people, and the reproaches leveled at her in the media and on social networks seemed to grow in resonance and virulence by the day.

Loves and Friendships in the Crosshairs

First, her breakup with British DJ Calvin Harris cemented her reputation as a calculating, man-hungry woman. Highly publicized, this split came more than a year into the relationship, in June 2016. Initially presented by both as friendly and respectful, it quickly turned into a settling of scores when the star, via her agents, let it be known that she had co-written with Harris, under the pseudonym Nils Sjöberg, one of his biggest hits: "This Is What You Came For" (April 2016), performed by Rihanna. While the DJ confirmed this revelation, he also made it known in a series of bruising tweets that he did not approve of it. Another episode added fuel to the fire in this feud: Taylor Swift was photographed barely a week after the official announcement of her separation on the arm of actor Tom Hiddleston, who is also British. Further proof, for some tabloids and the general public, that she was no longer the sweet young thing she had been at the start of her career.

Taylor Swift was also criticized for her friendships, judged elitist and at odds with the inclusive values she advocates in her music. In particular, it was deprecated that her squad—the group of celebrity friends she often highlights—was made up exclusively of young, beautiful, rich, famous, and slim women. They included singers, actresses, and models such as Selena Gomez, Hailee Steinfeld, Cara Delevingne, Gigi Hadid, Karlie Kloss, and Lily Aldridge. Taylor Swift, inclusivist in name only? Some people were beginning to think so.

#TaylorSwiftIsOverParty

A twist in the Kanye West affair, involving the rapper's then wife—businesswoman and model Kim Kardashian—would place Taylor Swift in the eye of a hate cyclone. In February 2016, Kanye West released "Famous," with lyrics that were, to say the least, controversial: "I feel like me and Taylor might still have sex / Why? I made that bitch famous" he raps in reference to his speech during Taylor Swift's onstage performance at the 2009 MTV Video Music Awards.

Shortly after the track's release, the TMZ website reported that Kanye West had obtained the singer's prior consent for the lyrics to be broadcast, which she denied. Through her agent Tree Paine, Taylor Swift assured the *New York Times* that she refused, and even warned him against releasing a song with such a strong misogynistic message. In mid-July 2016, after calling Taylor Swift a snake on Twitter, Kim Kardashian published a series of videos on Snapchat containing excerpts from the phone exchange between the pop star and the rapper. Edited in

Red and black express the conflict, revenge, and reinvention that mark this phase of Taylor Swift's career.

such a way as to transform reality in Kanye West's favor, the videos had the effect of a final assault on the young woman. Flooded with hate messages and "snake" emojis on the networks, she resigned herself to writing a final post in which she reiterated her version of events. The venom, alas, had already taken effect: the hashtag TaylorSwiftIsOverParty became the world's top Twitter trend. On August 29, 2016, Taylor Swift wrote just one sentence in her diary: "This summer is the apocalypse." The note would be included in the Deluxe Edition of *Lover* in August 2019.

A Year of Silence

By autumn 2016, Taylor Swift was at her lowest point and her public appearances were few and far between. She did, however, give two concerts, one in October 2016 at the Formula One Grand Prix Post-Race, and the other in February 2017 at Super Saturday Night, before the Super Bowl. She also released a duet with Zayn Malik, "I Don't Wanna Live Forever," which she created specially with Jack Antonoff for the soundtrack to the film *Fifty Shades Darker* (2017). But at the end of February 2017, faced with a feeling of total loss of control, she chose to disappear. In the media, on social networks, or even simply on the street, she no longer showed her face anywhere. In the documentary *Miss Americana* (2020), she confides that she felt extremely "alone" and "bitter" during this period, comparing her emotional state to that of "a wounded animal lashing out." "I figured I had to reset everything. I had to reconstruct an entire belief system for my own personal sanity," she adds. During her withdrawal, she moved to London, where she met the man with whom she would form a solid, peaceful, and discreet couple for six years, British actor Joe Alwyn.

Taylor Swift began recording *Reputation* in Nashville in September 2016. She opted for a two-team production: one with Jack Antonoff; the other with Max Martin and Shellback. Jack Antonoff's work plays a crucial role in the creation of this album, which is so different from its predecessors. With his unrivaled mastery of rich electronic textures, the art of silences, and dynamic shifts, the musician-producer provides the star with precious compact places for her highly esteemed narrative. He co-wrote and co-produced six tracks, including "Look What You Made Me Do" (co-produced with members of English pop band Right Said Fred) and "Getaway Car." For their part, Max Martin and Shellback co-wrote and co-produced nine, including the hit "Don't Blame Me" and the subtle "Delicate." Three musicians support them on certain tracks: Swedish producer and DJ Ali Payami ("...Ready for It?"), rapper Nayvadius Wilburn, aka Future ("End Game," written by Ed Sheeran), and Oscar Görres, another Swedish producer ("So It Goes..." and "Dancing with Our Hands Tied").

A Cathartic Album

Reputation, as its name suggests, was made in reaction to the events that marked Taylor Swift's public life between 2016 and its release in summer 2017. Tackling themes of revenge, image management, and rebirth, the album can be seen as a liberation of her voice after a period during which she no longer had the strength to express herself. For the first time in her discography, the atmosphere of this album is dark, both musically and aesthetically. As the

Taylor Swift uses smoke machines and the aesthetics of light and shadow to symbolize personal renewal and the reclaiming of her power.

track list progresses, however, the artist seems to leave the settling of scores behind in favor of her favorite theme, love. Tracks such as "Call It What You Want" and "New Year's Day" evoke the discreet, stable romance she had with Joe Alwyn at the time. Taylor Swift has said that her tracks have a linear chronology: The first express what she was feeling at the start of work on the album, while the last reflect her state of mind at the end of production. Sonically, *Reputation* is by far her most eclectic album. Marked by heavy beats, deep bass, and dark synths, many styles cohabit here: electro-pop, synthpop, trap, hip-hop, and R'n'B.

An Unforgettable Release

The announcement of the release of *Reputation* remains memorable for fans, and more broadly in the history of the music industry. On August 18, 2017, Taylor Swift deleted all her social media accounts, sparking a wave of speculation on the internet. A few days later, the clues started to drop down: short videos showing undulating snakes, all in black and white and silent, were posted without comment. On August 23, the star struck hard, unveiling the album's title and cover. On August 24, after almost a year's silence, the single "Look What You Made Me Do" was unveiled. Its music video, in which she appears from the very first images to have returned from the dead, was viewed more than 43.2 million times in its first day on YouTube, breaking the record for the most-viewed clip in twenty-four hours. The single climbed to number one on the Billboard Hot 100, posting the highest sales and streaming figures of 2017 in the US.

Commercially, the album was, as always, a huge success. It debuted at number one on the Billboard 200 in the US with over 1.2 million copies sold in its first week (2 million worldwide), making Taylor Swift the first artist to sell four consecutive albums at over a million copies in their first week. It would logically go on to become one of the best-selling albums of 2017. It also racked up the usual string of awards at the American Music Awards, taking Artist of the Year, Best Female Pop Rock Artist, Best Pop Rock Album, and Tour of the Year for her "Reputation Stadium Tour." In contrast, it was only nominated for a 2019 Grammy Award in the Best Pop Vocal Album category, won by Ariana Grande with "Sweetener."

Taylor Swift as an indomitable woman
in the single "...Ready for It?"

SINGLE

...READY FOR IT?

Taylor Swift, Max Martin, Shellback, Ali Payami / 3:28

Musicians
Taylor Swift: vocals, backing vocals
Shellback, Max Martin, Ali Payami: keyboards, programming
Recorded
MXM (Stockholm), 2017
Technical Team
Producers: Max Martin, Shellback, Ali Payami
Mixing: Serban Ghenea
Sound Engineers: John Hanes, Max Martin, Shellback
Mastering: Randy Merrill
Single Release
Digital Release: September 3, 2017
Best Rankings: Hot 100: 4; Mainstream Top 40: 12; Adult Pop Airplay: 10

Genesis

For the first song on her comeback album after a year's withdrawal from public life, Taylor Swift strikes hard. She slips into the skin of her alter ego, a sort of negative of the America's sweetheart of her early days, a vengeful superheroine, resolutely urban, sultry, and rebellious, whom she will take pleasure in embodying throughout the *Reputation* era. In "...Ready for It?" she imagines herself as a modern-day Bonnie, holding Clyde hostage or, conversely, captive to this love on a remote island, a bank robber, or a master thief. In a clever linguistic trick, she even compares this infernal duo to the tumultuous Hollywood couple of Richard Burton and Elizabeth Taylor, taking advantage of the homonymy between the famous actress's surname and her own first name: "And he can be my jailer, Burton to this Taylor."

Production

This musical firecracker is not called "...Ready for It?" for nothing: The atmosphere is brutal and the lyrics darker than usual. Taylor Swift wonders how fans and Swifties the world over will react to this radical change of direction. To produce this EDM (electronic dance music) track with pronounced trap and dancehall influences, she called on Max Martin and Shellback, now loyal collaborators since *Red*, released in 2012. Ali Payami, already featured on *1989*, is also on board. In the key of *E* minor, the arrangement begins with a synth bass sound (probably from a Roland TR-808) distorted to excess and loaded with sub bass (bordering on infrabass), quickly joined by a sharp trap rhythm over an 80 bpm tempo that allows Taylor Swift to lay down her first rap and dancehall flow. The chorus opens the horizon and takes the listener into tropical house and electro-pop territory. The soft groove of three synthesizer chords (*G* / *A* minor / *E* minor x 2) and the singer's voice, immersed in a mix of delays and long reverbs, create a dreamy, melodic atmosphere that contrasts with the harshness of the verses. A remix by artist BloodPop was released on December 10, 2017.

Ed Sheeran joins Taylor Swift at the 99.7 NOW! Poptopia in California, December 2017.

SINGLE

END GAME (FEAT. ED SHEERAN AND FUTURE)

Taylor Swift, Max Martin, Shellback, Ed Sheeran, Future / 4:04

Musicians
Taylor Swift: vocals, backing vocals
Shellback: keyboards, programming, bass, drums
Max Martin: keyboards, programming
Future, Ed Sheeran: vocals

Recorded
MXM (Stockholm and Los Angeles), Seismic Activities (Portland), Tree Sound (Atlanta), 2017

Technical Team
Producers: Max Martin, Shellback
Mixing: Serban Ghenea
Sound Engineers: John Hanes, Sam Holland, Michael Ilbert, Seth Firkins
Mastering: Randy Merrill

Single Release
Digital Release: November 14, 2017
Best Rankings: Hot 100: 18; Mainstream Top 40: 10; Adult Pop Airplay: 13

FOR DISCERNING SWIFTIES

In the second verse, sung by Ed Sheeran, the line "Something was born on the 4th of July" refers to the date on which Sheeran and his wife, Cherry Seaborn, began dating, and to Oliver Stone's film *Born on the Fourth of July* (1989), based on the autobiography of Vietnam War veteran Ron Kovic.

Genesis

For the second track on the album, Taylor Swift once again pulls out all the stops. No fewer than five composers are involved in the track's creation: Taylor Swift, Max Martin, Shellback, Ed Sheeran, and Nayvadius Wilburn (Future), two of whom appear as prestigious featuring artists: rapper Future and folk-pop star Ed Sheeran. Taylor, Sheeran, and Future each write and sing their own part. The track is divided into:

- Chorus and post-chorus 1: Taylor Swift and Future
- Verse 1: pre-chorus: Future; chorus: Taylor Swift and Future
- Verse 2: Ed Sheeran
- Pre-chorus 2, chorus, and post-chorus 2: Taylor Swift
- Verse 3: Taylor Swift; chorus: Taylor Swift, Future, and Ed Sheeran

Taylor Swift and Ed Sheeran came up with the idea of collaborating with Future on a drink-filled night out, when they realized they were both big fans of the rapper's work. Probably inspired by the singer's relationship with actor Joe Alwyn, "End Game" presents a distraught Taylor, who wants her partner to become her soulmate and see beyond an image unfairly tarnished by the media. From the second track (and third single) of *Reputation*, the listener is plunged into the heart of the matter; here, we leave our preconceived ideas in the closet.

Production

With a tempo of 80 bpm and a grid of simple but cleverly arranged chords (verse: *D* minor x 2 / *A* minor 7 / *G* and *D* minor x 2 / *C* / *G*; pre-chorus: *F* / *E* minor / *D* minor x 2; chorus: *F* x 2 / *C* / *G* and *D* minor / *C* / *G*), the three artists link flows and sung parts in an unusual, relatively linear arrangement. The deep bass synth sound (Moog-type) and the synthesizer chords, which in turn evoke the mellow sound of a Juno 106 or that of an icy Roland DX7, set the harmonic tone of the track. As for the rhythm, it mixes trip hop elements (the bass drum/snare drum pattern) and trap (the high hat with its fluctuating timing). All these elements evolve relatively little from start to finish on this pop rap and rhythm'n'blues production by Max Martin and Shellback.

HOAX

Modernity, sensuality, and power are the essential characteristics of the *Reputation* era in which Taylor Swift asserts her new public image.

I DID SOMETHING BAD

Taylor Swift, Max Martin, Shellback / 3:58

Musicians

Taylor Swift: vocals, backing vocals
Shellback: keyboards, programming
Max Martin: keyboards, programming

Recorded

MXM (Stockholm and Los Angeles), 2017

Technical Team

Producers: Max Martin, Shellback
Mixing: Serban Ghenea
Sound Engineers: John Hanes, Sam Holland, Michael Ilbert
Mastering: Randy Merrill

Genesis

In "End Game," Taylor Swift identifies with a Marvel villain. In "I Did Something Bad," she draws inspiration from the *Game of Thrones* series and its heroines, powerful and ruthless strategists, to shape this new character. Are the media casting her as a man-eating witch? No matter; she assumes the role in which she has been cast and enjoys playing the calculating, remorseless woman, expert in the art of manipulating narcissistic men. "I Did Something Bad" is also one of the few tracks where she uses a vulgar word (*shit*). However, the album does not carry the "explicit lyrics" sticker normally used in the US to indicate content unsuitable for a young audience.

Production

When Taylor wrote the framework for "I Did Something Bad" on the piano, she already had a good idea of what she had in store for this composition, some of whose arrangement ideas had come to her in a dream. Suffice to say, it was not going to end up as a piano and vocal bluette. With her accomplices Max Martin and Shellback, she manages to reproduce the epic EDM sounds she had in mind. The arrangement begins with two small keyboard sounds, one close to a pizzicato string ensemble and the other Rhodes-like, but with a streamlined attack and long resonance. Then, suddenly, a huge synthesizer sound (in unison over two distinct octaves) explodes on the chorus after a clever bass synth drop. Shellback is the source of this find: a rough timbre with an expressive, dubstep-like portamento, which Taylor humorously compares to the sound of a malfunctioning computer. Not unlike the lavish productions of Rihanna or Lady Gaga, the vocal gimmick "Ra-di-di-di-di-di-di-di-di-di-da-da," sampled, edited, processed, and pitched an octave lower, is frighteningly effective. Superbly enhanced by Serban Ghenea's mixing, the melody of the chorus is unstoppable and shows Taylor at the height of her art with syncopation and inspired vocal overdub. On the bridge, her voice is autotuned to the extreme, in the manner of 2010s hip-pop productions—a first for the singer. Max Martin and Shellback succeed in creating an orchestration that is both minimalist and massive, where the combination of acoustic drums and programmed percussion underlines the operatic dimension.

For the 2018 American Music Awards, Taylor Swift wore a spectacular Balmain dress made of mesh and metallic plates weighing approximately 20 pounds (9 kg).

DON'T BLAME ME

Taylor Swift, Max Martin, Shellback / 3:56

Musicians

Taylor Swift: vocals, backing vocals
Shellback: keyboards, programming, drums, bass, guitars
Max Martin: keyboards, programming, piano, backing vocals

Recorded

MXM (Stockholm and Los Angeles), 2017

Technical Team

Producers: Max Martin, Shellback
Mixing: Serban Ghenea
Sound Engineers: John Hanes, Sam Holland, Michael Ilbert
Mastering: Randy Merrill

Genesis

"Don't Blame Me" fits in perfectly with the theme of *Reputation*. Taylor Swift positions herself as an unabashed serial dater, based on the idea that only three things can really change someone: love, drugs, and religion. The last line of the second verse contains essentially concealed references to antagonistic cultural figures: "I once was poison ivy, but now I'm your daisy." Poison Ivy is a supervillain and sworn enemy of Batman in the DC Comics universe, and Daisy was Gatsby's great love in F. Scott Fitzgerald's 1925 novel *The Great Gatsby*. Taylor claims to have been inspired by this novel when writing the song "Delicate" (track 5 on *Reputation*) and quotes it in "This Is Why We Can't Have Nice Things" (track 7 on *Reputation*). The world of this novel, which incorporates passion, excess, and solitude, is conducive to Hollywood storytelling and has been adapted many times for the big screen. In the choruses, she seems to be addressing the media directly, while in the verses, it is clear that she is talking to her lover.

Production

Somewhere between EDM and gospel music, the lush production of "Don't Blame Me" stands out for its solemnity. The synthesizer sound, which shifts from a deep, cadenced tremolo to an expressive swell at the end of each harmonic cycle, is the most striking instrumental discovery in this arrangement by Max Martin, Shellback, and Taylor Swift. The programmed drums, simple and uncluttered, make their entrance on the second cycle of the first verse and hardly vary throughout the song. Only the addition of an open high-hat sound, superimposed on the snare drum, on the third beat of each bar lends a hand to the pulse of the choruses. With a ternary rhythm and a tempo of 136 bpm, the gospel side of "Don't Blame Me" is contained in the choir created by Taylor and Max by adding vocal overdubs, having sung most of the takes together in front of the same microphone.

AMERICAN MUSIC AWARDS
AMERICAN MUSIC AWARDS
AMERICAN MUSIC AWARDS

Striking a combination of power and femininity, Taylor Swift has not abandoned her glamorous image.

SINGLE

DELICATE

Taylor Swift, Max Martin, Shellback / 3:52

Musicians
Taylor Swift: vocals, backing vocals
Shellback: keyboards, programming
Max Martin: keyboards, programming, piano

Recorded
MXM (Stockholm and Los Angeles), 2017

Technical Team
Producers: Max Martin, Shellback
Mixing: Serban Ghenea
Sound Engineers: John Hanes, Sam Holland, Michael Ilbert
Mastering: Randy Merrill

Single Release
Digital Release: March 12, 2018
Best Rankings: Hot 100: 12; Top 40 Mainstream: 1; Adult Pop Airplay: 1; Dance / Mix Show Airplay: 4

Genesis

Taylor Swift created "Delicate" as the first "vulnerable" song on the album. Although the singer now knew how to protect herself and no longer allowed incessant jibes get to her, her status as a pop superstar was otherwise difficult to manage on the subject of love. She wonders how much the man she loves will be able to see beyond her media reputation and everything he may have heard before meeting her. Inspired by her reading of writer F. Scott Fitzgerald's *The Great Gatsby*, she keeps in mind the image of Gatsby frantically roaming his mansion in search of the woman he loved, Daisy, before leaving for the front to fight in the war. This vision infuses the entire writing process of "Delicate."

Production

The intro on "Delicate" hits hard, with a major first for Taylor: her voice is run through a vocoder, a device that analyzes sounds and synthesizes the voice. In this way, she pulses her phonemes to the sequence of chords of *C* / *D* minor / *A* minor / *F*, played by the synthesizer (not to be confused with the hard tune technique, which consists of creating a robotic voice by pushing the pitch correction settings to the extreme, as on "Don't Blame Me"). Paradoxically, the use of vocoder here produces an emotionally charged and sensitive effect in perfect keeping with the theme of "Delicate." This is the fifth consecutive track produced by Max Martin and Shellback (apart from the contributions of Ali Payami and Ilya Salmanzadeh). Set to a tempo of 95 bpm, this synthpop ballad gives pride of place to woozy synthesizers, while the swaying rhythm, supported by discreet sequences, distills an irresistible tropical house fragrance. Piano chords reinforce the texture of the synths, and Taylor's backing vocals embellish the refrains with distant echoes that inevitably evoke the mainstream electro-pop of the late 2010s.

At Jingle Ball 2017, Taylor Swift performed her new songs, such as "Look What You Made Me Do."

SINGLE

LOOK WHAT YOU MADE ME DO

Taylor Swift, Jack Antonoff, Richard Fairbass, Fred Fairbass, Bob Manzoli / 3:31

Musicians
Taylor Swift: vocals, backing vocals
Jack Antonoff: programming, instruments
Evan Smith: saxophone
Victoria Parker: violins
Phillip A. Peterson: cellos
Recorded
Rough Customer (Brooklyn, NY), 2017
Technical Team
Producers: Jack Antonoff, Taylor Swift
Mixing: Serban Ghenea
Sound Engineers: John Hanes, Laura Sisk
Mastering: Randy Merrill
Single Release
Digital Release: August 24, 2017
Best Rankings: Hot 100: 1; Top 40 Mainstream: 1; US Dance Mix / Show Airplay: 3; Dance Club Songs: 9

Genesis

"Look What You Made Me Do" is the first single from the *Reputation* album. As in "I Did Something Bad," Taylor Swift draws inspiration from the *Game of Thrones* series to build her character as a fearless avenger. More specifically, she takes her cue from Arya Stark and her kill list: "I've got a list of names and yours is in red, underlined." In the middle of the song, she inserts a fake answering machine message: "I'm sorry, the old Taylor can't come to the phone right now / Why? Oh, 'cause she's dead!" Since *Red*, her sense of humor and caustic lyrics have continued to sharpen. In terms of music, she draws heavily on the 1991 hit "I'm Too Sexy" by English pop group Right Said Fred. To cover the melody, the singer's management reportedly contacted the song's authors, Richard Fairbrass, Fred Fairbrass, and Rob Manzoli, to offer them a financial deal while preserving the anonymity of the artist who requested it. The day after the launch of the single "Look What You Made Me Do," the three songwriters, who had accepted the deal without protest, discovered the reference to their famous hit, clearly identifiable in the melody of the chorus, as well as the identity of the star. In an interview with *Rolling Stone* magazine, they later said they appreciated the cynicism of Taylor's song, which was totally in the spirit of their own.

Production

"Look What You Made Me Do" marks the return of Jack Antonoff and Taylor Swift as producers. After a very

cinematic intro, Taylor begins her flow over a minimalist electro beat that gradually builds up to the breakdown of the pre-chorus. Eighth-note hammered piano chords in the treble, abundantly distorted synth bass, and Taylor's backing vocals build up the tension until the chorus, again very stripped down. The "Look What You Made Me Do" lyrics repeat the melody of the 1991 hit "I'm Too Sexy." The second verse is more elaborate. High-pitched notes shoot out over a dissonant glissando, like a TR-808 pitched to the extreme. Abrupt, dubstep-like riser sounds and synthesizer stabs reminiscent of 1980s samplers frenetically punctuate this section, right up to the second pre-chorus. After the second chorus, the bridge repeats the intro's arrangement, sprinkled with synthesizers, organ, strings of all kinds, and ghostly backing vocals over which Taylor lays her vocal melody. This is followed by a short quotation of the chorus with a totally muffled vocal sound, followed by the spoken passage on which a frequency filter (equalization) is applied, cutting all the bass and a good part of the treble, to which a slight distortion is added to simulate the "telephone voice" effect. Taylor and Antonoff opt to conclude this breakneck arrangement with an evolving chorus ad lib. No doubt the listener will feel the compulsive urge to hum this heady ritornello from the very first listen.

At the Super Saturday Night Concert in February 2017 in Houston, Texas.

SO IT GOES...

Taylor Swift, Max Martin, Shellback, Oscar Görres / 3:47

Musicians
Taylor Swift: vocals, backing vocals
Shellback: keyboards, programming
Max Martin: keyboards, programming
Oscar Görres: keyboards, programming, piano

Recorded
MXM (Los Angeles and Stockholm), 2017

Technical Team
Producers: Max Martin, Shellback, Oscar Görres
Mixing: Serban Ghenea
Sound Engineers: John Hanes, Sam Holland, Michael Ilbert
Mastering: Randy Merrill

Genesis

After "Delicate" (track 5), "So It Goes..." is the next track on *Reputation* in which Taylor Swift is willing to reveal her vulnerable side. Probably inspired by her relationship with actor Joe Alwyn, she delivers her feelings without restraint and charges the atmosphere with a certain erotic tension. The track "So It Goes..." is a nod to the phrase popularized by American postmodern writer Kurt Vonnegut in his antimilitaristic science fiction novel *Slaughterhouse-Five; or, The Children's Crusade: A Duty-Dance with Death*, published in 1969. Taylor sometimes incorporates this song into the acoustic segments of the "Reputation Stadium Tour."

Production

Somewhere between synthpop, trap, and EDM, the production by Max Martin, Shellback, and Oscar Görres (also known as OzGo), a Swedish producer and songwriter who has collaborated with Maroon 5, Marina, Britney Spears, and Pink, is not a half-hearted one. The arrangement is based on a heavy rhythm, adorned with the fluctuating high hat typical of trap music. The slow tempo (75 bpm) is conducive to the muggy atmosphere created by the layering of grainy synthesizer sounds: distorted, octave-doubled bass synth, deep strings, and quarter-note piano chords plucked from the top of the keyboard. Taylor's voice is immersed in a set of effects consisting of several long delays and reverbs set to complement each other. Everything is done to give the listener the impression of floating in weightlessness, reflecting the intoxication described by the singer, at that time in the midst of a romantic idyll.

TIME

Max Martin co-wrote, co-produced, and performed on "Gorgeous."

Taylor Swift's appearance at the 2017 Jingle Ball on New York radio station Z100 marked her return to the stage after the release of *Reputation*.

SINGLE

GORGEOUS

Taylor Swift, Max Martin, Shellback / 3:52

Musicians
Taylor Swift: vocals, backing vocals
Shellback: keyboards, programming, guitars
Max Martin: keyboards, programming
James Reynolds: baby voice on the intro
Recorded
MXM (Stockholm and Los Angeles), 2017
Technical Team
Producers: Max Martin, Shellback
Mixing: Serban Ghenea
Sound Engineers: John Hanes, Sam Holland, Michael Ilbert
Mastering: Randy Merrill
Single Release
Digital Release: October 20, 2017
Best Ranking: Hot 100: 13

Genesis

In September 2016, Taylor Swift first wrote the chorus of "Gorgeous" on guitar, in her apartment on Cornelia Street in New York, while slightly befuddled. She wrote the rest of the song on the piano two weeks later, in Nashville. It was one of the first songs she wrote for the *Reputation* album. In it, she humorously describes how her attraction to Joe Alwyn disrupts her functioning, to the point of making her lose her mind a little. Taylor later revealed to her fans that all the positive love songs on *Reputation* are about the actor.

Production

The baby voice that exclaims the word *gorgeous* on the track's intro is that of young James Reynolds, the daughter of actors Blake Lively and Ryan Reynolds, Taylor's close friends. As she played her song on guitar in front of them, little James started repeating the word *gorgeous* at the top of her lungs. The singer found it so cute that she decided to record the child's voice on her phone and integrate it into the song's intro. Produced by Max Martin and Shellback, "Gorgeous" is a light, graceful electro-pop track, with a 92 bpm tempo. Between syncopated sequences and ethereal strings, synthesizers and a TR-808 drum machine dominate the arrangement. While the rhythmic programming is rather modern, the sounds used are mostly reminiscent of the 1980s. The arrangement is punctuated by risers typical of 2000s synthpop, and Taylor's voice is given a particularly dry treatment on the verses. This contrasts with the choruses and bridge, where the voice is bursting with delays and long reverbs.

Freedom, transgression, and the disillusionment evoked by a doomed relationship are the themes of "Getaway Car."

SINGLE

GETAWAY CAR

Taylor Swift, Jack Antonoff / 3:53

Musicians
Taylor Swift: vocals, backing vocals
Jack Antonoff: programming, instruments, backing vocals
Sean Hutchinson: drums
Victoria Parker: violins
Phillip A. Peterson: cellos
Recorded
Rough Customer (Brooklyn, NY), 2017
Technical Team
Producers: Jack Antonoff, Taylor Swift
Mixing: Serban Ghenea
Sound Engineers: John Hanes, Laura Sisk
Mastering: Randy Merrill

Genesis

If "...Ready for It?" implicitly alluded to the couple Bonnie and Clyde, in "Getaway Car," Taylor Swift and Jack Antonoff draw a direct comparison between the notorious criminals and the singer's recent jet-setting romance (presumably her relationship with actor Tom Hiddleston). Experienced as an outlet after her breakup with singer, songwriter, and DJ Calvin Harris, this fast-paced idyll is a necessary escape but doomed to failure. Hollywood-style banditry imagery (heists, chases, crime, escape) is one of the leitmotifs of the *Reputation* album, Taylor's way of showing just how difficult it is not to be crushed by the media steamroller. In an interview with *Rolling Stone* in 2021, Antonoff described the writing of the bridge—filmed by Taylor on her phone (the video soon became a Swiftian classic on the internet)—as the most intense moment of creative ping-pong he had ever experienced.

Production

Like "Delicate," produced by Max Martin and Shellback, "Getaway Car" begins with a voice run through a vocoder. Yet Antonoff's touch is palpable from the very first bars: a true aesthete of analog sound, he always seeks to infuse his productions with a retro charm. Grainy synthesizers, unstable oscillators, mellotron-like string treatment, and the juxtaposition of vintage and modern sounds have become his trademark. From the bridge onward, Antonoff hammers out piano chords on the quarter notes, stubbornly sticking to playing at the top of the keyboard to reinforce the sense of urgency. The drums played by Sean Hutchinson blend elegantly with the programmed percussion and synth bass sequence. There seems to be no stopping the rhythm section, whose binary drive is constantly renewed by variations in programming and playing on drums and high hat. Taylor moves effortlessly from restrained, sensitive vocals to a powerful, assertive full voice. To create the famous "choir" effect, Antonoff's backing vocals swell the ranks of the overdubs, the icing on the cake of this luminous, galvanizing arrangement.

Super Saturday Night Concert, February 2017, ten years after her appearance on the same show, one of her first televised performances.

The king in "King of My Heart" is a figure of support and protection, but also of gentle power. He is the image of a reliable and loving partner.

FOR DISCERNING SWIFTIES

On the "Reputation Stadium Tour" in 2018, Taylor Swift played "King of My Heart" every night without exception. Setting up the live version requires bringing out the heavy artillery, notably a very elaborate combination of percussion, programming sequences, and drums.

KING OF MY HEART

Taylor Swift, Max Martin, Shellback / 3:34

Musicians

Taylor Swift: vocals, backing vocals
Shellback: keyboards, programming, drums, bass
Max Martin: keyboards, programming

Recorded

MXM (Los Angeles and Stockholm), Conway Recording (Los Angeles), 2017

Technical Team

Producers: Max Martin, Shellback
Mixing: Serban Ghenea
Sound Engineers: John Hanes, Sam Holland, Michael Ilbert, Noah Passovoy
Mastering: Randy Merrill

Genesis

Taylor Swift had this idea for a while: to set out the different stages of a love relationship in a single, evolving, yet coherent and synthetic song. And this is exactly what she achieves on "King of My Heart." She describes the four main stages that every lover goes through: first, celibacy (in her case, comfortable and accepted), the meeting, the beginning of the relationship (which Taylor tries to keep secret for as long as possible), and then the celebration of a love that just might be the right one.

Production

The Max Martin, Shellback, and Taylor Swift team are together again for this pulsating electro-pop production. The singer composed "King of My Heart" on guitar, originally in *F#*, with a capo positioned on the fourth fret, that is, *F#* / *C#* / *A* flat minor / *B*, which she plays in the position of *D* / *A* / *E* minor / *G*. The album version was eventually recorded three tones higher, in favor of Taylor's energetic chest voice. The final chord grid (*C* / *G* / *D* minor / *F*) does not vary from start to finish. Over a 110 bpm tempo, the sophisticated rhythmic programming blends tribal percussion, bass drum, snare drum, high-hat trap, and hip-hop for an epic effect that would awaken the warrior instincts of the most peaceful of Swifties. The synth bass shakes the walls, the strings and risers open up the horizon, and the arpeggios seem to shimmer in the firmament. On the verses, Taylor switches from soothing vocals to a dense, syncopated flow. At the start of the second chorus, Shellback's strumming of an acoustic guitar, an instrument rarely used on *Reputation*, can be heard. With its legion of lead and backing vocals doubled by a vocoder, the chorus is perfectly suited to the stadiums.

During the *Reputation* era, "Dancing with Our Hands Tied" is part of the setlist at the 99.7 NOW! Poptopia concert in California.

FOR DISCERNING SWIFTIES

"Dancing with Our Hands Tied" is Taylor's brother Austin Swift's favorite song from the *Reputation* album.

DANCING WITH OUR HANDS TIED

Taylor Swift, Max Martin, Shellback, Oscar Holter / 3:31

Musicians
Taylor Swift: vocals, backing vocals
Shellback: keyboards, programming
Max Martin: keyboards, programming
Oscar Holter: keyboards, programming

Recorded
MXM (Los Angeles and Stockholm), 2017

Technical Team
Producers: Max Martin, Shellback, Oscar Holter
Mixing: Serban Ghenea
Sound Engineers: John Hanes, Sam Holland, Michael Ilbert
Mastering: Randy Merrill

Genesis

This is a recurring theme for Taylor Swift: how to experience a "normal" love relationship under the omnipresent and intrusive gaze of the media? In "Dancing with Our Hands Tied," the singer once again explores this issue, worried but full of the new hope inspired by her encounter with Joe Alwyn. Her inspiration came just before a writing session with fellow songwriters Max Martin and Shellback, as she was leaving the gym, while a paparazzo assailed her with an unkind remark about her weight. Once in the studio, Taylor burst into tears. After hiding months to rebuild her life, this attack was a blow. Writing "Dancing with Our Hands Tied" was to be her outlet.

Production

With its crystal-clear synthesizer chords and primitive beat racing ahead at 160 bpm, the production of "Dancing with Our Hands Tied" pulls no punches. The arpeggiators float weightlessly, the synth bass remains discreet, and Taylor's voice soars above, accompanied by her cohort of overdubbed backing vocals. To provoke a feeling of openness on the chorus, the binary rhythm programmed on a TR-808 performs a radical drop (the rhythm seems to suddenly slow down and halve the tempo). After the bridge, between 2:45 and 3:11, the singer performs some rather unusual acrobatic vocals, reaching the top of her register (successively F5 and G5) in a supple, chest-like voice. Max Martin, Shellback, and Oscar Holter provide a superbly precise arrangement.

During the *Reputation* stadium tour, Taylor Swift pays tribute to American dancer and actress Loie Fuller, who originated the serpentine dance at the end of the 19th century.

DRESS

Taylor Swift, Jack Antonoff / 3:50

Musicians
Taylor Swift: vocals, backing vocals
Jack Antonoff: programming, instruments

Recorded
Rough Customer (Brooklyn, NY), 2017

Technical Team
Producers: Jack Antonoff, Taylor Swift
Mixing: Serban Ghenea
Sound Engineers: John Hanes, Laura Sisk
Mastering: Randy Merrilll

Genesis

Even more so than "Delicate," the song "Dress" is full of sexual allusions. Inspired by her romance with Joe Alwyn, Taylor Swift dares to take erotic semantics to a new level. Irrespective of the singer's fascination with dresses of all kinds, the recurrent use of the word *dress*, evoking the purchase of a dress intended to be taken off, is a metaphor: Taylor is ready to bare herself before her lover, literally and figuratively, because she senses that he sees her as she really is, beyond her partially fabricated and uncontrollable media image. But for her, this is above all a love song, an ode to deep feeling and tenderness. The lines "Flashback when you met me, / Your buzzcut and my hair bleached" refer to Taylor and Alwyn's first meeting at the Met Gala in 2016.

Production

"Dress" is the third track on *Reputation* produced with Jack Antonoff. This sylph-like arrangement never seems to touch the ground. The rhythm is sketched out, the harmony is suspended, and everything here hangs on a thread: the synthesizers twirl, almost indecisive, and the percussive elements are plunged into a delay set to sixteenth notes, as if to imitate the palpitations of a heart in turmoil. The syncopated vocals on the verses and the falsetto of the choruses are reminiscent of Prince's edgy style. Despite the diaphanous musical atmosphere, the sexual tension is palpable. The orchestration is based on a precarious balance where everything is done to keep the listener on the edge of their seat.

THIS IS WHY WE CAN'T HAVE NICE THINGS

Taylor Swift, Jack Antonoff / 3:27

Musicians
Taylor Swift: vocals, backing vocals
Jack Antonoff: programming, instruments
Victoria Parker: violin and viola
Phillip A. Peterson: cellos

Recorded
Rough Customer (Brooklyn, NY), 2017

Technical Team
Producers: Jack Antonoff, Taylor Swift
Mixing: Serban Ghenea
Sound Engineers: John Hanes, Laura Sisk
Mastering: Randy Merrill

The short haircut and fringe mark the end of the *Reputation* era.

Genesis

As with the songs "Don't Blame Me" and "Delicate," Taylor Swift is once again inspired by *The Great Gatsby*, the seminal work by novelist F. Scott Fitzgerald. During the "1989 World Tour," she liked to throw extravagant parties and invite her favorite artists to share the stage with her, so that they could benefit from her success and strengthen her friendships. Always quick to criticize those who make the most of things, the media reproached her for having built up a kind of inner circle. Quibbles flew and invective multiplied, always unfair and unfounded. Exhausted by the gossip, Taylor decided to take a year off and withdraw completely from the media scene. However, it was not long before she was secretly preparing for her comeback. Beyond the Fitzgeraldian exuberance described in the first verse, "This Is Why We Can't Have Nice Things" evokes the fact that simple, essential things often seem beyond her reach. As Taylor has learned the hard way, friendship, trust, and outspokenness do not always mix well with the life of a star. Many have speculated that the text might be essentially about her feud with Kanye West.

Production

Inspired by the song "It's the Hard-Knock Life," from the musical *Annie*, in particular by the version produced by Greg Kurstin for the feature film released in 2014, Taylor Swift and Jack Antonoff hijack the codes of Broadway's own show tune style. Over a tempo of 82 bpm, the quadruple eighth-note high hat and all the rhythmic programming immediately put the listener in the mood: the dynamic duo are having a lot of fun in the studio and want it to be known (Taylor's hearty laughter at 2:32 is proof of this). With a high-pitched hammered piano, pizzicato, orchestral bells, and mellotron strings galore, eccentric choir-style vocal overdub and rumbling synth bass, this playful arrangement full of twists and turns exudes joie de vivre.

In the United States, "Call It What You Want" entered the Billboard Digital Song Sales chart at number one, with 68,000 digital copies sold.

CALL IT WHAT YOU WANT

Taylor Swift, Jack Antonoff / 3:23

Musicians
Taylor Swift: vocals, backing vocals
Jack Antonoff: programming, instruments, backing vocals
Recorded
Rough Customer (Brooklyn, NY), 2017
Technical Team
Producers: Jack Antonoff, Taylor Swift
Mixing: Serban Ghenea
Sound Engineers: John Hanes, Laura Sisk
Mastering: Randy Merrill

Genesis

Added at the last minute in fourteenth position on the standard edition of *Reputation*, "Call It What You Want" naturally finds its place on this album, which is constructed in a linear fashion, like a concept album. The first tracks reflect the frustration, anger, and need for rebellion felt by Taylor Swift at the time. When she meets Joe Alwyn, the tone begins to change. Their relationship evolves, his gaze soothes her, and the songs that follow show more vulnerability. Until the last tracks, when Taylor no longer hesitates to share her overflowing love, a vector of well-being and newfound comfort, sheltered from the media cyclone.

Production

Jack Antonoff and Taylor Swift's production oscillates between synthpop, rhythm'n'blues, and trap music. "Call It What You Want" evolves on a mid-tempo at the same pace as the previous track ("This Is Why We Can't Have Nice Things"): 82 bpm. A sense of calm is in the air. Four main elements dominate this arrangement: MPC-programmed rhythm, Taylor's sampled vocals, Roland DX7 chords, and bass synth. Mellotron strings (bowed and pizzicato) and sounds resembling a distorted guitar played backward and pitched an octave lower punctuate this inventive, ethereal orchestration. Taylor's phrasing moves seamlessly from scansion to vocals, all syncopated and supple, rhythm'n'blues style. "Call It What You Want" is one of the tracks Antonoff is most proud of, and one he would recommend fans listen to on headphones on a nocturnal stroll.

Through the snake, Taylor Swift transformed the negative image of a nickname given to her by detractors into a symbol of power.

SINGLE

NEW YEAR'S DAY

Taylor Swift, Jack Antonoff / 3:55

Musicians
Taylor Swift: vocals, backing vocals
Jack Antonoff: piano, guitar, bass, synthesizers
Recorded
Rough Customer (Brooklyn, NY), 2017
Technical Team
Producers: Jack Antonoff, Taylor Swift
Mixing: Serban Ghenea
Sound Engineers: John Hanes, Laura Sisk
Mastering: Randy Merrill
Single Release
Digital Release: November 27, 2017
Best Rankings: Hot Country Songs: 33; Country Airplay: 41; Digital Song Sales: 44

Genesis

"New Year's Day" is the fourth single and final song from the *Reputation* album. Like "Call It What You Want," it was originally intended for the Deluxe Edition. Taylor Swift draws inspiration from her previous New Year's Eve, spent in her London home. More specifically, she describes the day after this memorable party, happy not to wake up alone. Who, then, will have the heroic courage to cross the remnants of this Dionysian evening to bring her an Advil? In a burst of romantic enthusiasm, she hopes that her champion of difficult tomorrows will want to take a walk with her. In the meantime, she had carefully kept these two verses to one side: "Please don't ever become a stranger / Whose laugh I could recognize anywhere" and "Hold on to the memories, they will hold on to you." They eventually found their way into "New Year's Day."

Production

To close this eventful album, what could be better than a Joni Mitchell–style piano and vocal ballad? Comfortably seated behind his upright piano, with soft pedal engaged, Jack Antonoff accompanies Taylor with a sober, sensitive touch reminiscent of the minimalist playing of Neil Young. The first take was the right one. For the arrangement, a few acoustic guitar arpeggios, two synthesizer notes, and two vocal overdubs are all that were needed. In stark contrast to the massive, brutal sound of "...Ready for It?," the softness and purity of "New Year's Eve" mark a total appeasement.

Jack Antonoff was named Producer of the Year three years in a row: 2022, 2023, and 2024.

JACK ANTONOFF, SOULMATE IN MUSIC

To be very clear: it was not Taylor Swift who made Jack Antonoff a producer—although he insists she was the first artist to recognize him as such. One might also legitimately ask the question: without Jack Antonoff, would Taylor Swift have continued to reign as she does over the pop world? It is impossible to know, of course, but it is certain that their meeting influenced their respective destinies in equal measure.

Rock, Punk, and Folk Influences

Born on March 31, 1984, in Bergenfield, New Jersey, Antonoff owes his love of music to his father, a financier who he describes as "an incredible guitarist" in an interview with *Vogue France* in 2024. With his headphones firmly on, he grew up facing New York—which he felt both close to and isolated from—to the sound of rock bands from the 1970s and 1990s, often citing Phil Collins, Peter Gabriel, and the Strokes as the artists who forged him. Bruce Springsteen, whom he considers a master of musical storytelling, remains his greatest influence. Encouraged by his parents to follow this musical path, he began writing and composing at an early age. From the age of fifteen, he formed the punk band Outline, then, three years later, the more folk-oriented Steel Train. It was during this period that he suffered the tragedy that would haunt all his work: the death of his little sister Sarah, who died of brain cancer.

Mainly Female Collaborators

A decade and a move to New York later, with the band Fun—composed of Andrew Dost and Nate Ruess, and for whom he was the guitarist—he wrote the hit "We Are Young" (sung with Janelle Monáe), for which he won two Grammy Awards in 2013. The single already contains all his signature elements: eighties synths that know how to give pride of place to the piano; present, pared-down vocals; and a skillful blend of pop energy and melancholy. This immense success led him to write for others, starting with Lorde and Taylor Swift, with whom he forged a deep and solid friendship over the years and through his collaborations. The list of artists with whom he subsequently works is long and, surprisingly, all-female: It includes the names of Sia, Clairo, Carly Rae Jepsen, St. Vincent, and above all Lana Del Rey, most of whose discography he has produced to date—we owe him for the albums *Norman Fucking Rockwell!* (2019), *Chemtrails Over the Country Club* (2021), and *Did You Know That There's a Tunnel Under Ocean Blvd* (2023). To date, Jack Antonoff has won no fewer than eleven Grammy Awards, including Album of the Year for *1989* (2016) and *Folklore* (2021), and Producer of the Year, an award he won in 2022, 2023, and 2024.

A New Group

In 2014, Antonoff quietly put together Bleachers, which blends influences from pop, rock, eighties synthpop, and indie. He started this project, which is more personal than Fun, alone, surrounding himself with musicians for live performances and recording sessions. In 2023, musicians Mikey Freedom Hart, Sean Hutchinson, Evan Smith, Michael Riddleberger, and Zem Audu officially joined the band. As of 2024, Bleachers has four albums to its credit, the latest of which, released in March 2024 with the restrained title *Bleachers*, has won unanimous critical acclaim.

RELEASE DATE

United States: August 23, 2019

(ref.: Republic Records—B0030612-02)

Best Ranking: 1

ALBUM

Lover

I Forgot That You Existed · Cruel Summer · Lover · The Man · The Archer · I Think He Knows · Miss Americana & the Heartbreak Prince · Paper Rings · Cornelia Street · Death by a Thousand Cuts · London Boy · Soon You'll Get Better (feat. The Chicks) · False God · You Need to Calm Down · Afterglow · ME! (feat. Brendon Urie of Panic! At the Disco) · It's Nice to Have a Friend · Daylight · **Outtake:** All of the Girls You Loved Before

Above: Taylor Swift attends the 2019 Golden Globes afterparty in Beverly Hills.
Opposite: At the 2019 American Music Awards, Taylor Swift won the Artist of the Decade award.

BACK INTO THE LIGHT

The *Reputation* era was notable in Taylor Swift's career for two major reasons. First, its dark atmosphere marked a clean break with the luminous, romantic, and gentle universe to which the singer had previously accustomed her fans. The years 2017 and 2018 also saw Taylor disappear in an unprecedented way from the public sphere, as she made the choice—a salutary one, as she would later say on numerous occasions—not to grant interviews, express herself on social networks, or be seen on red carpets and sidewalks, where she was so often photographed by the paparazzi. The concerts on her gigantic "Reputation Stadium Tour"—a fifty-three-date worldwide tour that drew 2.55 million spectators and grossed over $345 million, making it the most profitable tour in US history at the time—were the only time she spoke from the heart, no doubt with the certainty that her words would not be truncated or misinterpreted. At the concert that opened the tour, on May 8, 2018, in Glendale, Arizona, she confided for the first time on the microphone about the events of the past months: "I went through some times when I didn't know if I was going to get to do this anymore. I wanted to send a message to you guys that if someone uses name-calling to bully you on social media, and even if a lot of people jump on board with it, that doesn't have to beat you. It can strengthen you instead." She completed her "Reputation Stadium Tour" in Tokyo on November 21, 2018, officially bringing to an end the most secluded—but also oh-so-lifesaving—era of her career.

Taylor Swift's performance at the 2019 Billboard Music Awards was an explosion of color, music, and dance.

A Change of Record Label

In late 2018, new rumors—this time totally unrelated to *Reputation*—began to circulate actively in the music industry and the media. On November 10, 2018, Taylor's fifteen-year contract with her label Big Machine Records expired, fueling speculation about the name of her future record label and a deal that promised to be one of the biggest in music history. The star did not keep the suspense going for long: on November 19, she announced that she was joining Republic Records, a subsidiary of Universal Music Group. Although the amount of the deal was not disclosed, *Forbes* magazine estimates that it could have been between $100 million and $200 million, a record for a female artist. (On the male side, the record is held by Bruce Springsteen, whose catalog was acquired in 2021 by Sony Music Entertainment for $550 million.) A clause—undoubtedly more important than the money for the singer—was also unveiled: the contract entitled Taylor to recover ownership of her future recordings five years after their respective releases, which was not the case with Big Machine. In the meantime, the artist had become one of the most financially successful of her generation, giving her ample opportunity to impose her conditions. Less than a year later, this type of musical property would become the center of an unprecedented controversy, when Big Machine sold all the masters produced by Taylor before 2019 (i.e., almost her entire discography) to businessman Scooter Braun, and she decided to rerecord all her albums to reclaim the rights.

Pastel Wave

On February 24, 2019, Taylor, as fond as ever of hidden messages launched without warning to her fans, posted on her Instagram account an enigmatic photo of a blue sky studded with sixty-one stars overlooking a hill. In this shot, seven palm trees stand out, with one in the middle. For Swifties, there was no doubt: in sixty-one days' time, on April 26, the star would be releasing her seventh album. The singer would later reveal that on the day this photo was published, she was indeed completing the recording of *Lover*.

Over the following weeks, her social networks were flooded with portraits or details of objects in pastel tones, launching her fans into a new game of chase. On April 25, a shot of Taylor Swift in front of a butterfly mural on a Nashville wall completed this series of visual clues. That

Brendon Urie, frontman of the band Panic! At The Disco, and Taylor Swift performing "ME!" at the 2019 Billboard Music Awards.

same evening, at midnight, she unveiled not a full album, but her very first single, "ME!"—a duet with Brendon Urie, the vocalist from the band Panic! At the Disco. The music video, in which we see a crawling snake explode into a flurry of pink butterflies in the very first seconds (the *Reputation* era is well and truly over, the metaphor explicitly declares), is just a big collection of Easter eggs designed to subliminally unveil *Lover*, starting with its title (the word appears in the form of a neon sign in the background).

A Serene Album

Reputation was night; *Lover* is undeniably day—first and foremost in its sound, which is much more organic than that of its predecessor. Acoustic guitars, synths, soft percussion, pianos...Taylor reintroduces the instruments that forged her identity. She also returns to her favorite subject, love; this time exploring it in all its forms. Romantic love, of which she now seems to have a calmer vision, of course has a major presence on this album—many of the tracks are inspired by her relationship with actor Joe Alwyn, with whom she had been in a relationship for around three years at this point ("Lover," "Cornelia Street," "Paper Rings"). It is also one of love for others, combined with the values of tolerance, benevolence, and self-esteem. In this way, Taylor ventures, as she has never done before, into social and political terrain, notably in "You Need to Calm Down," a catchy pop anthem in support of the LGBTQIA + community, and in "Miss Americana & the Heartbreak Prince," a dramatic ballad in which she shares her disillusionment and concern about the political situation in the United States, after four years of the Trump administration.

As her first album for Republic Records, *Lover* is definitely a symbol of freedom for the singer. For all that, she did not change her main collaborator: Jack Antonoff, who had worked with her since *1989*, co-produced a large number of tracks, including "Lover," "The Archer," and "Cornelia Street." She also called on Joel Little, a New Zealand producer known for his work with singer-songwriters Lorde and Gracie Abrams ("ME!" and "You Need to Calm Down"). The result is a commercial success, as always: The album started at number one on the Billboard 200, with almost 900,000 units sold worldwide in its first week, and it would be one of the best-selling albums of 2019.

Taylor Swift, in her Giambattista Valli haute couture dress, on the red carpet of the 2019 Billboard Music Awards.

I FORGOT THAT YOU EXISTED

Taylor Swift, Adam King Feeney, Louis Bell / 2:50

Musicians
Taylor Swift: vocals, backing vocals
Adam King Feeney: programming, guitar
Louis Bell: programming, keyboards
Frank Dukes: guitar, programming
Joe Harrison: guitar
David Urquidi: saxophone
Steve Hughes: trombone
Serafin Aguilar: trumpet

Recorded
Electric Feel (Los Angeles), 2019

Technical Team
Producers: Frank Dukes, Louis Bell, Taylor Swift
Mixing: Serban Ghenea
Sound Engineers: John Hanes, Louis Bell
Mastering: Randy Merrill
Best Rankings: Hot 100: 28; Rolling Stone Top 100: 5

Genesis

For a glorious opening to *Lover*, her seventh album, Taylor Swift decided to start with "I Forgot That You Existed," a song in which she definitively settles accounts with the past. She has turned the page and mourned her reputation: This was the avowed aim of her previous album, aptly titled *Reputation*. This long process enabled her to feel at home again. Now she was confident and at peace at last. From now on, any attack will leave her indifferent. The whole of *Lover* will be a declaration of love to love with a capital *L*, or it will not be. The lines "And I couldn't get away from ya / In my feelings more than Drake's" refer to the song "In My Feelings" by rapper and singer Drake. Taylor quoted the song in her essay on pop music, published in *Elle* magazine in February 2019. The lyrics "I thought that I would miss you but I didn't" sung on the voice memo piano and vocals version, appeared at number nineteen on the Deluxe version of *Lover*, are replaced by "I thought that it would kill me but it didn't" on the definitive version.

Production

By calling on producers Frank Dukes and Louis Bell, Taylor decided to try out an unprecedented partnership. Co-written with Adam King Feeney and Louis Bell, "I Forgot That You Existed" focuses on groove and clean lines. With its pitted, syncopated, high-pitched piano chords and sampled vocal gimmick, it is a far cry from the dense, brutal atmosphere of *Reputation*. The TR-808-style bass sticks to the piano like glue, the discreet high hat juggles the offbeats, and the finger snaps mark beats 2 and 4 of each bar—it takes no more than that to fire up the rhythm section and push the listener to take the first step onto the dance floor. Taylor's vocals bounce happily off this minimalist arrangement, opening the album with a touch of electro-pop that is light, sarcastic, and deliciously funky.

"Cruel Summer" was a runaway success four years after its 2019 release. Having gone viral on TikTok, the track climbed to the top of the charts in 2023.

SINGLE

CRUEL SUMMER

Taylor Swift, Jack Antonoff, Annie Clark / 3:55

Musicians
Taylor Swift: vocals, backing vocals
Jack Antonoff: drums, keyboards, vocoder, programming
Michael Riddleberger: drums
Annie Clark: guitars

Recorded
Electric Lady (New York), Conway Recording (Los Angeles), 2019

Technical Team
Producers: Jack Antonoff, Taylor Swift
Mixing: Serban Ghenea
Sound Engineers: John Hanes, Laura Sisk, Jack Antonoff
Mastering: Randy Merrill

Single Release
Digital Release: June 13, 2023
Best Rankings: Hot 100: 1; Adult Pop Airplay: 1; Top 40 Mainstream: 1; Dance / Mix Show Airplay: 12

Genesis

"Cruel Summer" is one of Taylor Swift's biggest hits. However, the story of its rise to the top of the charts is a rocky one, to say the least, since its acclamation took place four years after the release of the album *Lover.* Its release as a single was prevented by the COVID-19 pandemic in 2020. But the track, which broke listening records on digital platforms and was acclaimed by fans over the following years, was so successful that Taylor and her new label, Republic, decided to officially release it as a single on June 13, 2023. This second life, four years later, took the singer by surprise and stunned the music industry once again. Inspired by her encounter with Joe Alwyn, "Cruel Summer" recounts the brutal awakening of love during a torrid summer, at the end of a long period of turmoil. Intentionally portrayed as a hopeless, doomed romance, love blossomed and eventually led the singer to peace. Co-written with Jack Antonoff and Annie Clark (better known by her performing artist name as St. Vincent), who contributes her electro-cubist guitar signature, Taylor admitted in 2023 that "Cruel Summer" is the song on the album with which she is most satisfied.

Production

While they may have seemed to be touching the percussive instruments with their fingertips on "I Forgot That You Existed," Taylor and Antonoff have no hesitation in really going for it on "Cruel Summer." Set to a tempo of 170 bpm, the eighth-note synth bass sequence, bubbling and gritty to perfection, drives this driving synthpop production. The snare drum's singular sound seems to be made up of two main elements: a dry brush stroke (heard alone at the very beginning of the track), doubled by a more resonant rimshot-type sample. Firmly at the helm of the vocoder, Captain Antonoff develops a rich, inventive part, taking charge of the main gimmick ("Yeah, yeah, yeah, yeah"), giving expressiveness to the chords and responding to the lead vocal on the verses. As for the synthesizers, arpeggiators, risers, and strings follow one another in breathless succession, and Annie Clark's electric guitar skillfully blends into this outpouring of sparkling textures.

Taylor Swift performs at the iHeartRadio Wango Tango in 2019.

SINGLE

LOVER

Taylor Swift / 3:41

Musicians
Taylor Swift: vocals, backing vocals
Jack Antonoff: drums, bass, keyboards, piano, acoustic guitars, percussion, programming
Recorded
Electric Lady (New York), 2019
Technical Team
Producers: Jack Antonoff, Taylor Swift
Mixing: Serban Ghenea
Sound Engineers: John Hanes, Laura Sisk, Jack Antonoff
Mastering: Randy Merrill
Single Release
Digital Release: August 16, 2019
Best Rankings: Hot 100: 10; Adult Pop Airplay: 6; Top 40 Mainstream: 16

Genesis

Taylor Swift composed "Lover" on the piano one evening, alone in her Nashville home. She knew immediately that this song would be the title track of her new album. Once the lyrics were complete, she recorded a first draft as a voice memo (included at the twentieth position of the Deluxe version of *Lover*), which she sent to Jack Antonoff. The very next day, she headed off to join Antonoff and Laura Sisk in the studio. Everything was wrapped up in six hours. Galvanized by her romance with British actor Joe Alwyn, she imagined two lovers learning to live under the same roof for the first time. Although the verses and choruses came easily to her, the bridge gave her more trouble. Yet Taylor manages to live up to her ambitions, infusing the song with an element of enchantment and a wealth of detail that she feels has been lacking until now. For example, she takes her inspiration from newlyweds who have fun personalizing their wedding vows. Along with "Cornelia Street" and "Daylight," this is one of the three tracks on the album that she wrote entirely on her own. Like the rest of the album, "Lover," the first "pure" love song of which the star is truly proud, is timeless and truly intimate.

Production

Like "Sad Beautiful Tragic" (released in 2012 on the *Red* album), the laid-back verses of "Lover" are reminiscent of Mazzy Star's classic "Fade into You." Created by Antonoff and Taylor, the stripped-down indie-folk arrangement of this slow waltz gradually fleshes out. As a notable one-man band exponent, Antonoff plays all the instruments: acoustic guitar, drums on brushes, tambourine, electric organ, minimalist piano, and bass played with a palm mute pick, Paul McCartney style (in Paul's own words). As with an instant classic, the chorus melody is particularly irresistible. From the second cycle onward, the lead vocal is supported by an overdubbed backing vocal ensemble, and Mellotron strings (pizzicati and holds) appear from nowhere to sublimate the bridge, a true model of the genre. The reverb-laden production also evokes the heyday of 1960s bubblegum pop, and Phil Spector's wall of sound is not far off. The "slow dance" sticker, which record companies sometimes stuck on 45 rpm records as a marketing pitch, would suit this timeless acid ballad perfectly. On November 13, 2019, Taylor announced the release of a duet version with singer and songwriter Shawn Mendes (who writes his own verses). Shortly afterward, an orchestral remix entitled "Lover (First Dance Remix)" was released on November 26, 2019.

When "The Man" was released, some critics praised the feminist message in the song.

SINGLE

THE MAN

Taylor Swift, Joel Little / 3:10

Musicians
Taylor Swift: vocals, backing vocals
Joel Little: drums, keyboards, programming
Recorded
Electric Lady (New York), Golden Age West (Auckland), 2019
Technical Team
Producers: Joel Little, Taylor Swift
Mixing: Serban Ghenea
Sound Engineers: John Hanes, Joel Little
Mastering: Randy Merrill
Single Release
Digital Release: January 27, 2020
Best Rankings: Hot 100: 23; Adult Pop Airplay: 9; Top 40 Mainstream: 20

Genesis

In "The Man," the fourth single from the album *Lover*, Taylor Swift imagines how her choices and every move would have been perceived had she been a man. Taking this astute idea as her basic premise, she describes a series of situations in which her condition as a woman has made her task prodigiously difficult. To denounce this injustice, she draws not only on her own experience, but also on the many other testimonials she gathers online from her fans. In the verses "Let the players play / I'd be just like Leo / In Saint-Tropez," Taylor takes actor Leonardo DiCaprio, archetype of the prevailing sexism, as an example. A feminist song par excellence, "The Man" points the finger at patriarchal society with a sense of humor and relevance that has been very well received by the critics. Once again, Taylor Swift hits the nail on the head with this satirical ritornello, perfectly in tune with the zeitgeist.

Production

For the arrangement of this synthpop firecracker, Taylor called on the talents of Joel Little, a New Zealand producer and songwriter who has collaborated with Lorde, Imagine Dragons, and Shawn Mendes. Punchy yet airy, the verses are essentially based on the pairing of rhythmic programming and a minimalist synth bass, in perfect synchronicity. Taylor Swift's voice hovers over the top, passed through a long delay that elegantly fills the empty space. On the chorus, the instrumental gimmick is played by a synthesizer whose nasal timbre (made up of two slightly out-of-tune voices) evokes that of a duo of asthmatic trumpets, while an icy-sounding synthesizer layer opens up the stereo field. On the second chorus, the layer is doubled by a track of mellotron backing vocals immersed in a long reverb, then, on the coda of the third chorus, Joel Little decides to call in the mellotron strings to the rescue to densify the top of the harmonic spectrum. The entire piece is based on the chord sequence *F / G / C / A* minor. The vocal melody, syncopated and particularly catchy, serves the text perfectly. To get her message across as clearly as possible, Taylor was keen to create a chorus that would be easily memorized and easy to sing along to—a successful gamble for this new interplanetary hit.

In concert in Shanghai, on the eve of Singles' Day 2019. This unofficial Chinese holiday, which celebrates single people on November 11, is a veritable online shopping event, said to exceed the sales of Black Friday in the United States.

SINGLE

THE ARCHER

Taylor Swift, Jack Antonoff / 3:31

Musicians
Taylor Swift: vocals, backing vocals
Jack Antonoff: keyboards, programming

Recorded
Electric Lady (New York), 2019

Technical Team
Producers: Jack Antonoff, Taylor Swift
Mixing: Serban Ghenea
Sound Engineers: John Hanes, Laura Sisk, Jack Antonoff
Mastering: Randy Merrill

Single Release
Digital release (promotional pre-album single): July 23, 2019
Best Rankings: Hot 100: 38; Rolling Stone Top 100: 23

Genesis

"The Archer" refers to Taylor Swift's astrological sign, Sagittarius, sometimes called the Archer (she was born on December 13, 1989). Darker and more introspective than in previous tracks, the singer uses the archer metaphor to take stock: Sometimes the hunter, often hunted, she describes her struggles and past relationships, some tragically short-lived. Written in less than two hours by Taylor and Jack Antonoff while both were in California, "The Archer" respects the Swiftian tradition of the "vulnerable" song placed fifth on each of her albums. In an intimate tone and with palpable anxiety, Taylor talks about the need to unlearn the lessons of the past induced by patriarchal society. In the bridge, she even parodies the English nursery rhyme *Humpty Dumpty*, as if to reveal the common thread of her existential angst.

Production

Jack Antonoff is back at the helm for this production, halfway between synthwave and dream pop. Yamaha DX7 strings and Juno-6 sequences, firmly anchored on a creeping, grainy bass synth (also from a Juno-6), are superimposed in a tense flow over a 125 bpm tempo. Programmed on a LinnDrum electronic drum machine, the bass drum enters discreetly on the first chorus and remains the only percussive element in this arrangement. The sound swells and builds progressively, without the slightest boost or interruption, to create an anxious, breathless atmosphere, perpetually fed by the synthesizers and the bass drum pulse. Taylor's melody and vocal performance—immersed in a long reverb—recall the heyday of 1980s new wave and cold wave. This solemnity, flirting with grandiloquence, distills distant echoes of Cocteau Twins, Dead Can Dance, Depeche Mode, and Cyndi Lauper.

I THINK HE KNOWS

Taylor Swift, Jack Antonoff / 2:53

Musicians

Taylor Swift: vocals, backing vocals

Jack Antonoff: keyboards, acoustic and electric guitars, programming

Recorded

Electric Lady (New York), 2019

Technical Team

Producers: Jack Antonoff, Taylor Swift

Mixing: Serban Ghenea

Sound Engineers: John Hanes, Laura Sisk, Jack Antonoff

Mastering: Randy Merrill

Best Ranking: Hot 100: 51

Genesis

In "I Think He Knows," Taylor Swift confidently projects herself into a budding romance. She expresses her admiration for the man's quiet strength and the certainty of their mutual feelings. Probably inspired by her relationship with Joe Alwyn, she enjoys describing her lover's natural assurance and the calm he exudes—his childlike gaze disarms her and makes her flustered, just as it did when she was seventeen.

Production

Taylor and Jack Antonoff must have had a lot of fun producing and arranging "I Think He Knows." Set to a tempo of 100 bpm, this upbeat electro-pop track exudes joie de vivre. Right from the intro, the combination of round, syncopated synth bass and finger clicks on beats 2 and 4 is enough to set the tone. The star's vocals, half chanted, twirl over this minimalist groove and already communicate an irrepressible hip-shaking impulse. On the chorus, the flashy, acid synthesizers; the straight, dry, percussive disco rhythm (programmed on a LinnDrum); and the lead vocals and falsetto backing vocals create an ensemble reminiscent of the glamorous, vibrant Minneapolis sound pioneered by Prince in the late 1970s. Electric guitar, risers, backing vocal overdubs, and a whole arsenal of electronic percussion gradually flesh out this luminous, danceable arrangement.

In "Miss Americana & the Heartbreak Prince," Taylor sings of her disillusionment with the political climate in the United States.

MISS AMERICANA & THE HEARTBREAK PRINCE

Taylor Swift, Joel Little / 3:54

Musicians
Taylor Swift: vocals, backing vocals
Joel Little: drums, keyboards, programming
Recorded
Golden Age (Los Angeles), Golden Age West (Auckland), 2019
Technical Team
Producers: Joel Little, Taylor Swift
Mixing: Serban Ghenea
Sound Engineers: John Hanes, Joel Little
Mastering: Randy Merrill
Best Rankings: Hot 100: 49; Rolling Stone Top 100: 16

Genesis

To set the scene for her first clearly politicized song, Taylor Swift chose to use the world of high school and its famous prom night as a metaphor for American society. Written a few months after the 2018 midterm elections, during which the singer dared for the first time to take a stand and publicly support the Democratic candidates in her native Tennessee, "Miss Americana & the Heartbreak Prince" paints a picture of a moribund, violent, and misogynistic conservative America. Employing elements drawn from low-budget horror films, Taylor's dystopia is a direct denunciation of President Donald Trump's anti-democratic policies. "Miss Americana & the Heartbreak Prince," introduced by the phrase "It's been a long time coming but / it's you and me, that's my whole world," was chosen as the first song on the "Eras Tour" set list to celebrate Taylor Swift's reunion with her fans after the COVID-19 pandemic.

Production

"Miss Americana & the Heartbreak Prince" is the second track on the album *Lover* produced by Taylor and Joel Little. Introduced by an unidentified string ensemble superimposed over a synthesizer layer, this synthpop production immediately stands out for its cinematic dimension and heavy ambience. The programmed bass drum and Taylor's voice enter simultaneously, right from the start of the first verse. Propelled by a whirring synth bass, the rhythm gradually thickens, like a sinister fanfare that nothing seems able to stop. Synthesizers and strings mingle in a symbiotic dance, and Joel Little hammers piano chords in the top register of the keyboard. Taylor's lead vocals are supported by numerous backing vocals that punctuate the narrative, like a team of funereal cheerleaders. Her interpretation is more distanced than usual, as if to mark her disenchantment and blur the boundaries between irony, sarcasm, and deadpan literalism.

Lover

Taylor Swift performing on *Good Morning America* in New York City's Central Park, August 2019.

PAPER RINGS

Taylor Swift, Jack Antonoff / 3:42

Musicians

Taylor Swift: vocals, backing vocals, percussion
Jack Antonoff: keyboards, acoustic and electric guitars, bass, drums, percussion, piano, backing vocals, programming

Recorded

Electric Lady (New York), Metropolis (London), 2019

Technical Team

Producers: Jack Antonoff, Taylor Swift
Mixing: Serban Ghenea
Sound Engineers: John Hanes, Laura Sisk, Jack Antonoff
Mastering: Randy Merrill
Best Ranking: Hot 100: 45

Genesis

In "Paper Rings," Taylor Swift describes the beginnings of a love affair, the way in which people play cat-and-mouse with each other before daring to take the plunge. She lists a series of fond memories and describes a story that transcends convention and all material considerations. She draws inspiration from her relationship with Joe Alwyn, whom she would be willing to marry with two paper rings as wedding bands, despite her taste for pomp. For the decorum, she imagines herself as part of a ballroom band circa 1978, performing the love songs requested by the newlyweds.

Production

An upbeat song par excellence, "Paper Rings" stands out with its fast tempo (208 bpm) and pop-punk feel. Yet, apart from the first verse, the electric guitars remain very much in the background and the keyboards dominate this lively, colorful arrangement. Drums, tambourine, and claps take up the slack, helping to maintain the rhythmic tension right to the end. Inspired by outspoken female punk bands who sing and shout in the chorus, Taylor has no hesitation in asking Jack Antonoff to chant "Hey," "Ho," and "One, two, three, four" to simulate the energy of a rock concert in a small, crowded venue. To add to the illusion, her lead vocals are deliberately saturated and degraded, as if passed through a lo-fi (harmonica) microphone. The singer, who excels in the subtle art of vocal overdub, creates her own choir in the tradition of 1990s girl groups. On the choruses, the piano part and the brilliance of the synthesizers evoke an overdrive version of heartland rock from the late 1970s, a style already touched on in the song "Holy Ground," released on the *Red* album in 2012.

Taylor Swift, Ciara, and Shania Twain backstage with dancers at the 2019 American Music Awards. The singers presented a strong symbol of unity and female power in the music industry.

CORNELIA STREET

Taylor Swift / 4:47

Musicians
Taylor Swift: vocals, backing vocals
Jack Antonoff: keyboards, drums, piano, programming
Recorded
Electric Lady (New York), Metropolis (London), 2019
Technical Team
Producers: Jack Antonoff, Taylor Swift
Mixing: Serban Ghenea
Sound Engineers: John Hanes, Laura Sisk, Jack Antonoff
Mastering: Randy Merrill
Best Ranking: Hot 100: 57

Genesis

Along with "Lover" and "Daylight," "Cornelia Street" is one of three tracks on the album written entirely by Taylor Swift. It is also one of her most personal songs. In it, the singer refers to her townhouse on Cornelia Street in New York's Greenwich Village. She rented this house between 2016 and 2017, in the midst of a relationship with Joe Alwyn, while awaiting the renovation of her Tribeca residence. She nostalgically recounts the good times spent with the actor, the poetry of everyday life, and the reconciliation. The house is almost personified, transcended by Taylor's romanticism and the amount of detail employed in her description. "Cornelia Street" remains one of her favorite songs to this day, and it is a much-anticipated moment for fans during acoustic segments or surprise songs in concert.

Production

Taylor wrote "Cornelia Street" in her favorite chord progression: *C* / *G* / *A* minor / *F*. As on most of the album, production is by Jack Antonoff and Taylor. Antonoff plays and programs all the instruments. Piano chords released to resonate and a pulsating synthesizer (with a sound reminiscent of a flute) are the two founding elements of this exuberantly romantic pop orchestration. Set to a tempo of 102 bpm, the mix of acoustic drums and programmed percussion (the snare drum slams almost exaggeratedly) drives this deliberately linear arrangement, punctuated by quiet beats and various rhythmic and textural relaunches. To inject a dose of vulnerability and maintain the listener's attention, Taylor sings the last four verses of each chorus in falsetto. Reverb-drenched backing vocals and distant synth layers share the depth of field and atmospheric contours of this reverie-inducing production.

DEATH BY A THOUSAND CUTS

Taylor Swift, Jack Antonoff / 3:18

Musicians

Taylor Swift: vocals, backing vocals
Jack Antonoff: keyboards, synthesizers, guitar, programming

Recorded

Electric Lady (New York), 2019

Technical Team

Producers: Jack Antonoff, Taylor Swift
Mixing: Serban Ghenea
Sound Engineers: John Hanes, Laura Sisk, Jack Antonoff
Mastering: Randy Merrill
Best Ranking: Hot 100: 67

Genesis

At the time of *Lover*, Taylor Swift was happily in love with Joe Alwyn. So the inspiration for "Death by a Thousand Cuts" came not from her own life but from watching *Someone Great*, a romantic comedy by Jennifer Kaytin Robinson, released in 2019. In comparing breaking up in love to a slow agony, the singer pulls no punches and finds reassurance that she can still write dark, desperate breakup songs, while her life is all joy and enchantment. Funnily enough, director and writer Jennifer Kaytin Robinson, herself a Swiftie from the start, confesses to having found comfort and inspiration in listening to *1989*, especially the song "Clean," while writing her screenplay.

Production

After a surprising intro featuring a choir of sampled voices, a clave played on the quarter note beat, and rhythmic programming reminiscent of the sound of brushes played on eighth notes, this upbeat electro-pop production sets off with an orchestration that contrasts with the song's theme. The electric guitar arpeggio (which appears as early as the second intro cycle), played by Jack Antonoff on a clear, dry, and slightly compressed sound, drives the particularly shimmering verses. On the choruses, the piano arpeggios merge with a sort of hammered dulcimer (derived from the Persian santur, a trapezoidal instrument whose metal strings are struck by wooden hammers) to compete in brilliance with the vibrato-laden violin sounds and the army of backing vocals recorded in overdub. To support Taylor's dense, syncopated vocals, the mix of acoustic drums and programming rolls over a creeping synth bass, all accompanied by muffled vocal samples that give the impression of bouncing on the offbeats, as if weightless.

Taylor Swift presents *Cats*, a film adaptation of the musical by Tom Hooper (released in 2019) set in London.

LONDON BOY

Taylor Swift, Jack Antonoff, Cautious Clay, Mark Anthony Spears / 3:10

Musicians
Taylor Swift: vocals, backing vocals
Jack Antonoff: keyboards, bass, percussion, programming
Mikey Freedom Hart: keyboards
Evan Smith: keyboards, saxophone
Sean Hutchinson: drums
Idris Elba: guest intro
James Corden: guest intro

Recorded
Metropolis (London), Electric Lady (New York), Conway Recording (Los Angeles), 2019

Technical Team
Producers: Jack Antonoff, Taylor Swift
Coproducer: Sounwave
Mixing: Serban Ghenea
Sound Engineers: John Hanes, Laura Sisk, Jack Antonoff
Mastering: Randy Merrill
Best Ranking: Hot 100: 62

Genesis

In "London Boy," Taylor Swift declares her love both for London and for her boyfriend of the moment, British actor Joe Alwyn. She describes the British capital from her perspective as a Tennessee girl and draws a parallel between American popular culture and a somewhat clichéd vision of English culture. In the line "Like a Tennessee Stella McCartney," she even compares herself to an American version of the famous designer and daughter of Paul and Linda McCartney. Never short of marketing ideas, Taylor took advantage of her stay in London to visit the designer and play her song for her. The designer was thrilled and offered to collaborate on the merchandising of the album, which led to the creation of a line of clothing bearing the "sustainable development" label derived from the *Lover* graphic style.

Production

Produced by Taylor and Jack Antonoff with the help of Sounwave (an American producer and songwriter known for his regular collaborations with rapper Kendrick Lamar, and whose real name is Mark Anthony Spears), this reggae-tinged bubblegum pop track is introduced by the voice of English actor Idris Elba (from 2017's *The Late Late Show with James Corden*) with a short interjection from host James Corden. "London Boy" contains an interpolation of the track "Cold War" by American singer and songwriter Cautious Clay, released in 2017. Unlike a sample, an interpolation is a note-for-note rerecording of a musical passage. It can be very faithful to the original or reinterpreted, and its commercial use requires only the agreement of the publishing rights holders. "London Boy" is a tribute to Britpop in the broadest sense of the term. Set to a tempo of 158 bpm, its swaying rhythm, sunny horn sounds, hammered eighth-note keyboards, shimmering synthesizers, and dancehall bridge make this arrangement a perfect summer hit.

Taylor Swift has a very close relationship with her mother. Here they embrace after Taylor wins Songwriter of the Year and Artist of the Year at the Nashville Songwriters Hall of Fame ceremony in 2011.

SOON YOU'LL GET BETTER (FEAT. THE CHICKS)

Taylor Swift, Jack Antonoff / 3:21

Musicians
Taylor Swift: vocals, backing vocals
Jack Antonoff: keyboards, acoustic guitar, piano, Wurlitzer
Emily Strayer: banjo, harmonies
Martie Maguire: fiddle, harmonies
Natalie Maines: harmonies

Recorded
Electric Lady (New York), 2019

Technical Team
Producers: Jack Antonoff, Taylor Swift
Mixing: Serban Ghenea
Sound Engineers: John Hanes, Laura Sisk, Jack Antonoff
Mastering: Randy Merrill
Best Rankings: Hot 100: 63; Hot Country Songs: 10; Rolling Stone Top 100: 31

Genesis

"Soon You'll Get Better" is without doubt the most serious and personal song on the *Lover* album. In it, Taylor Swift sings about both of her parents having cancer. For her father, diagnosed in 2013, remission was relatively quick, but her mother had to battle the disease from 2015 to 2019. The singer recounts how she managed to cope, never contemplating the worst, with strength and hope. The opening lines, "The buttons of my coat were tangled in my hair / In doctor's office lighting, I didn't tell you I was scared," are particularly evocative and representative of the American songwriter's eye for detail. She was quick to send the demo of "Soon You'll Get Better" to the famous all-girl country band the Dixie Chicks (now known simply as the Chicks), who gladly agreed to take part in the recording of the

"Soon You'll Get Better," a song featuring the country group The Chicks, is an emotionally charged ballad.

studio version. Despite the difficulty of performing such an emotionally charged song, Taylor agreed to perform it alone at the piano, in front of the camera, for the television event *One World: Together at Home*, broadcast on April 18, 2020. Presented by Lady Gaga, this program created at the initiative of Global Citizen raised funds for the World Health Organization, in response to the COVID-19 pandemic.

Production

The country and bluegrass arrangement of this heartfelt ballad marks a genuine return to her roots for the Tennessee girl, who had been emancipated from her label as America's sweetheart for several years by this time. The acoustic production by Jack Antonoff and Taylor is particularly sensitive, with a close proximity of the instruments, which sound as if they were recorded live by the fireside. Only the singer's voice and the Chicks' backing vocals benefit from perceptible reverb. The fundamentals of American roots music are present: picking acoustic guitar, banjo, fiddle, piano, and soulful vocal harmonies. In the background of the mix, the vibraphone gracefully spreads its mauve, cottony veil. This is probably a virtual instrument, the only one in this orchestration, where each musician's touch is superbly enhanced. "Soon You'll Get Better" prefigures the purity of *Folklore*, the artist's next album, which would be released less than a year later.

The Versace outfit that Taylor Swift wears to the 2019 MTV Video Music Awards is a statement of color.

FALSE GOD

Taylor Swift, Jack Antonoff / 3:20

Musicians
Taylor Swift: vocals, backing vocals
Jack Antonoff: keyboards, programming, backing vocals
Michael Riddleberger: drums
Evan Smith: saxophone
Brandon Bost: backing vocals
Mikey Freedom Hart: backing vocals
Cassidy Ladden: backing vocals
Ken Lewis: backing vocals
Laura Sisk: backing vocals

Recorded
Electric Lady (New York), 2019

Technical Team
Producers: Jack Antonoff, Taylor Swift
Mixing: Serban Ghenea
Sound Engineers: John Hanes, Laura Sisk, Jack Antonoff
Mastering: Randy Merrill
Best Ranking: Hot 100: 77

Genesis

Sometimes, to keep a relationship at arm's length, sublimation and false promises are necessary. "False God" deals with this and shows how Taylor Swift manages to eroticize absence to overcome missing someone. Religious symbolism, sexual metaphors bordering upon rapture, and blind faith are all used to fuel the flame of her love for Joe Alwyn, whose acting career is mainly focused on Europe and the UK.

Production

With this production, somewhere between R'n'B, chill pop, and neosoul, Taylor and Jack Antonoff venture into new musical territory. The harmony, made up of two single chords—*E* minor 7 / *D* major 7—has a jazzy texture that is highly unusual for the singer. Then there are the chill wanderings of Evan Smith on saxophone, whose highly manipulated timbre (distortion, sampling, time stretching, reverb…) can sometimes be mistaken for hiccupping vocal samples. To add nuance to this slow, ascetic groove (80 bpm), the rhythm section is played live by Michael Riddleberger on electronic drums. The whole thing hangs by a thread, resting on a keyboard whose iridescent texture evokes that of an artificial cloud, in the image of the paradises promised by this tawdry god. Taylor Swift's performance is astonishingly convincing in this sensual soul register, whose sophistication is reminiscent of the world of English musician James Blake.

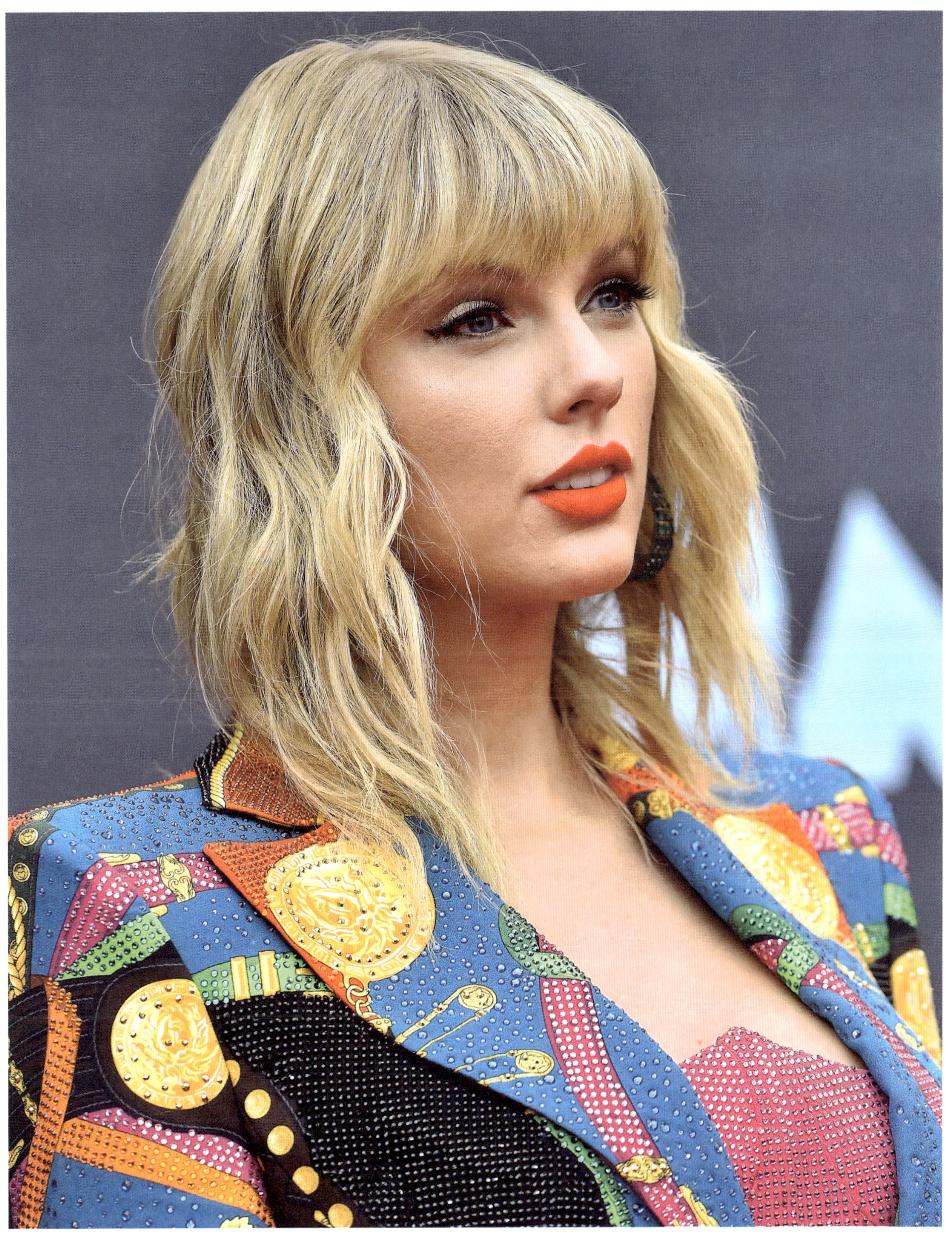

SINGLE

YOU NEED TO CALM DOWN

Taylor Swift, Joel Little / 2:51

Musicians
Taylor Swift: vocals, backing vocals
Joel Little: keyboards, programming

Recorded
Golden Age (Los Angeles), Golden Age West (Auckland), 2019

Technical Team
Producers: Joel Little, Taylor Swift
Mixing: Serban Ghenea
Sound Engineers: John Hanes, Joel Little
Mastering: Randy Merrill

Single Release
Digital Release: June 14, 2019
Best Rankings: Hot 100: 2; Adult Pop Airplay: 3; Top 40 Mainstream: 9

Genesis

For the second single from the *Lover* album, Taylor Swift decides to respond to her detractors and the trolls in the world with a fanfare. Composed with Joel Little, this joyously committed hit is structured in three parts: the first verse mocks trolls and cancel culture, the second settles the score with homophobes and protesters against LGBTQIA+ rights, and the bridge denounces the media practice of pitting female celebrities against each other. Directed by Taylor and Drew Kirsch, the music video—exuberant, colorful, saturated with prestigious guests and drag queens dressed as pop stars (including Jade Jolie as Taylor)—is equal to the challenge. With this track, Taylor equals the record of six hit singles to reach number two in the charts, previously held by Madonna. "You Need to Calm Down" also marks the start of her official stance in support of LGBTQIA+ rights, including support for the Equality Act and financial backing for GLAAD.

At the 2019 MTV Video Music Awards, Taylor Swift performs "You Need To Calm Down," which won Video of the Year and Best Pop Video awards.

Production

Having already co-produced "The Man," Joel Little is back at the helm on the production of this mainstream electro-pop track. With its medium tempo (85 bpm) and reduced number of tracks, the arrangement of "You Need to Calm Down" is remarkably clear. Each instrument plays its part, and everything is in its right place in the harmonic spectrum. The grainy synth bass, barely accompanied by a distant synth pad in the verses, naturally occupies the low frequencies and part of the lower mid-range. The programmed drums occupy three distinct frequency groups: the subs (very low frequencies, generally between 20 and 50 Hz) with the bass drum, the highs with the high hat in disco mode, and part of the high mid-range with its abundantly reverberant snare drum. The precious midrange is reserved for the pulsating synthesizer layer in sidechain; Taylor's voice, placed just above it; and the backing vocals, which occupy what space remains in the upper spectrum. Everything is designed to enhance Taylor's timbre and push the narrative to the fore. The hook on the chorus, with its overlapping "Oh ohs" rising an octave in groups of two notes (*E* < *D* / *G* < *F#* / *A* < *G* / *B* < *A* / *E* < *D*) on the *D* major scale, is a particularly catchy melodic find.

GLAAD, an American media watchdog association working to denounce discrimination and attacks on LGBTQIA+ people, is quoted in the second verse as a pun: "Why are you mad when you could be GLAAD?"

For "You Need To Calm Down," the singer also receives the Video for Good award (formerly called Best Video with a Message).

"ME!" is a joyful ode to self-confidence and self-esteem.

AFTERGLOW

Taylor Swift, Adam King Feeney, Louis Bell / 3:43

Musicians

Taylor Swift: vocals, backing vocals
Adam King Feeney: guitar
Joe Harrison: guitar
Matthew Tavares: guitar

Recorded

Electric Feel (Los Angeles), 2019

Technical Team

Producers: Frank Dukes, Louis Bell, Taylor Swift
Mixing: Serban Ghenea
Sound Engineers: John Hanes, Louis Bell
Mastering: Randy Merrill
Best Ranking: Hot 100: 75

Genesis

As with "I Forgot That You Existed," "It's Nice to Have a Friend," and "All of the Girls You Loved Before," "Afterglow" was composed by the trio of Taylor Swift, Adam King Feeney, and Louis Bell. After an argument with her partner Joe Alwyn, the singer wrote the lyrics and texted them to him, in a bid for reconciliation and appeasement. Here, *afterglow* specifically evokes the imagery of the remaining glow that illuminates the sky long after the sun has set. For Taylor, it is a metaphor for the calm after the storm. Nine years after "Back to December," released on the *Speak Now* album in 2010, she once again felt the need to write and sing a "letter of apology," showing that she knows how to admit when she was wrong. Meanwhile, "The Great War," released on the *Midnights* album in 2022, evokes the same conflict.

Production

In "Afterglow," electric guitars reign supreme. Gorged with choruses and reverbs, the six strings are superimposed on a primitive rhythmic programming centered on the pounding sound of a tom bass. To complete the ensemble, a throbbing synth bass, an intensely reverberated snare drum, and a discreet synthesizer (clearly heard at the end of the track, from 3:16 onward) contribute to thickening the sound of the choruses. This instrumental ambience, torn between earthiness and evanescence, is reminiscent of the dreamy pop of the Scottish band Cocteau Twins (active from 1979 to 1997). Taylor's vocals, however, are a different matter altogether. Her fast, syncopated delivery makes "Afterglow" unmistakably a reflection of her time. A few overdubbed backing vocals sprinkle this dream pop production, which could have come from a parallel world, a world where people still like to slow dance in new wave style.

FOR DISCERNING SWIFTIES

The song's title first appears in the "Lover" music video, when a hand places the words *after* and *glow* during a game of Scrabble. The game board is titled "King of Hearts" in a nod to her song "King of My Heart," released on *Reputation* in 2017. This hint suggests that the two titles are about the same person: Joe Alwyn.

SINGLE

ME! (FEAT. BRENDON URIE OF PANIC! AT THE DISCO)

Taylor Swift, Joel Little, Brendon Urie / 3:13

Musicians
Taylor Swift: vocals, backing vocals
Joel Little: keyboards, guitars, drum programming, synthesizers
Brendon Urie: vocals

Recorded
Electric Lady (New York), Golden Age West (Auckland), 2019

Technical Team
Producers: Joel Little, Taylor Swift
Mixing: Serban Ghenea
Sound Engineers: John Hanes, Joel Little
Mastering: Randy Merrill

Single Release
Digital Release: April 26, 2019
Best Rankings: Hot 100: 2; Adult Pop Airplay: 5; Top 40 Mainstream: 7

Genesis

Drafted as a piano and vocal ballad, "ME!" became the first single from the album and the first track to be released on Taylor Swift's new label, Republic. To make a strong impact, the singer invited Brendon Urie, lead singer of Panic! At the Disco, to sing with her. He co-wrote the track with Joel Little and Taylor. "ME!" is a joyous ode to self-confidence and self-esteem. Conceived as a letter to oneself, the song encourages listeners to think of themselves as their own best friend and to celebrate their uniqueness. It is also Taylor's first single to include a guest performer.

Production

Launched on a pulsating rhythm reminiscent of high school marching bands, the production by Joel Little and Taylor is all about the upbeat, driving factor. On the intro, a vocoder voice is superimposed on the singer's own, as if to symbolize her own reflection, that double we look to when seeking courage. On the verse, a synth bass creeps discreetly into the background, pauses for a pre-chorus composed exclusively of vocals and percussion, then comes the chorus, which explodes with a fanfare. There are no half measures here: the high-pitched trumpet discants, the acoustic guitar strumming in symbiosis with the sixteenth-note tambourine, and the eighth-note hammered piano chords stun the listener. Behind them, backing vocals galore, compressed drums, and ultra-hammering snare drums hold their own. Brendon Urie makes his entrance on the second verse and breathes new energy into this dense, clarion arrangement. He shares the microphone with Taylor until the end of the track, for an explosive duet.

At the Amazon Music Prime Day concert, New York, 2019.

IT'S NICE TO HAVE A FRIEND

Taylor Swift, Adam King Feeney, Louis Bell / 2:30

Musicians
Taylor Swift: vocals
Adam King Feeney: programming
Louis Bell: programming, songwriting, guitar
Regent Park School of Music: vocal sample

Recorded
Electric Feel (Los Angeles), 2019

Technical Team
Producers: Frank Dukes, Louis Bell, Taylor Swift
Mixing: Serban Ghenea
Sound Engineers: John Hanes, Louis Bell
Mastering: Randy Merrill
Best Ranking: Hot 100: 92

Genesis

Divided into three parts, "It's Nice to Have a Friend" tells the story of a love affair born of friendship. Two and a half minutes and three verses are enough for Taylor Swift to plunge the listener into the intimacy of a relationship through time. In the style of Big Star's song "Thirteen," the first verse recounts the blossoming of a friendship in elementary school. The second verse describes the moment, a few years later, when their hands touch for the first time. This is the time of adolescence. And finally, the third verse depicts the grand wedding and the beginnings of married life. The singer says she had fun writing her first song without a chorus—although the repetition of "It's nice to have a friend" between each verse might qualify as one. Knowing Taylor's penchant for nods and hidden messages, it is not impossible that the track once again makes reference to Joe Alwyn, her boyfriend at the time. The name Alwyn, probably of Scandinavian origin, includes the etymologically linked element *win* (Old English *wine/vän/venn/ven/vinur*), meaning "friend."

Production

Introduced by the children's choir from Toronto's Regent Park School of Music (the birthplace of producer Frank Dukes) and a pizzicato string ensemble doubled by crystal-clear steel drums, this pointillist orchestration floats like a kite. The purity of the children's voices, abundantly reverberated, evokes a church choir. After the second chorus, the instrumental part is embellished with a delightful trumpet gimmick. At the end of the cycle, the addition of a single orchestral bell note cleverly prefigures the lyrics "Church bells ring," which open the final verse, about the wedding. Taylor's precise, understated performance conveys a gentle nostalgia.

In 2019, during iHeartRadio Wango Tango, in California.

DAYLIGHT

Taylor Swift / 4:53

Musicians

Taylor Swift: vocals, backing vocals
Jack Antonoff: electric guitar, keyboards, pianos, programming

Recorded

Metropolis (London), Electric Lady (New York), 2019

Technical Team

Producers: Jack Antonoff, Taylor Swift
Mixing: Serban Ghenea
Sound Engineers: John Hanes, Laura Sisk, Jack Antonoff
Mastering: Randy Merrill
Best Rankings: Hot 100: 89

Genesis

"Daylight" is the third and final song on *Lover* that is written by Taylor Swift on her own. It is also the last and longest track on the album, at four minutes and fifty-three seconds. In it, the singer recounts her failures in love, her bad luck, and her doubts, until she meets Joe Alwyn, the light at the end of the tunnel, the man who will light up her love life for good. In short, the message of "Daylight" is that it is essential not only to recognize one's mistakes but also to understand that the damage done and the pain suffered in the past are not determinative. *Daylight* was the intended title for this seventh album, but the singer found it too sentimental, preferring instead *Lover*, which is more accurate and interesting, as the idea it conveys is more malleable.

Production

Jack Antonoff has the honor of co-producing the last track on *Lover*. "Daylight" is a synthpop ballad whose old-fashioned charm does not detract from its modernity. The track opens with a stripped-down first verse in which Taylor lays her voice over the deliciously retro sound of a Yamaha DX7. Over a 75 bpm tempo, the bass synth sequence and primitive drum machine carry the arrangement on their broad shoulders, while synth layers and risers gradually blossom. As soon as the second chorus comes out, Antonoff is quick to employ the tubular bells to add luster to the already rich orchestration. After the third and final chorus, the intensity suddenly drops, giving way to eighth-note piano chords, backed by a DX7 on the quarter note. At 4:10, the fade-out begins, along with a recording of Taylor's spoken voice, the words and sound quality of which suggest that it comes from a telephone interview. Despite its subdued statement and bittersweet tones, this closing track carries a message of love and hope.

"All of the Girls You Loved Before," leaked before its official release on March 17, 2023, becomes a favorite during the "Eras Tour."

EP

ALL OF THE GIRLS YOU LOVED BEFORE

Taylor Swift, Adam King Feeney, Louis Bell / 2:30

Musicians
Taylor Swift: vocals, backing vocals
Adam King Feeney: programming
Louis Bell: programming
Frank Dukes: guitar, keyboards
Joe Harrison: guitar
Matthew Tavares: guitar
Recorded
Electric Feel (Los Angeles), 2019
Technical Team
Producers: Frank Dukes, Louis Bell, Taylor Swift
Mixing: Serban Ghenea
Sound Engineers: Bryce Bordone, Louis Bell
Mastering: Randy Merrill
Single Release
Digital Release: March 17, 2023
Best Rankings: Hot 100: 12; Top 40 Mainstream: 35

Genesis

"All of the Girls You Loved Before" was originally intended for the *Lover* album but would not be officially released until 2023 on the *The More Lover Chapter* EP, having been leaked in February on the social network TikTok (under the title "All of the Girls"). In it, Taylor Swift describes how past relationships, even the most disastrous, are rich in valuable lessons. She thanks her partner's exes and mother for making him the man she loves today. However, the singer makes it clear that she loves him the most—"I'm so thankful for all of the girls you loved before / But I love you more."

Production

The theme and musical color of "All of the Girls You Loved Before" would not have been out of place on the *Lover* album. Produced in 2019 by Frank Dukes, Louis Bell, and Taylor Swift, the track features the dream pop sounds of "Afterglow," with an added touch of groove. A certain sensuality emanates from this synthpop waltz. The padded sound of the main keyboard, the ethereal synth layers, and the clean electric guitar rhythm (halfway between jerky strumming and chops) immerse the listener in a comfortable ambience. The unobtrusive synth bass rests on a bouncy three-quarter rhythmic programming, whose filtered sound on the verses unfolds during the choruses. Taylor's syncopated vocals benefit from a particularly long delay and reverb, which blend harmoniously with the resonance of the synth chords. From the end of the bridge onward, Taylor demonstrates the full range of her vocal tessitura, reaching for the highest notes of her register in a chest voice.

In October 2018, the star reveals for the first time her political concerns, particularly regarding gender equality and the fight against racial discrimination.

WHEN MUSIC TAKES A STAND: FROM THE STAGE TO THE POLITICAL ARENA

From her early days and for many years, Taylor Swift has carefully avoided divulging her political opinions, being aware that taking a progressive stance on controversial issues would alienate some of her audience. One should remember the singer's origins: country music, a genre inextricably linked with conservative values, particularly in the American South. And she is not the only one to adopt this apolitical stance: In her documentary *Miss Americana* (2020), she confides that to safeguard her image, her professional entourage has always encouraged her to steer clear of any political debate. Until 2018, she carefully avoided speaking out on sensitive issues. However, ten years into her career, this neutrality began to attract criticism, particularly during the 2016 presidential election. Worse still, her silence was fueling speculation and a range of interpretations, some of them emanating from extremist groups seeking to associate her with their ideologies.

A Long-Awaited Change of Direction

The artist chose to speak out clearly one evening in October 2018, with midterm elections due to take place a month later in the state of Tennessee. In a message posted on Instagram, Taylor Swift endorsed political figures for the first time, in this case Democratic candidates Phil Bredesen and Jim Cooper. She also voiced her concerns about women's rights, LGBTQ+ equality, and the fight against racial discrimination, thereby marking her entry onto the political scene. She looks back on this moment in *Miss Americana*. "I need to be on the right side of history," she declared, almost in tears, in front of the camera, as she posted her message on Instagram on October 8, 2018, finally making the change in direction so long awaited by some of her fans and observers: "It's time to take the tape off my mouth. For good."

Taking a Stand and Activism

From that time, now liberated, Taylor Swift has continued to take a stand on a multitude of issues. In 2019, she publicly voiced her support for abortion rights, and in 2022, she strongly criticized the US Supreme Court's decision to revoke this federal right. She has also been committed to the rights of LGBTQ+ people, calling for the adoption of the Equality Act, and has taken part in iconic events such as WorldPride NYC 2019 at the Stonewall Inn, a historic site of the gay rights movement. In May 2020, as President Donald Trump threatened protesters against police violence in a tweet (following the murder of George Floyd, a black man killed by police), Taylor Swift responded directly, concluding her message with a sentence: "We will vote you out in November @realdonaldtrump." On October 7, 2020, she officially announced her support for Joe Biden for president of the United States. In the 2024 presidential election, she renewed her support for Democratic candidate Kamala Harris.

It is undeniable that the artist's assumed commitment has had a considerable impact on electoral mobilization, particularly among young people. In 2018 and 2023, Taylor Swift's calls to register to vote triggered waves of new registrations within hours of her messages. This influence, dubbed the "Taylor Swift effect," quickly became a veritable media phenomenon, underlining the power of popular culture in political mobilization.

TEAM
USA

RELEASE DATES
Worldwide: July 24, 2020 (Republic Records)
*** "In the Trees" Deluxe Edition: August 4, 2020** (Republic Records—ref. B0032711-02)
Best Ranking: 1

ALBUM

Folklore

The 1 · Cardigan · The Last Great American Dynasty · Exile (feat. Bon Iver) · My Tears Ricochet · Mirrorball · Seven · August · This Is Me Trying · Illicit Affairs · Invisible String · Mad Woman · Epiphany · Betty · Peace · Hoax · The Lakes*

In 2020 at the Golden Globes, Taylor Swift set the red carpet on fire in an Etro haute couture dress.

Folklore: The Long Pond Studio Sessions, a documentary film set in Aaron Dessner's studio, located in the wilderness of the Hudson Valley, New York, was released on Disney+ on November 25, 2020. It is a behind-the-scenes look at the making of the album and includes an intimate live performance.

THE ART OF THE NARRATIVE AT ITS PEAK

In 2020, just as Taylor Swift was about to embark on her "Lover Tour," her sixth worldwide tour, the entire planet froze: The COVID-19 pandemic forced billions of people to isolate themselves at home, including international stars. The "Lover Tour" was postponed (and eventually canceled), and for the first time since she was a teenager, the singer found herself spending long weeks in the privacy of her own home, surrounded by her loved ones. But the hardworking Taylor Swift never let up. Unable to take a break, she used this enforced free time to secretly concoct her eighth studio album, *Folklore*.

From One Surprise to Another

In many respects, this album would take her audience completely by surprise. First, because it was announced just sixteen hours before its official release on July 24, 2020, just eleven months after *Lover*. Until then, Taylor Swift had meticulously planned every one of her releases, creating long teasing periods packed with riddles and other clues. With *Folklore*, she did the complete opposite: no teasers, and a simple series of black-and-white photos posted on social networks as the only promotional material (these shots were taken in May 2020 in a forest in New York's Hudson Valley by photographer Beth Garrabrant, with no other presence than that of the young woman). This was the first time the singer had released two projects less than a year apart. She confided in a December 2020 interview with *Entertainment Weekly* that only Joe Alwyn (her boyfriend at the time), members of her family, and her production team were aware of the project. *Folklore* is also a radical departure from the upbeat pop sound of *Lover*. Her music had never been so stripped down, with arrangements sometimes reduced to a single guitar and piano, even though drum machines and digital synths are not entirely absent from the production. For the first time, the album was classified as indie folk, electro-folk, and even, at times, alternative rock.

GOLDEN
GLOBE
AWARDS

The National in their recording studio. This is where the music documentary *Folklore: The Long Pond Studio Sessions* (2020) was filmed.

A New Kind of Introspection

Taylor Swift probably owes this desire for simplicity to a number of factors. After all, fifteen years of a very busy career is more than enough to justify any artist's desire for minimalism. But the *Folklore* departure seems even more introspective. Since *Lover*, the singer had aspired to a form of musical and personal appeasement. This new album is the natural expression of this state of mind: an album with a peaceful atmosphere, whose lyrics, often written in the third person, are to be taken as imaginary narratives in their own right, and no longer as reflections of the states of mind of a pop star tormented as much by her relationships as by her celebrity status. Taylor Swift tells the stories of a wealthy eccentric widow harshly judged by society ("The Last Great American Dynasty"), of a seven-year-old who loses her innocence through the trials endured by a friend ("Seven"), and of a ghost who watches the person responsible for his death ("My Tears Ricochet"). Three of the tracks—"Cardigan," "August," and "Betty"—depict a fictitious love triangle, dubbed the "teenage love triangle," formed by Betty, James, and an anonymous woman, who in turn express their nostalgia and regrets at different moments in their lives.

In an unprecedented way, a gentle melancholy inhabits and dresses this eighth album. The singer herself said in *Rolling Stone* that "sadness can be cozy" and that she sees these tracks as a means of soothing her audience's anxieties in the very particular context of this pandemic period.

Aaron Dessner, the Guide Toward Indie Folk

Conscious of the fact that such a folk shift could not succeed without a specialist in the field, Taylor Swift called upon Aaron Dessner, principal composer, guitarist, and keyboardist with indie rock band the National, to steer the production alongside her now loyal collaborator Jack Antonoff. Aaron Dessner co-wrote and co-produced the majority of the tracks on *Folklore*, giving the album its definitive indie folk color and introspective character. This work was carried out within the constraints of that time—that is, remotely, through proposals for compositions and arrangements that the two artists sent to each other in turn. Aaron Dessner also enabled the singer to refresh the usual structure of her songs. On certain tracks ("Seven," "Epiphany"), for example, he suggested moving away from the traditional verse-chorus-verse form in favor of atmosphere and narrative. Finally, it was he who facilitated the star's collaboration with singer Justin Vernon from the electro-folk indie band Bon Iver on the track "Exile." In a dialogue, two ex-partners express their pain, confusion, and regret at the end of their relationship.

Planetary Success Earned by a Work Created in Isolation

On its release, the album was a worldwide hit. It sold over 2 million units in its first week, including 1.3 million on its launch day. The album went straight to the top of the charts in the USA, giving the singer her seventh consecutive number one position, and also topped the charts in

Aaron Dessner, guitarist for The National, co-wrote and co-produced most of the tracks on *Folklore*.

many countries around the world, suggesting that the artist was now as much in demand abroad as in her own country. All sixteen tracks on the album entered the Billboard Hot 100 simultaneously, including three in the top 10. "Cardigan," chosen as the first promotional single, landed at number one.

Critically, *Folklore* was described by most of the media as the quintessential album of lockdown, and even as a genuine ray of hope in the anxiety-inducing context of the time. With five nominations for the 2020 Grammy Awards and a win for Album of the Year, Taylor Swift became the first woman in history to win the award three times (after her triumphs with *Fearless* in 2010 and *1989* in 2016). She also secured four nominations at the 2020 American Music Awards—Artist of the Year, Favorite Female Pop/Rock Artist, Favorite Music Video for "Cardigan," and Favorite Pop/Rock Album for *Folklore*—and won in the first three categories, extending her record as the most awarded artist in the show's history with a new total of thirty-two American Music Awards. This was also the third year in a row—and sixth overall—that she was crowned Artist of the Year, making her the first (and so far only) artist to achieve this.

Taylor Swift breaks a record previously held by Michael Jackson at the 2019 American Music Awards, where she wins 29 trophies. A year after this performance, she announces the release of *Folklore*.

FOR DISCERNING SWIFTIES

Perfectly in keeping with the delicacy and grace of the *Folklore* album (like *Evermore*), all tracks are written in lowercase letters.

SINGLE

THE 1

Taylor Swift, Aaron Dessner / 3:30

Musicians
Taylor Swift: vocals, backing vocals
Aaron Dessner: electric and acoustic guitars, mellotron, OP-1, piano, synth bass, synthesizer, drum programming
Bryce Dessner: orchestration
Jason Treuting: percussion
Thomas Bartlett: OP-1, synthesizer
Yuki Numata Resnick: violin, viola

Recorded
Long Pond (Hudson Valley, NY), 2020

Technical Team
Producer: Aaron Dessner
Mixing: Jonathan Low
Sound Engineers: Kyle Resnick, Laura Sisk, Jason Treuting, Jonathan Low, Aaron Dessner, Thomas Bartlett
Mastering: Randy Merrill

Single Release
Digital Release: October 9, 2020
Best Rankings: Hot 100: 4; Rolling Stone Top 100: 2

Genesis

The opening track and second single from the album, "The 1" is one of the last two songs (along with "Hoax") written by Taylor Swift for *Folklore*. According to producer and composer Aaron Dessner, the song is not autobiographical. Rather, it depicts the feelings of a friend addressing her childhood sweetheart. It is difficult to determine the full meaning of this song, in which the narrator alternates between optimism and confidence in the future, nostalgia, and confession, all tinged with a certain irony.

Production

Two chiming piano chords, *F* and *C*, are sufficient to carry this supple, elegant, and gently swaying production through to the end. This is the first time the listener discovers the subtle touch of Aaron Dessner, a member of the rock band the National since 1999. A great admirer of the artist and his band, Taylor Swift decided to call on him and his friend Jack Antonoff to produce her new album, in the midst of a period of pandemic lockdown. Aaron's twin brother, Bryce Dessner, is responsible for the string arrangement, which gradually comes to haunt this impressionistic orchestration. Over a 70 bpm tempo, the ostinato acoustic guitar chop chords stretch a thread between rhythmic programming, discreet synthesizers, and the magical fluctuations of the OP-1 synthesizer.

Taylor Swift in 2009, wearing one of her famous cardigans.

Often associated with the minimal techno of the 1990s, glitch is based on sounds derived from filtered and distorted samples, textures, or synthesizer sounds that evoke parasites such as dusty vinyl cracks or digital bugs.

SINGLE

CARDIGAN

Taylor Swift, Aaron Dessner / 3:59

Musicians
Taylor Swift: vocals, backing vocals
Aaron Dessner: electric guitar, bass, mellotron, OP-1, piano, percussion, synthesizer, drum programming
Bryce Dessner: orchestration
Benjamin Lanz: modular synthesizer
Dave Nelson: trombone
James McAlister: drum programming
Yuki Numata Resnick: violin, viola
Clarice Jensen: cello

Recorded
Kitty Committee (Los Angeles), Long Pond (Hudson Valley, NY), 2020

Technical Team
Producer: Aaron Dessner
Mixing: Jonathan Low
Sound Engineers: Kyle Resnick, Laura Sisk, Jonathan Low, Aaron Dessner, Bella Blasko
Mastering: Randy Merrill

Single Release
Digital Release: July 27, 2020
Best Rankings: Hot 100: 1; Top 40 Mainstream: 17; Adult Pop Airplay: 8; Hot Rock & Alternative Songs: 1; Rolling Stone Top 100: 1

Genesis

"Cardigan" is the first song Aaron Dessner and Taylor Swift wrote for the album. It all began when Swift asked Dessner to send her an anthology of his recent sketches and musical experiments, including the instrumental "Maple" (originally composed for his band the National), which immediately inspired her. A few hours later, she sent him "Cardigan"—the magic happened! This song became what fans interpreted as the final part of the "teenage love triangle" trilogy, which includes the songs "Betty," "August," and "Cardigan," written respectively in the voices of three fictional characters: Betty, Augustine (or Augusta), and James. "Cardigan" is narrated by Betty in a series of snapshots, distant but detailed and vivid memories, like that old woolen sweater you will never part with. For Aaron Dessner and Taylor Swift, it was clear: This first musical collaboration, touched by grace, gives them the way forward, and the foundations for *Folklore* are laid. "Cardigan" was chosen as the lead single from the singer's eighth album.

Production

Aaron Dessner's rich, delicate arrangement goes straight to the heart of the matter. Played softly, the piano gimmick rolls over a sophisticated rhythmic carpet made up of a mix of percussion and programming that sometimes evokes glitch. On bass, Aaron Dessner moves freely and harmoniously from low to high, echoing the piano notes. Bryce Dessner's orchestration gradually fleshes out the whole, in symbiosis with the synthesizer layers and the OP-1's degraded reverse sounds. In total coherence, Taylor Swift miraculously finds her way into this dreamlike musical universe, as if this arrangement had been custom-built around her voice.

Rebekah Harkness, here in her office in 1964, supported women through her patronage of the arts. Harkness is the inspiration behind "The Last Great American Dynasty."

THE LAST GREAT AMERICAN DYNASTY

Taylor Swift, Aaron Dessner / 3:51

Musicians
Taylor Swift: vocals, backing vocals
Aaron Dessner: electric guitar, bass, piano, percussion, keyboards, synthesizer, drum programming, slide guitar
Bryce Dessner: orchestration
Rob Moose: orchestration, violin
JT Bates: drums

Recorded
Kitty Committee (Los Angeles), Long Pond (Hudson Valley, NY), 2020

Technical Team
Producer: Aaron Dessner
Mixing: Jonathan Low
Sound Engineers: Laura Sisk, Jonathan Low, Aaron Dessner
Mastering: Randy Merrill
Best Rankings: Hot 100: 13; Rolling Stone Top 100: 6

Genesis

For some time—since 2013, to be precise—Taylor Swift had wanted to write the story of Rebekah Harkness (1915–1982), the first owner of her luxurious Holiday House in Watch Hill, Rhode Island. Known as Betty, she was a patron of the arts and heiress to the fortune of her husband William (Bill) Harkness, an oil tycoon who died in 1954. Taylor Swift identifies with this character of a free-spirited, exuberant woman out of step with the society of the time and scandalous in spite of herself. The moment she discovered Aaron Dessner's instrumental track, inspired by the electric guitar intricacies in Radiohead's *In Rainbows* (2007), she immediately sensed that she had finally found the right support for her song. Dessner's upbeat rhythm and atmospheric production were perfect, and the singer laid down her text and melody in a flash. Through the eyes of a mysterious character who is part of the Harkness entourage, "The Last Great American Dynasty" recounts the life of the wealthy socialite with a remarkable sense of detail. This spirit of synthesis has as much to do with American classicism as with the great storytellers of folk and country music. Only Taylor Swift could pull off this tour de force.

Production

Introduced by an ostinato piano note, a D played with the tip of the finger and the damper pedal engaged, this lively, lighthearted arrangement seems to flow naturally. Set to a tempo of 148 bpm, Bates's rhythmic programming and drums whirl under the piano chords, while the electric guitars, caught up in an increasingly dizzying dance, intertwine harmoniously. To flesh out the ensemble, Bryce Dessner and Rob Moose's orchestration gradually swells, providing the cinematic dimension essential to the song's narrative. As with "Cardigan," Taylor Swift makes Aaron Dessner's production her own with disconcerting ease. For the duration of the song, the listener is taken on a journey into the past, an immersion in the lavish life of Rebekah Harkness.

Justin Vernon of Bon Iver is featured on "Exile."

SINGLE

EXILE (FEAT. BON IVER)

Taylor Swift, Justin Vernon, William Bowery / 4:45

Musicians
Taylor Swift: vocals, backing vocals
Justin Vernon: vocals
Aaron Dessner: electric guitar, piano, synthesizer, songwriting
Rob Moose: violin, viola

Recorded
Kitty Committee (Los Angeles), April Base (Fall Creek, WI), 2020

Technical Team
Producers: Aaron Dessner, Joe Alwyn
Mixing: Jonathan Low
Sound Engineers: Laura Sisk, Jonathan Low, Aaron Dessner, Justin Vernon
Mastering: Randy Merrill

Single Release
Digital release (promotional single): August 3, 2020
Best Rankings: Hot 100: 6; Hot Rock & Alternative Songs: 2; Rolling Stone Top 100: 3

Genesis

The mysterious William Bowery credited on the liner notes is none other than Taylor Swift's partner Joe Alwyn. He wrote the piano part and the first verse, sung by Justin Vernon of Bon Iver. The young woman soon realized that the song would have to be a duet, and Joe Alwyn, an amateur singer with a deep but unconfident voice, called for a real performer, comfortable in the baritone register. Aaron Dessner thought of Justin Vernon, whom he knew well. After listening to the song, the indie-folk singer and songwriter accepted the proposal and co-wrote the track. A great admirer of Vernon's work, Taylor Swift nevertheless doubted for a while whether the collaboration would actually come to fruition. Structured in a question-and-answer format, "Exile" depicts a conflictual relationship that collapses into a dialogue of the deaf, with the two protagonists competing in bitterness. One blames the other for moving on too quickly, and the other blames the first for knowingly ignoring the signs of their dysfunction.

Production

This augmented "piano ballad" features the voices of Justin Vernon and Taylor Swift. Aaron Dessner, still at the helm, plays all the instruments except the violin and viola parts, provided by Rob Moose. Vernon's rich timbre enables him to cover a wide range of emotions. Starting out as a dark baritone on the verses, his voice opens up on the refrains and sets out on airy falsettos on the instrumental passages, where he seems to join Taylor Swift, as if in hope of reconciliation. This play of contrasts and superimpositions influences the singer's interpretation as she effortlessly slips into the skin of her character. In the background, synthesizers and strings gradually sketch out the contours of an atmospheric orchestration that comes into its own on the final chorus and outro.

Scarlett Johansson and Adam Driver, in Noah Baumbach's *Marriage Story* (2019), a movie that explores the complexities of a relationship and becomes the inspiration for "My Tears Ricochet."

MY TEARS RICOCHET

Taylor Swift / 4:15

Musicians
Taylor Swift: vocals, backing vocals
Jack Antonoff: backing vocals, live drums, percussion, electric guitar, keyboards, piano, bass
Evan Smith: saxophones, keyboards, programming
Bobby Hawk: strings

Recorded
Kitty Committee (Los Angeles), Long Pond (Hudson Valley, NY), 2020

Technical Team
Producers: Jack Antonoff, Joe Alwyn, Taylor Swift
Mixing: Serban Ghenea
Sound Engineers: Laura Sisk, Jack Antonoff
Mastering: Randy Merrill
Best Rankings: Hot 100: 16; Rolling Stone Top 100: 7

Genesis

"My Tears Ricochet" is the first song Taylor Swift composed for the *Folklore* album. It describes the point of view of a female ghost who sees her murderer mourn at her own funeral. The opening lines are inspired by the film *Marriage Story* (written and directed by Noah Baumbach and released in 2019), a dark tale of divorce. Taylor Swift, who was perfectly happy in her love life with Joe Alwyn at the time, deals with the themes of betrayal and separation without specifying whether they are romantic or friendly. She imagines that the person she has trusted most in her life suddenly becomes her worst enemy, her nemesis. Her need to broach this painful subject no doubt responds to her recent setbacks with Big Machine, her former label, and more directly with Scott Borchetta, who sold the masters of her back catalog to Scooter Braun. The line "And when you can't sleep at night (you hear my stolen lullabies)" seems to confirm this idea. Darker than its predecessors, this track was not placed in fifth position without careful consideration: The vulnerability is there, in the great Swiftian tradition. Aaron Dessner, who did not produce this track, says that it is one of his favorite songs of the *Folklore* era, saluting in passing the work of Jack Antonoff and Taylor Swift.

Production

Taylor Swift wrote "My Tears Ricochet" on her own. It is the first track on the album to be produced by Jack Antonoff. Joe Alwyn is also credited with production. Sampled and heavily edited, the intro's ghostly vocals haunt this neo-Gothic arrangement from start to finish. In the background, an electric organ with a granular, padded, almost lo-fi sound provides the harmonic context, set to a 130 bpm tempo. The rest of the instruments gradually enter, backing vocals fill in, and Evan Smith's saxophone blends in with the sound design elements. The rhythm section only makes its entrance on the bridge, at 2:27. Played live by Antonoff but immersed in an eighth-note delay, the drums follow the pulse of the synth bass sequence, as if to illustrate a wave propagating on water after a series of ricochets. To top it all off, Bobby Hawk's strings shed a dark light on this delicately orchestral funereal playlet. Taylor Swift strikes just the right tone for an interpretation perfectly balanced between detachment and palpable emotion.

MIRRORBALL

Taylor Swift, Jack Antonoff / 3:29

Musicians

Taylor Swift: vocals, backing vocals
Jack Antonoff: backing vocals, drums, Hammond B3, percussion, electric and acoustic guitars, keyboards

Recorded

Kitty Committee (Los Angeles), Rough Customer (Brooklyn, NY), 2020

Technical Team

Producers: Jack Antonoff, Taylor Swift
Mixing: Serban Ghenea
Sound Engineers: John Hanes, Laura Sisk, Jack Antonoff
Mastering: Randy Merrill
Best Rankings: Hot 100: 26; Hot Rock & Alternative Songs: 6

Genesis

In "Mirrorball," Taylor Swift compares celebrity to a mirrorball that shines only in the public eye. During the COVID-19 pandemic, artists were deprived of their light like a mirrorball broken into a thousand pieces and left in the dark. Yet, despite the pandemic, by achieving the feat of composing, producing, recording, and releasing the *Folklore* album in just a few months, the singer and her team managed to remain productive and quickly reestablish that precious link with the fans. *Evermore* was released six months later. For the singer and the Swifties, the disco ball never really stopped spinning.

Production

Written by Jack Antonoff and Taylor Swift, this ethereal production, with its dream pop and jangle pop flavors, gives pride of place to guitars. Always quick to put his one-man-band talents to good use, Antonoff plays all the instruments. The acoustic guitar strumming discreetly drives the ensemble, comfortably set to a 110 bpm tempo, and the electric guitar arpeggios, bursting with choruses and tremolos and abundantly reverberated, melt into the soaring sound of the Hammond organ pad. The drums seem to be played with fingertips and supported by the eighth-note tambourine, largely responsible, along with the brilliance of the electric guitars and the high-pitched vibraphone, for the jangle pop color. Relaxed and confident, Taylor Swift sings softly. She knows that she will be back with her fans soon and tiptoes back toward them, ready to shine brightly.

ON YOUR HEADPHONES

On the verses, Taylor Swift sings in a semi-falsetto, letting a lot of air pass through her voice. This technique, highly unusual for her, inevitably recalls the female voices of 1960s folk and pop music.

SEVEN

Taylor Swift, Aaron Dessner / 3:28

Musicians

Taylor Swift: vocals, backing vocals
Aaron Dessner: acoustic guitar, piano, bass, synthesizer, drum programming
JT Bates: drums
Bryce Dessner: orchestration
Bryan Devendorf: drum programming
Clarice Jensen: cello
Yuki Numata Resnick: violin, viola

Recorded

Long Pond (Hudson Valley, NY), 2020

Technical Team

Producer: Aaron Dessner
Mixing: Jonathan Low
Sound Engineers: Kyle Resnick, Jonathan Low, Aaron Dessner, JT Bates, Bryan Devendorf, Clarice Jensen
Mastering: Randy Merrill
Best Rankings: Hot 100: 35; Hot Rock & Alternative Songs: 7; Rolling Stone Top 100: 11

Genesis

"Seven" deals with child abuse as seen through the eyes of a seven-year-old girl who, driven by her protective instincts, struggles to understand the familial violence suffered by her young friend. Logically positioned in seventh place, this track is an ode to the purity of children's friendships. The singer takes up the pen of the little girl she was when she naively advised her friend to run away to India ("We'll move to India forever") or to come and live with her, explaining that together they would become formidable pirates. With great tenderness and poetry, Taylor Swift positions herself as a defender of children's rights.

Production

Aaron Dessner takes over the reins of this nostalgic, uncluttered production. His right hand gracefully canters over the piano with a supple, alert touch that sets the rhythmic pulse of this predominantly acoustic arrangement. Folk guitar strumming accentuates this light gallop, along with programmed percussion, bass, and JT Bates's ultra-sober drumming. The particularly resonant bass drum evokes the sound of 1920s big bands, giving us the strange impression of plunging into the heart of rural Pennsylvania. Bryce Dessner's impressionistic orchestration and Yuki Numata Resnick's glissandi-like playing recall the dreamlike style of American songwriter and violinist Andrew Bird.

SINGLE

AUGUST

Taylor Swift, Jack Antonoff / 4:21

Musicians
Taylor Swift: vocals, backing vocals
Jack Antonoff: live drums, Hammond B3, programmed percussion, electric and acoustic guitars
Evan Smith: saxophone, flute, electric guitar, keyboards
Bobby Hawk: strings
Jonathan Low: synth bass

Recorded
Kitty Committee (Los Angeles), Rough Customer (Brooklyn, NY), 2020

Technical Team
Producers: Jack Antonoff, Taylor Swift, Joe Alwyn
Mixing: Jonathan Low
Sound Engineers: Laura Sisk, Jack Antonoff, Mike Williams, Jon Gautier
Mastering: Randy Merrill

Single Release
Digital Release: July 24, 2020
Best Rankings: Hot 100: 23; Hot Rock & Alternative Songs: 5; Rolling Stone Top 100: 8

"August" is an ode to the summer romance.

Genesis

Positioned between "Cardigan" and "Betty," "August" belongs to the "teenage love triangle" trilogy. The song is written by a female narrator whose name Taylor Swift withholds, as if to underline the fact that she counts for little in the eyes of her transient lover (we do know, however, that the singer mentally represents her as Augustine or Augusta). The young man's name is James. He is seventeen years old. The song recounts his romance with the narrator, even though he is already in a relationship with Betty. The story takes place under the blazing August sun, in a suburb or small provincial town, potentially a seaside resort, where the air is "salty" ("salt air"). In Taylor Swift's mind, this love triangle comes to an end with summer, as James and Betty find each other again. Shy and insecure, the narrator will mourn her love for her handsome lover.

Production

Produced by Jack Antonoff, Taylor Swift, and Joe Alwyn, this airy ballad is arguably the most pop-oriented of the *Folklore* era. In sixteenth notes over a 90 bpm tempo, the strumming of the acoustic guitar and the drums played with brushes are a reminder of the album's indie folk lineage. In perfect symbiosis, this rhythmic duo drives the arrangement with lightness, while Evan Smith's electric guitars, Hammond organ, flute, and saxophone embroider a supple, evanescent harmonic backdrop. The string ensemble, played and arranged by Bobby Hawk, pulls the sonic spectrum upward, and the synth bass, played by Jonathan Low himself, anchors this padded instrumentation to the ground. It would not take much for everything to take off. Taylor Swift, unfurling her melody in an alert, poised voice, seems to leap from one cloud to another. A bittersweet dream pop ode to the holiday romance.

Bobby Hawk, on the strings starting with *Folklore*, performs here at a fundraiser organized by Jack and Rachel Antonoff (The Ally Coalition) for the LGBTQ+ community.

THIS IS ME TRYING

Taylor Swift, Jack Antonoff / 3:15

Musicians

Taylor Swift: vocals, backing vocals
Jack Antonoff: live drums, keyboards, bass, backing vocals, electric organ, percussion, programming
Evan Smith: saxophones, keyboards
Bobby Hawk, Lorenzo Wolff: strings

Recorded

Kitty Committee and Conway Recording (Los Angeles), Electric Lady (New York), Pleasure Hill Recording (Portland, ME), Restoration Sound (Brooklyn, NY), 2020

Technical Team

Producers: Jack Antonoff, Taylor Swift, Joe Alwyn
Mixing: Serban Ghenea
Sound Engineers: John Hanes, Laura Sisk, Jack Antonoff
Mastering: Randy Merrill
Best Rankings: Hot 100: 39; Hot Rock & Alternative Songs: 9; Rolling Stone Top 100: 13

Genesis

The song "This Is Me Trying" is a reflection on the period 2016–2017, when Taylor Swift felt at her lowest ebb. The song gives voice to three narrators behind whom the singer barely hides: In the first verse, the character goes through an existential crisis and struggles to save her relationship; in the second, she ruins her potential, lapses into alcohol, and lacks self-control; and, in the bridge, she is a burned-out woman, overwhelmed by a bereavement in love, who can no longer socialize.

Production

The trio of Jack Antonoff, Taylor Swift, and Joe Alwyn are once again at work to produce this dream pop track imbued with orchestral solemnity. Initially driven by an electric organ in a Leslie cabinet pushed to its limits, drums that seem to have been run through a delay set to eighth notes, and a bass also played to eighth notes, this arrangement is swept away by a deluge of backing vocals, strings, and brass that seems unstoppable. To accentuate the feeling of the inexorable progression of this fateful wall of sound, the electric bass is gradually joined by a sequence on throbbing synth bass. The singer's voice is overdubbed in unison and immersed in a reverb that places her at the back of the mix, as though caught in the eye of the cyclone. Despite its epic dimensions, the anxious atmosphere of "This Is Me Trying" is a catharsis of Taylor Swift's sabbatical year—a period of torment and necessary rest between the end of the *1989* world tour, in December 2015, and the release of the album *Reputation*, on November 10, 2017.

Mikey Freedom Hart, a multi-instrumentalist who appears on "Illicit Affairs," has been collaborating with Taylor Swift since *1989 (Taylor's Version)*.

ILLICIT AFFAIRS

Taylor Swift, Jack Antonoff / 3:10

Musicians

Taylor Swift: vocals, backing vocals
Jack Antonoff: live drums, keyboards, bass, electric guitar, percussion programming, backing vocals
Evan Smith: accordion, electric guitar, keyboards, saxophone, backing vocals
Mikey Freedom Hart: pedal steel

Recorded

Kitty Committee (Los Angeles), Rough Customer and Hook and Fade (Brooklyn, NY), Pleasure Hill Recording (Portland, ME)

Technical Team

Producers: Jack Antonoff, Taylor Swift, Joe Alwyn
Mixing: Serban Ghenea
Sound Engineers: John Hanes, Laura Sisk, Jack Antonoff, Evan Smith
Mastering: Randy Merrill
Best Rankings: Hot 100: 44; Rolling Stone Top 100: 13

Genesis

The text of "Illicit Affairs" is written in the form of an instruction manual for maintaining an extramarital relationship discreetly. The narrator evolves in a narrow world where she is ready to do anything to satisfy her addiction, while preparing herself for an inevitable downfall. Taylor Swift does not glorify betrayal and lies; on the contrary, she describes a grim reality. As is often the case in *Folklore*, this song is written by a fictional narrator. During this period of lockdown, the singer felt the need to step outside of herself and broaden her palette as a songwriter.

Production

From a purely formal point of view, "Illicit Affairs" is not far removed from the archetypal traditional folk song. The acoustic guitar and vocal base, the narrative flow, and the discreet chorus like an extension of the verses, recall the sometimes raw and direct style of the great North American songwriters. At 3:10, it is the shortest song on the album. The deceptively minimalist production by Jack Antonoff, Taylor Swift, and Joe Alwyn underscores the song's purpose with finesse. The soundscape created by Evan Smith, Antonoff, and Mikey Freedom Hart gradually fleshes out, like an ominous yet colorful shadow hanging over the main character. Accordion, saxophone, electric guitar, pedal steel, and backing vocals melt into an expressive, shifting sonic mix that breathes as the narrative unfolds, to the haunting accompaniment of Taylor Swift's performance.

Fender Coronado Bass II
Fender
Fender

"Invisible String" is believed to refer to Taylor Swift's relationship with Joe Alwyn.

INVISIBLE STRINGS

Taylor Swift, Aaron Dessner / 4:12

Musicians
Taylor Swift: vocals, backing vocals
Aaron Dessner: electric and acoustic guitars, bass, mellotron, piano, percussion, synthesizer, drum programming
James McAlister: drum programming
Yuki Numata Resnick: violin, viola
Clarice Jensen: cello

Recorded
Long Pond (Hudson Valley, NY), La Gaîté Lyrique (Paris), 2020

Technical Team
Producers: Aaron Dessner
Mixing: Jonathan Low
Sound Engineers: Kyle Resnick, Jonathan Low, Aaron Dessner
Mastering: Randy Merrill
Best Rankings: Hot 100: 37; Rolling Stone Top 100: 12

Genesis

Unlike most songs from the *Folklore* era, "Invisible Strings" is autobiographical. When she speaks of the invisible ties that bind two soulmates, enabling them to find each other again after years of separation as on the first day, Taylor Swift is surely thinking of her relationship with actor Joe Alwyn. The chorus evokes the existence of a kind of coincidence, a destiny in love. "Invisible Strings" is one of the few pure love songs on the album. According to Jonathan Bate, professor of English literature, the lines "And isn't it just so pretty to think / All along there was some invisible string / Tying you to me" refer to two classics of Anglo-Saxon literature: Ernest Hemingway's *The Sun Also Rises* (1926) for the line "Isn't it pretty to think so?" and Charlotte Brontë's *Jane Eyre* (1847) for its resonance with the phrase "It is as if I had a string somewhere under my left ribs, tightly and inextricably knotted to a similar string situated in the corresponding quarter of your little frame."

Production

Aaron Dessner and Taylor Swift come together once again to compose and produce this delicate, lively folk-pop ditty. For the guitar arpeggio, the musician uses one of his favorite instruments, the rubber bridge acoustic guitar, which enables him to produce a short percussive sound—akin to a violin played in pizzicato—while playing freely, without trying to muffle the strings with the palm of his right hand. The sound is particularly lively and shimmering, driving the whole arrangement with lightness. Small brush-played drums and programmed percussion

underpin the nuanced rhythm, while Clarice Jensen's cello and Yuki Numata Resnick's strings gracefully underscore the harmony. Surprisingly, and quite unusually, part of the recording was made at La Gaîté Lyrique in Paris. This probably involves either Yuki Numata Resnick's strings or Clarice Jensen's cello, or both. The synthesizer and mellotron layers discreetly accentuate the depth of field and highlight Taylor Swift's voluble vocals. Finally, a few notes of electric guitar, which seem to be played with an EBow (a kind of electric bow that produces a magnetic field that vibrates the steel strings without touching them and sounds like a violin) or with the help of a volume pedal to soften the attack and create a reverse effect, embellish this pocket-sized orchestration with a touch of pop dreaminess, fluid, colorful, and subtle.

Cellist Clarice Jensen, who performs on "Mad Woman," also contributes to the sound engineering on some of Taylor Swift's tracks.

MAD WOMAN

Taylor Swift, Aaron Dessner / 3:57

Musicians
Taylor Swift: vocals, backing vocals
Aaron Dessner: electric and acoustic guitars, bass, piano, percussion, synthesizer, drum programming
Bryce Dessner: orchestration
James McAlister: beat programming, synthesizer, hand percussion, drums
Yuki Numata Resnick: violin, viola
Clarice Jensen: cello

Recorded
Long Pond (Hudson Valley, NY), 2020

Technical Team
Producers: Aaron Dessner
Mixing: Serban Ghenea
Sound Engineers: Jonathan Low, Kyle Resnick, Aaron Dessner, James McAlister, Clarice Jensen
Mastering: Randy Merrill
Best Rankings: Hot 100: 47; Hot Rock & Alternative Songs: 10

Genesis

As soon as she heard the first notes of Aaron Dessner's piano, Taylor Swift, seriously perturbed by her dispute with businessman Scooter Braun over the purchase of her master tapes, wanted to give her voice to angry women. The anguish conveyed by this instrumental ritornello inspires this satirical, denunciatory text. In the mythopoeic vein of *Folklore*, Taylor Swift takes on the guise of a marginal widow seeking revenge on the town that ostracized her. Men are warned: "there's nothing like a mad woman." Whereas "The Man" was satirical and cheeky, "Mad Woman" denounces patriarchal society and gaslighting in a more direct, dark, and vituperative way.

Production

Composed and produced by Aaron Dessner, the arrangement of "Mad Woman" is essentially based on the piano melody and the accompanying fast-picking acoustic guitar arpeggio. Around it, the instruments intertwine in a subdued atmosphere. The pizzicati of the violin, viola, and cello keep up the pace, and the electric guitar licks twirl over a slightly crunchy sound superimposed on EBow-style playing. In symbiosis with Bryce Dessner's orchestration, synthesizers add depth of field and embellish the sophisticated sonic texture of this indie folk firebrand. In an array of discreet glitch sounds, the beat programming, which drives the overall sound as it gradually builds, is reinforced by the acoustic drums, tambourine, and various handheld percussion instruments played by James McAlister. Taylor Swift's edgy performance exudes restrained rage and steely determination.

In 2020 at the Sundance Film Festival, promoting the documentary *Miss Americana*, around the time Taylor Swift was recording "Epiphany."

EPIPHANY

Taylor Swift, Aaron Dessner / 4:49

Musicians

Taylor Swift: vocals, backing vocals
Aaron Dessner: electric guitar, mellotron, piano, synthesizers, drum programming
Bryce Dessner: orchestration
Dave Nelson: trombone
Yuki Numata Resnick: violin, viola
Kyle Resnick: trumpet
Clarice Jensen: cello
JT Bates: drums

Recorded

Kitty Committee (Los Angeles), Long Pond (Hudson Valley, NY), 2020

Technical Team

Producer: Aaron Dessner
Mixing: Jonathan Low
Sound Engineers: Kyle Resnick, Laura Sisk, Jonathan Low, Aaron Dessner, Benjamin Lanz, JT Bates
Mastering: Randy Merrill
Best Rankings: Hot 100: 57; Hot Rock & Alternative Songs: 11; Rolling Stone Top 100: 24

2020

Genesis

Composed by Taylor Swift and Aaron Dessner, "Epiphany" pays tribute to the nurses, medics, and all those who continued to work in the field during lockdown. The song describes the untenable and traumatic conditions under which these heroes fought to save lives in the midst of the COVID-19 pandemic. With particular reference to her grandfather Dean, a veteran of the bloody battle of Guadalcanal, Taylor Swift draws a comparison with what soldiers endured during World War II.

Production

Not unlike the ethereal productions of British musician Brian Eno, this ambient pop arrangement is based on four main chords (*C# / A♭ / B♭* minor / *F#*) played by an ensemble of strings, brass, synthesizers, piano, and electric guitar that seems carved from a single block. Identifiable from 1:37 onward, the only truly rhythmic element is driven by a synthesizer sequence spinning, unperturbed, in the background. Played with mallets and tuned excessively low, an orchestral kettledrum, large Japanese taiko, or tom bass–sounding percussion solemnly marks the opening beats of each bar. Taylor Swift, whose voice is charged with emotion, soars over this evanescent orchestration, casting her benevolent gaze on the heroes of the pandemic.

Jack Antonoff (left) and Evan Smith of Bleachers collaborate on "Betty."

FOR DISCERNING SWIFTIES

The first line of the outro, "Standing in your cardigan," is a nod to "Cardigan."

SINGLE

BETTY

Taylor Swift, William Bowery / 4:54

Musicians
Taylor Swift: vocals, backing vocals
Jack Antonoff: drums, bass, electric and acoustic guitars, backing vocals, electric organ, percussion, keyboards, mellotron
Aaron Dessner: electric guitar, high string guitar, piano, bass, percussion, songwriting
Mikey Freedom Hart: pedal steel, mellotron, Wurlitzer, harpsichord, vibraphone, electric guitar
Josh Kaufman: harmonica, electric guitar, lap steel guitar
Evan Smith: saxophone, clarinet

Recorded
Kitty Committee (Los Angeles), Rough Customer and Hook and Fade (Brooklyn, NY), Pleasure Hill Recording (Portland, ME)

Technical Team
Producers: Jack Antonoff, Aaron Dessner, Taylor Swift
Mixing: Serban Ghenea
Sound Engineers: John Hanes, Laura Sisk, Jonathan Low, Jack Antonoff, Evan Smith, Aaron Dessner, Josh Kaufman
Mastering: Randy Merrill

Single Release
Digital Release: July 24, 2020
Best Rankings: Hot Country Songs: 6; Hot 100: 42; Country Airplay: 32; Rolling Stone Top 100: 19

2020

Genesis

In the track listing order of *Folklore*, "Betty" is the third and final track in the "teenage love triangle" trilogy. In narrative chronology, it is actually the second chapter, as it gives voice to James, who is trying to make amends with Betty for cheating on her. "August" was the voice of Augustine (or Augusta), James's young lover, and "Cardigan" comes full circle from Betty's point of view. In the album's thread, the narrative thus begins at the end, but this is probably a choice linked more to marketing than artistic constraints, since Taylor Swift and her team generally position the biggest singles in the top five and "Cardigan" had been chosen as the lead single for *Folklore*.

After hearing Joe Alwyn (aka William Bowery) singing the chorus of "Betty" at the other end of the apartment, the

singer asked him if he would help her finish writing her song. She considered that a young man's opinion was a welcome addition to the staging of James's apology.

Production

"Betty" is the only track on *Folklore* that brings together the two producers, Aaron Dessner and Jack Antonoff. Surprisingly, this clash of the titans is played out within the framework of a song that could have appeared on *Fearless*, or even Taylor Swift's debut album. With its "Mr. Bojangles"–style descending chord progression (Jerry Jeff Walker's 1968 classic, covered by the Nitty Gritty Dirt Band and Nina Simone), the singer returns to the country-folk fundamentals of her early career. Nathan Chapman, the main producer of Taylor Swift's first three albums, would not have disowned this masterwork rooted in the Americana and classic rock of the 1960s and 1970s. The combination of picking and strumming acoustic guitars, the intricacies of electric guitars and lap steel, the primitive harmonica à la Bob Dylan, the tremulous Hammond organ, and the breezy piano plunge the listener into a postcard of faded colors. The triumphant sound of orchestral bells crowns this nostalgic, bittersweet arrangement where hope clearly dominates. Taylor Swift almost sounds as if she were seventeen again, when she was still Nashville's rising star, the age of the three characters in her love trilogy.

Violinist Rob Moose, from yMusic, contributes in several ways in the making of "Hoax."

PEACE

Taylor Swift, Aaron Dessner / 3:54

Musicians

Taylor Swift: vocals, backing vocals
Aaron Dessner: bass, piano, percussion, keyboards, synthesizer, field recording, mellotron, drone
Justin Vernon: pulse

Recorded

Kitty Committee (Los Angeles), Long Pond (Hudson Valley, NY), 2020

Technical Team

Producer: Aaron Dessner
Mixing: Jonathan Low
Sound Engineers: Laura Sisk, Jonathan Low, Aaron Dessner
Mastering: Randy Merrill
Best Rankings: Hot 100: 58; Hot Rock & Alternative Songs: 12; Rolling Stone Top 100: 25

Genesis

"Peace" is the third song Taylor Swift and Aaron Dessner wrote together for the *Folklore* album. Following the usual modus operandi, Dessner sends an instrumental track to the singer, who writes her text and melody over it; she then returns the track to him so that he can integrate it into his arrangement and fine-tune the whole, either on his own or with the help of other musicians. According to Taylor Swift, "Peace" is the most personal track of the *Folklore* era. The singer speaks directly to Joe Alwyn, her partner at the time, expressing her willingness to commit herself fully to their relationship despite her fear of not being up to scratch and dragging him down. At issue is her superstar status, which is difficult to reconcile with a stable, serene, and peaceful relationship.

Production

Launched by a synthesizer sequence, an eighth-note C ostinato reminiscent of composer Laurie Anderson's sonic explorations, Aaron Dessner's arrangement is built around an electric bass duet: two delicately harmonized lines over which Taylor Swift lays her vibrant, emotionally charged voice. The piano enters at 1:54. Dessner first sketches an impressionistic arpeggio, then embroiders a cascading sequence of chords on the upper part of the keyboard. Justin Vernon of Bon Iver is credited on the pulse. This is probably the muted beat that can be heard on the intro and outro, a subliminal pulse that underpins the C ostinato (or drone). Combined with a collage of Dessner's own field recordings (using a portable recorder), an evanescent synthesizer layer and piano chords played backward complete this masterly work. Somewhere between confession and prayer, "Peace" calls for introspection and resonates long after the end, as though suspended in time.

HOAX

Taylor Swift, Aaron Dessner / 3:40

Musicians

Taylor Swift: vocals, backing vocals
Aaron Dessner: bass, piano, electric and acoustic guitars, OP-1, synth bass
Rob Moose: orchestration, violin, viola

Recorded

Long Pond (Hudson Valley, NY), 2020

Technical Team

Producer: Aaron Dessner
Mixing: Jonathan Low
Sound Engineers: Laura Sisk, Jonathan Low, Aaron Dessner, Rob Moose
Mastering: Randy Merrill
Best Rankings: Hot 100: 71; Hot Rock & Alternative Songs: 14; Rolling Stone Top 100: 13

Genesis

To some extent acting as bookends for the songs on the *Folklore* album (standard edition), "The 1" and "Hoax" were written last. Contrary to their usual modus operandi, Taylor Swift sent the text of "Hoax" to Aaron Dessner a few days before the album's release, so that he could set it to music. One guideline: The musician must follow his instincts and do what comes most naturally. Most of the subjects addressed in *Folklore* are brought together in this last track: confessions, emotional instability and ambiguity, complicated love relationships. For Dessner, "Hoax" and "Peace" are the two songs that most realistically depict the gravity of the human condition. Having gone through phases of depression himself, Dessner is particularly sensitive to the desire to share the burdens of loved ones and the hope that persists no matter what.

Production

On reading "Hoax," Aaron Dessner, immersed in a meditative state that brings him great calm and comfort, immediately turns to the piano to sketch out the contours of this ritornello. Rob Moose lays down his violin and viola flourishes with expressive harmonics, glissandi, and sul ponticelli tonalities, meticulously orchestrated and articulated. The synth bass imposes the laws of gravity, and the ambient sounds of the OP-1 blend with the electric guitar notes produced, it would seem, by an EBow. Taylor Swift's tight vibrato, breath, and asperities of timbre are a perfect match for this intimate arrangement, a veritable indie folk and chamber pop miniature chiseled from a block of raw emotion.

On "The Lakes," Evan Smith plays flute, saxophone, and clarinet, drawing elegant arabesques.

SINGLE

THE LAKES

Taylor Swift, Jack Antonoff / 3:31

Musicians
Taylor Swift: vocals, backing vocals
Jack Antonoff: keyboards, acoustic guitar, mellotron, percussion, programming, piano
Evan Smith: saxophone, keyboards, clarinet, flute, bass
Bobby Hawk, Lorenzo Wolff: strings

Recorded
Kitty Committee (Los Angeles), Rough Customer (Brooklyn, NY), 2020

Single Release
Digital Release: August 18, 2020

Technical Team
Producers: Jack Antonoff, Taylor Swift
Mixing: Jonathan Low
Sound Engineers: Laura Sisk, Jack Antonoff, Jon Gautier, Mike Williams
Mastering: Randy Merrill

An orchestral version, matching Jack Antonoff's epic arrangement on the original demo, was released as a promotional single on July 24, 2021, to commemorate the first anniversary of *Folklore*.

Genesis

"The Lakes" shows Taylor Swift's fascination with the English Lake poets. After a retreat around Lake Windermere, England's largest lake, in the Lake District National Park, the singer developed a particular interest in this early nineteenth-century poetic movement, particularly William Wordsworth and John Keats. *The Tortured Poets Department* (the Taylor Swift album released on April 19, 2024) was particularly influenced by the romantic power of these poets exiled to the north of England.

A few weeks after the release of *Folklore*, the singer realized that "Hoax" was not the ideal closing song. So, to coincide with the release of the Deluxe Edition, she decided to add a single bonus track, "The Lakes," which she felt better encapsulated the album's themes. Introspection, the need to escape, and the desire to protect her mental health and her relationship are all evoked by the young woman, as is her romantic fantasy of retiring for good to a cottage in the Lake District.

Production

In the end, it was Jack Antonoff who had the honor of co-producing the final installment of the *Folklore* era with Taylor Swift. The lush arrangement of "The Lakes" is introduced by the old-fashioned charm of mellotron strings, delicately framed by the pizzicato playing of Bobby Hawk and Lorenzo Wolff. As if evoking the wisteria referred to in the second verse of the bridge—"I want to watch wisteria grow"—Antonoff paints an English-style sound garden where climbing plants and wildflowers seem to grow and bloom everywhere. Evan Smith's clarinet, flute, and saxophone describe elegant arabesques, and Antonoff's acoustic guitar unfurls its arpeggios, dispensing a few shimmering turnarounds along the way. Taylor Swift's performance oscillates between strength on the choruses and vulnerability on the verses and bridge.

Won over by Aaron Dessner's sensitive approach to songwriting and his sense of arrangement, by 2025, Taylor Swift and Dessner write or produce around 60 songs together.

Aaron Dessner founds The National in the early 2000s. He is the main composer for the group.

AARON DESSNER, THE SENSITIVE ASSET

Since their very first collaboration on the album *Folklore*, created remotely in the midst of the COVID-19 pandemic in 2020, Aaron Dessner and Taylor Swift have worked in perfect synergy, forging strong bonds of friendship in the process. Aaron Dessner told *People* magazine that Taylor Swift is "one of the greatest songwriters" he has ever met. In return, as related in *Us Weekly*, the singer is equally effusive in her praise for him: "This is someone I'd categorize as a soulmate collaborator. He's an incredible musician, instrumentalist, songwriter, producer, and without him this whole tour wouldn't have happened," she told the crowd at an "Eras Tour" concert in Pittsburgh, Pennsylvania, on April 14, 2023, as she brought the musician onstage to perform "Seven" (co-written with Aaron Dessner and featured on *Folklore*) with her.

The Indie Folk Melancholy of the National

Born on April 23, 1976, in Cincinnati, Ohio, Aaron Dessner grew up with his twin brother, Bryce Dessner, in a family with a passion for music. Both played several instruments from an early age, but it was in the early 2000s that they formed the National, an indie folk rock band, with Matt Berninger, Scott Devendorf, and Bryan Devendorf. Aaron soon became the band's main songwriter, alongside the more lyrically focused Matt Berninger. His sensitive approach to composition and his sense of rich, textured arrangements soon became the band's signature sound. The National finally came to prominence with their third album, *Alligator* (2005), which received rave reviews, but it was *Boxer* (2007) that really catapulted the band into the realms of success with "Fake Empire" and "Mistaken for Strangers." Poetic lyrics, hypnotic rhythms, and ethereal guitars exude an ambient melancholy that has been the band's trademark since *Boxer*. Subsequently, *High Violet* (2010) and *Trouble Will Find Me* (2013) consolidated the musicians' reputation as major players on the indie rock scene, notably with "Bloodbuzz Ohio" and "I Need My Girl." In 2017, *Sleep Well Beast* received the Grammy Award for Best Alternative Music Album.

Two Collectives for Creative Freedom

In 2016, Aaron Dessner embarked on a side project: Together with Justin Vernon of Bon Iver, he created the PEOPLE collective, a collaborative platform whose aim is to offer artists an independent space to promote musical projects. Two years later, the two friends set up Big Red Machine, a duo that combines electronic, folk, and indie

experimentation. In the same spirit as their platform, Big Red Machine quickly became a space for creative freedom, where both could give free rein to their musical wishes without the constraints of their respective bands.

To date, Big Red Machine has produced two albums: The first, released in 2018, bears the band's name and features contributions from Phoebe Bridgers and Lisa Hannigan, among others; and the second, *How Long Do You Think It's Gonna Last?* (2021), involved a number of artists, including Anaïs Mitchell, Sharon Van Etten, Ben Howard, Fleet Foxes, and Taylor Swift, who lent her voice to two tracks: "Renegade" and "Birch."

It was undoubtedly Aaron Dessner's musical depth that won Taylor Swift over in the long run. Following the release of *The Tortured Poets Department: The Anthology* in April 2024, of which Aaron produced about half, the two artists now have to their credit some sixty songs written and/or produced together.

RELEASE DATES

Worldwide: December 11, 2020 (Republic Records)

***Deluxe Edition: December 18, 2020** (Republic Records – B0033405-02)

Best Ranking: 1

ALBUM

Evermore

Willow · Champagne Problems · Gold Rush · 'Tis the Damn Season · Tolerate It · No Body, No Crime (feat. Haim) · Happiness · Dorothea · Coney Island (feat. the National) · Ivy · Cowboy Like Me · Long Story Short · Marjorie · Closure · Evermore (feat. Bon Iver) · Right Where You Left Me* · It's Time to Go*

Two years after the release of *Evermore*, Taylor Swift performs at the 2022 Nashville Songwriter Awards, where she is named Artist of the Decade.

FOR DISCERNING SWIFTIES

For both *Folklore* and *Evermore*, Taylor Swift drew inspiration from the Lakeists, a group of early-nineteenth-century English poets whose romanticism was rooted in the picturesque Lake District.

AN EXTENDED TRIP INTO THE LAND OF *FOLKLORE*

2020

On December 10, 2020, on Twitter, Taylor dropped another bombshell: Less than five months after the release of *Folklore*, its sister album, *Evermore*, would be released at midnight (Eastern time). She adopted the same communications strategy for this "surprise" album (times two) as for her previous one: no advance promotion, just a simple message to announce its imminent availability. The maneuver makes sense, since *Evermore*, as she explained following her tweet, is a natural extension of *Folklore*. Indeed, the singer and her team just could not stop writing songs. It was as if they were at the edge of the folk forest, forced to either turn back or to venture yet further into this music. For once, they chose the latter option. In the past, albums constituted unique epochs, and Taylor Swift waited for the release of one before planning the next.

A Twin in Chiaroscuro

For the first time in her career, Taylor Swift extended one of her famous "eras," so much so that she seemed to feel at ease with it. The only change to the woodsy, cottage-core-inspired universe in which she had coiled up is the season. Folklore spring is followed by wintry melancholy (in fact, she associates *Folklore* with spring and summer, and *Evermore* with autumn and winter).

Like *Folklore*, *Evermore* was written and produced in collaboration with Aaron Dessner of the National, Jack Antonoff, and, more spontaneously, Joe Alwyn. Like *Folklore*, the album was partly recorded at Dessner's Hudson Valley stronghold, Long Pond Studio. And like *Folklore*, it tells, in a style more alternative, folk, and indie rock than previous albums, stories that the songwriter

A poster of the London, Midland & Scottish Railway invites travelers to the Lake District, the inspiration for Taylor Swift's "The Lakes."

can no longer seem to contain within herself. Indeed, this ninth album continues the narrative approach of its twin, with tales told mostly in the third person, evoking the often tragic fates of fictional characters.

Dramas and Noir Fiction

The themes of *Evermore* are similar to those of its predecessor: love, fidelity, loss, regret, and nostalgia dominate. In the ballad "Champagne Problems," the singer evokes the painful rejection of a marriage proposal and the judgment passed on the person responsible (considered deranged). In "Coney Island," a melancholy duet with Matt Berninger, lead singer of the National, she explores the remorse of a relationship worn down by time and life's events. While she does not go so far as to reuse the "teenage love triangle" triptych model, she once again has fun interweaving the narratives. For example, "'Tis the Damn Season," which describes a young woman's return to her hometown and her falling in love with her childhood sweetheart, is connected to "Dorothea," sung by a young man who saw the aforementioned Dorothea leave her provincial town to fulfill her ambitions. Taylor Swift's narrative experiments do not stop there: As a great enthusiast for true crime (she told *Entertainment Weekly* she consumes numerous documentaries and podcasts dealing with criminal cases), she ventures into the genre of noir fiction or film noir, which she transposes—with a measure of success—into music. "No Body, No Crime," a sort of murder ballad, features a woman who decides to avenge her friend Este's murder at the hands of her husband.

A Clear Extension

Taylor Swift and Aaron Dessner did not expect to be recording a new album so soon after *Folklore*. However, the process began almost unconsciously back in the summer of 2020, when they were both working remotely on potential tracks for Big Red Machine, the band that grew out of Dessner's collaboration with Bon Iver's Justin Vernon. Taylor Swift took a particular interest in two instrumental tracks Dessner had shared with her, and used them

The National in full force: (left to right) Aaron Dessner, Scott Devendorf, Matt Berninger, Bryan Devendorf, and Bryce Dessner.

as inspiration for two songs, "Closure" and "Dorothea." But the real turning point came at the end of July 2020, just after the release of *Folklore*, when Dessner sent her a new instrumental that he casually titled "Westerly," the Rhode Island town where one of Taylor Swift's homes is located—in this case, the former home of composer and socialite Rebekah Harkness (the same person who inspired the track "The Last Great American Dynasty" on *Folklore*). The singer quickly e-mailed back "Willow," which became the first single and first track on the album. In the space of a few weeks, sixteen other tracks would eventually see the light of day.

Although most of the work was done remotely despite the lifting of health restrictions at the time, Taylor Swift did record most of her vocals with Aaron Dessner at Long Pond Studio in September 2020, on the heels of filming the docu-concert *Folklore: The Long Pond Studio Sessions*. Unlike *Folklore*, she wanted to include more duets: In addition to featuring Matt Berninger ("Coney Island"), we find Justin Vernon on "Evermore" and the Haim sisters, from the group of the same name, on "No Body, No Crime."

Like all its predecessors, *Evermore* was an instant success. It sold a million copies worldwide in its first week of release, becoming Taylor Swift's third album in sixteen months to pass the million mark in seven days (it was preceded by *Lover* and *Folklore*), and her eighth consecutive studio album to do so. It is also the singer's second album to top the Billboard 200 in 2020 and her eighth consecutive number one, making her the third woman in history to have eight of her albums ranked number one, after Barbra Streisand with eleven albums and Madonna with nine albums. When *Folklore* reached number three, the star also became the first woman in the history of the chart to have two albums on the podium at the same time. Last but not least, Taylor Swift entered *Guinness World Records* with a rather technical record: She is the female artist with the shortest gap between two number one albums on the Billboard 200—140 days—ever recorded.

SINGLE

WILLOW

Taylor Swift, Aaron Dessner / 3:34

Musicians

Taylor Swift: vocals, backing vocals
Aaron Dessner: keyboards, piano, synthesizer, drum machine programming, bass, electric and acoustic guitars, percussion
Bryce Dessner: orchestration
James McAlister: synthesizer, drum machine programming
Bryan Devendorf: horn, drum machine programming
Clarice Jensen: cello
Yuki Numata Resnick: violin
Josh Kaufman: electric guitar
Jason Treuting: glockenspiel
Alex Sopp: flute
CJ Camerieri: horn
Thomas Bartlett: keyboards, synthesizers
Benjamin Lanz: synthesizer (in the music video only)

Recorded

Long Pond (Hudson Valley, NY), 2020

Technical Team

Producer: Aaron Dessner
Mixing: Jonathan Low
Sound Engineers: Kyle Resnick, Jonathan Low, Aaron Dessner, James McAlister, Thomas Bartlett, CJ Camerieri, Alex Sopp
Mastering: Greg Calbi, Steve Fallone

Single Release

Digital Release: December 11, 2020
Best Rankings: Hot 100: 1; Top 40 Mainstream: 1; Adult Pop Airplay: 1; Hot Rock & Alternative Songs: 1; Rolling Stone Top 100: 11

Genesis

The opening song and lead single from the album, "Willow" is one of the first tracks co-written by the singer and Aaron Dessner, just a few months after the release of *Folklore*. A highly productive artist, Dessner decided to call his latest creation "Westerly," after the town (in Rhode Island) where Taylor Swift owns her famous Holiday House, the home that inspired her song "The Last Great American Dynasty." He sent his new demo to the singer, not expecting her to use it. Barely ten minutes later, reported *People* magazine, Taylor Swift sent him a voice memo that included the melody and full text of "Willow": "I guess we are making another album." This artistic dazzlement shook the multi-instrumentalist producer like an earthquake. In the text, Taylor Swift compares her life to a willow tree. Carried along by her collaborator's arrangement, whose bewitching ambience evokes a strange spell, a sort of musical love potion, she speaks of intrigue and the complexity of amorous desire. The mystical dimension of *Evermore* is thus announced.

Production

The swaying acoustic guitar, percussion, and light rhythmic programming are as reminiscent of Latin music as they are of tropical pop. Yet everything here remains sketchy: The synth bass hums under the pulse of the bass drum and shaker, the skins and strings are brushed, and Taylor Swift's vocals are often close to a whisper. Overdubbed backing vocals snake around the lead, as if to hypnotize the listener. Jason Treuting's glockenspiel evokes the exotic sound of a steel drum or marimba (this part may have been overdubbed or replaced by a virtual instrument whose color better suited the track's atmosphere). Halfway through the track, horn and flute mingle with violin and cello in a sensual dance orchestrated by Bryce Dessner, largely responsible for the chamber pop dimension of this exotic ritornello. The song's arrangement undulates over an 84 bpm tempo into which the singer slips effortlessly, with all the ease and suppleness for which the Swifties know her. Aaron Dessner and Taylor Swift were definitely destined to work together. The naturalness with which the one manages to immerse themself in the other's universe is uncanny.

Three different remixes were released in quick succession, as a promotional support for the first single from *Evermore*. On December 13, 2020, "Willow (Dancing Witch Version)," a dark, aggressive electro-pop version, was remixed by Elvira Anderfjärd (aka Elvira). Then on December 15 and 16, 2020, Aaron Dessner himself released two remixes: a stripped-down guitar and piano version called "Lonely Witch," followed by another textured synth-pop version called "Moonlit Witch."

CHAMPAGNE PROBLEMS

Taylor Swift, William Bowery / 4:04

Musicians
Taylor Swift: vocals, backing vocals
Aaron Dessner: acoustic guitar, piano, synthesizer, synth bass, songwriting
Logan Coale: double bass

Recorded
Kitty Committee (Los Angeles), Long Pond (Hudson Valley, NY), 2020

Technical Team
Producers: Aaron Dessner, Taylor Swift
Mixing: Jonathan Low
Sound Engineers: Jonathan Low, Aaron Dessner
Mastering: Greg Calbi, Steve Fallone
Best Rankings: Hot 100: 21; Hot Rock & Alternative Songs: 3; Rolling Stone Top 100: 7

Genesis

Taylor Swift wrote this sentimental ballad through the prism of a young girl who declines her suitor's proposal of marriage because she does not feel ready for commitment. The boy and his entourage blame her psychological problems for her refusal—the girl's difficulties are perceived as a sum of false problems, or "champagne problems." The song owes its melody and overall structure to the singer's partner at the time, Joe Alwyn (aka William Bowery). The couple worked on it together. In this case, the bridge is a world in itself, a narrative that can stand on its own. An expert in the subtle art of writing "keystone" bridges, the singer describes "Champagne Problems" as one of her proudest numbers.

Production

Produced by Aaron Dessner and Taylor Swift, this lo-fi ballad benefits from a minimalist arrangement centered around an upright piano played oompah style (very basic playing consisting of alternating chords with the left hand in the lower register and the right hand in the upper register, generally in eighth notes as here). The listener can clearly discern the crackling of the loud pedal and a few other artifacts preserved in the mix to accentuate the intimate effect. Played at the high end of the neck by Logan Coale, the double bass makes a grand entrance after the first chorus. It is interesting to note how the sound of this double bass riff resembles that of an electric bass. Supported by Taylor Swift's ethereal backing vocals, the riff returns at 2:02, precisely halfway through the song. This instrumental part heralds the river bridge, which does not really reach its climax until 3:02, on the lines: She would've made such a lovely bride / What a shame she's fucked in the head. Taylor Swift is already looking forward to her live show and hopes that fans will sing along to these words for a moment of communion and thrills worthy of "All Too Well." The double bass, progressively reinforced by the synth bass, marks the tonics in the round. To energize the bridge, Logan Coale switches to bowing on a staccato quarter note. Combined with small percussive glitch sounds, a discreet pulse underpins the whole sound on the sixteenth note, right from the start of the first chorus. Taylor Swift's performance exudes a sense of urgency, an intensity that deliberately contrasts with the fragile balance of this arrangement.

Previous page spread: The Swiftie community is one of the largest fan bases in the world, with millions in every country. The hashtag #Swifties is one of the most used on social networks.

GOLD RUSH

Taylor Swift, Jack Antonoff / 3:05

Musicians
Taylor Swift: vocals
Jack Antonoff: programming, bass, acoustic bass, drums, slide and electric guitars, piano, mellotron, percussion, backing vocals
Evan Smith: horns
Mikey Freedom Hart: synthesizer, celesta, Fender Rhodes, electric guitar
Sean Hutchinson, Michael Riddleberger: drums
Bobby Hawk: violin, viola
Patrik Berger: synthesizers
Recorded
Rough Customer (Brooklyn, NY) and Electric Lady (New York), 2021
Technical Team
Producers: Jack Antonoff, Taylor Swift
Mixing: Jonathan Low
Sound Engineers: Laura Sisk, Evan Smith, Mikey Freedom Hart, Sean Hutchinson, John Rooney, Jon Gautier
Mastering: Greg Calbi, Steve Fallone

2020

Genesis

Taylor Swift usually associates the color gold with Joe Alwyn, her partner at the time, but in "Gold Rush," she uses the word *gold* to symbolize envy and jealousy. This analogy with the gold rush that began in mid-nineteenth-century California transforms her story into a dreamlike, timeless fable. She imagines that the man she desires is so coveted that he will inevitably escape her grasp, and that she must therefore stop thinking about him. The narrator loses herself in this reverie (revealing her emotional insecurity), from which she emerges, moments later, a little dazed. The lines "My mind turns your life into folklore / I can't dare to dream about you anymore" refer to *Folklore*, the sister album to *Evermore*, released less than five months earlier.

Production

"Gold Rush" is the only song on *Evermore* produced by Jack Antonoff, Taylor Swift having left it to Aaron Dessner to produce the other sixteen tracks on the album (fifteen tracks in the standard version and seventeen in the Deluxe version). As with recent collaborations between Aaron Dessner and the young woman, it all begins with Jack Antonoff's instrumental track. "Gold Rush" is arguably the most "pop"-sounding song of the *Evermore* era. At 3:05, it is just five seconds longer than the album's shortest track, "Closure." Launched at an upbeat tempo (112 bpm) and packed with dream pop sounds, its breathless arrangement gives the listener the sensation of plunging into a waking dream, an enchanted journey as brief as it is strange and anxiety-inducing. After the nursery rhyme intro, in which angelic voices mingle with evanescent strings and synthesizers, the bass drum beats out the measure unrelentingly, from the first chorus to the outro, almost a carbon copy of the intro. Bobby Hawk marks the cadence with big bow strokes, and the electric guitar passes into a rhythmic delay that merges with the piano loops and synthesizer sequences. Mikey Freedom Hart's celesta and Fender Rhodes scatter notes from on high, like so many stars that Taylor Swift seems to catch on the fly, transforming them into a cloud of sparkling words.

In 2020 violinist Yuki Numata Resnick is sought by Taylor Swift for her dreamlike playing, here full of vibrato.

'TIS THE DAMN SEASON

Taylor Swift, Aaron Dessner / 3:49

Musicians
Taylor Swift: vocals, backing vocals
Aaron Dessner: piano, synthesizer, drum machine programming, bass, electric and acoustic guitars
Clarice Jensen: cello
Yuki Numata Resnick: violin
Josh Kaufman: harmonium, lap steel guitar
Nick Lloyd: Hammond B3
Thomas Bartlett: keyboards, synthesizers
Benjamin Lanz: horn arrangements, trombone

Recorded
Kitty Committee (Los Angeles), 2020

Technical Team
Producer: Aaron Dessner
Mixing: Jonathan Low
Sound Engineers: Kyle Resnick, Jonathan Low, Aaron Dessner, Thomas Bartlett, Benjamin Lanz
Mastering: Greg Calbi, Steve Fallone
Best Rankings: Hot 100: 39; Hot Rock & Alternative Songs: 6; Rolling Stone Top 100: 13

Aaron Dessner treasured this instrumental piece until he could find a suitable match. In an interview with Billboard.com, he explains how Taylor Swift wrote the lyrics and melody for the track in one night, after their first day of rehearsals for the music documentary *Folklore: The Long Pond Studio Sessions.*

Genesis

This song is written through the eyes of the character of Dorothea, the eponymous heroine of the ninth song on *Evermore*. In it, Taylor Swift portrays a young girl who has abandoned her small provincial town to take on Hollywood. "'Tis the Damn Season" recounts how Dorothea reconnects with her childhood sweetheart during a short vacation visit to her family in Tupelo, Mississippi (this location is indicated in one of the verses in "Dorothea"). The narrator tells her ex-boyfriend that she will soon have to leave again and tries to deal as best she can with their mutual feelings and this painful separation.

Production

This arrangement by Aaron Dessner is essentially based on a melancholy electric guitar arpeggio with a slightly crunchy sound. Programmed percussion hammers away at the offbeats and, on the chorus mainly, on beats 2 and 3. This dramatic effect is reinforced by Clarice Jensen's cello and Yuki Numata Resnick's violin, whose vibrato-laden playing seeks to strike a chord with the listener. In the background, the harmonium and Hammond organ merge to create a layer of asperity, mingled with Benjamin Lanz's brass instruments. Once again, this instrumental piece seems tailor-made for the voice and lyrics of Taylor Swift, whose edgy interpretation resonates with Aaron Dessner's electric guitar.

The pop star shares a special moment with a young fan.

An Epiphone acoustic guitar, featuring graphics from *Evermore* and signed by Taylor Swift, is auctioned to benefit Musicares.

TOLERATE IT

Taylor Swift, Aaron Dessner / 4:05

Musicians

Taylor Swift: vocals, backing vocals
Aaron Dessner: keyboards, piano, synthesizer, drum machine programming, bass, percussion
Bryce Dessner: orchestration
James McAlister: synthesizer, keyboards, drum machine programming, drums
Bryan Devendorf: percussion, drum machine programming
Clarice Jensen: cello
Yuki Numata Resnick: violin, viola
Josh Kaufman: electric guitar
Jason Treuting: percussion

Recorded

Long Pond (Hudson Valley, NY), 2020

Technical Team

Producer: Aaron Dessner
Mixing: Jonathan Low
Sound Engineers: Kyle Resnick, Jonathan Low, Aaron Dessner, James McAlister
Mastering: Greg Calbi, Steve Fallone
Best Rankings: Hot 100: 45; Hot Rock & Alternative Songs: 8

2020

Genesis

The source of inspiration for "Tolerate It" is Daphne du Maurier's 1938 novel *Rebecca*. In this classic of English literature, first adapted for the screen in 1940 by Alfred Hitchcock, the main character, Edythe Van Hopper, seeks to impress her husband with her efforts and goodwill. But, haunted by the memory of his late first wife, Rebecca, he merely tolerates his new wife's presence. Taylor Swift identifies with the character of Edythe Van Hopper, having felt herself to be in a similar situation several times before with a man who paid little attention to her once the relationship was established. Following in the great Swiftian tradition of the "vulnerable" ballad, "Tolerate It" is fifth on the track listing.

Production

Aaron Dessner's instrumental track is based on a piano part with an odd meter time signature: 10/8. This unusual meter creates a sensation of permanent imbalance, as if Taylor Swift's character were falling and catching herself in extremis at the end of each cycle. A sophisticated sonic backdrop gradually swells in the background: Light percussion mingles with the cavalcade of programmed glitch sounds; the purity of the string ensemble orchestrated by Bryce Dessner clashes with the deep, distorted sound of the bass, while the electric guitar and synthesizers distill a multitude of swell and reverse-textured sounds. A sense of urgency emanates from Taylor Swift's voice, in perfect harmony with the intensity of the arrangement.

Este Haim, Taylor Swift's friend long before *Evermore*, onstage during the *1989* world tour.

SINGLE

NO BODY, NO CRIME (FEAT. HAIM)

Taylor Swift / 3:35

Musicians

Taylor Swift: vocals, backing vocals
Danielle Haim: backing vocals
Este Haim: backing vocals
Aaron Dessner: mandolin, keyboards, piano, synthesizers, field recording, bass, acoustic and electric guitars
Josh Kaufman: electric and lap steel guitars, electric organ, harmonica
JT Bates: drums

Recorded

Long Pond (Hudson Valley, NY), Ariel Rechtshaid's house studio (Los Angeles), 2020

Technical Team

Producers: Aaron Dessner, Taylor Swift
Mixing: Jonathan Low
Sound Engineers: Jonathan Low, Matt DiMona, Ariel Rechtshaid, JT Bates
Mastering: Greg Calbi, Steve Fallone

Single Release

Digital Release: Republic Records in partnership with MCA Nashville, January 11, 2021
Best Rankings: Hot Country Songs: 2; Hot 100: 34; Country Airplay: 54; Rolling Stone Top 100: 12

2020

Genesis

"No Body, No Crime" is what one might call a murder ballad, a subgenre of traditional ballads that tell dark murder stories. It is the only song on *Evermore* composed entirely by Taylor Swift. Inspired by her obsession with crime documentaries and podcasts typical of the true-crime genre, the singer has written a veritable film noir script. Written from the point of view of the friend of a woman murdered by her cheating husband, the story is full of twists and turns—the murdered woman is named after one of Taylor Swift's close friends, whom she invites to sing backing vocals: Este (Haim). The narrator decides to avenge her friend's death by killing the culprit: the husband. But the husband's mistress is found guilty of this second murder, having collected her lover's life insurance money.

Production

"No Body, No Crime" opens with the sound of police car sirens and Taylor Swift's voice declaiming "He did it, he did it." Launched by three notes on the mandolin, Aaron Dessner's orchestration immediately transports the listener a few years back in time. All the guitars are out on show, and this arrangement plays on the fundamentals of mainstream American country rock. The snare drum slams like a late-nineties production, and the lap-steel guitar licks between the vocal phrases. Acoustic guitar strumming, subtly crunchy electric guitar, bass, and drums drive the overall solid, bouncy mid-tempo groove. The echo of Taylor Swift's voice accentuates the feeling of going back in

time twenty years. The backing vocals of the Haim sisters soberly support the singer's interpretation, well ensconced within her comfort zone.

Active since 2007, the American rock band Haim is made up of the three sisters Danielle, Este, and Alana Haim. Since their collaboration with Taylor Swift on "No Body, No Crime"—a latecomer given their lifelong relationship—the three rockers have officially considered the star as "the fourth Haim sister."

FOR DISCERNING SWIFTIES

Before recording this knowing song for her friend Este Haim, and having no doubt that she would appreciate the idea, Taylor Swift texted her to ask the name of her favorite chain restaurant. And so Olive Garden appears in the first verse of the second couplet.

In 2020, Taylor Swift, who has just taken control of her catalog by re-recording her first six albums, is named the Best Solo Act in the World by the NME Awards. The statue's middle finger represents the rebellious attitude of rock music and the British magazine *New Musical Express*.

HAPPINESS

Taylor Swift, Aaron Dessner / 5:15

Musicians

Taylor Swift: vocals, backing vocals
Aaron Dessner: piano, synthesizer, drum programming, keyboards, bass, electric and acoustic guitars
Bryce Dessner: orchestration
Yuki Numata Resnick: violin
Thomas Bartlett: keyboards, synthesizers
JT Bates: drums
Ryan Olson: drum programming (high hat)

Recorded

Long Pond (Hudson Valley, NY), 2020

Technical Team

Producer: Aaron Dessner
Mixing: Jonathan Low
Sound Engineers: Kyle Resnick, Jonathan Low, Aaron Dessner, Thomas Bartlett, JT Bates, Ryan Olson, Robin Baynton
Mastering: Greg Calbi, Steve Fallone
Best Rankings: Hot 100: 52; Hot Rock & Alternative Songs: 9

Genesis

At 5:15, "Happiness" is the longest track on the album. It is also the last track to be included in the track listing of the standard edition of *Evermore*. Taylor Swift wrote the lyrics and melody a week before the album went to the Sterling Sound studio for mastering. Aaron Dessner had been working on this composition since 2019, intending it for Big Red Machine, the collaborative art–pop music project (featuring many notable artists) of which he and Justin Vernon have held the reins since 2008. Touched by the beauty of this instrumental piece, Taylor Swift wrote bespoke lyrics, proposed the result to her partner, and won his support. Inspired by the situation of a friend coming out of a long and trying relationship, she writes "Happiness" from the (fictional) pen of a young woman seeking to restructure, to find herself again, after years of living together. In her view, the line "I haven't met the new me yet" sums up the song's central concept. Every relationship brings changes, and being alone implies a new relationship with the world, a transformation. Subtle references to F. Scott Fitzgerald's novel *The Great Gatsby*, one of Taylor Swift's bedside books, can be heard just beneath the surface.

Production

Aaron Dessner's folk-ambient production lends a special flavor to this bittersweet, luminous ballad. The mix of synthesizer lead sounds and electric guitar playing on EBow recalls the textures developed by Brian Eno and the Frippertronics technique (playing based on the superimposition of tape recorder loops) invented by guitarist Robert Fripp (founder of progressive rock band King Crimson) in the 1970s. The piano and Bryce Dessner's pizzicato and staccato orchestration progressively add the organic touch. The rhythmic programming plays an essentially atmospheric role. To underline the bridge's tonal shift, the cadence becomes more pronounced, and the swirling high hat programmed by Ryan Olson responds to glitch sounds and acoustic percussion. Taylor Swift's warm timbre, set in the lower half of her wide register, radiates a pleasant sense of benevolence and hope.

NME AWARDS
BEST SOLO ACT IN THE

The piano in "Dorothea" is originally part of the closing music of an episode of *Bob's Burgers*.

FOR DISCERNING SWIFTIES

The piano part in "Dorothea" is the same one used three years earlier by Aaron Dessner for "Give It to Teddy," his band the National's contribution to the closing credits of the American animated series *Bob's Burgers* ("Thanks-hoarding," episode 5, season 8, 2017).

DOROTHEA

Taylor Swift, Aaron Dessner / 3:45

Musicians

Taylor Swift: vocals, backing vocals
Aaron Dessner: piano, bass, electric and acoustic guitars, tambourine
Josh Kaufman: electric and acoustic guitars
Thomas Bartlett: piano, keyboards, synthesizers
Benjamin Lanz: modular synthesizer
JT Bates: drums, percussion

Recorded

Long Pond (Hudson Valley, NY), 2020

Technical Team

Producer: Aaron Dessner
Mixing: Jonathan Low
Sound Engineers: Laura Sisk, Jonathan Low, Aaron Dessner, Thomas Bartlett, JT Bates
Mastering: Greg Calbi, Steve Fallone
Best Rankings: Hot 100: 67; Hot Rock & Alternative Songs: 13; Rolling Stone Top 100: 40

2020

Genesis

This is the song that introduces Dorothea, the character invented by Taylor Swift and already featured on "'Tis the Damn Season." Through the eyes of Dorothea's former lover, Taylor Swift paints the portrait of a young girl who left Tupelo, a small provincial town in Mississippi, for Hollywood, with a head full of dreams. Her ex-boyfriend, who has remained in her hometown, casts a sympathetic eye on the irresistible rise of the woman he loved so much. On TV, in magazines, Dorothea is everywhere. But the young man's flame is not extinguished. Patient, he remains hopeful that Dorothea's flame also still burns brightly. To find out what happens next, one must go back as far as "'Tis the Damn Season," four songs earlier.

Production

Launched on a ternary rhythm at 120 bpm, this instrumental piece by Aaron Dessner immediately gives pride of place to the vocals. Dessner's upright piano, a central element of the arrangement, gracefully carries the tune from beginning to end. JT Bates provides a disjointed drum part, a weightless groove that enables this orchestration to gradually gain in intensity. The acoustic guitar strumming gradually builds in power, and the electric guitars weave an increasingly animated dialogue between EBow, arpeggios, and melodic licks. Behind them, the synthesizer layers expand and deepen the field. Taylor Swift's light interpretation gently lulls the listener, torn between hope and disbelief.

SINGLE

CONEY ISLAND
(FEAT. THE NATIONAL)

Taylor Swift, Aaron Dessner, Bryce Dessner, William Bowery / 4:35

Musicians
Taylor Swift: vocals, backing vocals
Matt Berninger: vocals
Aaron Dessner: keyboards, piano, acoustic and electric guitars, synthesizer, drum machine programming, bass, percussion
Bryce Dessner: piano, synthesizer, orchestration
Bryan Devendorf: drum machine programming, drums
Scott Devendorf: bass, piano
Clarice Jensen: cello
Yuki Numata Resnick: violin
Jason Treuting: drums, percussion

Recorded
Long Pond (Hudson Valley, NY), Scarlet Pimpernel (London), Knobworld (Los Angeles), 2020

Technical Team
Producers: Aaron Dessner, Bryce Dessner
Mixing: Jonathan Low
Sound Engineers: Kyle Resnick, Jonathan Low, Aaron Dessner, Robin Baynton, Sean O'Brien
Mastering: Greg Calbi, Steve Fallone

Single Release
Digital Release: January 18, 2021
Best Rankings: Hot 100: 63; Hot Rock & Alternative Songs: 12; Rolling Stone Top 100: 32

Genesis

The third single from the *Evermore* era, "Coney Island" is an opportunity to invite the full band the National, of which Taylor Swift is an unconditional fan. This guest appearance—long-awaited, since Aaron Dessner is one of the permanent members of the Cincinnati, Ohio–based rock band—finally becomes a reality. While frantically writing the lyrics with her partner at the time, Joe Alwyn (aka William Bowery), Taylor Swift immediately thought of Matt Berninger (lead singer of the National) as the male vocalist for the song. She had already touched on the subject of the erosion of feelings in a couple in "Tolerate It," but here she delves deeper into guilt and regret after years spent together, with the accompanying litany of routine and indifference. The estranged couple recall their memories of Coney Island.

With great admiration and humor, Matt Berninger testifies (on Instagram) to his collaboration with Taylor Swift, saying: "It was like dancing with Gene Kelly. She made me look good and didn't drop me once."

Production

Based on a repetitive riff—three notes played in unison on guitars and keyboards, and a creeping rhythm played with mallets on toms in the drum kit—this hushed, atmospheric arrangement bears the hallmark of the National's most reflective works. To reinforce the main riff, Aaron Dessner superimposes a light strumming and a second acoustic guitar riff doubled with dotted notes on the Rhodes. Clarice Jensen and Yuki Numata Resnick's straight, reverberating held string notes envelop the whole, leaving the voices of Taylor Swift and Matt Berninger plenty of room. The warmth of the singer's mezzo timbre and the richness of his baritone voice blend perfectly. As if in evidence of this, their alchemy admirably serves the narrative, carried by the ensemble of tribal percussion on Prozac that imperceptibly builds in intensity right to the end of the track. The spark of the couple embodied by the two artists has been extinguished, but for the listener, the magic remains.

Fans will recognize Ivy from the soundtrack of the TV series *Dickinson* (2019), whose heroine is played by actress Hailee Steinfeld.

FOR DISCERNING SWIFTIES

This is the list of quill pen songs, as compiled by Taylor Swift for an exclusive Apple Music playlist: "Anti-Hero," "Carolina," "Cowboy Like Me," "Epiphany," "Evermore (feat. Bon Iver)," "Happiness," "Hoax," "Ivy," "Mastermind," "My Tears Ricochet," "Peace," "Red," "Sad Beautiful Tragic," "Snow on the Beach," "The Last Great American Dynasty," "Tolerate It," and "Willow."

IVY

Taylor Swift, Aaron Dessner, Jack Antonoff / 4:20

Musicians

Taylor Swift: vocals, backing vocals
Aaron Dessner: piano, synthesizer, drum machine programming, percussion, bass, synth bass, electric and acoustic guitars, rubber bridge acoustic guitar, and twelve-string guitar
Justin Vernon: backing vocals, triangle, drums, banjo, electric guitar
Bryce Dessner: orchestration
Bryan Devendorf: drum machine programming, drums
Clarice Jensen: cello
Yuki Numata Resnick: violin, viola
Kyle Resnick: trumpet
JT Bates: drums
Josh Kaufman: lap steel guitar
Thomas Bartlett: synthesizers
Benjamin Lanz: trombone, modular synthesizer
Logan Coale: double bass

Recorded

Long Pond (Hudson Valley, NY), 2020

Technical Team

Producer: Aaron Dessner
Mixing: Jonathan Low
Sound Engineers: Kyle Resnick, Jonathan Low, Aaron Dessner, Thomas Bartlett, Justin Vernon, JT Bates, Benjamin Lanz
Mastering: Greg Calbi, Steve Fallone
Best Rankings: Hot 100: 61; Hot Rock & Alternative Songs: 11; Rolling Stone Top 100: 13

Genesis

For Taylor Swift, "Ivy" falls into the category of quill pen songs—that is, songs composed in a slightly pompous classical style, inspired by Charlotte Brontë, Emily Dickinson, or period films in which the characters all wear puffed sleeves and corsets. The fans developed a whole mythology around this song after the release of *Evermore*, whose date corresponds to Emily Dickinson's birthday almost to the day. In fact, Alena Smith obtained the singer's agreement to include the song in the soundtrack of her *Dickinson* TV series, which depicts the poet's life. Taylor Swift portrays the torments of a woman prey to impossible love, as she is promised to another. By candlelight, the character writes to her lover, begging him to stop feeding her fantasies, while fanning the flames of their desire in spite of herself.

Production

"Ivy" is the only song on *Evermore* that Taylor Swift co-wrote with her two producers of that time, Aaron Dessner and Jack Antonoff. Nevertheless, production is entirely Aaron Dessner's responsibility. The arrangement of this indie folk ritornello relies mainly on an interweaving of strings of all kinds: acoustic guitars, violin, viola, cello, double bass, banjo, lap steel, and electric guitar. To achieve this scintillating texture, Dessner uses no fewer than three types of acoustic guitar (standard, rubber bridge, and twelve-string). He is supported by fellow musician Justin Vernon of Bon Iver on banjo, electric guitar, backing vocals, and triangle pulse. In the background, the percussion swirls, while brass and synthesizers gradually thicken the spectrum of this whirling, airy orchestration. Taylor Swift tiptoes through her light, voluble melody, as if to counterbalance the emphasis of these quill-written words from another time.

Dickinson

Taylor Swift's dream of inviting Marcus Mumford of the band Mumford & Sons to sing with her comes true in "Cowboy Like Me."

COWBOY LIKE ME

Taylor Swift, Aaron Dessner / 4:35

Musicians

Taylor Swift: vocals, backing vocals
Aaron Dessner: piano, synthesizer, drum machine programming, percussion, synth bass, keyboards, electric and acoustic guitars, bass
Marcus Mumford: backing vocals
Justin Vernon: drums, electric guitar
Bryce Dessner: orchestration
Clarice Jensen: cello
Yuki Numata Resnick: violin
Josh Kaufman: lap steel guitar, harmonica, mandolin
Logan Coale: double bass

Recorded

Long Pond (Hudson Valley, NY), Scarlet Pimpernel (London), 2020

Technical Team

Producer: Aaron Dessner
Mixing: Jonathan Low
Sound Engineers: Kyle Resnick, Jonathan Low, Aaron Dessner, Justin Vernon, Robin Baynton
Mastering: Greg Calbi, Steve Fallone
Best Rankings: Hot 100: 71; Hot Rock & Alternative Songs: 15

Genesis

"Cowboy Like Me" falls into the Swiftian category of "mini-movie script" songs. In it, Taylor Swift portrays two ambitious crooks engaged in a kind of love ballet. They challenge each other and play a game of cat-and-mouse, waiting to find their next victim. Due to the COVID-19 pandemic, *Evermore* was partially recorded at Scarlet Pimpernel, the home studio installed in Marcus Mumford's second home in London. A huge fan of the Mumford & Sons front man, Taylor Swift had long dreamed of inviting the singer-songwriter to sing on her album. She and Aaron Dessner were hard at work on "Cowboy Like Me" when Mumford walked through the studio door and hummed a harmony. The singer seized the opportunity and asked him if he would like to take part in the recording: Mumford readily agreed.

Production

Eleventh on the *Evermore* track listing, "Cowboy Like Me" is probably the track most representative of contemporary Americana. Aaron Dessner's broad, pure production evokes the soul of classic American folk and rock music. His sensitive piano touch and strumming, laid-back acoustic guitar playing lay the foundations for this organic arrangement. Josh Kaufman's engaging lap steel is reminiscent of David Lindley (a multi-instrumentalist of genius, best known for his work with Jackson Browne). Justin Vernon's mandolin, harmonica, and brush drums add depth to the instrumentation. Orchestrated by Bryce Dessner, the strings of Yuki Numata Resnick and Clarice Jensen accompany the changes in intensity in successive, supple waves. In the background, a synthesizer drone, omnipresent yet constantly oscillating in volume, evokes the dramatic ending of Radiohead's classic "Karma Police" (1997). Taylor Swift's restrained interpretation leaves plenty of room for Marcus Mumford's backing vocals. The listener is plunged into a slow-motion road trip where everything seems to happen in the blinking of an eye.

Gibson

Bryan Devendorf of The National is on drums in "Long Story Short."

LONG STORY SHORT

Taylor Swift, Aaron Dessner / 3:35

Musicians

Taylor Swift: vocals, backing vocals
Aaron Dessner: keyboards, synthesizer, drum machine programming, bass, synth bass, percussion, acoustic and electrical guitars
Bryce Dessner: orchestration, electric guitar
James McAlister: drum machine programming, synthesizers
Bryan Devendorf: drums
Clarice Jensen: cello
Yuki Numata Resnick: violin
Kyle Resnick: trumpet
Jason Treuting: crotales, metallic percussion

Recorded

Long Pond (New York), 2020

Technical Team

Producer: Aaron Dessner
Mixing: Jonathan Low
Sound Engineers: Kyle Resnick, Jonathan Low, Aaron Dessner, Bryce Dessner
Mastering: Greg Calbi, Steve Fallone
Best Rankings: Hot 100: 68; Hot Rock & Alternative Songs: 14; Rolling Stone Top 100: 42

Genesis

In "Long Story Short," Taylor Swift looks back on the darkest period of her life. Between 2016 and 2020, she had to deal with a media lynch mob and a number of disputes. As if to close this painful chapter once and for all, she pays tribute to Joe Alwyn, with whom she was gradually finding her anchorage. The quiet strength and unfailing love of her companion helped her to get through these trials and concentrate on the essentials. With her newfound confidence, Taylor Swift announces that she has left her torments behind her.

Production

To underline her point, what better than an up-tempo indie pop setting? Powered by a mix of drums and percussion programmed at 158 bmp, "Long Story Short" pulls no punches. Aaron Dessner's arrangement is as much about the taut rhythm as it is about the layers of ethereal synthesizers and layered electric guitars. Jason Treuting's metallic percussion melts into the brilliance of the electric piano sound, and Bryce Dessner's orchestration adds its dose of dramatic tension. Aaron Dessner graces the listener with an elaborate bass line and some particularly shimmering harmonized shots, notably on the second half of the third verse. Taylor Swift's natural flow does the rest: syncopated, dynamic, and relaxed.

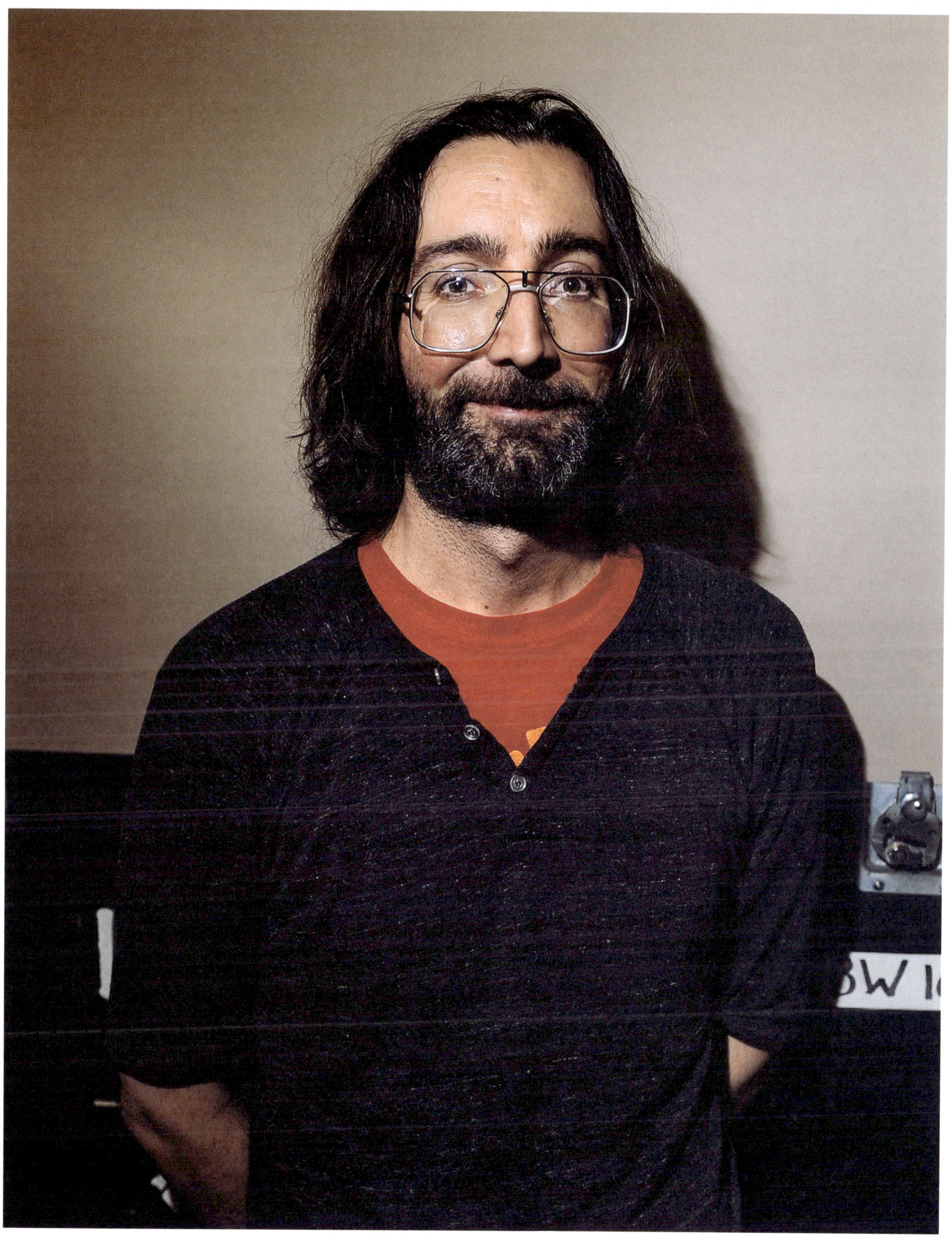

ON YOUR HEADPHONES

The instrumental version of "Marjorie" precedes that of "Peace" (released six months earlier on *Folklore*), the drone and main thread of the latter echoing the pulsating drone sample heard in the distance on the bridge of the former (if you listen closely).

MARJORIE

Taylor Swift, Aaron Dessner / 4:17

Musicians

Taylor Swift: vocals, backing vocals
Marjorie Finlay: backing vocals
Aaron Dessner: piano, synthesizer, drum machine programming, synth bass, drone, percussion, acoustic guitar
Justin Vernon: backing vocals, synthesizer (Prophet 5)
Bryce Dessner: orchestration
James McAlister: percussion, synthesizer (Vermona pulse)
Bryan Devendorf: percussion, drums, drum machine programming
Clarice Jensen: cello
Yuki Numata Resnick: violin
Jason Treuting: chord stick, percussion
Ryan Olson: drum programming (high hat)

Recorded

Long Pond (Hudson Valley, NY), 2020

Technical Team

Producer: Aaron Dessner
Mixing: Jonathan Low
Sound Engineers: Kyle Resnick, Jonathan Low, Aaron Dessner, Ryan Olson
Mastering: Greg Calbi, Steve Fallone
Best Rankings: Hot 100: 75; Hot Rock & Alternative Songs: 16; Rolling Stone Top 100: 56

Genesis

"Marjorie" is Taylor Swift's tribute to her grandmother Marjorie Finlay, a former opera singer who died in 2003. In it, the star lists the invaluable advice of her grandmother, whose presence she still feels strongly, and regrets not having spent more time with her, and not having asked her more questions. Aaron Dessner had been saving this instrumental piece for some time. In his opinion, it is one of the most experimental compositions on *Evermore*, an ideal medium for this benevolent ghost story.

Production

The arrangement for "Marjorie" is based on a superimposition of synthesizer sequences and a piano played in placed chords. The orchestration gradually swells: solemn vibrato held string notes, drones, heady guitar loops, played percussion, and swirling programming. Taylor Swift miraculously finds her way through this maze of sound. Through the magic of musical sampling, the soprano voice of her grandmother, Marjorie Finlay, echoes in the distance. On backing vocals and synthesizer, Justin Vernon once again makes his contribution. A specialist in atypical instruments, Jason Treuting has the brilliant idea of recording a chord stick track (a four-string instrument akin to a dulcimer) to infuse the synthesizer sequences with organic color. The melody, the words, and Taylor Swift's interpretation manage to give a pop twist to this textural and formally complex piece.

The National photographed in their recording studio in Long Pond, upstate New York.

CLOSURE

Taylor Swift, Aaron Dessner / 3:00

Musicians

Taylor Swift: vocals, backing vocals
Aaron Dessner: piano, synthesizer, drum machine programming, synth bass, percussion
Justin Vernon: drums, synthesizer (Messina system)
Bryce Dessner: orchestration, piano
James McAlister: drums, synthesizer
Gabriel Cabezas: cello
Yuki Numata Resnick: violin
Dave Nelson: trombone
Kyle Resnick: trumpet
Trever Hagen: trumpet, electronic performance (no-input mixing)
Jason Treuting: chord stick, percussion
Logan Coale: double bass

Recorded

Long Pond (Hudson Valley, NY), 2020

Technical Team

Producers: Aaron Dessner, BJ Burton, James McAlister
Mixing: Jonathan Low
Sound Engineers: Kyle Resnick, Jonathan Low, Aaron Dessner, Justin Vernon, James McAlister, Gabriel Cabezas, Bryce Dessner, Dave Nelson, Trever Hagen
Mastering: Greg Calbi, Steve Fallone
Best Ranking: Hot 100: 82

Genesis

In the writing of "Closure," Taylor Swift assumes the role of a young woman whose ex-boyfriend cannot stand the idea that she has forgotten him for good. She replies firmly that she needs neither his explanations nor his pseudo-friendship, because she knows that he is only trying to clear his conscience.

Production

Introduced by 5/4 rhythmic programming from metal band Nine Inch Nails' Trent Reznor (a producer notably renowned for his discovery of Marilyn Manson), the industrial folk production of "Closure" is an oddity on *Evermore*. The piano duet, performed by Aaron Dessner and his twin Bryce, gracefully hovers over this jerky, abundantly distorted hyperpop rhythm. Justin Vernon, clearly very involved in the production of this album, handles the running of Taylor Swift's voice through a digital harmony generator developed by his friend and collaborator Chris Messina. The result can be compared to the effect produced by a vocoder. To top it all off, Trever Hagen produces random electronic sounds in no-input mixing. Strings and brass appear and disappear in successive waves, like taut lines between each burst of vocals. The acid treatment of this arrangement fits well with the song's subject and can be seen as a way of illustrating the difficult management of a breakup.

Swifties form a real community, united by their love for music and the personality of their idol.

EVERMORE
(FEAT. BON IVER)

Taylor Swift, Justin Vernon, William Bowery / 5:04

Musicians
Taylor Swift: vocals, backing vocals
Aaron Dessner: piano, synthesizer, drum machine programming
Stuart Bogie: alto and contrabass clarinets, flute
Justin Vernon: vocals, synthesizer, field recording
Joe Alwyn (aka William Bowery): piano
Bryce Dessner: orchestration
James McAlister: drums, synthesizer
Gabriel Cabezas: cello
Clarice Jensen: cello
Yuki Numata Resnick: violin
Jason Treuting: percussion
Josh Kaufman: lap steel guitar
Logan Coale: double bass
Alex Sopp: flute

Recorded
Long Pond (Hudson Valley, NY), 2020

Technical Team
Producers: Aaron Dessner, Taylor Swift
Mixing: Jonathan Low
Sound Engineers: Kyle Resnick, Jonathan Low, Aaron Dessner, Stuart Bogie, Justin Vernon, Gabriel Cabezas, Robin Baynton, Alex Sopp
Mastering: Greg Calbi, Steve Fallone
Best Ranking: Hot 100: 57

Genesis

"Evermore" is both the title track and the closing track on the standard edition of *Evermore*. As with "Exile," the fourth track on *Folklore*, which was also a duet with Justin Vernon, the genesis of "Evermore" began with the piano part, composed by Joe Alwyn. Taylor Swift laid down her melody and lyrics on the verses and choruses, and asked Justin Vernon to take charge of the bridge. The two narrators describe a seemingly endless period of depression and suffering, but ultimately find hope.

Production

Unlike "Exile," on which Aaron Dessner performed the piano part for technical reasons, Joe Alwyn recorded his part himself. For Taylor Swift and Dessner, this decision was a conscious one. It was a matter of respecting the composer's sensibility as far as possible and making the piece as lively as possible. With this in mind, "Evermore" is recorded without a click (metronome) and the bridge accelerates so much that it changes tempo completely. This allows Justin Vernon to launch into an extended litany sung in falsetto, on which he opts to double his voice to gain in intensity (unless this is the Messina effect described in "Closure"). Coupled with the synthesizer layers, Bryce Dessner's distant orchestration gives this highly theatrical piano ballad a cinematic dimension. Against this autumnal backdrop, the emotionally charged performance of Taylor Swift and Justin Vernon reaches its climax on the breathless verbal ping-pong of the second half of the bridge. Somewhere between a story with an ending and one without, the long journey of *Evermore* draws to a close.

Swifties are very creative. They make fan art, write fan fiction, and compose songs as a tribute to their idol.

RIGHT WHERE YOU LEFT ME

Taylor Swift, Aaron Dessner / 4:05

Musicians

Taylor Swift: vocals, backing vocals
Aaron Dessner: piano, synthesizer, keyboards, acoustic and electric guitars, banjo, bass, drum machine programming
Bryce Dessner: orchestration
James McAlister: drums
Jonathan Low: drum machine programming
Yuki Numata Resnick: violin
Josh Kaufman: electric guitar, harmonica, harmonium
Nick Lloyd: Hammond B3
Thomas Bartlett: piano, keyboards
JT Bates: percussion

Recorded

Long Pond (Hudson Valley, NY), Scarlet Pimpernel (London), 2020

Technical Team

Producer: Aaron Dessner
Mixing: Jonathan Low
Sound Engineers: Kyle Resnick, Jonathan Low, Aaron Dessner, Robin Baynton, JT Bates, Nick Lloyd, James McAlister, Thomas Bartlett
Mastering: Greg Calbi, Steve Fallone

Genesis

Taylor Swift wrote "Right Where You Left Me" in the words of a young girl with a broken heart. Life seems to have stopped: Around her, the world keeps spinning, but she remains inconsolable, as though frozen. The songwriter painted this sadly surreal picture over an instrumental piece by Aaron Dessner, a few days before the mastering phase. This is the first of two bonus tracks included on the Deluxe Edition of *Evermore*, the second being "It's Time to Go."

Production

The arrangement of "Right Where You Left Me" is driven by acoustic guitar strumming and Aaron Dessner's banjo work. Progressively joined by a set of electric guitars with a highly processed, spatialized sound, the instrumentation rushes forward and gradually thickens. Layers of synthesizers, Hammond organ, harmonium, and Bryce Dessner's orchestration transform this country-folk-pop composition, taking it into alternative and indie folk territory, very much in the spirit of *Evermore*.

Taylor Swift with model Karlie Kloss for the Victoria's Secret fashion show in 2014.

IT'S TIME TO GO

Taylor Swift, Aaron Dessner / 4:14

Musicians

Taylor Swift: vocals, backing vocals
Aaron Dessner: piano, synthesizer, keyboards, electronic drums, drum machine programming, bass, electric and acoustic guitars, synth bass
Justin Vernon: bass, electric and acoustic guitars
Bryan Devendorf: electronic drums, drum machine programming
JT Bates: drums, percussion
Bryce Dessner: orchestration
Thomas Bartlett: piano, synthesizer, keyboards
Clarice Jensen: cello
Yuki Numata Resnick: violin
Dave Nelson: trombone
Kyle Resnick: trumpet
Jason Treuting: chord stick, percussion

Recorded

Long Pond (Hudson Valley, NY), 2020

Technical Team

Producer: Aaron Dessner
Mixing: Jonathan Low
Sound Engineers: Kyle Resnick, Jonathan Low, Aaron Dessner, Justin Vernon, Dave Nelson, JT Bates, Thomas Bartlett
Mastering: Greg Calbi, Steve Fallone

2020

Genesis

Located at the seventeenth and final position on the track listing of the Deluxe version of *Evermore*, the aptly named "It's Time to Go" is also the album's second bonus track. Here, Taylor Swift lists a number of situations in which her intuition has saved her. The first verse seems to mention her dispute with model Karlie Kloss, her ex–best friend, and the third undoubtedly refers to her dispute with Scott Borchetta, the boss of her former label Big Machine Records. Thus, the *Evermore* era ends with this final piece of advice: You have to listen to your instincts and have the courage to leave when it's time to go.

Production

Introduced by a pulsating eighth-note sound, this bowed instrument sequence (cello, violin, or an unidentified virtual string instrument) runs through the entire arrangement on a C drone, gradually reinforced by a synthesizer sequence. The upright piano provides the harmonic structure: *C / A* minor / *F / G*. The cadence changes only in the middle of the chorus (*C / G / A* minor / *F*), between the last two cycles of the post-chorus and the first two cycles of the outro (*F / A* minor / *C / G*). After an arpeggio at the upper end of the neck, the bass lays down the gimmick of the post-chorus, before soon being doubled by the acoustic guitar. Essentially based on bass drum and high hat, the rhythmic programming is quickly joined by JT Bates's acoustic drums. Synthesizers, strings, lap steel guitar, and brass open up the spectrum. Taylor Swift's voice undulates over Aaron Dessner's swaying production, creating a hushed ambience for this gentle farewell.

Taylor Swift and director Lana Wilson at the preview of *Miss Americana* (2020).

THE MASTERS CONTROVERSY

Conflicts between artists and record companies are not uncommon in the music industry, but few have been as high-profile as the one that, from 2019, pitted Taylor Swift against Big Machine Records. The artist was only sixteen when she signed her very first contract with the independent label in 2006. The label had just been founded in Nashville by Scott Borchetta with the aim of promoting emerging artists in the country and pop country genres, at a time when digital platforms were booming. Launching such a young artist was a risky gamble, but it quickly paid off: As soon as her first single, "Tim McGraw," was released, the teenager began to enjoy success. Two years later, in 2008, her second album, *Fearless*, propelled her to superstar status in the USA.

Big Machine Records, Six Albums and Thirteen Years

According to her contract, Taylor Swift had to produce a total of six albums with Big Machine. From 2006 to 2017, she released the albums that would make her one of pop's biggest stars: *Taylor Swift* (2006) and *Fearless* (2008), as well as *Speak Now* (2010), *Red* (2012), *1989* (2014), and *Reputation* (2017). Like most record company contracts, the one between the artist and Big Machine stipulated that the label—and not the singer herself—owned the original recordings, or masters, of all the tracks. Taylor Swift, on the other hand, owns the copyright to her lyrics and compositions. In other words, she does not receive any direct income from the recordings when they are used in commercials or films or broadcast on the radio, and cannot freely exploit these masters without Big Machine's agreement.

A Stab in the Back

In November 2018, the artist's contract with Big Machine came to an end. Again, as is usual in the music world, she wanted to free herself from her first label and find new freshness in another record company. She told Scott Borchetta that she wanted to acquire full ownership of the masters of her first six albums. But no agreement was reached, the producer being aware that even by selling them back to the singer at a high price, he was depriving himself of the monumental revenues that the tracks would continue to generate in the future. (Taylor Swift would later reveal that Scott Borchetta had offered to give her back her masters in exchange for the renewal of her contract with him.) At the same time, the singer signed with Republic Records, a subsidiary of Universal Music Group, this time negotiating full ownership of her future masters into the contract.

On June 30, 2019, she received a real hammer blow when she learned that Big Machine had been sold to Ithaca Holdings, a company owned by entrepreneur Scooter Braun, for around $300 million. The news was all the more shocking given that Braun was the former manager of Kanye West. He was the man who, behind the scenes, played a major role in the conflict that pitted her against the rapper. As soon as the sale was announced, Taylor Swift denounced the acquisition in a post on Tumblr: "I learned about Scooter Braun's purchase of my masters as it was announced to the world. All I could think about was the incessant, manipulative bullying I've received at his hands for years." For her, the deal was a real betrayal on the part of Big Machine and Scott Borchetta, obviously aware of the bullying the artist had been subjected to. In November 2019, the producer posted a statement titled "So, It's Time for Some Truth..." on the Big Machine website. In the aftermath, several celebrities, including Demi Lovato and Sia, publicly pledged their support. Others, however, came to Taylor Swift's defense: Brendon Urie, leader of Panic! At the Disco, spoke of an appalling acquisition, while Iggy Azalea railed on Twitter against men's control over women's work in the music industry.

Taylor Swift Takes Back Control

After this major blow, Taylor Swift decided on a radical course of action: In August 2019, she announced her intention to rerecord her first six albums in their entirety to regain control of them. After all, American copyright law allows for this: An artist can rerecord their works after a certain period and thus produce new masters under their full ownership. But the pop star went even further than this. Because she had become the most influential personality in the music world, she had no trouble convincing the streaming platforms to feature her own versions when they became available, to the detriment of her original albums. And even though some of her fans admit to treasuring the sound of the first records, which often marked their childhood or adolescence, they followed their idol's instructions: to favor listening to the Taylor's Versions.

In November 2019, the tone became even harder between the artist and Big Machine. This time, she accused Scooter Braun and Scott Borchetta of preventing her from performing her old songs—on the pretext that they were protected by the rights of her former masters—at the 2019 American Music Awards ceremony, and from broadcasting them in her documentary *Miss Americana*, due for release in 2020. Big Machine denied this, but evidence of the label's good faith was lacking. A year later, Scooter Braun ended up selling all the singer's recordings to another company, Shamrock Holdings, without making any real profit (the transaction would have amounted to $300 million, the same sum he had put on the table a year earlier to buy the singer's catalog). Taylor Swift, for her part, announced that she had been approached by Shamrock Holdings to propose a transaction. She declined the offer, determined to pursue her project of reappropriating her music. Her first rerecording, *Fearless (Taylor's Version)*, was released in April 2021 and, not without some surprise on the part of the singer herself, was a huge commercial success. The others followed, each time generating the same public enthusiasm: *Red (Taylor's Version)* in November 2021, *Speak Now* in July 2023, and *1989* in October 2023.

Repercussions

This conflict between Taylor Swift and her former record company has had the merit of shedding light on industry practices considered unfair by many, notably with respect to contracts that leave little control to emerging artists, who are often forced to relinquish their rights to gain a foothold in the industry. And while Prince had previously publicly campaigned for the right to regain control of his masters, Taylor Swift's voice will have found more resonance, no doubt buoyed by debates on the treatment of artists in the age of streaming.

RELEASE DATES

United States: October 21, 2022 (Republic Records—ref. 2445790111)
Version: "3am Edition": October 22, 2022 (Taylor Swift)
Version: "The Til Dawn Edition" and CD "The Late Night Edition"
(Republic Records—ref. 2455761781)**: May 26, 2023**
Best Ranking: 1

ALBUM

Midnights

Lavender Haze · Maroon · Anti-Hero · Snow on the Beach (feat. Lana Del Rey) · You're on Your Own, Kid · Midnight Rain · Question...? · Vigilante Shit · Bejeweled · Labyrinth · Karma · Sweet Nothing · Mastermind · The Great War* · Bigger Than the Whole Sky* · Paris* · High Infidelity* · Glitch* · Would've, Could've, Should've* · Dear Reader* · You're Losing Me (From the Vault)** · Hits Different*** ·

** bonus Midnights (3am Edition)*
*** bonus Midnights (The Late Night Edition)*
**** bonus Midnights (The Til Dawn Edition)*

Promotional poster for *Midnights* in front of an HMV music store in the UK.

At the 2022 MTV Video Music Awards, Taylor Swift announces the release of *Midnights* in a spectacular Oscar de la Renta dress.

This was the fifth time that Taylor had called on photographer Beth Garrabrant, with whom she had collaborated since *Folklore* in 2020, on the design of the *Midnights* album cover. Garrabrant has made a significant contribution to the visual aesthetics of the artist's recent projects.

INTROSPECTION

2022

The year 2021 marked the realization of a crucial project in Taylor Swift's career from an artistic and commercial point of view: the rerecording of her first six albums, announced with great fanfare in 2019 as part of her feud with Scooter Braun. *Fearless (Taylor's Version)* was released in April 2021 and *Red (Taylor's Version)* in November. The singer's fan base was convinced that she would release at least one if not two Taylor's Versions in 2022, to ensure continuity in the defense of her discography. In reality, this was not to be. In the summer of 2022, there was still no sign of an imminent third rerecorded album.

Another Surprise Announcement

On the evening of August 28, 2022, Swift once again surprised her fans, the music industry, and the media by announcing at the MTV Video Music Awards—where she won three awards for her fifteen-minute video *All Too Well: The Short Film*—that she would be releasing her tenth studio album on October 21, 2022. Jubilation took hold of social networks as soon as the singer spoke. That same evening, at midnight, she revealed on her personal accounts the title—*Midnights*—and its concept. In an interview on SiriusXM Hits 1, she said, "This is a collection of music written in the middle of the night, a journey through terrors and sweet dreams. The floors we pace and the demons we face." Her poetic text hints that the album will be tinged with the same lyricism as the previous two.

A Compilation of Insomnias

Midnights is a concept album, as the tracks together form a collection of stories about "13 sleepless nights scattered throughout my [Taylor's] life." Thirteen tracks, in which the artist reflects on her fears, insecurities, and moments of clarity, all occurring during the night. She describes the album as an exploration of insomnia, during which she was forced to confront the thoughts that haunted her. "I think that I've always been fascinated with sleeplessness. [...] It's a time when I've written a lot of my songs. It's a time when the catharsis of songwriting has helped me the most," she explained in an interview with SiriusXM Hits 1, just before the album's release.

Far more personal than the melancholy tales of the "Folkmore" era (a contraction of *Folklore* and *Evermore* adopted by the Swifties), these nocturnal reflections oscillate between retrospection and projection into the future. The themes dear to the artist are guilt and regret ("Midnight Rain," "Mastermind"), nostalgia, and the gaze of others ("Anti-Hero") and, of course, love ("Snow on the

Midnights receives the Album of the Year and Best Pop Vocal Album awards.

Beach," "Sweet Nothing"), all of which continue to inspire her, album after album. The first track on the track list, "Lavender Haze," which recounts the external pressures she had to deal with during her relationship with Joe Alwyn, largely sets the tone. The track is a reflection, but also a confession, on the romantic relationship she has worked so hard to preserve over the previous six years. As she announces from the very first seconds, *Midnights* is an album in which she lays herself bare once again, with the hindsight and wisdom that her past experiences have given her. In several tracks—including the singles "Anti-Hero" and "Bejeweled"—she does not hesitate to open a real window on her psyche: "Anti-Hero" humorously addresses the way she perceives herself and manages her anxiety, while "Bejeweled" looks back on periods in her life when she may have felt overshadowed or undervalued.

2022

A Muted Pop

The concept of the nocturnal album, in which it is easy to move from an introspective track that stems from insomnia to the tale of a festive late night, might seem perfectly tailored to accommodate a variety of sounds and moods. But *Midnights* does not seem to want to take advantage of this largesse. On the contrary, its atmosphere is seamlessly coherent, certainly due to the delicate, uncluttered, and formidably effective production by Jack Antonoff, once again at the helm (although Aaron Dessner contributed to the writing of "Would've, Could've, Should've" and "High Infidelity").

Deep bass lines, soft beats, enveloping keyboard layers, and the sounds of bells and chimes remind us, as does the clock in Cinderella's castle, that after midnight, the night sets in, with its possible insomnia. *Midnights* is a textured, spellbinding album that does not fail in its aim: to immerse its listener in the theme of night. Such an effect is undeniably due to the magic of analog sound that Jack Antonoff is so fond of. He exploits the full potential of his tape equipment and vintage synthesizers.

Midnights also marks a clear return to pop, after the indie folk of *Folklore* and *Evermore*, even though it is far, far removed from the supercharged energy of *1989* or the revanchist electro-trap of *Reputation* (perhaps *Lover* is its closest relative). One might be tempted to call it dream pop and synthpop, but it is hard to categorize it in a precise genre, as it seems to be the culmination—and, why not also the synthesis—of a sixteen-year career.

Taylor Swift takes the stage at the 2024 Grammy Awards.

Commercial and Cultural Dominance

Immediately following the announcement of its release, *Midnights* was heavily promoted, once again breaking with the "Folkmore" era, during which communications operations around the albums had been minimalist, due to the pandemic. Between September 21 and October 7, 2022, Swift unveiled the track list in a series of thirteen videos posted on TikTok, titled "Midnights Mayhem with Me." In each video, set to elevator music, she draws numbers in a lottery cage to gradually reveal the titles of her unreleased songs. In addition to the standard vinyl version, she offered three sleeve variants, each showing a quarter of a dial on its reverse side. The four parts form a (real) clock to be built with a mechanism sold separately. But the singer's finest marketing coup was undoubtedly the release of an extended edition, *Midnights (3am Edition)*, featuring seven bonus tracks, just three hours after the classic version (released on October 21 at midnight). This would be complemented in the spring by two further bonus editions, *The Late Night Edition* and *The Til Dawn Edition*.

As always, the album was an immediate success. But *Midnights* stands out from the rest with a series of records broken in terms of physical sales and streaming. In particular, it broke Spotify's all-time record for most listened-to album in a single day, with 186 million streams on its first day on the platform, surpassing the previous record of 155 million streams set by Drake's *Certified Lover Boy* in 2021 (note that this record would be broken again in April 2024 by another of the singer's albums: *The Tortured Poets Department*).

Swift also became the most listened-to artist in a single day on Spotify, with 228 million streams across her entire catalog, as well as the first to break the 200 million mark. The album also broke Apple Music and Amazon records for most listened-to pop album in a single day (and in a single week for Amazon) and was the first album to reach over 700 million listens on Spotify in a single week. In the charts, Swift's dominance was so overwhelming that she became the first artist in history to control the entire top 10 of the Billboard Hot 100 with ten tracks present simultaneously.

Republic Records would later claim that *Midnights* sold over 6 million units worldwide in two months. Media pundits the world over were asking, how far will Taylor Swift's hegemony extend? And Anna Nicolaou of *Financial Times* asked, will she be the last pop superstar?

The writing of "Lavender Haze" is a collective work to which Zoë Kravitz contributed.

SINGLE

LAVENDER HAZE

Taylor Swift, Jack Antonoff, Zoë Kravitz, Sounwave, Jahaan Sweet, Sam Dew / 3:22

Musicians
Taylor Swift: vocals, backing vocals
Jack Antonoff: drums, synthesizers, Juno 6, backing vocals, Wurlitzer, percussion, programming
Zoë Kravitz: backing vocals
Sounwave: programming
Jahaan Sweet: bass, synth bass, flute, Juno
Sam Dew: backing vocals
Dominik Rivinius: snare drum

Recorded
Rough Customer (Brooklyn, NY), Electric Lady (New York), Henson Recording (Los Angeles), 2021–2022

Technical Team
Producers: Jack Antonoff, Taylor Swift, Sounwave, Jahaan Sweet, Braxton Cook
Mixing: Serban Ghenea
Sound Engineers: Laura Sisk, Ken Lewis, Jack Antonoff, Jahaan Sweet
Mastering: Randy Merrill
Vinyl Mastering: Ryan Smith

Single Release
Digital Release: November 29, 2022
Best Rankings: Hot 100: 2; Top 40 Mainstream: 5; Adult Pop Airplay: 4; Dance / Mix Show Airplay: 6

2022

Genesis

"Lavender Haze" is the opening track and second single from Taylor Swift's tenth studio album. The singer wrote it with Jack Antonoff, Zoë Kravitz (daughter of Lenny Kravitz), Sounwave (Marc Anthony Spears), Jahaan Sweet, and Sam Dew. She first heard the expression *lavender haze* (which translates as "being on cloud nine" when in love) in an episode of *Mad Men* and, struck by its evocative sound, decided to explore its meaning. She uses it to illustrate the need she feels to take refuge in a kind of emotional cocoon (lavender in color), away from the prying eyes of the media.

Production

The "Lavender Haze" instrumental track is the result of writing sessions with Jack Antonoff, Sounwave, and Sam Dew for Swift's long-time friend Zoë Kravitz's first solo album. The arrangement is based on a short synthpop and rhythm'n'blues loop populated by atonal ambient sounds. Created by Jahaan Sweet (an American producer close to Britney Spears, who has collaborated with Drake, Eminem, and Kehlani), the loop was strange enough to immediately inspire Jack Antonoff. Jazz musician Braxton Cook, a friend of Sweet's, provided the vocal sample that became the song's main gimmick. The creeping, abundantly distorted synth bass anchors this instrumentation in a deep, infectious groove. Taylor Swift's interpretation deftly juggles falsettos, flows, and rhythm'n'blues vibes, scansions, and vocoder-harmonized passages. The choral production of this opening track immerses the listener in a nocturnal ambience full of sensual vibrations. The atmosphere of *Midnights* is perfectly set. To support the single release of "Lavender Haze," four remixes were produced. A tropical house remix by German DJ Felix Jaehn was released on February 10, 2023, followed by three other versions: the "Tensnake Remix," the "Jungle Remix," and the "Snakehips Remix," all released on March 3, 2023. On streaming platforms, the four remixes were combined in the *Lavender Haze (Remixes)* EP.

MAROON

Taylor Swift, Jack Antonoff / 3:38

2022

Musicians
Taylor Swift: vocals, backing vocals
Jack Antonoff: modular synthesizer, Juno 6, piano, electric guitar, bass, percussion, programming
Evan Smith: electric organ, flute, saxophone, clarinet

Recorded
Rough Customer (Brooklyn, NY), Electric Lady (New York), 2021–2022

Technical Team
Producers: Jack Antonoff, Taylor Swift
Mixing: Serban Ghenea
Sound Engineers: Laura Sisk, Jack Antonoff, Evan Smith
Mastering: Randy Merrill
Vinyl Mastering: Ryan Smith
Best Ranking: Hot 100: 3

Genesis

In "Maroon," Taylor Swift compares the deterioration of a love relationship to a color chart that ranges from bright red (the color of *Red*) to maroon. Once at the bottom of this scale, all that remains is a vague memory of happy days, when the intensity of feelings was still shared. *Midnights* is an immersion in Swift's nocturnal thoughts, the kind that keep her awake and tormented for years. "Maroon" is one of these thoughts, a palette of tenacious memories made up of embarrassing, funny, or magical moments.

Production

Somewhere between synthpop and dream pop, this Jack Antonoff production evokes the heyday of English cold wave in the late 1980s. The primitive drum machine, the modular synthesizer sequences, the grainy synth bass, and the effects-laden electric guitar—everything is here. Immersed in a long, icy reverb, Swift's voice passes through a subtly dosed vintage vocoder in the middle of the choruses. The electric bass passes through a chorus effect and reinforces the synth bass with large pick strokes. We find a number of ingredients already present on *1989*. Only the singer's phrasing and the bass drum's rich bass register this production in its actual time.

At the 2024 Grammy Awards, Taylor Swift wears a Schiaparelli strapless dress.

There are no fewer than six official "Anti-Hero" remixes: "Anti-Hero" (feat. Bleachers), released on November 7, 2022; "Anti-Hero" (Roosevelt Remix) on November 9, 2022; "Anti-Hero" (Kungs Remix), on November 10, 2022; and "Anti-Hero" (Jayda G. Remix) and "Anti-Hero" (Acoustic Version), both released on November 19, 2022. A final version was released on November 17, 2022: "Anti-Hero" (ILLENIUM Remix).

"Anti-Hero" is awarded Song of the Year at the 2023 iHeartRadio Music Awards.

SINGLE

ANTI-HERO

Taylor Swift, Jack Antonoff / 3:20

Musicians
Taylor Swift: vocals, backing vocals
Jack Antonoff: modular synthesizer, Juno 6, Prophet-5, mellotron, Wurlitzer, bass, acoustic guitar, backing vocals, percussion, LinnDrum programming
Bobby Hawk: violin

Recorded
Rough Customer (Brooklyn, NY), Electric Lady (New York), 2021–2022

Technical Team
Producers: Jack Antonoff, Taylor Swift
Mixing: Serban Ghenea
Sound Engineers: Jon Gautier, Laura Sisk, Jack Antonoff
Mastering: Randy Merrill
Vinyl Mastering: Ryan Smith

Single Release
Digital Release: October 21, 2022
Best Rankings: Hot 100: 1; Top 40 Mainstream: 1; Adult Pop Airplay: 1; Dance / Mix Show Airplay: 3

Genesis

As the lead single from *Midnights*, "Anti-Hero" was co-written with Jack Antonoff (as are almost all the songs from the *Midnights* era). In it, Taylor Swift shares her deepest nightmares and insecurities. In particular, she fears that her superstar status is robbing her of her personality. In an uncompromising self-portrait, she is self-critical. The singer had warned Antonoff: This text is too strange and personal to be a hit. Fans the world over proved her wrong, as "Anti-Hero" broke all records.

Production

The introduction, with its LinnDrum (drum machine) programming, instantly recalls Prince's productions from his "Kiss" period (1985–1986). Effects-laden electric guitars, distorted synth bass, and synthesizer strings and sequences blend to propel this arrangement into synthpop territory. The icy reverb on Swift's voice contributes to the flamboyance of this arrangement, created from scratch by *Midnights* mastermind Antonoff.

"Snow on the Beach" is co-written by and features the singing talents of Lana Del Rey.

FOR DISCERNING SWIFTIES

The penultimate line of the bridge, "Now I'm all for you like Janet," is a nod to singer Janet Jackson and her 2001 song "All for You."

SNOW ON THE BEACH (FEAT. LANA DEL REY)

Taylor Swift, Lana Del Rey, Jack Antonoff / 4:16

Musicians
Taylor Swift: vocals, backing vocals
Lana Del Rey: vocals
Jack Antonoff: Juno 6, mellotron, bass, acoustic and electric guitars, backing vocals, drums, percussion, programming
Bobby Hawk: violin
Dylan O'Brien: drums
Evan Smith: synthesizers

Recorded
Rough Customer (Brooklyn, NY), Electric Lady (New York), Henson Recording (Los Angeles), 2021–2022

Technical Team
Producers: Jack Antonoff, Taylor Swift
Mixing: Serban Ghenea
Sound Engineers: Laura Sisk, Jack Antonoff, Dave Gross, Evan Smith
Mastering: Randy Merrill
Vinyl Mastering: Ryan Smith
Best Ranking: Hot 100: 4

2022

Genesis

"Snow on the Beach," featuring Taylor Swift and Lana Del Rey, was one of the most eagerly awaited female duets of the previous ten years. A great admirer of Del Rey's work, Swift considers her participation a huge honor. As for Jack Antonoff, he had already worked on three albums by this melancholic singer and songwriter with her suave voice. So it was only natural that the three artists co-wrote and recorded "Snow on the Beach." The song describes a mutual love at first sight, an emotional shock so strong that at first it seems unreal. As if it were suddenly snowing on the beach.

Production

As if to evoke falling snowflakes, "Snow on the Beach" begins with a shower of pizzicato strings. To give the lead to the two singers, ethereal synthesizers and electric guitars discreetly adorn this dream pop ballad. Played by Dylan O'Brien (the actor who co-stars with Sadie Sink in *All Too Well: The Short Film*), the drums are deliberately positioned far back in the mix, and the twinkling sound of the bell evokes Christmas music. Lana Del Rey's voice is in the background, too much so for her fans, who voiced their frustration en masse. The two singers responded by recording a new version, humorously titled "Snow on the Beach (feat. More Lana Del Rey)," included at number 22 on *Midnights (The Til Dawn Edition)*. Lana Del Rey sings the first half of the second verse on lead, and her voice is mixed more forward overall. Bobby Hawk's string arrangement is also highlighted.

Taylor Swift and Stevie Nicks share a stage at the 2010 Grammy Awards.

YOU'RE ON YOUR OWN, KID

Taylor Swift, Jack Antonoff / 3:14

Musicians
Taylor Swift: vocals, backing vocals
Jack Antonoff: Juno 6, mellotron, Moog, electric guitar, bass, backing vocals, percussion, programming
Evan Smith: synthesizers
Sean Hutchinson: drums, percussion

Recorded
Rough Customer (Brooklyn, NY), Electric Lady (New York), 2021–2022

Technical Team
Producers: Jack Antonoff, Taylor Swift
Mixing: Serban Ghenea
Sound Engineers: Laura Sisk, Jack Antonoff, Evan Smith, Sean Hutchinson
Mastering: Randy Merrill
Vinyl Mastering: Ryan Smith
Best Ranking: Hot 100: 8

2022

Genesis

"You're on Your Own, Kid" describes the transition to adulthood, unrequited love, and the torments of adolescence. Taylor Swift mentions her eating disorders and her already clear ambition to pursue a career in music. The song was one of the favorites of Stevie Nicks, the legendary lead singer of American soft rock band Fleetwood Mac. After the death of her close friend and collaborator Christine McVie in November 2022, Nicks explained how much the song had helped her in her grief and publicly thanked Taylor Swift at a concert in 2023. The line "So make the friendship bracelets" is the origin of a fan-initiated trend: Before concerts, Swifties exchange multicolored bracelets inscribed with various messages—references to Taylor Swift's songs and albums—which they sometimes give to celebrities. Jennifer Garner, Jennifer Lawrence, Nicole Kidman, and Keith Urban, for example, have publicly displayed them. A remix titled "You're on Your Own, Kid (Strings Remix)" is available exclusively on the physical version of *Midnights (3am Edition)*, at track number 15.

Production

With its electric guitar intro played with palm mute on the tonics, "You're on Your Own, Kid" kicks off with a very pop-rock arrangement. The drum machine and synthesizers gradually join the party, and Jack Antonoff's production turns into a flamboyant synthpop anthem. With deep strings, risers, synthesizer sequences, and grainy synth bass; fluctuating oscillators; and resonant leads immersed in delay, the listener is swept up in a whirlwind of galvanizing electronic textures. As evidenced by her sensitive, relaxed vocal performance, Taylor Swift is in her favorite element.

Taylor Swift attends a 2022 MTV Video Music Awards afterparty in New York.

MIDNIGHT RAIN

Taylor Swift, Jack Antonoff / 2:54

Musicians
Taylor Swift: vocals, backing vocals
Jack Antonoff: modular synthesizer, Juno 6, Moog, Prophet-5, drums, percussion
Recorded
Rough Customer (Brooklyn, NY), Electric Lady (New York), 2021–2022
Technical Team
Producers: Jack Antonoff, Taylor Swift
Mixing: Serban Ghenea
Sound Engineers: Laura Sisk, Jack Antonoff
Mastering: Randy Merrill
Vinyl Mastering: Ryan Smith
Best Ranking: Hot 100: 5

2022

Genesis

In "Midnight Rain," Taylor Swift reflects on one of her love affairs. She explains that life as a stay-at-home mom stuck in a small provincial town is not for her. She realizes that her desire to pursue a musical career will break her boyfriend's heart, but she continues to dream in CinemaScope, realizing that nothing can stop her from fulfilling her destiny. On one of her sleepless nights, she wonders what her ex-boyfriend, now a good family man, might think of her now. "Midnight Rain" is an excellent illustration of the central concept of *Midnights*: thirteen sleepless nights during which Swift anxiously delves into the past.

Production

"Midnight Rain" begins with Swift's voice pitched an octave lower and using formant shifting (a configuration usually associated with a vocal corrector) heavily manipulated. The production by the singer and Jack Antonoff, suspended on hi-hat programming that fluctuates between triplets and sixteenth notes, oscillates between rhythm and blues and electro-pop. Everything seems to unfold in slow motion. Antonoff plays and programs all the instruments: The shimmering Juno 6 clashes with the whirring bass of the Moog, and sounds passed in reverse constantly haunt this excessively slow (70 bmp) and deliberately destabilizing arrangement. Through pitch effects, Swift seems to establish a dialogue with her transfigured double, as if to illustrate the distorted view her ex had of her.

QUESTION...?

Taylor Swift, Jack Antonoff / 3:30

Musicians
Taylor Swift: vocals, backing vocals
Jack Antonoff: Juno 6, mellotron, backing vocals, percussion, programming, applause
Dominik Rivinius: drums
Evan Smith: synthesizers
Sean Hutchinson: drums, percussion
Rachel Antonoff: applause
Austin Swift: applause
Dylan O'Brien: applause
Recorded
Rough Customer (Brooklyn, NY), Electric Lady (New York), Abbey Road (London), 2021–2022
Technical Team
Producers: Jack Antonoff, Taylor Swift
Mixing: Serban Ghenea
Sound Engineers: Laura Sisk, Jack Antonoff, Ken Lewis, Evan Smith
Mastering: Randy Merrill
Vinyl Mastering: Ryan Smith
(Non-Single) Release
Digital release (limited-time digital download): October 25, 2022
Best Ranking: Hot 100: 7

Genesis

Perfectly in keeping with the theme of *Midnights*, "Question...?" returns once again to an old love. Unlike "Midnight Rain," this is a fundamental, incomparable relationship. Speaking directly to her ex-lover, the singer asks him about the intensity of his feelings for his girlfriend, while hoping that they never exceed their own.

Production

Launched on a 109 bpm tempo by a filtered drum machine, the arrangement of "Question...?" is quickly joined by chords from Juno 6 with a largely clipped attack and a distant synthesizer layer, but only really takes off at 1:50, on the second chorus. On drums, Dominik Rivinius and Evan Smith on synth are consistently fleshed out. Then the instrumentation moves on rails until the bridge, where Taylor Swift's voice passes through a suite of harmonizer and/or vocoder treatments. Due to a number of musical and textual similarities with the song "Out of the Woods," the fans deduce that the singer is addressing her ex Harry Styles here.

VIGILANTE SHIT

Taylor Swift / 2:44

Musicians
Taylor Swift: vocals, backing vocals
Jack Antonoff: Juno 6, Moog, Wurlitzer, percussion, programming
Dominik Rivinius: drums
Evan Smith: synthesizers
Recorded
Rough Customer (Brooklyn, NY), Electric Lady (New York), 2021–2022
Technical Team
Producers: Jack Antonoff, Taylor Swift
Mixing: Serban Ghenea
Sound Engineers: Laura Sisk, Jack Antonoff, Ken Lewis, Evan Smith
Mastering: Randy Merrill
Vinyl Mastering: Ryan Smith
(Non-Single) Release
Digital Release (limited-time digital download): October 25, 2022
Best Ranking: Hot 100: 10

Genesis

This time, Taylor Swift's nocturnal brooding awakens a fantasy of cosplay-style revenge. "Vigilante Shit" is a film noir scenario, a stylistic exercise in which the singer derives great pleasure and particularly excels. Swift imagines herself the accomplice of an intrepid woman who takes revenge for her husband's infidelity by murdering him without a trace. According to some music critics, this dark story could be related to her feud with rapper Kanye West or her dispute with Scooter Braun.

Production

To illustrate this dark tale of revenge, Swift and Jack Antonoff set out on a dark pop production that incorporates elements of hip-hop and rhythm'n'blues. Based on an *A* minor key, rhythmic programming adds the trap touch, while synth bass played on the Moog reinforces the 808 bass. The synthesizers, distilled in impressionistic strokes, are responsible for the dark pop color and recall the minimalist quality of some of singer Billie Eilish's productions. Swift's voice passes through a vocoder on carefully chosen phrases, and the bridge contrasts sharply with its eerie nursery rhyme melody.

Taylor Swift backstage at the 2022 MTV Europe Music Awards in Germany.

BEJEWELED

Taylor Swift, Jack Antonoff / 3:14

Musicians

Taylor Swift: vocals, backing vocals
Jack Antonoff: Juno 6, DX7, OB-1, Moog, kalimba, acoustic guitars, bass, backing vocals, percussion, programming
Evan Smith: synthesizers
Mikey Freedom Hart: keyboards

Recorded

Rough Customer (Brooklyn, NY), Electric Lady (New York), 2021–2022

Technical Team

Producers: Jack Antonoff, Taylor Swift
Mixing: Serban Ghenea
Sound Engineers: Laura Sisk, Jack Antonoff, Evan Smith, David Hart
Mastering: Randy Merrill
Vinyl Mastering: Ryan Smith
Best Ranking: Hot 100: 6

Genesis

In "Bejeweled," Taylor Swift tackles the delicate subject of the loss of self-esteem in an imbalanced, even toxic, love relationship. By analogy, she evokes her anxiety at the idea of returning to the arena of mainstream, flamboyant pop. After two intimate albums, *Folklore* and *Evermore*, produced back-to-back in the midst of the pandemic, she wrote this song to give herself courage and regain confidence. It was time once more for her to bring out her luminous attire and her aura of incandescent superstardom.

Production

From the intro, the brilliance of the synthesizer arpeggio evokes a cascade of diamonds (one might swear it had been played on the pad of an OM-27 Omnichord). Midway between synthpop and disco pop, Swift and Jack Antonoff's production shines brightly. Set to a tempo of 82 bpm, the synthesizers reign supreme: layers of pulsating sequences, deep Moog bass, shimmering Juno 6 arpeggiators, and satin strings. Almost primitive, the rhythmic programming perfectly follows the contours of this deliberately flashy arrangement. With its army of backing vocals and sophisticated processing (multiple meticulous reverb automations), vocal production takes center stage.

Chinese billboard for the film-concert *Taylor Swift: The Eras Tour*, distributed from October 2023 for a limited period in more than 100 countries around the world.

LABYRINTH

Taylor Swift, Jack Antonoff / 4:07

Musicians
Taylor Swift: vocals, backing vocals
Jack Antonoff: Juno 6, OB-8, Moog, Realistic Synth, electric guitars, backing vocals, percussion, programming
Recorded
Rough Customer (Brooklyn, NY), Electric Lady (New York), 2021–2022
Technical Team
Producers: Jack Antonoff, Taylor Swift
Mixing: Serban Ghenea
Sound Engineers: Laura Sisk, Jack Antonoff
Mastering: Randy Merrill
Vinyl Mastering: Ryan Smith
Best Ranking: Hot 100: 14

Genesis

"Labyrinth" describes the exhilarating yet dizzying sensation of falling in love too quickly, when you've barely recovered from your previous relationship. In the first pre-chorus, the lines "You know how scared I am of elevators / Never trust it if it rises fast / It can't last" evoke Taylor Swift's phobia of elevators—the ideal metaphor for vertigo in love. In the second pre-chorus, the lines "You know how much I hate that everybody just expects me to bounce back / Just like that" help the listener understand that this song also expresses the oppression felt by the star. However combative Swift may be, the feeling of constantly having to bounce back up to meet the expectations of insatiable fans and media must be exhausting.

Production

This Jack Antonoff and Taylor Swift production paints a synthpop landscape populated by atypical sounds. The expressiveness of the synthetic textures and the singer's ethereal voice plunge us into a strange, anxiety-inducing reverie. The pulsating synthesizer sequence and sampled vocal interjections, soon joined by a lead synth gimmick that sounds like the trumpeting of an alien elephant, set the ball rolling. But Antonoff does not stop there; with the anemic electric guitar, distant orchestral bells, wind ensemble and choir, both filtered mellotron-style, everything is done to keep the listener between daydreaming and alertness. On the pre-chorus and second verse, Swift's natural voice is discreetly doubled by a vocoder track. At 2:54, the arrangement of this song suddenly takes a rather different turn: the bass drum pattern changes, the rhythmic programming intensifies, and Swift's voice is pitched an octave lower. After the very mainstream "Bejeweled," the craftsmanship of "Labyrinth" feels like surreal experimentation.

TAYLOR SWIFT
THE ERAS TOUR
泰勒·斯威夫特·时代巡回演唱会 观影之旅

Ice Spice featured on "Karma," in *Midnights (The Til Dawn Edition)*.

SINGLE

KARMA

Taylor Swift, Jack Antonoff, Sounwave, Jahaan Sweet, Keanu Beats / 3:24

Musicians
Taylor Swift: vocals, backing vocals
Jack Antonoff: drums, Juno, Omnichord, percussion, programming
Sounwave: programming
Keanu Beats: synthesizers
Jahaan Sweet: keyboards, synth pad

Recorded
Rough Customer (Brooklyn, NY), Electric Lady (New York), Henson Recording (Los Angeles), 2021–2022

Technical Team
Producers: Jack Antonoff, Taylor Swift, Sounwave, Jahaan Sweet, Keanu Beats
Mixing: Serban Ghenea
Sound Engineers: Laura Sisk, Jack Antonoff, Keanu Beats, Jahaan Sweet, Sounwave
Mastering: Randy Merrill
Vinyl Mastering: Ryan Smith

Single Release
Digital Release: May 1, 2023
Best Rankings: Hot 100: 2; Top 40 Mainstream: 1; Adult Pop Airplay: 1; Dance / Mix Show Airplay: 13

2022

Genesis

For the album's third single, Taylor Swift and her team chose "Karma," one of the most positive songs of the *Midnights* era. Unusually, it is filled with an immense sense of joy and pride in the middle of the night. The singer is deeply convinced that doing good creates the conditions for positive karma. She tells herself that she deserves to be happy and that sometimes one just has to stop being hard on oneself.

For the "Karma (feat. Ice Spice)" version, positioned at number 23 on *Midnights (The Til Dawn Edition)*, New York rapper Ice Spice, a Swiftie since her youth, contacted Taylor Swift to express her desire to record a duet with the star. As luck would have it, Swift had made Ice Spice her new favorite artist. She immediately proposed a starring role on "Karma." The rapper accepted and recorded her part in a flash; the remix was released on May 26, 2023.

Production

Set to a 90 bpm tempo, the song's synthpop and disco pop production distills an infectious energy. In the realm of the disco ball, synthesizers are king. The Omnichord's characteristic cascades of notes illuminate this beat-based arrangement, the result of a collaboration between Sounwave and Australian producer Keanu Beats. This time, the Omnichord, played by Jack Antonoff, is mentioned in the liner notes (unlike on "Bejeweled," whose intro seems to feature an Omnichord chime). Jahaan Sweet, who also worked on "Lavender Haze," contributes keyboards and synthesizers. The arrangement of the "Karma (feat. Ice Spice)" version is generally very similar to the original until the second verse, when the rhythmic programming takes a trap and dancehall turn to accompany Ice Spice's unstoppable flow.

"Sweet Nothing" is inspired by Sir Paul McCartney.

After "Exile" and "Betty" on *Folklore* (2020), and "Champagne Problems," "Coney Island," and "Evermore" on *Evermore* (2020), "Sweet Nothing" is the sixth song co-written by Taylor Swift and Joe Alwyn (under the pseudonym of William Bowery).

SWEET NOTHING

Taylor Swift, William Bowery / 3:08

Musicians

Taylor Swift: vocals, backing vocals
Jack Antonoff: modular synthesizer, Juno 6, Moog, Prophet-5, piano, programming, drums, percussion
Evan Smith: electric organ, flute, saxophone, clarinet

Recorded

Rough Customer (Brooklyn, NY), Electric Lady (New York), 2021–2022

Technical Team

Producers: Jack Antonoff, Taylor Swift
Mixing: Serban Ghenea
Sound Engineers: Laura Sisk, Jack Antonoff, Evan Smith
Mastering: Randy Merrill
Vinyl Mastering: Ryan Smith
Best Ranking: Hot 100: 15

2022

Genesis

Taylor Swift and Paul McCartney had been friends since they first met in 2010. In 2018, the former Beatle wrote "Who Cares," a song inspired by Taylor Swift's special relationship with her fans. In turn, the singer and her partner Joe Alwyn co-wrote "Sweet Nothing" to allude to the legendary Sir Paul. In the text, the singer expresses her gratitude for the sweet and loving life Alwyn has given her. But the reference to the Irish town of Wicklow, not far from where Paul and his family took their summer vacation in 1971, just after the Beatles officially split up, is surely also a tribute to the mythical couple formed by Linda and Paul McCartney.

Production

The arrangement of "Sweet Nothing" is centered on the Fender Rhodes part. The clean production of this ballad draws its DNA from the supple, generous style of 1970s soft rock. Evan Smith's saxophone and clarinet, often paired with Swift's backing vocals, punctuate this delicate instrumentation right up to the climax of the final chorus. Omnichord, electric organ, and synthesizers discreetly contribute to the enveloping atmosphere. Swift's performance shifts from fragility to intensity, as her delivery becomes more dense. The sweetness of "Sweet Nothing" is a breath of fresh air in *Midnights*, a pop album that relies heavily on the intensive use of synthesizers and rhythmic programming.

In "Mastermind," the songwriter is the architect of her personal and professional lives.

MASTERMIND

Taylor Swift, Jack Antonoff / 3:11

Musicians

Taylor Swift: vocals, backing vocals
Jack Antonoff: Juno, Minimoog, electric guitars, backing vocals, percussion, programming, drums
Bobby Hawk: violin
Evan Smith: synthesizers, saxophones
Michael Riddleberger: drums
Mikey Freedom Hart: Minimoog, programming
Zem Audu: saxophones

Recorded

Rough Customer (Brooklyn, NY), Electric Lady (New York), 2021–2022

Technical Team

Producers: Jack Antonoff, Taylor Swift
Mixing: Serban Ghenea
Sound Engineers: Laura Sisk, Jack Antonoff, Evan Smith, Jon Gautier, David Hart, Michael Riddleberger, Zem Audu
Mastering: Randy Merrill
Vinyl Mastering: Ryan Smith
Best Ranking: Hot 100: 13

2022

Genesis

The thirteenth and final track on the standard edition of *Midnights*, "Mastermind" returns to the issue of the opposition of fate against control. Unlike "Invisible String," which dealt with the invisible forces of fate, Taylor Swift demonstrates here that she leaves nothing to chance, that she is both the architect and the great strategist of her love and professional life. In this way, "Mastermind" is the cornerstone of the album: Childhood and adolescence have left their marks, wounds that sometimes come back to haunt the young woman in the middle of the night, even though she now has total self-control.

Production

"Mastermind" opens with a duet of sixteenth-note arpeggiators that immediately sets the breathless tone of this orchestral electro-pop production. Jack Antonoff's Minimoog bass sounds like short bursts of seismic tremors, with a very slow attack. Rhythmic programming relies heavily on a relentlessly hammering black bass drum. A few drum rolls and very occasional snare drum punctuations help to reinforce the pulse, and transitions are marked by razor-sharp cymbal tones. From the very first chorus, the organic contributions of Bobby Hawk's violin and Evan Smith and Zem Audu's brass gradually flesh out the instrumentation, culminating in the bridge's cinematic climax. Contributing almost subliminally to the orchestral dimension of this arrangement, softly attacking tubular bells mark the entrance to the second verse and the bridge. Shielded from all this grandeur, the treatment of the lead vocals remains deliberately dry, as if to emphasize the eminently confessional aspect of the lyrics.

THE GREAT WAR

Taylor Swift, Aaron Dessner / 4:00

Musicians

Taylor Swift: vocals, backing vocals
Aaron Dessner: keyboards, synth bass, piano, electric guitar, percussion, drum programming, synthesizer
Thomas Bartlett: piano, synthesizer
Kyle Resnick: trumpet
James McAlister: drum programming, percussion
Yuki Numata Resnick: violin

Recorded

Long Pond (Hudson Valley, NY), 2021

Technical Team

Producers: Aaron Dessner, Taylor Swift
Mixing: Serban Ghenea
Sound Engineers: Aaron Dessner, Bella Blasko, Jonathan Low
Mastering: Randy Merrill
Vinyl Mastering: Ryan Smith
Best Ranking: Hot 100: 26

Genesis

"The Great War" is the first bonus track on the *3am Edition* and *The Til Dawn Edition* of *Midnights*. Produced by Aaron Dessner, this track did not pass the rigorous selection of the thirteen tracks on the standard edition, all produced or co-produced by Jack Antonoff. Taylor Swift uses the imagery of the First World War as a metaphor for conflict in love, to represent the violence of emotions. This is also a way of illustrating the courage, even heroism, of the man who takes the blows and manages, despite everything, to get out of the trenches and save his loved one from their destructive instincts.

Production

Somewhere between indie pop and synthpop, this production by Dessner is not out of place in the *Midnights* era. A central element of this arrangement, the martial rhythmic programming seems to be doubled by drums played with brushes. At 2:53, a real snare drum, played marching band–style, replaces the drum machine and sets the pace for the third and final verse. The brilliance of the layered synthesizers illuminates this ethereal, enveloping orchestration. Taylor Swift's interpretation is marked by nonchalance, as if the young woman herself wished to distance herself from her self-criticism and the war metaphors she uses.

BIGGER THAN THE WHOLE SKY

Taylor Swift / 3:38

Musicians

Taylor Swift: vocals, backing vocals
Jack Antonoff: synthesizer; acoustic, electric, and slide guitars; piano; bass; programming

Recorded

Rough Customer (Brooklyn, NY), Electric Lady (New York), 2021–2022

Technical Team

Producers: Jack Antonoff, Taylor Swift
Mixing: Serban Ghenea
Sound Engineers: Laura Sisk, Jack Antonoff
Mastering: Randy Merrill
Vinyl Mastering: Ryan Smith
Best Ranking: Hot 100: 21

Genesis

Written by Taylor Swift alone, "Bigger Than the Whole Sky" describes the difficulty of having to mourn someone who left too soon, without having had time to partially or fully realize their potential. In the second verse of the second couplet, "Did some force take you because I didn't pray?," Swift shares her traumatic relationship with religion. What influence does religion have on the grieving process? Some fans believe that Swift wrote this song after her friend Claire Kislinger suffered a miscarriage. This is probably why "Bigger Than the Whole Sky" is often used to introduce testimonials from women who share their experiences of miscarriage on social networks.

Production

The atmospheric production by Jack Antonoff and Swift sublimates this folk song that tackles a difficult subject. The deep, ethereal texture of the synthesizers, combined with the percussion plunged into reverb (from 1:15), infuses this arrangement with its share of solemnity. Antonoff's slide guitar contributes a bluesy, sad, but comforting edge. Swift's performance shifts from the bass half of her vocal range (on the verses) to the beginning of her high register (on the choruses), where she manages to contain the intensity of her chest voice, flirting with her head voice, without restricting herself to falsetto. This balancing act, requiring great technical mastery, results in a sensitive interpretation, always on the razor's edge, in perfect harmony with the song's theme.

At the 2022 American Music Awards, the singer won six awards. *Red (Taylor's Version)* won for Best Pop/Rock Album and Best Country Album.

FOR DISCERNING SWIFTIES

"Paris" is the third song to mention the name of a city in its title, after "Welcome to New York" (*1989*, 2014) and "London Boy" (*Lover*, 2019).

PARIS

Taylor Swift, Jack Antonoff / 3:16

Musicians
Taylor Swift: vocals, backing vocals
Jack Antonoff: synthesizer, piano, programming
Evan Smith: synthesizer, percussion
Mikey Freedom Hart: synthesizer, theremin, electric organ

Recorded
Rough Customer (Brooklyn, NY), Electric Lady (New York), 2022

Technical Team
Producers: Jack Antonoff, Taylor Swift
Mixing: Serban Ghenea
Sound Engineers: Laura Sisk, Jack Antonoff, David Hart, Evan Smith, Mikey Freedom Hart
Mastering: Randy Merrill
Vinyl Mastering: Ryan Smith
Best Ranking: Hot 100: 32

2022

Genesis

As the title suggests, "Paris" is a love song. In it, Taylor Swift describes two characters who dream of escapism and magical places. Their feelings for each other transcend the mundane, transforming the commonplace into the marvelous, table wine into champagne. In the first verse, the singer dismisses with a wave of her hand a piece of gossip about the behavior of one of her exes in a nightclub. Then, from the very first chorus, "Paris" is suddenly transformed into a love song. Swift's deliberately wry sense of humor marks her detachment from gossip and her desire to focus solely on the positive.

Production

Launched on a tempo of 111 bpm, Jack Antonoff and Taylor Swift's electro-pop production relies on an overlay of shimmering synthesizers and groovy rhythmic programming. The organic-sounding timbred bass drum pattern is particularly dense. A combination of snaps and shakers doubles the snare drum to reinforce the upbeat feel. The synthesizer layers literally overwhelm the end of the intro, the choruses, and the bridge, as if to illustrate the overflowing love felt by the two characters. Taylor Swift sits comfortably in the middle of her vocal range, delivering a performance with an intense, syncopated flow.

AMERICAN MUSIC AWARDS
AMERICAN MUSIC AWARDS
AMERICAN MUSIC AWARDS

German fans wait for the concert hall to open during the "Eras Tour" in Hamburg.

HIGH INFIDELITY

Taylor Swift, Aaron Dessner / 4:00

Musicians
Taylor Swift: vocals, backing vocals
Aaron Dessner: keyboards, piano, acoustic and electric guitars, synthesizer, percussion, drum programming, drums
Benjamin Lanz: drums, trombone
James Krivchenia: drums
James McAlister: drum programming, synthesizer
Thomas Bartlett: synthesizer

Recorded
Long Pond (Hudson Valley, NY), 2021

Technical Team
Producers: Aaron Dessner, Taylor Swift
Mixing: Jonathan Low
Sound Engineers: Aaron Dessner, Bella Blasko, Jonathan Low
Mastering: Randy Merrill
Vinyl Mastering: Ryan Smith
Best Ranking: Hot 100: 33

2022

With "Illicit Affairs," "August," and "Betty" on *Folklore*, and "No Body, No Crime" and "Ivy" on *Evermore*, "High Infidelity" continues the tradition of songs exploring the theme of infidelity.

Genesis

In March 2021, Taylor Swift composed "High Infidelity" and "Would've, Could've, Should've" with Aaron Dessner in her Los Angeles home, a few days before the Grammy Awards ceremony, during which *Folklore* won Album of the Year. As its title suggests, "High Infidelity" focuses on the damage caused by infidelity. The singer uses an array of hard-hitting phrases, often graphic and sometimes very direct.

Production

The arrangement begins with a minimalist synthesizer sequence, quickly joined by piano chords and Swift's vocals on the first verse. The orchestration builds smoothly until the outro, at 3:21. The ensemble of rhythmic programming, percussion, and drums gradually gains in density, while the synthesizers are superimposed in successive layers (layers and sequences, including the synth bass). Aaron Dessner's delicate acoustic guitar brings an organic brilliance that complements the hushed roundness of the piano. At the crossroads between indie pop, electro-pop, and alternative folk, Dessner's second production on the extended versions of *Midnights* has the intricacy of lacework. This chiaroscuro instrumental balance allows Swift to interpret her lyrics in a nuanced way, despite her fast, syncopated flow.

After a first collaboration on "London Boy," Sounwave co-wrote "Glitch" with Taylor Swift.

GLITCH

Taylor Swift, Jack Antonoff, Sounwave, Sam Dew / 2:28

Musicians
Taylor Swift: vocals, backing vocals
Jack Antonoff: synthesizers, percussion, programming, bass, electric guitar
Sounwave: programming
Sam Dew: backing vocals
Zoë Kravitz: backing vocals
Recorded
Rough Customer (Brooklyn, NY), Electric Lady (New York), Henson Recording (Los Angeles), 2021–2022
Technical Team
Producers: Jack Antonoff, Taylor Swift, Sounwave
Mixing: Serban Ghenea
Sound Engineers: Laura Sisk, Jack Antonoff
Mastering: Randy Merrill
Vinyl Mastering: Ryan Smith
Best Ranking: Hot 100: 41

Genesis

"Glitch" comes from the same session as "Lavender Haze," the opening track on *Midnights.* So this is the same team at work (with the exception of Jahaan Sweet). At 2:28, this is the shortest track of the *Midnights* era and of Taylor Swift's entire discography before the release of "Now That We Don't Talk" (2:26) on Taylor's Version of *1989,* in 2023. In it, the singer describes a friendship that turns into a love affair, with nothing premeditated. Like a bug in the matrix, this romance still blossoms, against all odds.

Production

The electro-pop and chamber pop production by Jack Antonoff, Taylor Swift, and Marc Anthony Spears (aka Sounwave) is the most experimental of the *Midnights* era. The floating sensation created by the microtonal modulation of the electric guitar and the filtered backing vocals of Zoë Kravitz and Sam Dew transport the listener into a strange world, an expressionist trip-hop setting crossed by the psychedelic vapors of modern soul. The omnipresent glitch sounds coat the rhythmic programming with a layer of static dust—giving the instrumentation its lo-fi color. In symbiosis with the arrangement, Taylor Swift's vocals oscillate between sensuality, laid-back nonchalance, and an acid falsetto.

Taylor Swift and John Mayer sing together at the 2009 Z100 Jingle Ball.

FOR DISCERNING SWIFTIES

The fourth line of the bridge and outro, "Stained glass windows in my mind" refers to the windows in John Mayer's apartment (a small New York church converted into a home) at the time of his romance with Taylor Swift.

WOULD'VE, COULD'VE, SHOULD'VE

Taylor Swift, Aaron Dessner / 4:20

Musicians

Taylor Swift: vocals, backing vocals
Aaron Dessner: piano, synthesizer, drum programming, bass, harmonica, electric and acoustic guitars
Bryce Dessner: electric guitar
James McAlister: drum programming, drums, synthesizer
Bryan Devendorf: drums
Thomas Bartlett: keyboards, synthesizer

Recorded

Long Pond (Hudson Valley, NY), 2022

Technical Team

Producers: Aaron Dessner, Taylor Swift
Mixing: Jonathan Low
Sound Engineers: Bella Blasko, Jonathan Low, Aaron Dessner, Justin Vernon
Mastering: Randy Merrill
Vinyl Mastering: Ryan Smith
Best Ranking: Hot 100: 20

2022

Genesis

Written around the same time as "High Infidelity," in March 2021, "Would've, Could've, Should've" is considered by fans to be the follow-up to the song "Dear John," released in 2010 on the *Speak Now* album. Then age nineteen, Taylor Swift openly addressed her ex-boyfriend John Mayer, thirteen years her senior. In 2021, eleven years later and at the age of thirty-two—the same age as John Mayer at the time of their relationship—she once again takes the floor to challenge him. The tone of "Would've, Could've, Should've" is more bitter, confused, and ambivalent than on "Dear John." The singer expresses her regrets and her feeling of having been robbed of a part of her youth. It is not over yet, and the wound remains open. In an interview for the *Broken Records* podcast in April 2023, Aaron Dessner described "Would've, Could've, Should've" as his most accomplished co-writing with Taylor Swift.

Production

Dessner and Swift's indie pop and soft rock production relies above all on the intensity of its rhythm section. James McAlister and Bryan Devendorf, launched into a 158 bpm tempo, reinforce the programming by pounding their drums; Dessner's eighth-note bass never falters. Electric guitars, divided between delay-laden clean and crunch, compete with synthesizers for the center of the spectrum. Taylor Swift firmly holds the reins of this arrangement in the form of a frantic cavalcade. Her taut, energetic flow takes listeners on an emotional whirlwind they will not soon forget.

Taylor Swift in a sparkling midnight blue dress at the 2023 Grammy Awards in Los Angeles.

DEAR READER

Taylor Swift, Jack Antonoff / 3:45

Musicians
Taylor Swift: vocals, backing vocals
Jack Antonoff: synthesizer, electric guitar, piano, bass, programming

Recorded
Rough Customer (Brooklyn, NY), Electric Lady (New York), 2021–2022

Technical Team
Producers: Jack Antonoff, Taylor Swift
Mixing: Serban Ghenea
Sound Engineers: Laura Sisk, Jack Antonoff
Mastering: Randy Merrill
Vinyl Mastering: Ryan Smith
Best Ranking: Hot 100: 45

2022

Genesis

To round off the *3am Edition* of *Midnights* in style, Taylor Swift directly addresses the listener—or rather, the reader, as the song's title suggests. The verses are full of sound advice, and one can tell that she is speaking from personal experience when the message on the chorus suddenly urges the audience, "Never take advice from someone who's falling apart"—that is, herself. As is often the case, the bridge takes a different turn. Swift paints a picture of her own lonely, twilight wanderings, and no longer addresses her audience directly. In the outro, she suggests that the reader should find a wiser mentor, despite her flamboyant aura. As in "Anti-Hero" and "The Great War," self-criticism and self-questioning are recurrent themes in *Midnights*, a veritable anthology of nocturnal ruminations.

Production

Quickly submerged by a wave of electronic sounds, the hushed upright piano of the intro gives way to ethereal synthesizers on the verses and takes its place again on the choruses, as if to signify a return to reality. "Dear Reader" navigates between indie pop, electro-pop, dream pop, and chamber pop, showing that Jack Antonoff and Taylor Swift's production eludes any attempt at categorization. Finely chiseled rhythmic programming is the backbone of this effortless arrangement. The vocal production also benefits from special attention (multiple reverbs, morphing, spatialization, and complex automations), a fine piece of work refined by Serban Ghenea at the mixing stage. In the outro, Taylor Swift's lead vocals are first pitched an octave lower, conveying the famous robotic effect. Antonoff then plays with the dynamic evolution of the formant, like so many alter egos corresponding to the singer's contradictions, assertive in the verses and severely self-critical in the choruses and outro.

At the premiere of the 2023 movie *Renaissance: A Film by Beyoncé*. Taylor Swift's song "Get Me to the Weekend" is part of the film's soundtrack.

YOU'RE LOSING ME (FROM THE VAULT)

Taylor Swift, Jack Antonoff / 4:37

Musicians
Taylor Swift: vocals, backing vocals
Jack Antonoff: drums, mellotron, piano, Wurlitzer, percussion, programming, synthesizers, cello
Bobby Hawk: violin

Recorded
Rough Customer (Brooklyn, NY), December 5, 2021

Technical Team
Producers: Jack Antonoff, Taylor Swift
Mixing: Serban Ghenea
Sound Engineers: Jack Antonoff, Laura Sisk, Oli Jacobs
Mastering: Randy Merrill
Vinyl Mastering: Ryan Smith

Single Release
Digital Release: November 29, 2023
Best Ranking: Hot 100: 27

2022

Genesis

"You're Losing Me" is the only From the Vault track from the *Midnights* era. Added as a bonus track to *The Late Night Edition*, released exclusively on CD in May 2023, this track was made available six months later as a digital version. According to a story he posted on Instagram, Jack Antonoff wrote and recorded the song at home with Swift on December 5, 2021, in the middle of their work period on the *Midnights* tracks. "You're Losing Me" was not, however, chosen for the standard edition of the album. In it, Swift deals, in all likelihood, with her breakup with Joe Alwyn, despite her best efforts to pick up the pieces. To express this sense of tragic, inescapable loss, she uses a lexical field borrowed from the field of medical emergencies.

Production

Taylor Swift and Jack Antonoff's pop production, gently launched at a tempo of 103 bpm, contrasts with the gravity of the theme. As in "Wildest Dreams," released in 2014 on *1989*, an authentic recording of Taylor Swift's heartbeat transformed into a rhythmic loop is used to produce the pulse of the intro, chorus beginnings and outro. First played in pizzicato, the violin responds to the high-pitched Wurlitzer, before the mix of drums and programmed percussion kicks in to energize the second verse. Bobby Hawke then builds up a veritable string ensemble, which expands as the intensity of the arrangement rises. The piano comes into its own on the bridge, with its plated, sweeping, authoritative chords. The instrumentation at the start of each chorus is drastically stripped down. As if to illustrate the narrator's situation of imminent death, all that remains is Taylor Swift's voice, doubled by a vocoder track, and her heartbeat.

Taylor Swift is believed to be singing about her irreversible breakup with Joe Alwyn in "You're Losing Me."

HITS DIFFERENT

Taylor Swift, Aaron Dessner, Jack Antonoff / 3:54

Musicians

Taylor Swift: vocals, backing vocals
Jack Antonoff: synthesizer, acoustic and electric guitars, piano, bass, percussion, programming
Aaron Dessner: synthesizers, bass, electric guitar
James McAlister: drums, synthesizer sequencing
Sean Hutchinson: drums, percussion
Evan Smith: synthesizers
Thomas Bartlett: synthesizers, OP-1

Recorded

Long Pond (Hudson Valley, NY), Rough Customer (Brooklyn, NY), Electric Lady (New York), Conway Recording and Sharp Sonics (Los Angeles), 2022

Technical Team

Producer: Jack Antonoff, Aaron Dessner, Taylor Swift
Mixing: Serban Ghenea
Sound Engineers: Laura Sisk, Jonathan Low, Aaron Dessner, Jack Antonoff, Sean Hutchinson, Evan Smith, Thomas Bartlett
Mastering: Randy Merrill
Vinyl Mastering: Ryan Smith
Best Ranking: Hot 100: 27

2022

Genesis

"Hits Different" is the twenty-first and final original composition from *Midnights (The Til Dawn Edition).* Co-written by Taylor Swift, Jack Antonoff, and Aaron Dessner, this is the only song from the *Midnights* era to come from a collaboration between the two producers. This clash of the titans had already taken place on the track "Betty" from *Folklore* (2020), the only difference being that Antonoff and Dessner had not participated in the writing of the track, which was written by Swift and William Bowery (aka Joe Alwyn). Swift describes the disastrous state in which she finds herself after a breakup. Heartbroken and unable, as usual, to move on. Written in a blatantly hyper-realistic style, the singer distils sarcastic punchlines and is not afraid to show her flaws, with all the self-mockery and false casualness for which we know her. As is often the case, the bridge passage assumes another dimension, becoming a song within a song, both epic and tragic.

Production

With its new-wave bass and eighth-note picking in the style of Simon Gallup (The Cure), this pop-rock production by Jack Antonoff, Aaron Dessner, and Taylor Swift shines brightly. Over a tempo of 106 bpm, crystalline electric guitars and acoustic guitar strumming combine with synthesizer sequences to underpin the rhythmic pulse. The programmed drums and percussion set off on a bouncy groove reminiscent of the heyday of 1990s pop. The acid melody and Taylor Swift's interpretation echo the ardor and spontaneity of her debut, on a much less polished text. Undoubtedly, Big Machine Records, her record label at the time, would not have approved of this uninhibited outspokenness. The bridge occupies a good third of the structure, and the lyrics, on a double-revolution composition, take a reflective, poetic, even metaphysical turn.

RELEASE DATE

United States: April 19, 2024 (Republic Records—602468003496)

Best Ranking: 1

ALBUM

The Tortured Poets Department

Fortnight (feat. Post Malone) · The Tortured Poets Department · My Boy Only Breaks His Favorite Toys · Down Bad · So Long, London · But Daddy I Love Him · Fresh Out the Slammer · Florida!!! (feat. Florence and the Machine) · Guilty as Sin? · Who's Afraid of Little Old Me? · I Can Fix Him (No Really I Can) · loml · I Can Do It with a Broken Heart · The Smallest Man Who Ever Lived · The Alchemy · Clara Bow · The Black Dog · imgonnagetyouback · The Albatross · Chloe or Sam or Sophia or Marcus · How Did It End? · So High School · I Hate It Here · thanK you aIMee · I Look in People's Windows · The Prophecy · Cassandra · Peter · The Bolter · Robin · The Manuscript

Seven days after its release, *The Tortured Poets Department* was streamed more than 1.76 billion times on Spotify, a world record.

2024

A FREE ALBUM

In March 2023, Taylor Swift launched her sixth tour, the "Eras Tour," marking her return to the stage after a five-year absence. For the first time, the artist embraced her entire discography, revisiting each of her musical eras through a series of concerts in which each album was given a distinct visual and sonic identity. This ambitious project quickly established itself as one of the most lucrative tours in music history, breaking ticket sales records. But it also highlighted certain flaws in online distribution systems, particularly in the United States, where dynamic pricing—adjusted according to supply and demand—reached dizzying levels.

The phenomenal success of the "Eras Tour" goes beyond music, becoming a veritable object of study in marketing, economics, and sociology. Its particularity lies in the length and structure of the show: On the 152 scheduled dates, spectators are treated to a show lasting over three hours, with no downtime. Even though three concerts were canceled in Austria in August 2024, following a foiled terrorist attack, its global impact remains undeniable. Each era of the artist is thus transformed into a kind of mini brand, with its own visual codes and unique sounds, making the tour particularly attractive to an intergenerational audience, and especially to long-standing fans.

Stratospheric

In the summer of 2023, Taylor Swift released Taylor's Version of *Speak Now*, which was once again a huge commercial success. A few months after her separation from actor Joe Alwyn—apparently amicable and gentle, according to information gathered by celebrity magazines—the artist began a new relationship with football star Travis Kelce. Their highly publicized romance was confirmed in September, when she was spotted at a home game of Kelce's team, the Kansas City Chiefs, at the Arrowhead Stadium in Missouri. Never before in her career had Swift been so acclaimed. In the autumn of 2023, her coronation was complete when she became the first artist in history to pass the billion-dollar mark in assets generated solely by her music.

It was in this state of paroxysmal grace that Swift announced, at the sixty-sixth Grammy Awards on February 4, 2024, the release of a new and eleventh original studio album, on which she had begun work in

The "Eras Tour" sells 3.5 million tickets, with each show lasting more than three hours.

FOR DISCERNING SWIFTIES

Despite its poetic lyrics, *TTPD* is paradoxically the Taylor Swift album containing the most profanity by far. On the social network Reddit, fans have drawn up a graph showing that the number of swear words in her lyrics increases exponentially with each album.

2022, and the completion of her work on *Midnights*. *The Tortured Poets Department* was released on April 19 by Republic Records.

A "Lifeline"

Against all expectations, this album was a far cry from the appeasement that pervaded the previous three albums, and above all, it was a separation from the radiant, powerful image that the singer was projecting of herself at the time. The star confessed at one of her concerts in Melbourne, in February 2024, that *The Tortured Poets Department*, commonly abbreviated *TTPD*, had been a "lifeline" in a difficult phase of her personal life. It was so necessary and cathartic for her to write it, in fact, that it could not be limited to the sixteen tracks of the standard version. Just two hours after it went online, *TTPD* was expanded by fifteen tracks to form a double album titled *The Tortured Poets Department: The Anthology*.

TTPD: The Anthology (and even to some extent *TTPD* in its short version) is not a record designed for listeners unfamiliar with Taylor Swift's universe. Long, and less homogeneous than its predecessors, it seems a little repetitive at times, and it contains no obvious hits, at least none identifiable as such upon first hearing. However, it is undeniably the most spontaneous and personal album the singer has ever delivered, the one with the greatest emotional depth, carried by a skillful mastery of songwriting.

Lyricism, Vulnerability, and Disorder

"Once we have spoken our saddest story, we can be free of it," Taylor Swift wrote in a message posted on Instagram on the day of the album launch. Indeed, *TTPD* is a deeply melancholy album, in which love, fame, and mental health are approached from the darkest angle. Love, in particular, appears as a force capable of isolating, paralyzing, and bringing tears to the eyes without warning, even in the most innocuous moments. In short, love can plunge a normally resilient person into an unprecedented abyss of grief. "Down bad, waking up in blood / Staring at the sky, come back and pick me up," she sings in an almost weary voice in "Down Bad." The ballad "So Long, London," a reflection on the end of a relationship she tried to save (most likely the one with Joe Alwyn), is also one of her most heart-rending songs: "Every breath feels like rarest air / When you're not sure if he wants to be there."

TTPD is as easy to decipher as it is to listen to. Rich in references to significant events in Taylor Swift's life and parallels with her past works, it stands out as a journey with no fixed landmarks in the vast Swiftian lore. Track after track, it almost comes close, at times, to a feverish delirium in its abundance of lyrics, or even a liberating automatic writing session. The songs on *TTPD: The Anthology* in particular, often sung in the lower midrange, sometimes sound like incantations where

choruses and verses no longer matter. This is also the first time the singer has used such a sarcastic, sometimes crude tone. Her lyrics spare no one: not her detractors, not her former companions, not her public, and not even herself.

TTPD features a relatively small list of contributors in its credits. Jack Antonoff and Aaron Dessner—alongside Taylor Swift, of course—are in complete control. The former is the main producer of the standard, resolutely synthpop edition, while the latter is responsible for producing the more folk-sounding *Anthology*. A number of musical personalities have also contributed their personal touch to various tracks: singer and rapper Post Malone, a long-standing friend of Swift's, with whom she forms a rather unexpected duet on "Fortnight," the album's first track; Florence Welch of Florence and the Machine, who sings and plays several instruments on "Florida!!!"; Glenn Kotche, from the band Wilco, on drums on ten tracks; musicians from Jack Antonoff's creative project Bleachers; and Louis Bell, a songwriter and regular collaborator with Post Malone.

Historic Performance

When the album was released, reviews were mixed, although all praised its high quality of writing. Some considered *TTPD* to be one of the artist's best, while others criticized it for lacking coherence and for being too dense. Some journalists and influencers nevertheless reversed their initial judgments after a few days, conceding that *TTPD* is an album whose thirty-one tracks cannot be fully appreciated in one or two listens, but should instead be allowed to infuse slowly.

In terms of commercial reception, *TTPD* was a veritable tidal wave. It became the most listened-to album in a single day on Spotify, surpassing 300 million streams and breaking the all-time record previously held by her other album, *Midnights*. It is also the first album to accumulate a billion streams on Spotify in a single week, in just five days. After seven days, the counter stood at 1.76 billion streams worldwide—another all-time record. Unsurprisingly, it immediately climbed to the top of the Billboard 200, where it remained for a record fifteen weeks. It is also the third album in history and the first by a female artist to spend twelve consecutive weeks at the top of the chart. Finally, it should be noted that all thirty-one songs on the extended version of the album entered the Billboard Hot 100, and at one point songs from the album simultaneously occupied the top 14 positions for the first time in history! Taylor Swift no longer needed to prove it, but with *The Tortured Poets Department*, she reminds anyone who still doubts it: She is not only the greatest pop star of all time, but also one of the most prolific, independent, and free-spirited artists the music industry has ever known.

Taylor Swift and Post Malone win Video of the Year for "Fortnight" at the 2024 MTV Video Music Awards.

SINGLE

FORTNIGHT

(FEAT. POST MALONE)

Taylor Swift, Jack Antonoff, Austin Post / 3:48

Musicians
Taylor Swift: vocals, backing vocals
Post Malone: vocals
Jack Antonoff: drums, Juno, Korg M1, electric and acoustic guitars, percussion, programming
Sean Hutchinson: drums

Recorded
Conway Recording and Electric Feel (Los Angeles), Electric Lady (New York), 2023

Technical Team
Producers: Jack Antonoff, Taylor Swift
Mixing: Serban Ghenea
Sound Engineers: Laura Sisk, Oli Jacobs, Bryce Bordone, Michael Riddleberger, Louis Bell, Sean Hutchinson
Mastering: Randy Merrill
Vinyl Mastering: Ryan Smith

Single Release
Digital Release: April 19, 2024
CD Release: April 26, 2024 (ref. 602465345193)
Best Rankings: Hot 100: 1; Mainstream Top 40: 5; Adult Pop Airplay: 1; Dance/Mix Show Airplay: 13

2024

Genesis

The Tortured Poets Department kicks off in style with this high-flying duet. A great admirer of songwriter Post Malone, Taylor Swift had no hesitation in contacting him to suggest a four-handed writing session. Won over by the singer's creativity and generosity, Post Malone (whose real name is Austin Malone) enthusiastically accepted her proposal. The result is "Fortnight," an introduction to the album's themes of fatalism, longing, melancholy, and broken dreams. *The Tortured Poets Department* explores the tragic dimensions of love and grief, playing with the codes of theatrical drama and poetic ennui inspired by the English Romantics. "Fortnight" paints a grim picture of two former lovers turned neighbors, both trapped in unhappy marriages. The character played by the singer fantasizes about murdering her ex-lover's wife. Then she discovers that her husband is cheating on her, giving her a renewed impulse to murder. For his part, the character played by Post Malone imagines their escape to Florida (a motif revisited in the song "Florida!!!," the eighth track on the album). The hyperbolic line "I love you, it's ruining my life" sums up the spirit of Taylor Swift's eleventh studio album.

Production

With Jack Antonoff back at the helm, Swift returns to her favorite creative cocoon. The song's downtempo synthpop arrangement (96 bpm) begins on tiptoe but sets the tone for the first part of the *Tortured Poets* era. Taylor Swift's vocals fly over a Korg M1 overlay and a minimalist Juno sequence enhanced by a subtle filter opening effect. The ascetic drum machine, the pulsating eighth-note synth bass, and Post Malone's echoing backing vocals successively join this gentle start. From then on, the instrumentation becomes progressively more dense: Layers of synthesizers are superimposed and drums reinforce the rhythmic programming. Post Malone harmonizes his partner's vocals and takes the lead on the first half of the outro. Taylor Swift's nonchalant, almost lascivious tone of voice and the heady melody make this summit encounter an ideal lead single, a perfect introduction to the atmosphere of this opus, which extends the nocturnal wanderings of *Midnights*.

In "TTPD," the inaccessible figure of the poet Dylan Thomas is evoked, as is that of Patti Smith.

THE TORTURED POETS DEPARTMENT

Taylor Swift, Jack Antonoff / 4:53

Musicians

Taylor Swift: vocals, backing vocals
Jack Antonoff: Juno, pocket piano, cello, M1, programming, backing vocals
Michael Riddleberger: drums
Mikey Freedom Hart: bass, acoustic and electric guitars, piano, B3 organ
Zem Audu: synthesizers
Evan Smith: synthesizers

Recorded

Conway Recording (Los Angeles), Electric Lady (New York), 2023

Technical Team

Producers: Jack Antonoff, Taylor Swift
Mixing: Serban Ghenea
Sound Engineers: Laura Sisk, Oli Jacobs, Bryce Bordone, Sean Hutchinson, Michael Riddleberger, Mikey Freedom Hart, Evan Smith, Zem Audu
Mastering: Randy Merrill
Vinyl Mastering: Ryan Smith
Best Ranking: Hot 100: 4

2024

Genesis

A number of clues, such as the typewriter that has become one of the album's symbols, suggest that this song is addressed to Matty Healy, a British singer-songwriter and former companion of the singer, who confessed to a passion for typewriters. Taylor Swift's tumultuous relationship with this tormented artist seems to have left a deep impression on her. In an outburst of candor, she seeks to bring her ex-boyfriend back to reality, evoking the unattainable figures of poet Dylan Thomas and iconic singer and poet Patti Smith: "You're not Dylan Thomas, I'm not Patti Smith." With a critical eye on their relationship, she describes the couple as "modern idiots." The singer also inserts a nod to her contemporaries: Charlie Puth, American singer and songwriter, as well as to those close to her, mentioning Lucy (presumably her friend Lucy Dacus, a talented singer and songwriter) and Jack (surely Jack Antonoff, her longtime collaborator).

Production

This flamboyant synthpop production by Antonoff and Swift transports the listener to the heart of the 1980s. The primitive drum machine and cascade of glittering synthesizers are reinforced by acoustic and electric guitars, bass, piano, and B3 organ, all played by Mikey Freedom Hart, multi-instrumentalist emeritus and loyal Swift collaborator. Inhabited by a particularly intense romantic breath, Swift's interpretation is poignant. Her army of overdubbed backing vocals forms a complex orchestration that, combined with Serban Ghenea's masterful reverb work, contributes greatly to the intoxicating impression of floating in the middle of a cathedral of sound.

Promotional poster in the UK.

2024

MY BOY ONLY BREAKS HIS FAVORITE TOYS

Taylor Swift / 3:23

Musicians

Taylor Swift: vocals, backing vocals

Jack Antonoff: electric guitars, drums, bass, Moog, Juno, M1, programming

Recorded

Conway Recording (Los Angeles), Electric Lady (New York), 2023

Technical Team

Producers: Jack Antonoff, Taylor Swift

Mixing: Serban Ghenea

Sound Engineers: Laura Sisk, Oli Jacobs, Bryce Bordone

Mastering: Randy Merrill

Vinyl Mastering: Ryan Smith

Best Ranking: Hot 100: 6

Genesis

Taylor Swift wrote "My Boy Only Breaks His Favorite Toys" alone at the piano. In this song, she draws a parallel between the way a boy treats his girlfriend and the behavior of a child who, after breaking his favorite toy, ceases to be interested in it. Already explored in "Hits Different," an original composition from the *Midnights* era, the metaphor of the Ken doll, the male counterpart of the Barbie, returns here. In "Hits Different," Swift evoked the habit of replacing one Ken with another ("I used to switch out these Kens"), while in "My Boy Only Breaks His Favorite Toys," she sings: "I felt more when we played pretend / Than with all the Kens." In an interview for Amazon Music, the star confided that this song is about the denial that keeps us in a toxic, dysfunctional relationship, nurturing the illusory hope of improvement.

Production

Like "The Tortured Poets Department," the previous song, "My Boy Only Breaks His Favorite Toys" uses a sound palette largely borrowed from the 1980s. However, Jack Antonoff employs a few different production techniques, starting with the famous gated snare, the grainy synth bass sequence programmed in sixteenth-notes on a Moog, and the shimmering arpeggiator line. The treatment of lead and backing vocals is very similar to that of *The Tortured Poets Department* and, with the exception of the Moog for the bass, the two main synthesizers are the same: the Juno and the Korg M1. With its unusual structure, the synth-pop and new wave ambience is perfectly in keeping with Swift's lexical field and materialistic metaphors.

DOWN BAD

Taylor Swift, Jack Antonoff / 4:21

Musicians
Taylor Swift: vocals, backing vocals
Jack Antonoff: Moog, Juno, piano, M1, mellotron, drums, percussion, programming
Mikey Freedom Hart: DX7, M1, mellotron
Sean Hutchinson: percussion
Zem Audu: saxophones
Evan Smith: saxophones
Recorded
Conway Recording (Los Angeles), Electric Lady (New York), 2023
Technical Team
Producers: Jack Antonoff, Taylor Swift
Mixing: Serban Ghenea
Sound Engineers: Laura Sisk, Oli Jacobs, Jack Manning, Bryce Bordone, Sean Hutchinson, Michael Riddleberger
Mastering: Randy Merrill
Vinyl Mastering: Ryan Smith
Best Ranking: Hot 100: 2

Genesis

The expression *down bad* can mean both "feeling down" and "being madly in love." In "Down Bad," Taylor Swift skillfully plays on this potential dual meaning, fusing the two interpretations. With a great deal of second-degree humor, she compares love to a kind of Stockholm syndrome tinged with conspiracy theories. She tells an alien abduction story, in which the narrator, a teenage girl enchanted by her interstellar journey, is brought back to Earth against her will. This harsh return to reality shatters her illusions: She understands that this love story will have no future and that the flying saucer will not be coming back for her.

Production

Jack Antonoff's arrangement kicks off with retro-futuristic electronic sounds that illustrate Swift's borrowings from popular science-fiction imagery. The analog sound of LinnDrum programming; a flickering synthesizer drone with pulsating tremolo; a weightless arpeggiator; the icy, sparkling sound of the M1; and lead vocals doubled by a vocoder track are enough to set the scene for "Down Bad": a teenage romance that turns to disillusionment against the backdrop of an encounter of the third kind.

SO LONG, LONDON

Taylor Swift, Aaron Dessner / 4:22

Musicians
Taylor Swift: vocals, backing vocals
Aaron Dessner: piano, electric guitar, synthesizer, drum programming
Benjamin Lanz: synthesizer
Recorded
Long Pond (Hudson Valley, NY), 2023
Technical Team
Producers: Aaron Dessner, Taylor Swift
Mixing: Serban Ghenea
Sound Engineers: Bella Blasko, Jonathan Low, Benjamin Lanz, Bryce Bordone, Aaron Dessner
Mastering: Randy Merrill
Vinyl Mastering: Ryan Smith
Best Ranking: Hot 100: 5

Genesis

Taylor Swift began writing the songs that would make up *The Tortured Poets Department* as soon as *Midnights* was released, in 2022. She managed to nurture her creative process during the first phase of the "Eras Tour," in early 2023. It was at this point that the media announced her separation from Joe Alwyn, after a six-year relationship. "So Long, London" is a farewell to her ex-partner, but also to London, a city now close to her heart.

Production

"So Long, London" is Aaron Dessner's first contribution to the album. Performed solo by Swift, the intro sounds like a choirboy canon, its rhythm evoking the ringing of church bells, anchored in London's typical soundscape. Unusually fast, the tempo is marked by a 160 bpm bass drum and supported by a pulsating synthesizer sequence. The rest of the arrangement and the vocal line seem to float above, on a halved tempo. This shift creates a sense of urgency, as if to evoke Taylor Swift's need to move on without waiting any longer. The piano's placed chords ring out solemnly, little ornamental OP-1-like counterpoints and a rumbling synth bass pop up from time to time, while the electric guitar arpeggio accompanies the chorus and its echoing backing vocals. Despite Swift's breathy, almost whispered rendition, the listener can feel just how irrevocable this goodbye is. A farewell in song, benevolent and resolute.

At the 2024 MTV Video Music Awards, Taylor Swift wins seven awards, including Artist of the Year.

BUT DADDY I LOVE HIM

Taylor Swift, Aaron Dessner / 5:40

Musicians
Taylor Swift: vocals, backing vocals
Jack Antonoff: Juno, mellotron, cello, electric and acoustic guitars, bass, programming, synthesizers, backing vocals
Aaron Dessner: acoustic guitars
Sean Hutchinson: drums
Mikey Freedom Hart: synthesizers
Zem Audu: synthesizers
Evan Smith: synthesizers
Bobby Hawk: strings

Recorded
Conway Recording (Los Angeles), Electric Lady (New York), 2023

Technical Team
Producers: Aaron Dessner, Jack Antonoff, Taylor Swift
Mixing: Serban Ghenea
Sound Engineers: Laura Sisk, Oli Jacobs, Bella Blasko, Jonathan Low, David Hart, Bryce Bordone, Sean Hutchinson, Michael Riddleberger, Mikey Freedom Hart, Evan Smith, Zem Audu
Mastering: Randy Merrill
Vinyl Mastering: Ryan Smith
Best Ranking: Hot 100: 7

Genesis

Co-written with Aaron Dessner, "But Daddy I Love Him" directly references an iconic scene from Disney's *The Little Mermaid* (1989), where Ariel, the little mermaid, rages against her father, King Triton, who disapproves of her feelings for the human Prince Eric. In this song, Taylor Swift assumes the role of Ariel, and the disapproving gaze is cast by judgmental fans as intrusive parental figures. The boisterous Matty Healy, meanwhile, seems to assume the traits of Prince Eric, as he crystallizes a controversial love affair that elicits backbiting and criticism. In this way, Taylor Swift responds to all those who feel entitled to comment on her private life with an attitude that is both infantilizing and intrusive in the guise of benevolence.

Production

The big production of "But Daddy I Love Him" is a real team effort. At 5:40, the track is the longest of *The Tortured Poets Department*. Somewhere between pop, folk rock, and electro-pop, its mainstream ambition required the collaboration of three producers: Aaron Dessner, Jack Antonoff, and Taylor Swift. At the heart of this remarkably dense composition is the arrangement, based above all on Dessner's acoustic guitar arpeggio. The layers and pulsating synthesizer sequences advance in symbiosis with the rhythmic programming and the drum duo played by Sean Hutchinson and Michael Riddleberger. The snare drum snaps almost exaggeratedly, while Antonoff helps create the epic dimension by layering some of his favorite instruments: cello, mellotron, Juno, saturated electric guitar, and backing vocals. The faithful Mikey Freedom Hart, Zem Audu, and Evan Smith are on synthesizers, and Bobby Hawk at the helm on strings takes things to a sublime level. Swift delivers a performance that is both intense and nuanced: Delicate on the verses, pre-refrains, and bridge, she unleashes all her power on the choruses, always at ease in the upper register with her full voice.

Opposite: Matty Healy of The 1975 will share Taylor Swift's life for a while after her breakup with Joe Alwyn.

FRESH OUT THE SLAMMER

Taylor Swift, Jack Antonoff / 3:30

2024

Musicians
Taylor Swift: vocals, backing vocals
Jack Antonoff: acoustic and electric guitars, drums, percussion, electric organ, synthesizer, DX7, M1, programming
Recorded
Conway Recording (Los Angeles), Electric Lady (New York), Esplanade (New Orleans), 2023
Technical Team
Producers: Jack Antonoff, Taylor Swift
Mixing: Serban Ghenea
Sound Engineers: Laura Sisk, Oli Jacobs, Bryce Bordone, Christopher Rowe
Mastering: Randy Merrill
Vinyl Mastering: Ryan Smith
Best Ranking: Hot 100: 11

Genesis

"Fresh Out the Slammer" evokes the feeling of confinement that Taylor Swift felt in her previous relationship. Oppressed by the media, fans, and her ex-partner (Joe Alwyn, in all likelihood), she nevertheless managed to free herself. This necessary escape led her into the arms of the tempestuous Matty Healy, and then soon into those of American football player Travis Kelce. But that is another story.

Production

With its atmospheric intro evoking the great American plains, the song's sophisticated production is adorned with dream pop, country rock, and Western overtones. Jack Antonoff and Taylor Swift orchestrate this desert-tinged ballad, which soars like an ode to freedom. The fast tremolo and spring reverb of the electric guitar, the strumming of the acoustic guitar, the acoustic drums with their cross-stick snare, the electric organ, and the cinematic synthesizers are all played by Antonoff. On the second verse, an ensemble of programmed strings bursts triumphantly into the high end of the spectrum, as if to herald the final change of direction. At 2:25, on the bridge, which also serves as an outro, the tempo slows down and suddenly drops from 88 to 75 bpm on a different rhythmic pattern. As the atmosphere darkens and the air seems to become rarer, it is time for Swift to explore new horizons.

Next page spread: A joyous look at Jack Antonoff at the 2025 Grammy Awards.

ANNIE
Fender

Florence Welch, frontwoman of Florence + The Machine, collaborates closely with Taylor Swift on "Florida!!!"

FLORIDA!!!
(FEAT. FLORENCE AND THE MACHINE)

Taylor Swift, Florence Welch / 3:35

Musicians
Taylor Swift: vocals, backing vocals
Florence Welch: vocals, drums, piano, percussion
Jack Antonoff: bass, cello, acoustic and electric guitars, drums, piano, Juno, M1, mellotron, Moog, programming
Emily Jean Stone: oddities

Recorded
Conway Recording (Los Angeles), Electric Lady (New York), Esplanade (New Orleans), Miloco (London), 2023

Technical Team
Producers: Jack Antonoff, Taylor Swift
Mixing: Serban Ghenea
Sound Engineers: Laura Sisk, Oli Jacobs, Bryce Bordone, Ben Loveland, Jon Sher
Mastering: Randy Merrill
Vinyl Mastering: Ryan Smith
Best Ranking: Hot 100: 8

Genesis

Inspired by the true-crime series *Dateline*, Taylor Swift chose Florida as the backdrop for her song, as bandits make a new life under a new identity to escape the authorities. She mentions it here as a symbol of an ideal refuge and a fresh start. To accompany her on this mad escape, she calls on Florence Welch, the singer-songwriter and frontwoman of the British indie rock band Florence and the Machine. In the second verse, the lines "The hurricane with my name when it came / I got drunk and I dared it to wash me away" sung by Welch refer to Hurricane Florence, which threatened the East Coast in September 2018. Taylor Swift also invites the actress Emma Stone, a friend of hers who is credited under her full name, Emily Jean Stone, to contribute her share of "oddities." It is hard to say whether this involves percussion, vocal interventions, or other mysterious contributions.

Production

Halfway between indie rock and arena rock, this Swift and Welch composition is all about dramatic intensity and a sense of urgency that runs through every note. The seven hammering strokes of the chorus contrast with the restrained tension of the verses, accentuated by the rapid vibrato of Welch's voice, which naturally puts her artistic stamp on the song. Jack Antonoff's production is equal to the challenge. Like the calm before the storm, the synthesizer layer flows gently over the verses; the sequences and rhythmic programming maintain the suspense, before the explosion of the choruses, tamed by the slow, deep tremolo of the electric guitar. Welch and Antonoff share the percussive elements to create the tribal ambience of the bridge. In terms of vocal production, backing vocals gush forth from all sides, harmonies are legion, and the lead performances of both singers live up to their promise. The listener would expect nothing less from a collaboration between two artists of this caliber.

FOR DISCERNING SWIFTIES

Florence Welch performed "Florida!!!" onstage with Taylor Swift during the three dates of the "Eras Tour" in Miami, on October 18, 19, and 20, 2024. At the end of the tour, the star declared: "My mystifyingly talented friend Florence came to Miami and each night we performed 'Florida!!!' in Florida!!!"

In "Guilty As Sin?" the singer evokes the melancholy of Paul Buchanan and his Scottish band The Blue Nile.

2024

GUILTY AS SIN?

Taylor Swift, Jack Antonoff / 4:14

Musicians
Taylor Swift: vocals, backing vocals
Jack Antonoff: acoustic and electric guitars, bass, drums, percussion, Juno, M1, programming
Bobby Hawk: strings

Recorded
Conway Recording (Los Angeles), Electric Lady (New York), Prime Recording (Nashville), 2023

Technical Team
Producers: Jack Antonoff, Taylor Swift
Mixing: Serban Ghenea
Sound Engineers: Laura Sisk, Oli Jacobs, Bryce Bordone, Christopher Rowe
Mastering: Randy Merrill
Vinyl Mastering: Ryan Smith
Best Ranking: Hot 100: 10

Genesis

In "Guilty as Sin?" the bored narrator, who feels trapped in her relationship, fantasizes about someone other than her partner. What follows is a reflection on guilt and desire. To illustrate her melancholy, Taylor Swift mentions the Blue Nile (a Scottish sophisti-pop and synthpop band active from 1981 to 2004) in the first line and, in the second line, their song "The Downtown Lights," the lead single from their 1989 album *Hats*.

Production

Co-written and co-produced by Swift and Jack Antonoff, "Guilty as Sin?" follows a rigid, relentless binary rhythm. Launched on a 95 bpm tempo, the guitars played in palm mute, eighth-note bass, and generously compressed straight drums recall the pop-rock sound of the 1990s. The slide guitar immersed in reverb, the tremolo guitar, the Juno layer, and Swift's melismas (melodic figures of several consecutive notes carrying the same syllable) on the chorus reinforce this impression. Antonoff plays most of the instruments. As for Bobby Hawk, he sprinkles pizzicato strings throughout, bringing a certain relief to the rhythm section. He also plays a number of discreet held notes, most noticeable on the outro.

Elizabeth Taylor in *Who's Afraid of Virginia Woolf?* directed by Mike Nichols in 1966.

WHO'S AFRAID OF LITTLE OLD ME?

Taylor Swift / 5:34

Musicians
Taylor Swift: vocals, backing vocals
Jack Antonoff: Juno, Moog, M1, mellotron, cello, electric guitars, piano, bass drums, programming
Aaron Dessner: piano
Michael Riddleberger: percussion
Mikey Freedom Hart: synthesizers
Zem Audu: synthesizers
Evan Smith: synthesizers
Sean Hutchinson: drums
Recorded
Conway Recording (Los Angeles), Electric Lady (New York), Esplanade (New Orleans), Long Pond (Hudson Valley, NY), 2023
Technical Team
Producers: Jack Antonoff, Taylor Swift
Mixing: Serban Ghenea
Sound Engineers: Laura Sisk, Oli Jacobs, Joey Miller, Jonathan Low, Jack Manning, Jozef Caldwell, Mikey Freedom Hart, Bryce Bordone, Michael Riddleberger, Sean Hutchinson, Zem Audu, Evan Smith, Bella Blasko
Mastering: Randy Merrill
Vinyl Mastering: Ryan Smith
Best Ranking: Hot 100: 9

2024

Genesis

After "Guilty as Sin?," "Who's Afraid of Little Old Me?" is the second interrogative track. The third, "How Did It End?" appears at number 21 on the *Anthology* version. In this track, Taylor Swift responds directly to the criticisms and rumors that have been circulating since the early days of her career, largely fueled by certain fans and the media. In a voice memo to Jack Antonoff about the demo for "Who's Afraid of Little Old Me?" she says: "Yeah, just a song about being crazy." This statement could be a reference to Edward Albee's 1962 play *Who's Afraid of Virginia Woolf?* and perhaps even more so to its 1966 film adaptation with Elizabeth Taylor and Richard Burton, directed by Mike Nichols. The singer has already quoted this pair of actors in the opening song of *Reputation*, "...Ready for It?" (another title in the form of a question), and she likes to distill Virginia Woolf references in her songs. So there is little doubt about the nod.

Production

As with "But Daddy I Love Him," the production on "Who's Afraid of Little Old Me?" brings out the big guns. With the exception of Bobby Hawk, the team of musicians is unchanged. Composed entirely by Swift and co-produced with Jack Antonoff, "Who's Afraid of Little Old Me?" verges on orchestral pop. With its dense, intricate instrumentation, this arrangement is certainly not lacking in depth. The arsenal of synthesizers is deployed: galloping sequences, grainy Moog bass, shimmering leads, swirling arpeggiators, seismic risers, and deep layers. Sean Hutchinson's drums mingle with Michael Riddleberger's percussion and programming, while Antonoff's electric guitar twang spices things up. At 5:34, this epic track is barely sixteen seconds shorter than "But Daddy I Love Him," the longest track of *TTPD*. On every last phrase of the chorus, "Who's afraid of little old me?!," Swift pushes her chest voice to the limit, as if in imitation of the frog that wants to be bigger than the ox, vehemently underlining the absurdity of the situation.

"I Can Do It with a Broken Heart" shares some of the same technical team as the award-winning "Fortnight."

I CAN FIX HIM (NO REALLY I CAN)

Taylor Swift, Jack Antonoff / 2:36

Musicians
Taylor Swift: vocals, backing vocals
Jack Antonoff: synthesizer, Juno, acoustic and electric guitars, percussion, bass, piano, mellotron, programming
Recorded
Conway Recording (Los Angeles), Electric Lady (New York), Rue Boyer (Paris), Prime Recording (Nashville), 2023
Technical Team
Producers: Jack Antonoff, Taylor Swift
Mixing: Serban Ghenea
Sound Engineers: Laura Sisk, Oli Jacobs, Bryce Bordone, Christopher Rowe
Mastering: Randy Merrill
Vinyl Mastering: Ryan Smith
Best Ranking: Hot 100: 20

2024

Genesis

In the category of songs that sound like mini movie scripts, "I Can Fix Him (No I Really Can)" moves away from film noir and into the world of the Western. The mood is set: a train, a small town, a saloon, a Texas highway, a pistol, and a woman in love with a dangerous man with calloused hands. At just 2:36, this is the shortest song on the standard album version. On the *Anthology* version, however, it is "I Look in People's Windows" that takes the prize, with a running time of 2:11.

Production

To bring this playlet to life, Taylor Swift and Jack Antonoff drew inspiration from the sounds that have shaped the Western imagination since Ennio Morricone helped to reinvent the genre in the 1960s. Except for the harmonica, nothing is missing: the deep tremolo of the rhythmic electric guitar, the twang and long spring reverb of the lead guitar, the orchestral bells, the rootsy sound of the acoustic guitar, the vibraphone and the assortment of metallic percussion that sometimes evokes the clank of stirrups, and sometimes the detonation of a gunshot. With her sensual, mysterious interpretation, Swift takes the listener on a one-way trip along the dusty roads of the Wild West.

LOML

Taylor Swift, Aaron Dessner / 4:37

Musicians
Taylor Swift: vocals, backing vocals
Aaron Dessner: pianos, synthesizers, synth bass, keyboards
Glenn Kotche: drums, percussion
Rob Moose: violin, viola
Recorded
Electric Lady (New York), Long Pond (Hudson Valley, NY), Prime Recording (Nashville), 2023
Technical Team
Producers: Aaron Dessner, Taylor Swift
Mixing: Serban Ghenea
Sound Engineers: Bella Blasko, Jonathan Low, Bryce Bordone, Christopher Rowe, Laura Sisk, Rob Moose
Mastering: Randy Merrill
Vinyl Mastering: Ryan Smith
Best Ranking: Hot 100: 12

Genesis

Usually, *loml* is an acronym for "love of my life." However, throughout her narrative, Taylor Swift observes the deterioration of her relationship, culminating in the dramatic conclusion of the final chorus where, in the last verse, she twists the meaning of this popular expression into a poignant "loss of my life." The song explores the evolution of a relationship from idealization to disillusionment. Swift, with her inventive pen, transforms an acronym of tenderness into a symbol of loss and emotional rupture.

Production

Swift and Aaron Dessner co-wrote and co-produced this piano ballad. Its minimalist arrangement relies essentially on the piano arpeggio and its subtly worked sound. At the end of verses and choruses, the sound seems to have been colored by a kind of chorus, as if the acoustic piano part had been identically doubled by an electric piano. Between distant layers, discreet ornaments, and throbbing synth bass, the synthesizers gradually open up the spectrum and swell to cinematic proportions. The backing vocals and Swift's soulful interpretation heighten the dramatic intensity.

SINGLE

I CAN DO IT WITH A BROKEN HEART

Taylor Swift, Jack Antonoff / 3:38

Musicians
Taylor Swift: vocals, backing vocals
Jack Antonoff: drums, Juno, M1, percussion, piano, programming
Oli Jacobs: backing vocals, percussion, programming, spoken word

Recorded
Conway Recording (Los Angeles), Electric Lady (New York), 2023

Technical Team
Producers: Jack Antonoff, Taylor Swift
Mixing: Serban Ghenea
Sound Engineers: Laura Sisk, Oli Jacobs, Bryce Bordone
Mastering: Randy Merrill
Vinyl Mastering: Ryan Smith

Single Release
Digital Release: July 2, 2024
Best Rankings: Hot 100: 3; Mainstream Top 40: 6; Adult Pop Airplay: 4

Genesis

"I Can Do It with a Broken Heart" is the second single from the album *The Tortured Poets Department.* Taylor Swift turns this song into a kind of pep talk for herself, to give herself courage in tackling the mammoth "Eras Tour."

Production

Introduced by a crazy arpeggiator, the arrangement sets off on a very upbeat electro-pop and dance-pop production that contrasts with the song's theme and the rather dark aesthetic of *The Tortured Poets Department.* Launched on a 130 bpm tempo, frenetic synthesizer sequences drive the entire instrumentation. Rhythmic programming shifts from a simple bass drum pulse in the black to a particularly flashy disco pop pattern, packed with toms fills and flashy, stinging percussive events. Combined with the keyboard sounds of the Korg M1, the piano part underpins the harmony almost subliminally. Swift's energetic, playful vocals add to the parodic, even sarcastic dimension of this overstimulating track. It's a way of underlining the cost of being constantly in the spotlight: having to shine by always being beautiful, successful, and smiling. Usually confined to the engineering aspects, Oli Jacobs is on backing vocals, percussion, and the recurring "1, 2, 3, 4" heard in the distance.

Taylor Swift attends the 2024 Golden Globe Awards in Beverly Hills, where she is nominated in the Box Office Achievement category for her concert film *Taylor Swift: The Eras Tour.*

THE SMALLEST MAN WHO EVER LIVED

Taylor Swift, Aaron Dessner / 4:05

Musicians

Taylor Swift: vocals, backing vocals
Aaron Dessner: bass, drum programming, electric guitar, piano, synthesizer
James McAlister: drums, electric guitar, percussion, synthesizers
Rob Moose: violin, viola, arrangements
Jason Slota: percussion

Recorded

Long Pond (Hudson Valley, NY), Tiny Telephone (Oakland, CA), Electric Lady (New York), 2023

Technical Team

Producers: Aaron Dessner, Taylor Swift
Mixing: Serban Ghenea
Sound Engineers: Bella Blasko, Bryce Bordone, Aaron Dessner, Laura Sisk, Beau Sorensen, James McAlister, Rob Moose
Mastering: Randy Merrill
Vinyl Mastering: Ryan Smith
Best Ranking: Hot 100: 14

2024

Genesis

"The Smallest Man Who Ever Lived" is a diatribe that Taylor Swift seems to be addressing to her ex-boyfriend, the boisterous Matty Healy. In the bridge, she amuses herself by using a number of words and expressions borrowed from the lexicon of the worlds of espionage and the police: "who wanted me dead," "gun underneath our bed," and "sleeper cell spy."

Production

In the spirit of Aaron Dessner and Taylor Swift's previous production, "loml," "The Smallest Man Who Ever Lived" begins as an augmented piano ballad. A monotone synthesizer sequence, a distant stratum, and a few reverse-passed piano chords gradually embellish the arrangement, which are soon joined by an eighth-note bass drum and Rob Moose's cinematic destringing arrangement, which swells until the bridge explodes with saturated electric guitars, hammered piano and martial drums, strings played in energetic staccato, and harmonized backing vocals that push to the top octave. The bridge of "The Smallest Man Who Ever Lived" is yet another fine example of a song within a song. Swift continues to explore the subtle art of expressing complex emotions.

THE ALCHEMY

Taylor Swift, Jack Antonoff / 3:16

Musicians

Taylor Swift: vocals, backing vocals
Jack Antonoff: drums, Juno, M1, electric guitars, backing vocals, percussion, cello, programming
Sean Hutchinson: drums

Recorded

Conway Recording (Los Angeles), Electric Lady (New York), Prime Recording (Nashville), 2023

Technical Team

Producers: Jack Antonoff, Taylor Swift
Mixing: Serban Ghenea
Sound Engineers: Laura Sisk, Oli Jacobs, Bryce Bordone, Sean Hutchinson, Christopher Rowe
Mastering: Randy Merrill
Vinyl Mastering: Ryan Smith
Best Ranking: Hot 100: 13

Genesis

With a host of sports metaphors, "The Alchemy" describes the emergence of a love that takes Taylor Swift by surprise, as she recovers from a painful breakup. The dates mentioned and the vocabulary used leave little doubt as to the identity of the person involved: American football player Travis Kelce. As Swift refuses to fight the chemistry, she decides to allow herself to be carried away by this mutually intoxicating and irresistible attraction.

Production

"The Alchemy" is a dreamlike pop-rock song, underpinned by a hybrid rhythm made up of programmed elements and rhythm'n'blues-style acoustic drums. Synthesizers and electric guitars vie for the middle of the spectrum in an overflow of variegated textures. The sixteenth-note synth sequence drives the choruses and the twang guitar, one of Antonoff's signature sounds, and spices up the song's open, ethereal arrangement. The sophisticated vocal production superbly showcases the performances of Swift and her army of backing vocals: They seem to float above this euphoric, electric orchestration.

Clara Bow was a silent movie star and a sex symbol of the Roaring Twenties.

CLARA BOW

Taylor Swift, Aaron Dessner / 3:37

Musicians

Taylor Swift: vocals, backing vocals
Aaron Dessner: piano, synthesizers, bass, percussion, drum programming, Fender VI
Glenn Kotche: drums, percussion
JT Bates: drums
Thomas Bartlett: synthesizers, keyboards, piano
James McAlister: synthesizers, percussion, keyboards
The London Contemporary Orchestra: symphony orchestra
Robert Ames: conductor
Bryce Dessner: orchestral arrangement

Recorded

Long Pond (Hudson Valley, NY), Air Studios (London), 2023

Technical Team

Producers: Aaron Dessner, Taylor Swift
Mixing: Serban Ghenea
Sound Engineers: Jonathan Low, Jeremy Murphy, Bryce Bordone, Thomas Bartlett, James McAlister, Bella Blasko
Mastering: Randy Merrill
Vinyl Mastering: Ryan Smith
Best Ranking: Hot 100: 21

2024

Genesis

The song "Clara Bow" denounces the music industry's tendency to fashion interchangeable female singers by flattering their egos and creating a climate of competition specifically reserved for the female star system. Clara Bow, a silent film actress, was a true icon of the Roaring Twenties and a sex symbol of her era. Through this mythical figure, Taylor Swift criticizes show business, pointing out that the same sexist patterns have persisted for over a hundred years. To support her point, she cites another of her models, closer to home, Stevie Nicks, the legendary singer of the protean band Fleetwood Mac, with whom she is sometimes compared. "Clara Bow" is structured as a series of quotations inspired by her conversations with executives and label heads, which she transcribes here with great irony. In the outro, the parallel between Swift and the actress expresses both the absurdity of this system and the idea that the singer has in turn become a figure to which young female artists are compared.

Production

Swift and Aaron Dessner's pop-rock production focuses on the electric bass duet in eighth-note palm mute. One of the two bassists plays the tonic while the other harmonizes delicately. The bass duo is one of Dessner's specialties (the arrangement of "Peace" on the *Folklore* album, is also a perfect illustration). The result, textural and particularly shimmering, drives the whole arrangement. In the distance, synthesizers deepen the field, and the strings of the London Contemporary Orchestra gradually flesh out this minimalist instrumentation with staccatos and airy outfits arranged by Bryce Dessner and conducted by Robert Ames. On drums, we find JT Bates, but it is above all the excellent Glenn Kotche, drummer for Wilco, the legendary American folk-rock band led by Jeff Tweedy, who stands out. Essentially based on toms, the drums build up in parallel with the orchestra and create the link with the bass duo. Swift delivers a precise, sensitive performance, comfortably installed at the center of her range.

FOR DISCERNING SWIFTIES

The various versions of the physical release of the standard edition of *The Tortured Poets Department* include one of the following four songs as a bonus track: "The Black Dog," "The Albatross," "The Bolter," or "The Manuscript."

THE BLACK DOG

Taylor Swift / 3:58

Musicians
Taylor Swift: vocals, backing vocals, piano
Jack Antonoff: acoustic and electric guitars, bass, Juno, M1, Polysix, cello, drums, mellotron, piano, Rhodes, vocoders, programming
Bobby Hawk: strings
Sean Hutchinson: drums
Recorded
Conway Recording (Los Angeles), Electric Lady (New York), 2023
Technical Team
Producers: Jack Antonoff, Taylor Swift
Mixing: Serban Ghenea
Sound Engineers: Laura Sisk, Michael Riddleberger, Oli Jacobs, Bryce Bordone, Sean Hutchinson, Jack Manning
Mastering: Randy Merrill
Vinyl Mastering: Ryan Smith
Best Ranking: Hot 100: 25

Genesis

Originally with the title "Old Habits Die Screaming" (as in the last line of each chorus), "The Black Dog" is the first song on *The Tortured Poets Department: The Anthology*. It is also included as a bonus track on one of the physical versions of the standard edition. Inspired by the turmoil of her personal life, Taylor Swift plays a heartbroken character who, in a fit of desperation, follows her ex-boyfriend (thanks to the shared geolocation of their phones) to a London pub. The place, which actually exists and where the singer and her ex-boyfriend Joe Alwyn used to hang out, is called the Black Dog. There, she observes her ex flirting with a much younger woman but struggles to understand why he does not miss her presence, when they have lived and shared so much together. In the chorus, Swift mentions the American alternative rock band the Starting Line, of which her former boyfriend is a fan, but with which his new girlfriend is unfamiliar because of her young age.

Production

Composed by Swift on her own and co-produced with Jack Antonoff, "The Black Dog" begins as a piano ballad. Acoustic guitar, Fender Rhodes, Bobby Hawk's strings, and synthesizers gradually flesh out the choruses, until the last verse explodes on the word *screaming*, in a sudden crash of saturated electric guitars and pounding drums. The bridge begins in stripped-down mode, and the instrumentation ramps up until the penultimate verse of the final chorus, when the tension suddenly drops, as if to spurn the brutality of previous chorus endings, perhaps marking the beginnings of acceptance and appeasement.

IMGONNAGETYOUBACK

Taylor Swift, Jack Antonoff / 3:42

Musicians

Taylor Swift: vocals, backing vocals
Jack Antonoff: drums, Juno 60, Prophet 6, M1, acoustic guitars, percussion, keyboard, piano, programming
Jack Manning: piano

Recorded

Electric Lady (New York), 2023

Technical Team

Producers: Jack Antonoff, Taylor Swift
Mixing: Serban Ghenea
Sound Engineers: Laura Sisk, Oli Jacobs, Bryce Bordone
Mastering: Randy Merrill
Vinyl Mastering: Ryan Smith
Best Ranking: Hot 100: 26

Genesis

With its title of words strung together, "imgonagetyouback" evokes a coded message. The main feature of this song is the ambiguity of "get you back" (which can mean either to rekindle a relationship or take revenge). The narrator wants her ex-boyfriend back, but she doesn't yet know whether she wants him back or revenge (Whether I'm gonna be your wife or / Gonna smash up your bike, I / Haven't decided yet / But I'm gonna get you back). The lack of breathing space in the title could also serve to underline the narrator's determination. Dressed in the short skirt that suits her so well, she devises a plan, detailing her intentions step by step.

Production

With its two-speed synthesizer sequence (or maybe a Rhodes with the tremolo depth pushed to the extreme and the speed set in automation?) and its sparse LinnDrum programming, Jack Antonoff's arrangement gives pride of place to Swift's siren-like vocals. On the choruses, the padded sound of Fender Rhodes arpeggios occupies the center of the spectrum, screening the stormy, jerky synth-pop production of the singer and Antonoff. Assertive and sexy, the backing vocals, flow, and melody of the singer's voice sail into rhythm'n'blues territory.

THE ALBATROSS

Taylor Swift, Aaron Dessner / 3:03

Musicians

Taylor Swift: vocals, backing vocals
Aaron Dessner: piano, synthesizers, percussion, drum programming, bass, acoustic and electric guitars, high strung guitar, keyboards
Benjamin Lanz: synthesizer
Glenn Kotche: drums, percussion
James McAlister: drum programming
The London Contemporary Orchestra: symphony orchestra
Robert Ames: conductor
Bryce Dessner: orchestral arrangement

Recorded

Long Pond (Hudson Valley, NY), Air Studios (London), 2023

Technical Team

Producers: Aaron Dessner, Taylor Swift
Mixing: Serban Ghenea
Sound Engineers: Jonathan Low, Jeremy Murphy, Bryce Bordone, Benjamin Lanz, James McAlister, Bella Blasko
Mastering: Randy Merrill
Vinyl Mastering: Ryan Smith
Best Ranking: Hot 100: 30

Genesis

"The Albatross" could almost be classed as a quill pen song. Assuming the guise of a doomsday oracle, Taylor Swift uses the metaphor of the threatening arrival of the albatross to evoke the ambivalence of amorous feelings: The bird symbolizes both the beauty and fragility of true love. It is only in the final chorus, in the first person, that the singer reveals the identity of the bird, enabling the listener to understand that this dreaded danger, which everything seems to point to, is herself. "The Albatross" is a poetic response to rumors, rarely benevolent.

Production

Taylor Swift and Aaron Dessner's ethereal folk-pop production is perfectly suited to the theme of "The Albatross." The acoustic guitar arpeggio drives the arrangement. This is soon joined by the synthesizers and strings of the London Contemporary Orchestra, conducted by Robert Ames and arranged by Bryce Dessner. Glen Kotche's percussive drums energize the ensemble, in symbiosis with the pulsating synthesizer sequence on the sixteenth note. Taylor Swift's performance is smooth and fluid. Her overdubbed backing vocals play the role of second voice on the verses and choruses, a harmonic reinforcement of the orchestra on the bridge and a melodic gimmick on the chorus and outro.

"Chloe or Sam or Sophia or Marcus" is a song about hope for recovery after a broken heart.

CHLOE OR SAM OR SOPHIA OR MARCUS

Taylor Swift, Aaron Dessner / 3:33

Musicians
Taylor Swift: vocals, backing vocals
Aaron Dessner: piano, synthesizer, bass, drum programming, acoustic and electric guitars, keyboards, mandolin
Benjamin Lanz: synthesizer, trombone
Glenn Kotche: drums, percussion
JT Bates: drums
Rob Moose: violin, viola, orchestral arrangement
Recorded
Long Pond (Hudson Valley, NY), Prime Recording (Nashville), 2023
Technical Team
Producers: Aaron Dessner, Taylor Swift
Mixing: Serban Ghenea
Sound Engineers: Jonathan Low, Bryce Bordone, Maryam Qudus, Benjamin Lanz, Christopher Rowe, Bella Blasko
Mastering: Randy Merrill
Vinyl Mastering: Ryan Smith
Best Ranking: Hot 100: 36

2024

Genesis

"Chloe or Sam or Sophia or Marcus" evokes romantic sadness through poetic metaphors in which Taylor Swift strings together powerful images of absence, pain, and loss. Haunted by memories, she sees holographic projections and ghosts of the past flash through her mind. The hope of a cure, of a healing of this open wound, is felt. The metaphor "scarlet maroon" recalls "Maroon," the second song on *Midnights* (her previous album, released in 2022), where the singer used the same terms to establish a palette of fading love, from scarlet to maroon. The third line of the second verse, "You needed me but you needed drugs more," seems to echo the dissolute lifestyle of the singer's ex-partner Matty Healy. It is safe to assume that Swift drew inspiration for this song from her relationship with the artist.

Production

In waltz time, this nostalgic ballad, imbued with the delicacy of the songs co-written and co-produced by Taylor Swift and Aaron Dessner, invites the listener to plunge into the singer's battered soul. Driven by the piano and its Erik Satie–like motif, the arrangement seems to flow naturally. The acoustic guitar and mandolin pull the cadence into a 6/8 rhythm, the electric guitar elegantly doubles and harmonizes the piano motif, and Rob Moose's violin and viola seem to light the dawn on this twilight instrumentation. On the opening beats of each bar, the bass drum passes through a delay set to eighth notes in 4/4, creating an increasingly intense and unsettling triplet sensation, like a beating heart. The bass oscillates between double-note playing in thirds and fifths, all the while sticking to the bass drum. Swift's rendition is at once restrained and breathless, at times verging on the whispered, until the end of the third verse. The backing vocals embellish the lead voice and finally break away to sketch out the melodic gimmick of the outro.

HOW DID IT END?

Taylor Swift, Aaron Dessner / 3:58

Musicians
Taylor Swift: vocals, backing vocals
Aaron Dessner: piano, synthesizer, drum programming, electric guitar, keyboards, synth bass
Glenn Kotche: drums, percussion
JT Bates: drums
James McAlister: synthesizers, Omnichord, drums, keyboards
Thomas Bartlett: synthesizer, keyboards, piano
The London Contemporary Orchestra: symphony orchestra
Robert Ames: conductor
Bryce Dessner: orchestral arrangement
Recorded
Long Pond (Hudson Valley, NY), Air Studios (London), 2023
Technical Team
Producers: Aaron Dessner, Taylor Swift
Mixing: Serban Ghenea
Sound Engineers: Jonathan Low, Jeremy Murphy, Bryce Bordone, James McAlister, Thomas Bartlett, Bella Blasko
Mastering: Randy Merrill
Vinyl Mastering: Ryan Smith
Best Ranking: Hot 100: 35

Genesis

"How Did It End?" deals with Taylor Swift's separation from Joe Alwyn. The singer denounces the media voyeurism that impinges upon her private life, constant scrutiny by tabloids eager for scandal, sensational headlines, and tears. While exploring the personal pain of this breakup, the song also questions the role of the media in constructing a distorted reality, where intimacy becomes a spectacle to be consumed.
Production

"How Did It End?" is an orchestral piano ballad written and produced by Taylor Swift and Aaron Dessner. Composed and played by Dessner, the arrangement relies on the delicacy of 3/4 piano arpeggios. Coupled with abundantly reverberant electric guitar and synthesizers, Bryce Dessner's orchestration, brilliantly performed by the London Contemporary Orchestra (conducted by Robert Ames), gradually swells to create an increasingly poignant atmosphere. Swift's vibrant voice reinforces this dramatic progression, adding a cinematic dimension to the whole. The rich, detailed production underscores the tension between the intimate pain of the breakup and the grandiose staging of the instrumentation.

SO HIGH SCHOOL

Taylor Swift, Aaron Dessner / 3:48

Musicians
Taylor Swift: vocals, backing vocals
Aaron Dessner: piano, synthesizers, percussion, drum programming, electric guitar, keyboards, synth bass, bass
James McAlister: synthesizers, drums, electric guitar, drum programming
Benjamin Lanz: modular synth, sequencer, synthesizers, trombone
Recorded
Long Pond (Hudson Valley, NY), 2023
Technical Team
Producers: Aaron Dessner, Taylor Swift
Mixing: Serban Ghenea
Sound Engineers: Jonathan Low, Bryce Bordone, James McAlister, Bella Blasko
Mastering: Randy Merrill
Vinyl Mastering: Ryan Smith
Best Ranking: Hot 100: 24

Genesis

"So High School" can be seen as a tribute to teenage love and the carefree days of the late 1990s. Probably motivated by her meeting with American professional football player Travis Kelce (they were both born in 1989), Taylor Swift makes numerous references to her first love and her high school life. In particular, she cites the film *American Pie* (1999) and the video game *Grand Theft Auto* (first released in 1997). "So High School" is a joyfully regressive pop song full of spirit.

Production

Taylor Swift and Aaron Dessner's pop-rock production is perfectly in tune with the song's theme. Immersed in reverb, sparkling electric guitars drive the arrangement. Dessner superimposes strumming tracks in a one-way motion and enhances the whole piece with shimmering arpeggios. Synthesizers accentuate the dream pop feel, and the bass marks the eighth-note tonics over a typical nineties drum pattern. Swift's interpretation and vocal melody flow naturally. With total ease, the singer alternates between low midrange and falsetto, via the top of her chest register.

In 2022, Taylor Swift receives an honorary doctorate of fine arts from New York University. During her speech, the star encourages young graduates to follow their dreams and never give up in the face of adversity.

I HATE IT HERE

Taylor Swift, Aaron Dessner / 4:03

Musicians
Taylor Swift: vocals, backing vocals
Aaron Dessner: piano, synthesizers, bass, drum programming, electric and acoustic guitars, high strung guitar, mandolin, banjo, percussion
Benjamin Lanz: synthesizer
Glenn Kotche: drums, percussion
James McAlister: synthesizers, acoustic guitar, bass, synth bass, percussion
Thomas Bartlett: synthesizers, keyboards, piano
The London Contemporary Orchestra: symphony orchestra
Robert Ames: conductor
Bryce Dessner: orchestral arrangement
Recorded
Long Pond (Hudson Valley, NY), Air Studios (London), 2023
Technical Team
Producers: Aaron Dessner, Taylor Swift
Mixing: Serban Ghenea
Sound Engineers: Jonathan Low, Bella Blasko, Jeremy Murphy, Bryce Bordone, James McAlister, Thomas Bartlett, Maryam Qudus, Benjamin Lanz
Mastering: Randy Merrill
Vinyl Mastering: Ryan Smith
Best Ranking: Hot 100: 34

Genesis

In "I Hate It Here," Taylor Swift expresses her need to escape the mediocrity of the real world. The singer plunges into a daydream, escaping into an idealized past (the 1930s), her secret garden, and imaginary moon valleys, as well as a planet where only the good souls survived. But she knows that nostalgia is a trap: "Nostalgia is a mind's trick / If I'd been there, I'd hate it."

Production

Acoustic guitar picking is at the heart of this orchestral folk-pop production by Swift and Aaron Dessner. Electric guitar, mandolin, and banjo twirl all around, Glen Kotche's drums and percussion gently set the pulse, and keyboards complement the acoustic guitar arpeggio. The combination of synthesizers and the London Contemporary Orchestra opens up the horizon and deepens the scope of this dense, luminous arrangement. Between bitterness and benevolence, seeming to float above the instrumentation, Swift's voice incites the listener to reverie and reflection.

Some see "Thank You Aimee" as a nod to Britney Spears's "If U Seek Amy" (2008).

FOR DISCERNING SWIFTIES

On August 15, 2024, in the live version of the song available as a paid download (it had been available for streaming the previous week), the title becomes "thank You aimEe." This typographical choice is interpreted as an allusion to rapper Kanye West, who officially changed his name to Ye in 2021.

FOR DISCERNING SWIFTIES

On August 15, 2024, in the live version of the song available as a paid download (it had been available for streaming the previous week), the title becomes "thank You aimEe." This typographical choice is interpreted as an allusion to rapper Kanye West, who officially changed his name to Ye in 2021.

THANK YOU AIMEE

Taylor Swift, Aaron Dessner / 4:23

2024

Musicians

Taylor Swift: vocals, backing vocals
Aaron Dessner: synthesizers, drum programming, acoustic guitar, mandolin, banjo, keyboards, synth bass, percussion
Jack Antonoff: electric guitar, cello, drums, percussion, backing vocals, programming
Glenn Kotche: drums, percussion
Thomas Bartlett: synthesizers, keyboards, piano
The London Contemporary Orchestra: symphony orchestra
Robert Ames: conductor
Bryce Dessner: orchestral arrangement

Recorded

Long Pond (Hudson Valley, NY), Sharp Sonic (Los Angeles, Air Studios (London), 2023

Technical Team

Producers: Aaron Dessner, Jack Antonoff, Taylor Swift
Mixing: Serban Ghenea
Sound Engineers: Jonathan Low, Bella Blasko, Jeremy Murphy, Bryce Bordone, Thomas Bartlett, Maryam Qudus, Laura Sisk, Oli Jacobs, Jack Antonoff
Mastering: Randy Merrill
Vinyl Mastering: Ryan Smith
Best Ranking: Hot 100: 23

Genesis

Because of its three capital letters forming the name Kim, this track is widely considered a diss track against Kim Kardashian. Born in the ashes of the 2009 MTV Video Music Awards scandal, the dispute between Taylor Swift and Kardashian dates back to 2016, when Kanye West, then married to Kardashian, released the single "Famous," in which he claims to have made the singer famous. Not without reason, Taylor Swift considers the "Famous" lyrics to be misogynistic. In her song "thanK you aIMee," she uses the character Aimee to symbolize a bully in high school. Marked by this painful experience, she emerges all the stronger for it. Aimee could also be a reference to Britney Spears's song "If U Seek Amy" (*Circus*, 2008), which plays on sexual innuendo.

Production

"But Daddy I Love Him" and "thanK you aIMee" are the only two songs from *The Tortured Poets Department* co-produced by Aaron Dessner, Jack Antonoff and Taylor Swift. The formula on "thanK you aIMee" is not far removed from that used on "I Hate It Here." The acoustic guitar arpeggio, supported by a synthesizer sequence and a rhythmic mix of programmed elements and played percussion, drives the arrangement. The instrumentation gradually becomes denser until the London Contemporary Orchestra enters, followed by keyboards, drums, and chimes, whose shimmering sound helps create the victorious mood of the choruses. On the intimate third verse, the banjo doubles the acoustic guitar arpeggio, and the mandolin rhythm is clearly visible in the pared-down outro.

Musician Patrik Berger, who had already collaborated on *Evermore*'s "Gold Rush," co-wrote "I Look in People's Windows" with Taylor Swift and Jack Antonoff.

2024

I LOOK IN PEOPLE'S WINDOWS

Taylor Swift, Jack Antonoff, Patrik Berger / 2:11

Musicians
Taylor Swift: vocals, backing vocals
Jack Antonoff: acoustic guitars, Juno, cello, programming
Patrik Berger: acoustic guitars
Recorded
Conway Recording (Los Angeles), Electric Lady (New York), 2023
Technical Team
Producers: Jack Antonoff, Patrik Berger, Taylor Swift
Mixing: Serban Ghenea
Sound Engineers: Laura Sisk, Oli Jacobs, Bryce Bordone
Mastering: Randy Merrill
Vinyl Mastering: Ryan Smith
Best Ranking: Hot 100: 39

Genesis

Taylor Swift co-wrote "I Look in People's Windows" with Patrik Berger and Jack Antonoff. In this song, she takes on the role of a character in the midst of the sadness of love, desperately looking for the image of her ex-boyfriend in people's windows. Set against the backdrop of the festive season, the narrator experiences an overwhelming solitude, observing the outside world through shop windows, in the vain and illusory hope of catching a glimpse of the one she still loves.

Production

A talented Swedish producer, Berger collaborated with Swift and Jack Antonoff on the writing and production of "Slut!," whose From the Vault version was released on Taylor's Version of *1989*, in October 2023. At 2:11, "I Look in People's Windows" is the shortest track of *The Tortured Poets Department*. Intimate and sophisticated, this arrangement features a duet of acoustic guitars played by Antonoff and Berger and a combination of plucked sounds. Scattered throughout the track, sound design elements dress up this intimate electro-folk production (reversed cello, birdsong, and layers of heavily manipulated samples): The acoustic guitar gimmick is in good company. Taylor Swift's voice passes through a subtly proportioned vocoder whose analog grain blends harmoniously with the backing vocals. The result of this skillful work immerses the listener in a world that is both fairy tale–like and disquieting, hybrid but always organic.

THE PROPHECY

Taylor Swift, Aaron Dessner / 4:09

Musicians

Taylor Swift: vocals, backing vocals
Aaron Dessner: drum programming, electric and acoustic guitars
Glenn Kotche: drums, percussion
James McAlister: synthesizers, Omnichord, percussion, drum programming, autoharp
JT Bates: drums
Thomas Bartlett: synthesizers, keyboards, piano
The London Contemporary Orchestra: symphony orchestra
Robert Ames: conductor
Bryce Dessner: orchestral arrangement

Recorded

Long Pond (Hudson Valley, NY), Air Studios (London), 2023

Technical Team

Producers: Aaron Dessner, Taylor Swift
Mixing: Serban Ghenea
Sound Engineers: Jonathan Low, Bella Blasko, Jeremy Murphy, Bryce Bordone, James McAlister, Thomas Bartlett
Mastering: Randy Merrill
Vinyl Mastering: Ryan Smith
Best Ranking: Hot 100: 32

Genesis

In "The Prophecy," Taylor Swift reveals her mystical side with a touch of second degree. Invoking a higher power, she implores it to change her destiny in love. She refuses to embody the cliché of the star who is happy in business but unhappy in love and would give her last penny for the oracle to announce that she will find her soulmate and feel reassured at last. Through this quest, she shows herself to be vulnerable and human, revealing her doubts and expectations of love. Far from fame, she seeks genuine comfort and the promise of lasting happiness.

Production

After "I Hate It Here," "thanK you aIMee," and "I Look In People's Windows," "The Prophecy" is the fourth song in a row to be arranged around acoustic guitar picking. In this case, the arrangement even features a trio of acoustic guitars, three tracks with similar but complementary playing, judiciously distributed to the left, center, and right of the stereo field. With the London Contemporary Orchestra's majestic interventions, the twirling electric piano, and Glen Kotche's mallet playing focused on drums and cymbals, this folk-pop production by Aaron Dessner and Taylor Swift takes off on the choruses, the bridge, and the instrumental outro. Swift, perfectly situated in the middle of her range, distills the backing vocals with her usual grace.

CASSANDRA

Taylor Swift, Aaron Dessner / 4:00

Musicians

Taylor Swift: vocals, backing vocals
Aaron Dessner: piano, synthesizers, electric guitar, keyboards, percussion, synth bass
Benjamin Lanz: modular synthesizer, trombone
Glenn Kotche: snare drum, vibraphone
James McAlister: synthesizers, modular synth, keyboards, percussion, drum programming
The London Contemporary Orchestra: symphony orchestra
Robert Ames: conductor
Bryce Dessner: orchestral arrangement

Recorded

Long Pond (Hudson Valley, NY), Air Studios (London), 2023

Technical Team

Producers: Aaron Dessner, Taylor Swift
Mixing: Serban Ghenea
Sound Engineers: Jonathan Low, Jeremy Murphy, Bryce Bordone, Bella Blasko, Pat Burns, James McAlister, Benjamin Lanz
Mastering: Randy Merrill
Vinyl Mastering: Ryan Smith
Best Ranking: Hot 100: 44

Genesis

With "Cassandra," Taylor Swift once again follows in the tradition of mythological references but approaches the theme of prophecy from a new angle. Inspired by the figure of Cassandra, the prophetess of Troy, she explores a deeply political subject: institutional betrayal and the hypocrisy of bigots. In mythology, Cassandra, known for her great beauty, receives the gift of prophecy from Apollo in exchange for her promise to offer herself to him. But although unable to refuse the god, she goes back on her promise, and in revenge, Apollo condemns her to a life in which no one will believe her. In this song, Swift pays tribute to whistle-blowers, who are often misunderstood and persecuted. She criticizes a society in denial, which prefers to ignore warnings and to blame the messenger rather than question its own interests, often guided by short-term profit.

Production

With its unison melody of piano and voice, the arrangement of "Cassandra" is above all pure. The combination of rhythmic programming and acoustic drums, atmospheric synthesizers and the London Contemporary Orchestra gradually flesh out the instrumentation. Staying within the comfort of her midrange, Swift delivers an intense, articulate performance that conveys her anger and frustration.

At the 2024 Grammy Awards, Taylor Swift wins Album of the Year (for *Midnights*) for the fourth time.

FOR DISCERNING SWIFTIES

Sur la version de l'album « The Anthology », 7 chansons sont des *piano ballads* augmentées : *Lolm*, *The Smallest Man Who Ever Lived*, *How Did It End?*, *Cassandra*, *Peter*, *Robin* et *The Manuscript*. *The Black Dog* (la seule produite par Jack Antonoff) et *Chloe Or Sam Or Sophia Or Marcus* sont réalisées dans un esprit similaire mais le piano perd sa place centrale au cours de l'arrangement.

PETER

Taylor Swift / 4:43

2024

Musicians
Taylor Swift: vocals, backing vocals
Aaron Dessner: piano, synthesizer, drum programming, keyboards, bass

Recorded
Long Pond (Hudson Valley, NY), 2023

Technical Team
Producers: Aaron Dessner, Taylor Swift
Mixing: Serban Ghenea
Sound Engineers: Jonathan Low, Bryce Bordone, Bella Blasko
Mastering: Randy Merrill
Vinyl Mastering: Ryan Smith
Best Ranking: Hot 100: 46

Genesis

The song may have been inspired by Taylor Swift's tempestuous ex-partner Matty Healy. The character of Peter is a reference to Peter Pan, the famous hero of J. M. Barrie's 1911 British novel. In a way, one could say that Healy suffered from Peter Pan syndrome, a malaise linked to the inability to come to terms with the idea of growing up. Swift, on the other hand, fully accepts this transition. She wants to thrive in the adult world and has no choice but to bid Peter farewell: "the woman who sits by the window has turned out the light."

Production

"Peter" falls into the category of augmented piano ballads. Largely represented in the second half of the *Anthology* version and always associated with the work of Aaron Dessner, the melancholy inherent in this category is perfectly suited to the expression of Swift's regret. Dessner's piano is once again at the heart of the arrangement, leading the way for the one and only waltz on this sprawling double album. Synthesizers and discreet percussion enhance this delicate, swirling waltz, supporting one of the prettiest melodies of *The Tortured Poets Department*. Before playing "Peter" live for the first time (in an acoustic version, on the Eras Tour, May 17, 2024, in Stockholm), Swift admitted to the audience that it was one of her favorite songs on the album.

"The Bolter" is inspired by the work of writer Nancy Mitford, photographed here in the 1970s.

FOR DISCERNING SWIFTIES

Of *The Anthology*, seven songs are augmented piano ballads: loml, The Smallest Man Who Ever Lived, How Did It End?, Cassandra, Peter, Robin, and The Manuscript. The Black Dog (the only one produced by Jack Antonoff), and "Chloe or Sam or Sophia or Marcus" are made in a similar spirit, but the piano loses its central place in the arrangement.

THE BOLTER

Taylor Swift, Aaron Dessner / 3:58

2024

Musicians

Taylor Swift: vocals, backing vocals
Aaron Dessner: piano, synthesizers, drum programming, electric and acoustic guitars, high strung guitar, bass, percussion
Glenn Kotche: drums, percussion
James McAlister: Omnichord, percussion, synthesizers
Thomas Bartlett: synthesizers, keyboards, piano
Rob Moose: violin, viola, orchestral arrangement
The London Contemporary Orchestra: symphony orchestra
Robert Ames: conductor
Bryce Dessner: orchestral arrangement

Recorded

Long Pond (Hudson Valley, NY), Air Studios (London), 2023

Technical Team

Producers: Aaron Dessner, Taylor Swift
Mixing: Serban Ghenea
Sound Engineers: Jonathan Low, Jeremy Murphy, Bryce Bordone, Bella Blasko, Thomas Bartlett, James McAlister, Rob Moose
Mastering: Randy Merrill
Vinyl Mastering: Ryan Smith
Best Ranking: Hot 100: 47

Genesis

Both autobiographical and inspired by Nancy Mitford's novel *The Pursuit of Love* (1945) as well as the life of Sylvia Plath, one of Taylor Swift's favorite authors, "The Bolter" describes a character who seeks love everywhere except in the right place. In the eyes of both Swift and Mitford, a bolter ("dissident") is a woman who voluntarily remains on the margins of traditional society. Marked by a near-death experience at the age of six, after nearly drowning in icy waters, the young girl described by the songwriter seems, as she grows older, to be drawn to the thrill of perilous situations. This endearing, mischievous, and charming "dissident" is not afraid to follow men she suspects of bad faith, while taking a malicious pleasure in pushing them away. She catches the "trophy hunters" at their own game, escaping them at every turn, sometimes risking her life in the process. The message is clear: A woman must belong only to herself. Despite some explicit lyrics, the sustained style of "The Bolter" places the song in the category of quill pen songs.

Production

With acoustic guitar strumming and forward vocals: Aaron Dessner and Taylor Swift's country-folk production does not beat about the bush. Set to a tempo of 92 bpm, the drums, percussion, and rhythmic programming only reinforce the rhythmic impulse of the folk guitars. The orchestra and synthesizers open up the harmonic spectrum, the piano hammers out the eighth note at the top of the keyboard, and Swift's stacked backing vocals contribute to the gradual densification of the instrumentation.

Like the song "Robin," Taylor Swift explores childlike joy, here during the 2024 AFC championship game between the Kansas City Chiefs and the Baltimore Ravens.

ROBIN

Taylor Swift, Aaron Dessner / 4:00

2024

Musicians

Taylor Swift: vocals, backing vocals
Aaron Dessner: piano, synthesizers, drum programming, electric guitar, bass, percussion, keyboards, drums
Benjamin Lanz: synthesizers
Glenn Kotche: drums, percussion
James McAlister: Buchla, clavas, synthesizer, percussion
Thomas Bartlett: synthesizers, keyboards, piano
The London Contemporary Orchestra: symphony orchestra
Robert Ames: conductor
Bryce Dessner: orchestral arrangement

Recorded

Long Pond (Hudson Valley, NY), Air Studios (London), 2023

Technical Team

Producers: Aaron Dessner, Taylor Swift
Mixing: Serban Ghenea
Sound Engineers: Jonathan Low, Bella Blasko, Jeremy Murphy, Bryce Bordone, Maryam Qudus, Benjamin Lanz, Thomas Bartlett, James McAlister
Mastering: Randy Merrill
Vinyl Mastering: Ryan Smith
Best Ranking: Hot 100: 55

Genesis

Conceived as a galvanizing speech populated with references to the childlike imagination, the song "Robin" is probably addressed to Robin Dessner, Aaron Dessner's son born in 2015. Taylor Swift and Dessner have composed an ode to the innocence, playfulness, and boundless imagination of children. The song invites us to celebrate the creativity and wonder that childhood inspires, while offering a gentle reflection on the passage of time and the gradual loss of that carefree spirit.

Production

The first piano chord is a fitting reminder of John Lennon's 1971 classic "Imagine." Typical of the augmented piano ballad, the arrangement of "Robin" revolves around Aaron Dessner's clean, supple playing. Swift's gentle interpretation, positioned very close to the microphone, accentuates the close effect. After the first chorus, Dessner delivers a particularly shimmering bass melody. His picking then slips into the gaps in the instrumentation to discreetly enhance the harmony. Together with the synthesizer layers and sequences, Bryce Dessner's orchestral arrangement opens up the horizon, while the combination of rhythmic programming, percussion, and drums elegantly supports the fairy tale–like edifice.

Left: Onstage at the 2024 MTV Video Music Awards.

Next page spread: At the Amazon Music Prime Day concert in New York, 2019.

THE MANUSCRIPT

Taylor Swift / 3:44

Musicians

Taylor Swift: vocals, backing vocals
Aaron Dessner: piano, synthesizer, synth bass
James McAlister: drum programming, synthesizer
Thomas Bartlett: synthesizer
The London Contemporary Orchestra: symphony orchestra
Robert Ames: conductor
Bryce Dessner: drum programming, filtered brass and winds, piano, synthesizer, orchestral arrangement

Recorded

Long Pond (Hudson Valley, NY), Air Studios (London), 2023

Technical Team

Producers: Aaron Dessner, Taylor Swift
Mixing: Serban Ghenea
Sound Engineers: Bryce Bordone, Jonathan Lowe, Bella Blasko, Bryce Dessner, James McAlister, Thomas Bartlett, Jeremy Murphy
Mastering: Randy Merrill
Vinyl Mastering: Ryan Smith
Best Ranking: Hot 100: 51

Genesis

"The Manuscript" concludes this dense, bracing Swiftian chapter with a touch of nostalgia, leaving behind the black-and-white spleen typical of *The Tortured Poets Department*. The manuscript in question tells the story of a torrid romance that, all too quickly, turns into agony. In particular, it explores the question of age difference, the female character being younger than the man in question (which could, according to some rumors, allude to Jake Gyllenhaal or John Mayer). In this third-person song, Taylor Swift, at the height of her powers, displays one songwriting feat after another. Subtle metaphors, innuendo, snatches of dialogue, and play on temporality: She juggles figures of speech and multiplies the levels of reading, combining irony, directness, and a sense of self-mockery.

Production

Extremely minimalist and airy, the arrangement of this final augmented piano ballad is divided into two relatively distinct parts. First, the suspended piano chords, plucked from the top of the keyboard, are linked by the resonance of the reverb, Swift's voice, the taut thread of the orchestra perched at the top of the spectrum, and the synthesizer layers. Then, from 2:01 onward, the 3/4 rhythm, led by the orchestra and piano, comes to life, and the intensity rises a notch before dropping back to the outro. This change of dynamic, albeit subtle, is Swift's way of signaling that she is finally serene, and this time she intends to stay that way.

Discography

LIVE ALBUMS

Speak Now World Tour—Live
Release Date: digital download, streaming, CD + DVD/Blu-ray, November 21, 2011, Big Machine

Live from Clear Channel Stripped 2008
Release Date: digital download, streaming, April 23, 2020, Big Machine

Lover (Live from Paris)
Release Date: Streaming, LP, May 19, 2020, Republic Records

Folklore: The Long Pond Studio Sessions
Release Date: digital download, streaming, LP, November 24, 2020, Republic Records

EP (*EXTENDED PLAYS*, WITH PHYSICAL RELEASE)

The Taylor Swift Holiday Collection
Release Date: CD, digital download, streaming, October 14, 2007, Big Machine

Beautiful Eyes
Release Date: CD + DVD, July 15, 2008 (Walmart exclusive), Big Machine

NON-ALBUM SINGLES AND CONTRIBUTIONS

You Don't Have to Call (0:45)
Taylor Swift

Digital release, May 2006
Telephone ring tone released as a free download promoting the Pepsi brand

Crazier (3:12)
Taylor Swift, Robert Ellis Orrall

Digital release, March 20, 2009, Big Machine Records
This song was co-written in 2002, when Taylor Swift was only 13. It was selected several years later for inclusion on the soundtrack of the film *Hannah Montana: The Movie* by Peter Chelsom (2009).

American Girl (4:10)
Tom Petty

Digital release, June 30, 2009, Big Machine Records
Cover of "American Girl" by Tom Petty and the Heartbreakers (1976), recorded during the "Fearless Tour," Taylor Swift's first tour

Today Was a Fairytale (4:02)
Taylor Swift

Digital release, January 19, 2010, Big Machine Records (Republic Records for television)
Promotional single taken from the soundtrack of the film *Valentine's Day* by Garry Marshall (2010)

Breathless (3:51)
Kevin Griffin

Digital release, January 23, 2010, MTV Networks
Live version recorded during the "Hope for Haiti Now: A Global Benefit for Earthquake Relief" telethon, included in the compilation "Hope For Haiti Now." "Breathless" was originally recorded by the American alternative rock trio Better Than Ezra.

Safe & Sound (4:01)

Taylor Swift, T. Bone Burnett, John Paul White, Joy Williams

Digital release, December 26, 2011, Big Machine Records (Republic Records for television)
Promotional single for the original soundtrack of the film *The Hunger Games: Songs from District 12 and Beyond* by Gary Ross (2012)

Eyes Open (4:04)

Taylor Swift

Digital release, March 27, 2012, Big Machine Records (Republic Records for television)
Promotional single for the original soundtrack of the film *The Hunger Games: Songs from District 12 and Beyond* by Gary Ross (2012)

Ronan (4:25)

Taylor Swift

Digital release, September 8, 2012, iTunes

Sweeter Than Fiction (3:54)

Taylor Swift, Jack Antonoff
Digital release, October 21, 2013, Big Machine Records (Republic Records for television). Promotional lead single for the original soundtrack of the film *One Chance* by David Frankel (2013). The album *One Chance (The Incredible True Story of Paul Potts: Motion Picture Soundtrack)* chronicles the life of opera singer Paul Potts (2013).

I Don't Wanna Live Forever (feat. Zayn Malik) (4:05)

Taylor Swift, Jack Antonoff, Sam Dew

Digital release, December 9, 2016, Universal Music Group
Single for the original soundtrack of the film *Fifty Shades Darker* by James Foley (2017)

September (3:07)

Earth, Wind & Fire, Maurice White, Allee Willis, Al McKay

Digital release, April 13, 2018, Big Machine Records
Cover of the song originally composed and recorded by Earth, Wind & Fire (1978)

Beautiful Ghosts (4:21)

Taylor Swift, Andrew Lloyd Webber

Digital release, November 15, 2019, Polydor
Promotional single for the film *Cats* by Tom Hooper (2019)

Christmas Tree Farm (3:48)

Taylor Swift

Digital release, December 6, 2019, Republic Records
Vinyl and picture disc single release, December 2020 (ref. B0033165-11), Republic Records
Single included in the compilation *Christmas Tree Farm (Old Timey Version)* (2021)

Only the Young (2:37)

Taylor Swift, Joel Little

Digital release, January 31, 2020, Republic Records
Outtake from the *Lover* album (2019). "Only the Young" was used as a soundtrack for the closing credits of the *Miss Americana* documentary by Lana Wilson (2020).

Carolina (4:25)

Digital release, June 24, 2022, Republic Records, Mercury Classics
Promotional single for the original soundtrack of *Where the Crawdads Sing* by Olivia Newman (2022). This film is an adaptation of the novel of the same name, written by Delia Owens and published in 2018.

Glossary

Americana: a musical genre blending American roots and musical traditions, such as folk, country, rhythm'n'blues, rock'n'roll, and bluegrass.

Andantino: a tempo indication denoting a pace slightly faster than the andante.

Arpeggio: notes of a chord quickly played in succession.

Arpeggiator: a tool included on some synthesizers enabling an arpeggio to be played from a chord held on the keyboard.

Automation: volume curve or any other parameter, programmed manually or other than in a mixing software or DAW [Digital Audio Workstation].

Bend: term generally used by guitarists to describe the act of pulling or pushing one or more notes on a stringed instrument to increase their tension and raise the pitch slightly.

Bluegrass: a musical genre that emerged in the United States as a branch of country music.

Bottleneck: metal or glass tube passed over one finger of the hand to slide over the strings on the neck side, steel guitar–style.

Cajon: the cajón, or cajon, is a musical instrument invented in Peru in the 18th century. Compared with the traditional cajon, the modern cajon generally has an additional element, the percussive timbre effect, which makes the sound similar to that of a snare drum. It is one of the few musical instruments on which the artist sits.

Celesta: a percussion instrument invented in 1886. This is a hybrid between the glockenspiel and the piano, with hammers actioned by keyboard keys striking metal strips.

Chamber pop: different than chamber classical music, this term defines a genre born in the early 1960s that combines rock with orchestral elements (strings, brass, piano, vocal harmonies) and emphasizes melody and texture. It is now considered a sub-genre of indie pop.

High hat: double cymbal that marks the tempo, operated by the foot.

Chord stick: a four-string instrument, closely related to the dulcimer, with a triangular soundbox reminiscent of the balalaika. The chord stick is played like a strummed guitar, but with a single finger to stop the chords on the neck.

Fender Rhodes keyboard: electric piano created by Fender Rhodes in the 1940s to reduce the weight and bulk of a real piano.

Clawhammer: guitar technique using the thumb and forefinger to attack the strings from top to bottom. This technique takes its name from the notion that the hand that strikes the strings, stiffened by farm work, assumes the shape of an eagle's claw or claw hammer.

Climax: high point of a musical arrangement or song.

Coda: word of Italian origin indicating the conclusion of piece of music.

Crossover single: single that achieves a ranking in two or more charts of different musical styles.

Delay: audio effect that reproduces the acoustic phenomenon of an echo. Integrated into an effects pedal or mixing console, the delay is used on vocals and instruments to regularly repeat a sound by shifting its signal in time. A *slapback delay* is a short delay that creates the sensation of note bounce or thickening of sound.

Distortion: sound effect created by degrading the quality of an audio signal through saturation of an amplifier channel. This is made possible by the amplifier's built-in distortion effect, or by means of a distortion pedal.

Dobro: a brand of guitar whose sound is amplified by a metal resonator. Its name comes from the contraction of the name of its American creators of Slovak origin, the Dopyera brothers.

Doo-wop: vocal style consisting of singing a melodious combination of onomatopoeia, often in close harmony. A typical group consists of a tenor accompanied by a trio or quartet.

Drone: a bourdon, or held note.

Drop: DJ technique for creating stimulus effects, often consisting of a build-up to a sudden stop, before pushing the music to its maximum intensity.

Dry: natural vocal processing, giving the impression that no reverb, delay or other artificial effects have been applied.

Dubstep: a musical style derived from electronic music that emerged in the 1990s and originated in South London. It developed from many related musical styles such as two-step garage, broken beat, drum and bass, and reggae.

EBow: a form of electric bow that produces a magnetic field that vibrates the steel strings without touching them, creating a sound similar to that of a bow on the strings of a violin.

Envelope filter: automated frequency sweep effect, generally used on bass and electric guitar.

EP: abbreviation for *Extended Player*, a record format consisting of more tracks than a single, and fewer tracks than on an album.

Fade-out: musical fade at the end of a piece.

Falsetto: a (male or female) "head" voice, as opposed to the full voice sometimes referred to as the "chest" voice, and which is higher than the normal range.

Field recording: audio recording made outdoors using a portable recorder.

Formant: parameter generally associated with a vocal corrector (Auto-Tune, Melodyne, or vocoder), which adds more or less low or high harmonics to a given voice or sound.

Frailing: technique halfway between clawhammer and picking.

Gated snare: a (reverb) mixing technique that gives a snare drum more fullness and power, while avoiding interference with other elements of the mix, discovered by accident during the recording of Peter Gabriel's (self-titled) third album in 1979.

Glitch: often associated with the minimalist music technology of the 1990s, glitch is based on sounds derived from filtered and distorted samples, textures, or synthesizer sounds that evoke unwanted artifacts, such as dusty vinyl crackles or digital bugs used in an intentionally noise-generating or rhythmically musical way.

Baritone guitar: guitar with a lower range than the standard guitar, with a longer neck, which enables it to be tuned at least a fourth (or even an octave) lower than the standard tuning.

Hook: recurring musical motif, and the main "hook" of the piece.

Interpolation: a term used in pop and urban music to designate a musical quotation that has been re-recorded, re-interpreted, and more or less transformed (unlike a sample). Interpolation often involves a financial arrangement with the original author and/or composer.

Jangle pop: a style that emerged in the mid-1960s, taking its name from the bright sounds of the tambourine and the electric 12-string guitar. Spearheaded by the Byrds.

Laid back: patterns (of cymbals, snare drum, or bass drum, for example) that incorporate strokes deliberately played outside the usual grid of sixteenth notes.

Lap steel: a kind of electric guitar, similar to pedal steel but more rudimentary, played on the lap with a bottleneck or steel bar sliding over the strings.

Lead single: first single chosen to represent the album. Like a locomotive, it is the song most promoted.

Licks: musical motif(s).

LinnDrum or Linn-LM1 (drum machines): the first programmable drum machine using digital samples of drum sounds, designed by Roger Linn in the late 1970s and produced by Linn Electronics in 1979.

Lo-Fi: emerging in the 1990s, this style defines the sound of bands from independent labels, recorded in more or less basic conditions, in contrast to the hi-fi sound of mainstream bands produced by the major labels. The groups Pavement and Sebadoh are among its best-known exponents.

Mashup: song created from one or two different pre-recorded songs, usually by superimposing the vocal part of one song over the instrumental part of another.

Mastering: in the production of a song or album, the stage following mixing, designed to give the recording an even quality and optimized sound levels (irrespective of the listening medium), and to homogenize the tracks.

Mid-tempo: music played at a moderate tempo.

MPC (Music Production Center): series of music workstations (sequencer and sampler with integrated pads) produced by the Akai brand. The MPC 60, the first model in the range, was created in 1988.

Layers: sustained notes or chords, played in particular by a synthesizer or string ensemble. Layers are often used as harmonic binders and placed in the background of the mix.

No-input mixing: technique using the feedback loops of an audio signal as a sound source to generate oscillation frequencies.

Octaver: pedal for the electric guitar that adds or substitutes one or more octaves above or below the original note.

Omnichord OM-27: a kind of electronic equivalent of the autoharp. The instrument (synthesizer and rhythm box) has been developed by Suzuki since 1981.

Hammond (B3) organ: electromechanical keyboard instrument invented in the 1930s by Laurens Hammond. The best-known model is the B3, developed in 1955 and still in use today.

Ostinato: insistent, repeated melodic or rhythmic motif, often forming the basis of a work.

Outro: end of a piece, the opposite of the intro.

Overdub: set of new recorded sounds (vocals and/or instruments) added to an existing recording.

Palm mute: guitar and bass technique that consists in muffling notes by placing the palm of the hand (right-handed for right-handed players, left-handed for left-handed players) on the strings close to the bridge. The aim is to mute the notes played with the pick.

UniVibe pedal: phase-modulating effect pedal for electric guitar, created in the late 1960s in Japan by Fumio Mieda.

Pitch: how high or low a sound is pitched.

Plucked: sounds with a pronounced attack and short resonance, often involving plucked strings, harmonic percussion, or keyboard sounds.

Bridge: sequence and transition between two passages in a song, usually between verse and chorus.

Portamento: sliding from one note to another.

Reed organ: musical instrument with keys, which produces sound when fine metal double reeds [anches] vibrate under the action of air pressure exerted mechanically by the foot or electrically. The harmonium and melodeon belong to the reed organ family. They differ from pipe organs, which are generally much larger.

Reverb: natural or artificial echo effect applied to an instrument or voice during the recording or mixing of a piece.

Reverse (sound): recorded sound played backward.

Riff: short, recurring fragment of a few notes in a piece. The origin of the word comes from the abbreviation of the expression *rhythmic figure*.

Rim shot: hitting the skin of the snare drum at the same time as the rim, producing a powerful, slamming sound.

Risers: synthesizer sounds that seem to rise upward to create a retro-futuristic musical effect.

Roland TR-808 (drum machine): electronic musical instrument in the drum machine family, manufactured between 1980 and 1983 by Roland.

Shouts: literally calling out.

Sidechain: compression circuit activated in parallel by another element, often the kick drum (electronic bass drum), which triggers synthesizers to create a rhythmic movement conducive to dancing.

Slide: the act of sliding from one note to the next on the neck of a stringed instrument (usually guitar or bass), either with a fingertip or a bottleneck.

Staccato: term generally used for violin, viola or cello, designating short bowing with a clean attack.

Stomp: percussion effect created by stamping a foot.

Strumming: guitar technique consisting of sweeping all the strings of the instrument up and down with the right hand for right-handed players, and with the left hand for left-handed players.

Shuffle: rhythmic figure that substitutes a ternary rhythm for a binary one. Common in blues, it adds flexibility and movement to the piece, broadening the creative horizon.

Sul ponticello: a bowing technique used on the violin, viola or cello, which involves playing very close to the bridge.

Swell: a sound whose slow, progressive attack seems to grow like a wave.

OP-1 synthesizer: designed by Teenage Engineering, this portable synthesizer with sampler and controller features additional functions (FM radio, G-Force sensors, etc.). The integrated tape recorder function enables everything to be recorded on four tracks, with overdubbing and reverse recording functions.

Tag: short musical intervention provided by an instrument.

Sustained: also referred to as a "held note," a term generally used for bowed instruments. As opposed to the short, lively sound of staccato playing, the held/sustained note lasts a certain length of time, with or without vibrato.

Tom: type of drum used mainly for breaks. There are usually three: the alto and medium (rack toms) are hung on the bass drum, and the floor tom is placed on the opposite side to the high hat.

Tonic: the tonic is the first degree of tonality in a scale, and therefore the most important. It gives its name to the key associated with it. The root gives its name to the chord.

Trigger: doubling with electronic drum sounds.

Tubular bells: orchestral bells (in tube form).

Turnarounds: short phrasing that enhances harmony with melodic counterpoints.

Twang: "accent," "vibration," or "nasal tone." On the electric guitar, a twangy sound ("clear," "brief," "vibrating," or "sharp") is obtained through a special playing technique using a felt pad wedged on the bridge, or note-to-note playing muffled by the palm of the hand holding the pick.

Up-tempo: music played at a fast tempo.

Upbeat: optimistic, good-humored [also the last beat in a bar leading straight into the following bar].

Vocoder: electronic device that produces synthetic sound by analyzing the main spectral components of the voice.

Wah-wah: audio effect produced by oscillating the sound frequency between low and high pitches. The resulting sound is reminiscent of a human voice repeating the onomatopoeia *wah*. Mainly used on electric guitars, this effect is produced using the pedal of the same name.

Wurlitzer: electric piano, a direct competitor of the Fender Rhodes, marketed by the Wurlitzer brand (who also made organs) from the early 1950s.

Index

Songs are in ***bold italic***. Albums are in **bold**, and pages with captions are in **bold**.

Photo Credits

AFP
© Jason Kempin / Getty Images North America / Getty Images via AFP **65**, © Rick Diamond / Getty Images North America / Getty Images via AFP **78-79**, © Jason Kempin / Getty Images North America / Getty Images via AFP **82**, © Terry Wyatt / Getty Images via AFP **365**.

Alamy
© Zuma Press, Inc. / Alamy Stock Photo **201**, © UPI / Alamy Stock Photo **469**.

Augustimage
© Austin Argrave **56-57**, © Art Streiber **370-371**.

Aurimages
© The Kobal Collection / Shutterstock **342**, © Mary Evans / All Film Archive / Fox Television Animation **380**, © Warner Bros / Everett **457**.

Bridgeman Art Library
© Gregorio Binuya / Everett Collection / Bridgeman Images **141**.

Dalle
© Andrew Orth / Retna Ltd.-Zuma / Dalle **7**, © Camera Press / Dean Chalkley / NME / Dalle **379**, © Sonia Moskowitz Gordon / Zuma / Dalle **437**.

Getty Images
© Aaron J. Thornton / WireImage **359**, © Allen Berezovsky / WireImage **270**, **281**, © Alo Ceballos / FilmMagic **115**, © Amy T. Zielinski / Redferns **234**, © Andreas Branch / Patrick McMullan **54**, © Axelle / Bauer-Griffin / FilmMagic **295**, **475**, © Axelle / Bauer-Griffin / WireImage **315**, © Barry Brecheisen / WireImage **21**, © Barry Chin / The Boston Globe **187**, © Bettman, Getty Images **463**, © Brad Smith / ISI **327**, © Brian Killian / WireImage **152**, © Brian Rasic **455**, © Bryan Bedder / WireImage **111**, © C Flanigan **387**, © C Flanigan / FilmMagic **259**, **279**, © Chen Dongjie / VCG **415**, © Chen He / Visual China Group **231**, **235**, © Chiaki Nozu / WireImage **195**, © Chris McKay **287**, © Christopher Polk / ACMA2011 / For ACM **117**, © Christopher Polk / Billboard **361**, © Cooper Neill / For TAS **207**, © Daniel Bockwoldt / Picture Alliance **424**, © Daniele Venturelli / WireImage **331**, **344**, © Dave Hogan / MTV **413**, © Dave J Hogan **154**, **155**, © David Becker / GC Images **353**, © David Benito **35**, **439**, © David Krieger / Bauer-Griffin / GC Images **162**, © Denise Truscello / For iHeartRadio **145**, © Denise Truscello / WireImage **220-221**, © Don Arnold / WireImage **239**, **375**, © Donato Sardella / For InStyle **290**, © Ed Rode / WireImage **47**, © Emma McIntyre / AMA2018 / For dcp **273**, © Erika Goldring / WireImage **385**, **449**, © Feature China / Future Publishing **219**, **244**, © FilmMagic **71**, © FilmMagic / FilmMagic / For Bonnaroo Arts And Music Festival **357**, © Francis Reiss / Picture Post / Hulton Archive **443**, © Frazer Harrison / AMA2011 **105**, © Fred Duval / FilmMagic **337**, © Frederick Breedon / FilmMagic **75**, **183**, © Frederick Breedon / WireImage **36**, **55**, © Frederick Breedon IV **312**, © Frederick Breedon IV / FilmMagic **133**, © Frederick Breedon IV / WireImage **23**, © Gabe Ginsberg / WireImage **223**, © Gary Miller / FilmMagic **93**, © Gilbert Flores / Variety **423**, © Gotham / GC Images **301**, **411**, © Graham Denholm / WireImage **29**, **58**, © Gregg DeGuire / FilmMagic **53**, © Gregg DeGuire / WireImage **157**, © Gus Stewart / Redferns **341**, © Hiroyuki Ito **373**, © J. Emilio Flores / Corbis **313**, © Jack Mitchell **339**, © James Devaney / GC Images **208**, **236**, **237**, © Jason LaVeris / FilmMagic **241**, © Jason Squires / WireImage **40-41**, **100**, © JB Lacroix / WireImage **165**, **257**, **260-261**, © JC Olivera / WireImage **400**, © Jeff Kravitz / For MTV **447**, **479**, © Jeff Kravitz / AMA2014 / FilmMagic **205**, **229**, © Jeff Kravitz / FilmMagic **19**, **73**, **89**, **245**, **425**, © Jeff Kravitz / FilmMagic / For dcp **321**, © Jeff Kravitz / FilmMagic / For iHeartMedia **99**, **323**, © Jeff Vespa / WireImage **213**, © Jeremy Drey / MediaNews Group / Reading Eagle **18**, © Jeremy Moeller **390**, © Jim Steele / Popperfoto **87**, © JJ / Bauer-Griffin / GC Images **169**, © JMEnternational / JMEnternational / For BRIT Awards **143**, © JMEnternational / For BRIT Awards **11**, © Joe Kohen / WireImage **9**, **107**, © John Shearer / For dcp **292**, © John Shearer / For DIRECTV **255**, **269**, © John Shearer / For MTV **441**, **459**, © John Shearer / For The Recording Academy **10**, **404**, **431**, **450-451**, © John Shearer / WireImage **17**, **25**, **174**, **472**, © Jon Kopaloff / FilmMagic **39**, **123**, **137**, **215**, © Kara Durrette **478**, © Karwai Tang / WireImage **393**, © Katja Ogrin / Redferns **417**, © Kevin Mazur **271**, **461**, © Kevin Mazur / For ABA **307**, © Kevin Mazur / For Amazon **297**, **322**, **325**, **480-481**, © Kevin Mazur / For dcp **293**, © Kevin Mazur / For DIRECTV **265**, **274-275**, **277**, © Kevin Mazur / For iHeartMedia **299**, **405**, © Kevin Mazur / For Jingle Ball 2012 **171**, **185**, © Kevin Mazur / For MTV / Paramount Global **399**, **467**, © Kevin Mazur / For Netflix **395**, © Kevin Mazur / For SiriusXM **348-349**, © Kevin Mazur / For The Recording Academy **429**, © Kevin Mazur / For The Rock and Roll Hall of Fame **199**, © Kevin Mazur / AMA2012 / WireImage **191**, © Kevin Mazur / AMA2018 / For dcp **12-13**, **280**, **285**, **495**, © Kevin Mazur / AMA2019 / For dcp **335**, © Kevin Mazur / WireImage **81**, **83**, **106**, **125**, **126-127**, **163**, **167**, **209**, **210-211**, **225**, **227**, **305**, **316-317**, **318-319**, **377**, **471**, © Kevin Mazur / WireImage / For Clear Channel Radio New York **135**, © Kevin Mazur / WireImage / For Parkwood **433**, © Kevin Mazur /WireImage **113**, © Kevin Winter / ACM2015 / For dcp **91**, © Kevin Winter / ACMA **45**, © Kevin Winter / WireImage **196**, **217**, © Kieran Frost / Redferns **453**, © Krissy Krummenacker / MediaNews Group / Reading Eagle **26**, © Kristy Sparow **407**, © Kurt Krieger / Corbis **291**, © Kyle Gustafson / for The Washington Post **333**, © Larry Busacca / For The Washington Post **332**, **367**, **389**, © Lester Cohen / WireImage **153**, **177**, © Liu Xingzhe / Visual China Group **139**, © Mark Reinstein / Corbis **70**, © MEGA / GC Images **420**, © Michael Caulfield / WireImage **76**, **409**, © Michael Loccisano / FilmMagic **49**, **85**, **159**, © Mick Hutson / Redferns **419**, © Mike Kemp / In Pictures **398**, **444**, © Mike Marsland / WireImage **179**, © Mike Windle / ACM2015 / For dcp **140**, © Mike Windle / WireImage **248-249**, © Noam Galai **95**, © Paul Marotta **360**, © Per Ole Hagen / Redferns **197**, © Photo by Apple TV+ / Kobal / REX **383**, © Rabbani and Solimene Photography **253**, © Randy Brooke / WireImage **129**, © Reg Lancaster / Express **477**, © Rich Fury / AMA2018 / For dcp **263**, © Rick Diamond / ACMA2013 / For ACM **61**, © Rick Diamond / WireImage **31**, **43**, **69**, © Rick Kern / WireImage **351**, © Rob Hill / WireImage **67**, © Robert Alexander **27**, © Robin L Marshall **374**, © Samir Hussein **161**, © Shirlaine forrest / WireImage **44**, © Skip Bolen / WireImage **104**, © Smiley N. Pool / Houston Chronicle **120**, © SSPL **366**, © Steve Gonzales / Houston Chronicle **206**, © Steve Jennings / WireImage **283**, © Steve Russell / Toronto Star **391**, © Taylor Hill / For Boston Calling **347**, © Taylor Hill / For The Ally Coalition **345**, **354-355**, © Taylor Hill / FilmMagic **24**, **62**, 181, **254**, **266-267**, **403**, © Theo Wargo / WireImage **233**, **311**, © Theo Wargo / WireImage / For Clear Channel Radio New York **427**, © Theo Wargo / WireImage / For New York Post **63**, **77**, © Tim Mosenfelder **131**, © Timothy Norris / FilmMagic **401**, © Tommaso Boddi / WireImage **309**, © Tony R. Phipps / FilmMagic **34**, © Tony R. Phipps / WireImage **33**, © VCG **303**, © Venturelli / WireImage **119**, © Wesley Lapointe / Los Angeles Times **8**.

At the 2018 American Music Awards, Taylor Swift wins, among others, the award for Best Pop/Rock Album for *Reputation*.

About the Authors

Damien Somville studied cinema and sound engineering before working for major record labels like Atmosphériques and Warner, all while developing his career as an author-composer and stage musician. In 2015, he opened his own studio in Paris, Plastic Folk Inventions, which supports artists in producing albums and composing music for film. From recording, mixing, and arranging to writing lyrics (in English or French), he has produced a series of productions (performed by Bats on a Swing, Lenha, ZO, Watine, Buzy, Gal Kuper, Emmanuelle Cadoret, Silly Jungsters, Sophie Darly), the *In Tenebris* podcast, and predominantly folk, rock, pop, and electro songs. Passionate about music, he tackles all styles both in his creations and in his arrangements. He is the co-author of *Dolly Parton All the Songs* and excels at telling the exceptional stories of artists such as Taylor Swift whose career he has followed since its beginnings.

Marine Benoit has been a print journalist for more than fifteen years. As a music editor, she contributed numerous general and specialized titles (*Le Monde*, *M Le Monde*, the American media Mashable in its French version or even *Sciences et Avenir*, where she currently works in the field of science). A fan of amateur indie rock folk, dream pop, alternative rock, slowcore, or even shoegaze and Americana, she loves monumental pop work just as much by Taylor Swift, whom she considers one of the most prolific and inspired of her generation.

Translation by Caroline Higgitt and Paul Ratcliffe by arrangement with Jackie Dobbyne of Jacaranda Publishing Services Limited

Cover design by Amanda Kain
Cover photographs: (front cover) Kryssia Campos via Getty Images; (back cover) Krista Schlueter/The New York Times/Redux

Original title: *La Totale Taylor Swift*
Published by Éditions E/P/A—Hachette Livre, 2025

Black Dog & Leventhal Publishers
Hachette Book Group
1290 Avenue of the Americas
New York, NY 10104
www.blackdogandleventhal.com
BlackDogandLeventhal @BDLev

First English-Language Edition: October 2025

Published by Black Dog & Leventhal Publishers, an imprint of Hachette Book Group, Inc. The Black Dog & Leventhal Publishers name and logo are trademarks of Hachette Book Group, Inc.

Additional copyrights/credits information is on page 494.

LCCN: 2025931290

ISBNs: 978-0-7624-8929-9 (hardcover), 978-0-7624-8930-5 (ebook)

Printed in China

10 9 8 7 6 5 4 3 2 1